HELP OR HINDRANCE?

The Economic Implications of Immigration for African Americans

HELP OR HINDRANCE?

The Economic Implications of Immigration for African Americans

Daniel S. Hamermesh
and
Frank D. Bean
editors

Russell Sage Foundation
New York

The Russell Sage Foundation

The Russell Sage Foundation, one of the oldest of America's general purpose foundations, was established in 1907 by Mrs. Margaret Olivia Sage for "the improvement of social and living conditions in the United States." The Foundation seeks to fulfill this mandate by fostering the development and dissemination of knowledge about the country's political, social, and economic problems. While the Foundation endeavors to assure the accuracy and objectivity of each book it publishes, the conclusions and interpretations in Russell Sage Foundation publications are those of the authors and not of the Foundation, its Trustees, or its staff. Publication by Russell Sage, therefore, does not imply Foundation endorsement.

Library of Congress Cataloging-in-Publication Data

Help or hindrance? : the economic implications of immigration for
    African Americans / [edited by]
        Daniel S. Hamermesh and Frank D. Bean.
            p.   cm.
        Includes bibliographical references and index.
        ISBN 0-87154-387-7
            1.   United States—Emigration and immigration—Economic aspects.
        2.   Alien labor—United States.   3.   Afro-Americans—Employment.
        I.   Hamermesh, Daniel S.   II.   Bean, Frank D.
        JV6471.H45   1998   97-46611
        331.6'396073—dc21   CIP

The paper used in this publication meets the minimum requirements of American National Standard for Information Sciences—Permanence of Paper for Printed Library Materials. ANSI Z39.48-1992.

Text design by Suzanne Nichols.

RUSSELL SAGE FOUNDATION
112 East 64th Street, New York, New York 10021
10 9 8 7 6 5 4 3 2 1

To our families

CONTENTS

CONTRIBUTORS

FRANK D. BEAN is Ashbel Smith Professor of Sociology and professor of public affairs at the University of Texas at Austin.

DANIEL S. HAMERMESH is Edward Everett Hall Centennial Professor of Economics at the University of Texas at Austin. He is also research associate of the National Bureau of Economic Research.

JULIAN R. BETTS is associate professor of economics at the University of California-San Diego.

GEORGE J. BORJAS is Pforzheimer Professor of Public Policy at the John F. Kennedy School of Government, Harvard University. He is also research associate of the National Bureau of Economic Research.

KRISTIN F. BUTCHER is assistant professor of economics at Boston College.

ROBERT W. FAIRLIE is assistant professor of economics at the University of California-Santa Cruz.

RICHARD B. FREEMAN is Herbert Ascherman Professor of Economics at Harvard University. He is also director of labor studies at the National Bureau of Economic Research and director of the Program for Discontinuous Economics at the London School of Economics.

JEFFREY T. GROGGER is professor in the School of Public Policy and Social Research at the University of California-Los Angeles. He is also faculty research fellow of the National Bureau of Economic Research.

CAROLINE M. HOXBY is Morris Kahn Associate Professor of Economics at Harvard University. She is also faculty research fellow of the National Bureau of Economic Research.

GEORGE E. JOHNSON is professor of economics at the Universiry of Michigan.

LINDA DATCHER LOURY is associate professor of economics at Tufts University. She is also fellow at the Institute on Race and Social Division at Boston University

BRUCE D. MEYER is Household International, Inc. Professor of Economics and faculty fellow of the Institute for Policy Research at Northwestern University. He is also research associate of the National Bureau of Economic Research.

CORDELIA W. REIMERS is professor of economics at Hunter College and the Graduate School of the City University of New York.

PETER H. SCHUCK is the Simeon E. Baldwin Professor of Law at Yale Law School.

MARTA TIENDA is professor of sociology and public affairs at Princeton University. She is also research associate of the Office of Population Research.

JEFFREY S. ZAX is professor of economics at the University of Colorado at Boulder.

Introduction

Daniel S. Hamermesh and Frank D. Bean

Immigration issues have in recent years risen once again to a prominent place on the public policy agenda of the United States (Teitelbaum and Weiner 1995). This is reflected not only in the results of
public opinion polls that show an increase in the number of people
who think current U.S. immigration levels are "too high" (Espenshade
and Belanger 1997; Espenshade and Calhoun 1993) but also in the cre-
ation of a special commission to recommend changes in U.S. immigration policy (U.S. Commission on Immigration Reform 1994) and in
the passage of legislation tightening restrictions on unauthorized migration (Bean et al. 1997). Such concerns on the parts of the public and
policymakers are in part the product of recent trends in the magnitude
and racial and ethnic mix of persons coming into the country compared to those at earlier times. They are also the result of economic
trends over the past twenty-five years that seem to suggest relatively di-
minished economic prospects for American workers, especially workers
with less than college educations (Bean, Cushing, and Haynes 1997).
Given each of these trends, and given that educational levels in the
African American population continue to lag behind those in the white
population (Farley 1996), questions about the economic implications
of immigration for blacks take on special resonance. This volume seeks
to address such questions.

One of the reasons for popular, public policy, and social-scientific
concern about the consequences of immigration derives from the volume of the flows, which has been rising since World War II. But even at
their recent sizable levels, immigration totals still are not as substantial
as they were during the first two decades of the century (see, for example, Bean, Vernez, and Keely 1989; Cafferty et al. 1983; Reimers 1985).
During the 1930s and 1940s, immigration numbers dropped tenfold
from these record-setting, early twentieth-century levels because of the
passage of the National Origins Quota Act in 1924, the Great Depres-
sion during the 1930s, and an unfavorable immigration climate during
World War II. Specifically, the number of entrants decreased from over
seven hundred thousand per year during the first twenty years of the

1

century to less than seventy thousand per year from 1925 through 1945 (U.S. Immigration and Naturalization Service 1996). After this lull, legal immigration again moved steadily upward, and by the late 1980s and early 1990s reached levels approaching the all-time highs set in the early part of the twentieth century. (If the legalizations resulting from the Immigration Reform and Control Act [IRCA] are included, the recent levels exceed all previous highs [U.S. Immigration and Naturalization Service 1996].)

The national origins of U.S. immigrants have also changed sharply. Prior to 1960, the vast majority came from European countries or Canada (often over 90 percent when examined on a decade basis). Even as late as the 1950s, over two-thirds (67.7 percent) of all arrivals were from these countries. Things changed rapidly during the 1960s, when family reunification criteria rather than national origin quotas became the basis for granting entry visas. By the 1980s, only 12.5 percent of legal immigrants came from Europe or Canada, whereas 84.4 percent came from Asian or Latin American countries (U.S. Immigration and Naturalization Service 1996).

These relatively recent changes in the national origin of immigrants have begun to convert the United States from a largely biracial society consisting of a sizable white majority and a small black minority (together with a very small American Indian minority of less than 1 percent) into a multiracial, multiethnic society consisting of several racial/ethnic groups (Passel and Edmonston 1994). This trend became discernible in the 1950s, but began to accelerate in the 1960s. By 1996, over a quarter of the U.S. population designated itself as either black, Hispanic, Asian, or American Indian (table I.1). And the growth of other groups has meant that the proportion of African Americans in the minority population has been declining. By 1990 blacks, no longer a majority of the minority population, made up only 48 percent of minorities (compared with 44 percent in 1996).

Because some observers think current concerns about immigration may be rooted in fears about the country's changing racial/ethnic composition and the role that immigration plays in contributing to that process, it is useful to examine more precisely the contribution of immigration per se to population growth and changing population composition. Table I.2 shows the contribution of immigration since 1900 to population growth (as opposed to growth resulting from an excess of births over deaths among pre-1900 natives) for the major racial/ethnic groups in 1990 (Passel and Edmonston 1994). Although post-1900 immigration has accounted for about 30 percent of the growth of the total U.S. population since 1900, its contribution to the growth of the

Table I.1   U.S. Population by Race/Ethnicity: 1990 to 1996
            (in Thousands)

Year	Total	Non-Hispanic White	Black	Hispanic	Asian	American Indian
Population						
1900	76,195	66,225	8,834	656	243	237
1910	93,879	82,049	10,255	999	299	277
1920	110,747	96,969	11,512	1,632	389	244
1930	127,585	111,543	12,736	2,435	527	343
1940	136,928	119,425	13,767	2,814	577	345
1950	155,156	134,351	15,668	4,039	739	357
1960	182,055	154,969	19,071	6,346	1,146	524
1970	205,567	170,371	23,005	9,616	1,782	793
1980	226,625	180,392	26,482	14,604	3,726	1,420
1990	248,712	187,139	29,986	22,354	7,274	1,959
1996	264,313	191,270	33,073	28,438	9,468	2,064
Percent						
1990	100.0	86.9	11.6	0.9	0.3	0.3
1910	100.0	87.4	10.9	1.1	0.3	0.3
1920	100.0	87.6	10.4	1.5	0.4	0.2
1930	100.0	87.4	10.0	1.9	0.4	0.3
1940	100.0	87.2	10.1	2.1	0.4	0.3
1950	100.0	86.6	10.1	2.6	0.5	0.2
1960	100.0	85.1	10.5	3.5	0.6	0.3
1970	100.0	82.9	11.2	4.7	0.9	0.4
1980	100.0	79.6	11.7	6.4	1.6	0.6
1990	100.0	75.2	12.1	9.0	2.9	0.8
1996	100.0	72.4	12.5	10.8	3.6	0.8

Sources: Adapted from table 2.3 in Passel and Edmonston (1994) and 1996 Current Population Survey.
Note: Populations include fifty states and District of Columbia.

various major racial/ethnic subgroups varies enormously, accounting for nearly all of the growth among Hispanics and Asians (85.7 percent and 97.3 percent, respectively), but virtually none of the growth among blacks.

Given that immigration has recently affected U.S. racial/ethnic composition, questions are often raised about what the racial/ethnic composition of the U.S. population will look like in the future if current immigration and other demographic trends continue. One answer is provided by population projections undertaken by the Bureau of the Census of current demographic trends. Although the bureau projects the Hispanic and non-Hispanic populations separately (Hispanics may be of any race, although almost all are white), it is useful to subtract the

Table I.2   Contribution of Post-1900 Immigration and 1990
Population for the Population of the United States
in 1990 by Race/Ethnicity (in Thousands)

Contribution from Component	Total	Non-Hispanic White	Black	Hispanic	Asian
Estimated population	248,712	187,139	29,986	22,354	7,274
1990 population	174,145	141,369	27,493	3,108	216
1st generation	8,534	8,184	29	301	20
2nd generation	35,574	34,118	392	956	108
3rd generation	38,547	36,735	941	869	2
4th + generations	90,055	60,868	26,151	991	85
Immigration since 1900	74,567	45,769	2,493	19,246	7,058
1900–1910 immigrants	17,286	16,398	125	606	157
1910–1920 immigrants	14,487	12,624	196	1,257	409
1920–1930 immigrants	9,305	6,661	167	2,182	295
1930–1940 immigrants	1,439	1,021	22	312	83
1940–1950 immigrants	3,590	2,389	68	1,055	77
1950–1960 immigrants	5,272	2,870	158	1,885	359
1960–1970 immigrants	5,214	1,930	266	2,433	584
1970–1980 immigrants	9,518	2,658	834	4,013	2,014
1980–1990 immigrants	10,756	1,341	774	5,525	3,116

Source: Adapted from Passel and Edmonston (1994, table 2.4).

Hispanic numbers from the numbers for non-Hispanic whites so that the totals for these two groups are mutually exclusive. Expressed as a percentage of the total population, the four largest racial/ethnic minority groups are projected to increase from 27.7 percent of the total population in 1996 to 37.5 percent in 2020 (Campbell 1994). Thus, given current trends (including immigration), the size of the U.S. minority population as measured by the Census Bureau would grow considerably in less than twenty-five years.

Such results sometimes cause alarm and fuel anti-immigration sentiment. The projections on which they are based, however, should be viewed with skepticism. Apart from their assumptions about demographic processes, projections about the future racial/ethnic composition of the U.S. population depend on two critical additional assumptions: first, that racial/ethnic categories are immutable; and second, that interracial and interethnic marriage patterns are unchanging and have little effect on racial/ethnic identification and thus on projections of future population composition. Neither of these assumptions seems totally warranted. In particular, rates of intermarriage have increased substantially in recent years, and depending on the self-identification of the offspring of such marriages, projections of racial/ethnic composition can vary substantially (Edmonston, Lee, and Passel 1994). The future racial/ethnic composition of the U.S. population thus is probably much less ascertainable than is often thought because of the blurring of racial/ethnic boundaries, including those between blacks and other groups. Nonetheless, it is likely that in the foreseeable future immigrants to the United States will continue to be made up of large numbers of Asians and Hispanics, thus keeping African Americans a minority within the subpopulation of racial/ethnic minorities. Such a secondary minority position may deflect attention away from the continuing disadvantaged status of segments of the African American population, a possibility that reaffirms the importance of studying the economic implications of immigration for blacks.

At a general level, the question of the economic consequences of immigration has recently been addressed by a study conducted by the National Research Council of the National Academy of Sciences (Smith and Edmonston 1997). The major conclusions are that immigration: (1) benefits the U.S. economy overall and exerts only a small adverse impact on the wage and employment opportunities of competing native groups (pp. 5–34); (2) that it benefits high-skilled workers and the owners of capital but not low-skilled workers; and (3) that it imposes overall a small fiscal burden (measured as the difference between the cost of services received and the amount of taxes paid) on taxpayers, a burden that is larger the greater the number of low-skilled (generally low-education) immigrants. The report had little to say on the question of the economic implications of immigration for blacks, noting that "none of the available evidence suggests that [blacks] have been particularly hard-hit on a national level" (p. S-5).

The importance of this question and its relative lack of study are the main reasons for this book. In order to investigate further the economic implications of immigration for African Americans and other minorities, we assembled a group of economists and charged them with the task of producing innovative research projects on various aspects of the relationship between immigration to the United States and the economic circumstances of African Americans. A few of the authors had already produced substantial research on a variety of topics in the area of immigration. Indeed, the group comprises many of the leading experts who study the economics of immigration. For most of the authors, however, immigration had not been the major focus of their research. Instead, they had concentrated on some particular labor-market outcome more generally and were convinced that the interrelations between it and immigration to the economic situations of African Americans were important and potentially fruitful research topics. After this group completed its work, we also asked another group of scholars and policy analysts to consider broadly the results of the research studies and place them not only in the context of recent economic and social trends in the United States, but also in the context of the country's changing policies toward immigration and racial/ethnic relations.

The first set of papers (the research studies) are divided into two main groups that make up the first two parts of this volume. The first group deals either directly or by implication with the impact of immigration on the labor-market outcomes experienced by African Americans and other minorities. The overarching theme of this group of studies is the extent to which immigrants substitute for native minority workers in employment. This means that the studies consider how immigration affects employment, various dimensions of work time, wage rates and earnings, and how these effects differ among various minority workers distinguished by educational attainment or geographic location. The studies also examine how our inferences about these impacts are affected by the nature of the ownership of capital and other inputs into production that cooperate with minority, immigrant, and other labor in the United States.

A huge literature on labor demand demonstrates that the degree of substitution between workers of different types is altered by the amount of capital that employers use. Thus, in his simulation of the labor market in the United States, George E. Johnson recognizes that one must account for the degree to which employers can substitute capital for workers of different skills and ethnicities. He therefore constructs a simulation model that uses the best available estimates of the parameters describing substitution among these groups of labor and capital, of the sizes of the populations of workers and their earnings, and of the capital stock and the returns to it. The strongest conclusion from this careful simulation is that immigration of the type that predominated in the United States from the mid-1970s to the mid-1990s *does* reduce the earnings of unskilled workers, particularly African Americans. The effects are not, however, very large, partly because immigration has not been that large relative to the size of the low-skilled and minority populations. Nonetheless, the theoretical derivations show that accounting for substitution between capital and labor would not alter the conclusion from the empirical studies presented later in the volume that recent immigration has to some extent imposed a burden on low-skilled African Americans.

In a second theoretical study George J. Borjas asks how the results are affected when we recognize that capital is not just some disembodied input, but is instead a factor of production that is owned by *people*, and in the United States owned disproportionately by native whites. Because he focuses on this aspect of the market for inputs and the distribution of returns to providing labor and owning capital, he examines in a different way than Johnson the nature of substitution between capital and workers of different types. Recognizing that a disproportionate ownership of capital exists, however, is crucial to understanding the implications of immigration for African Americans because they control relatively much more labor than capital. Thus, if low-skilled immigration benefits owners of capital, as the National Research Council study recently argued (Smith and Edmonston 1997), it will benefit native whites disproportionately. Recognizing the ethnic identity of the ownership of capital in a formal simulation model leads to the interesting conclusion that most of the cost to African Americans of low-skilled immigration comes because blacks do not reap much of the higher returns to capital that it generates. Borjas estimates that recent immigration has reduced the average personal income of African Americans by about 0.5 percent, specifically, around one hundred dollars per person. The main point is that, even if one finds very small direct labor-market impacts on minorities, those effects are exacerbated by the disproportionate benefits that unskilled immigration has conferred upon native whites through their ownership of capital.

In his study of labor-market disamenities, Daniel S. Hamermesh examines whether the preconditions for substitution between immigrants and natives exist. In particular, he considers whether it is possible, as many scholars believe, that immigrants wind up in jobs that natives would not accept and that would not otherwise be filled because their nonwage conditions are so repugnant to natives. He studies this by measuring immigrant-native, white-minority differences in a variety of nonwage outcomes, all else equal, including the timing of work—when during the day the worker is on the job—injury rates and durations, and expressed satisfaction with various aspects of the job. Using data from the Current Population Surveys for May and June 1991, he finds that there is little difference between native whites and immigrants in the timing of their work during the day. Otherwise identical immigrants are also in jobs where injuries are less frequent and of shorter duration than in jobs held by native whites. The real difference in these nonwage outcomes is between minorities, especially African Americans, and immigrants and native whites. The results suggest that the preconditions for substitution between immigrants and natives do exist, but also that there is a major dimension—nonwage job characteristics—along which outcomes are worse for African Americans than for otherwise observationally identical native and immigrant workers.

Cordelia W. Reimers uses the 1980 and 1990 Censuses of Population to examine the wages of low-skilled native workers, after adjusting them for the observable characteristics such as education and age that we know cause wages to differ among workers. She looks at the impacts of differential changes over this decade in the geographic dispersion of low-skilled immigrants on how well low-skilled native workers, particularly high school dropouts, fared in the labor market. The novel foci of the study are a concentration on high school dropouts and an examination of workers arrayed by their position in the distribution of earnings. This allows Reimers to examine how immigration has affected minority workers distinguished explicitly by their labor-market productivity. She finds some evidence that, where recent immigration has been greater, the wage rates of African Americans rose less during the 1980s. This impact was, however, greater among the higher-paid high school dropouts than among the lower-paid. In other words, the findings imply that the immigrants of the 1980s generally substituted most heavily for minority workers slightly above the bottom of the distribution of skills. The labor-market prospects of the most marginal minority employees—those who had dropped out of high school and fared worst in the labor market among all high school dropouts—were less severely affected by immigration.

Kristin F. Butcher uses a similar methodology to answer a different, and in some ways more general, question: How did the migration of the 1980s affect labor-market outcomes of minorities more generally, not only lower-skilled minorities? She uses the same data on the relative size of changes in immigration across metropolitan statistical areas (MSAs) during the 1980s, but examines how these differential changes affected the changing gap between native whites and African Americans in such outcomes as employment, annual weeks worked, wage rates, and annual earnings. Her estimates demonstrate that there is little evidence that differential changes in immigration affected the white-minority gaps in most of these outcomes generally. The gap in annual earnings was increased, however; and in each of the outcomes the effect on the gap was greater among less-educated minority workers than among others. To some extent these results corroborate Reimers's, in that they indicate the labor-market burden generated by recent immigrants has been felt particularly heavily among workers near the bottom of the distribution of skills in the minority population. They also suggest, since the biggest impacts are on annual earnings, that the main effect on low-skilled minorities may have been to reduce their weekly hours of work.

Taken together, the studies in the first part of the volume provide by far the clearest and most comprehensive evidence of the direct labor-market impacts of the immigration of the 1970s and 1980s on the situations of African Americans. They make it clear that there has been a negative impact, not especially large overall, but clearly identifiable. Moreover, the impact has been especially felt by the lowest-skilled African American workers (as opposed to all blacks, since people with very little attachment to the labor force are not directly affected). Much of the overall impact is the result of African Americans benefiting only slightly from the higher rate of return to the ownership of capital that low-skilled immigration has induced. Perhaps most important, the studies suggest that the impacts are crucially dependent on the skill composition of immigration: Had recent immigration been higher-skilled, the impact on African Americans would very probably have been smaller and perhaps even positive.

Immigration can affect the economic circumstances of African Americans in a variety of ways that are not directly part of the employment relationship. These include pre–labor-market effects, such as those that occur through the accumulation of knowledge in formal education; effects on non–labor-market activities, such as housing choices and criminal activities; and impacts on workers' choices of whether to enter employment or to become self-employed instead. Part two of the volume provides economic analyses of these other activities. Since there has been even less research on these topics than on the labor-market effects of immigration on African Americans, the knowledge gleaned from these studies stands entirely alone in forming the basis from which future research must depart.

One of the most incendiary issues in American cities is the role of small-scale immigrant enterprises in primarily African American residential areas. In their contribution Robert W. Fairlie and Bruce D. Meyer shed light on this controversy by examining the extent to which immigration reduces the likelihood that African Americans enter self-employment. They thus examine a substitution question, but here substitution in self-employment rather than in the wages and employment opportunities that were the focus of the studies in Part I. As in several of those studies they use Census of Population data for 1980 and 1990 and compare both levels of and changes in the importance of immigrants across MSAs to the self-employment propensities of minorities. Their results indicate at most weak evidence that immigration reduces the self-employment opportunities of African Americans: The latter are almost as likely to be self-employed in those metropolitan areas where immigration has been more important, and their self-employment has grown more rapidly than is the case elsewhere. This is true even if one accounts for the differing propensities of various immigrant groups to be self-employed. To put it concretely, the well-publicized Asian grocer in the inner city does not appear to be deterring in any substantial way the entrepreneurial instincts of the local residents.

One of the most persistent concerns about minority employment is that residential segregation has coupled with the changing spatial distribution of job opportunities to make it increasingly difficult for minorities to gain access to jobs. Many people believe that the suburbanization of jobs, along with the concentration of African Americans in inner cities, has contributed to their rising unemployment. Jeffrey S. Zax asks the next question in this line of argument: How does immigration affect spatial relationships in the labor market for minority workers? Again using the 1980 and 1990 censuses, Zax compares levels and changes in immigration across MSAs to the changing relationship between minority residential segregation and outcomes reflecting the economic well-being of minorities. The evidence makes it absolutely clear that residential segregation and poorer economic outcomes among African Americans go together; but where immigration has been more rapid recently, minority residential segregation is less, and minority outcomes are better. It may simply be that more dynamic areas are the ones to which immigrants are attracted and which generate better outcomes for minorities, natives, and the immigrants themselves. A more optimistic interpretation of Zax's results, however, is that the influx of immigrants generates a fillip to labor demand in the local area that provides minorities the ability to improve their housing situation by relocating nearer to where jobs are located.

An immense amount of research in the study of economic development and of labor markets has demonstrated the central role of education—of the accumulation of human capital through formal schooling—in generating growth and improving workers' well-being. For that reason we included two studies examining the relationships between immigration and minorities' educational opportunities in this book. In the first of these Julian R. Betts asks whether there is "educational substitution" between immigrants and African Americans in the completion of secondary schooling. Immigration can be viewed as raising the cost of education for other lower-income groups, since it increases competition for the public funds that finance high schools. Also, however, an influx of low-skilled workers raises the returns to education by making skill relatively more scarce. The net impact on minorities' incentives to complete school is thus unclear and must be settled by examining the data.

Betts does this, again using 1980 and 1990 census data by MSA, in this case comparing the immigration data to changes in the fraction of young African Americans completing high school. Accounting for differences in the characteristics of both the individual workers and the MSAs, Betts finds clear evidence that increased immigration has had a substantial negative effect on young African Americans' likelihood of completing high school. The effect on Mexican Americans is much less clear. The results imply that, if we are to ease the burden of immigration, local public authorities must accommodate it by ensuring that sufficient funding is available for schools so that immigration does not reduce the educational opportunities of the minorities with whom the children of immigrants apparently compete for access.

As Caroline M. Hoxby explains, the analysis of access is more complicated in the case of higher education, where there is much greater heterogeneity in the nature of educational institutions. These may reduce native minority enrollment by relying on foreign students to satisfy pressures for affirmative action programs that put minorities in their classrooms. Underprepared foreign students may also compete with poorly prepared native students for the limited resources available for remedial college-level programs.

Hoxby considers both of these issues using a triennial survey of students and institutions in 1986, 1989, and 1992. Because affirmative action pressures are most visible at the institutions of higher education that have students with the highest standardized test scores, while the need for remedial programs is greatest at schools with students with lower scores, Hoxby examines these two possibilities by stratifying institutions according to a measure of student quality (average SAT score). She finds that a greater presence of immigrant/foreign students substitutes for native minorities at the most selective schools, but not elsewhere, through competition for access to affirmative action programs. Obversely, they substitute for native minorities at mid-level schools in terms of access to remedial programs (which are mostly absent at the top schools). By inference foreign students displace the higher-educational opportunities of native minorities, but the negative impact does not come at the expense of the least-qualified minority high school graduates.

Jeffrey T. Grogger uses an argument similar to Betts's to analyze the impact of immigration on the propensity of young male African Americans to engage in criminal activities. More immigration of low-skilled workers increases competition with natives for access to criminal opportunities; but the low-skilled immigration also may reduce low-skilled natives' labor-market opportunities (as Reimers and Butcher show), thus increasing the relative returns to criminal activities by native minorities. To examine the relative importance of these opposing effects Grogger links information from the National Longitudinal Survey of Youth on the amount of income a youth (age fifteen to twenty-two) had in 1980 from criminal activities, and on whether the youth was incarcerated at any time between 1979 and 1982, or between 1988 and 1992, to Census of Population data from 1990 on the size of the immigrant population in each MSA. No matter how he tweaks the data Grogger finds no differential impact of immigration on the measures of crime by young African American men.

No doubt there are more problems of mismeasurement in these data reflecting criminal activity than in many of the other outcomes we examine in this volume. Nonetheless, these are the best data available, and the study examines them extremely carefully. By inference the results suggest that any effects of immigration on crime by minorities cancel out. We need not worry that somehow the labor-market displacement that is demonstrated in the studies in Part I is leading minorities into lives of crime.

This initial view of the non–labor-market impacts of immigration on African Americans yields decidedly mixed conclusions. The research finds no (or small) adverse effects of immigration on African Americans' propensities to engage in crime and to start their own businesses. The effects are perhaps positive on the tendency to be housed nearer to jobs. But studies of the crucial pre–labor-market outcome—educational attainment—find substantial displacement of minorities by immigrants. Since education has been so important in enabling African Americans (and others) to escape poverty, these findings are especially worrisome.

Taken all together, the results of the various research projects indicate that recent immigration to the United States appears to have exerted small negative effects on the economic situations of African Americans. Each of the effects uncovered by the individual research projects is small. If viewed in isolation, none of them would be thought to constitute strong evidence about adverse effects from immigration on African Americans. As a group, however, they add up to more compelling documentation that the positive economic effects of immigration emphasized by the National Research Council (Smith and Edmonston 1997) are substantially less likely to extend to African Americans. This is perhaps not surprising given that the NRC study also found that such benefits were concentrated among the highly skilled and among the owners of capital, both of whom involve disproportionately few African Americans.

It must be emphasized, however, that the observed effects are small. In Part III an invited group of commentators (Marta Tienda, Richard B. Freeman, Peter Schuck, and Linda Datcher Loury) remind us that it is one thing to try to estimate both the economic effects of immigration in general and those effects on African Americans in particular, but an altogether different thing to try to estimate the effects of immigration on the country's overall social welfare, as Freeman in particular notes. Small negative effects of immigration on economic variables may be offset by small (or large) positive effects on other aspects of social welfare. And even if the overall balance of such effects proved negative, thus pointing to an apparent need to find policies to curtail immigration, knowledge of the costs of implementing restrictive policy options is severely limited, thus making it difficult to know the degree to which the costs of implementing immigration controls might exceed the social welfare costs of the immigration itself. The process of selecting among policy options is thus inherently complex. Such complexities and uncertainties, however, should not obscure the fact that the results of the research reported here clearly suggest that African Americans do not appear to have benefited economically from immigration to the same degree as native whites.

REFERENCES

Bean, Frank D., Rodolfo O. de la Garza, Bryan R. Roberts, and Sidney Weintraub, eds. 1997. *At the Crossroads: Mexico and U.S. Immigration Policy.* Lanham, Md.: Rowman and Littlefield.

Bean, Frank D., Robert Cushing, and Charles W. Haynes. 1997. "The Changing Demography of U.S. Immigration Flows: Patterns, Projections, and Contexts." In *Migration Past, Migration Future: Germany and the United States*, edited by Klaus Bade and Myron Weiner. Providence R.I.: Berghahn Books.

Bean, Frank D., George Vernez, and Charles B. Keely. 1989. *Opening and Closing the Doors: Evaluating Immigration Reform and Control.* Washington, D.C.: The Urban Institute Press.

Cafferty, Phyllis, Barry R. Chiswick, Andrew Greeley, and Teresa A. Sullivan. 1983. *The Dilemma of American Immigration.* New Brunswick, N.J.: Transaction.

Campbell, Paul R. 1994. *Population Projections for States, by Age, Sex, Race, and Hispanic Origin: 1993–2020.* Washington, D.C.: U.S. Bureau of the Census, P25-1111.

Edmonston, Barry, Sharon M. Lee, and Jeffrey S. Passel. 1994. "Ethnicity, Ancestry, and Exogamy in U.S. Population Projections." Paper presented at the Population Association of America meetings. Miami (May 5–7, 1994).

Espenshade, Thomas J., and Maryann Belanger. 1997. "U.S. Public Perceptions and Reactions to Mexican Migration." In *At the Crossroads: Mexico and U.S. Immigration Policy*, edited by Frank Bean, Rodolf O. de la Garza, B.R. Roberts, and Sidney Weintraub. Lanham, Md.: Rowman and Littlefield.

Espenshade, Thomas J., and Charles A. Calhoun. 1993. "An Analysis of Public Opinion Toward Undocumented Migration." *Population Research and Policy Review* 12 (3): 189–224.

Farley, Reynolds. 1996. *The New American Reality: Who We Are, How We Got Here, Where We Are Going*. New York: Russell Sage Foundation.

Passel, Jeffrey S., and Barry Edmonston. 1994. "Immigration and Race: Recent Trends in Immigration to the United States." In *Immigration and Ethnicity: The Integration of America's Newest Arrivals*, edited by Barry Edmonston and Jeffrey S. Passel. Washington, D.C.: The Urban Institute Press.

Reimers, David M. 1985. *Still the Golden Door*. New York: Columbia University Press.

Smith, James P., and Barry Edmonston, eds. 1997. *The New Americans: Economic, Demographic, and Fiscal Effects of Immigration*. Washington D.C.: National Academy Press.

Teitelbaum, Michael S., and Myron Weiner, eds. 1995. *Threatened Peoples, Threatened Borders: World Migration and U.S. Policy*. New York: Norton.

U.S. Commission on Immigration Reform. 1994. *U.S. Immigration Policy: Restoring Credibility*. Washington, D.C.: U.S. Government Printing Office.

U.S. Immigration and Naturalization Service. 1996. *Statistical Yearbook of the U.S. Immigration and Naturalization Service, 1995*. Washington, D.C.: U.S. Government Printing Office.

PART I

IMPLICATIONS FOR EARNINGS AND INCOME

CHAPTER 1

The Impact of Immigration on Income Distribution Among Minorities

George E. Johnson

The purpose of this paper is to address several methodological issues associated with the question of the likely impact of immigration policy on the level and distribution of aggregate income. Given the high rate of immigration during the past twenty years—especially the immigration of people with relatively low levels of labor-market skill—it seems likely that the earnings of the low-skilled segment of the domestic population have been adversely impacted. On the other hand, other groups, people with relatively high labor-market skills and the owners of nonlabor factors, have probably benefited from the new immigration. Of particular interest in this paper is the degree to which different ethnic groups (African Americans, incumbent Hispanic Americans, and "Others" (all other ethnic groups) have been affected differently by the new immigration.

The quantitative magnitude and the form of the impact of immigration on the level and distribution of income depend on the "model" one applies to the problem and the values of key parameters. The major modeling issues include the aggregation of different age/education/gender/ethnic groups in the aggregate production function, the labor supply elasticities of different labor groups, and the way the supplies of nonlabor factors are affected by wage changes caused by immigration. Having specified such a model, the likely quantitative effects of a given amount and form of immigration depend on the values of certain behavioral parameters.

The next section explores modeling issues in detail. It must be true that an increase in the aggregate labor force through immigration causes some change in aggregate output (ΔY), and this increased output is equal to the earnings of the new immigrants (ΔY_m) plus the change in the income of the owners of nonlabor inputs (ΔY_k) plus the change in the earnings of all domestic labor groups ($\Sigma \Delta Y_{di}$). The focus of the models in this paper is on the size and distribution of the right hand side of $\Delta Y - \Delta Y_m = \Delta Y_k + \Sigma \Delta Y_{di}$ for a given amount and form of immigration.

I then illustrate some of the major modeling issues by asking what we would reasonably expect to happen in response to a hypothetical increase in the adult low-skilled population of ten million immigrants in 1993. The age/gender/education distribution of these immigrants is assumed to approximate that of all Hispanic immigrants to the United States between 1983 and 1992 and who were between the ages of eighteen and sixty-five in 1993. The ten million figure was chosen because it seems a reasonable estimate of the total amount (legal and otherwise) of low-skilled immigration into the United States that actually occurred during the preceding ten years. Thus, the effects of the hypothetical immigration discussed in the third section may be considered as rough estimates of the effects of low-skilled immigration since the early 1980s.

The effects of this immigration scenario depend, needless to say, on the specification of the underlying model of labor-market equilibrium and the values of specific parameters. A fairly robust result, however, is that low-skilled immigration results in what is in effect an income transfer from lower- to higher-skilled members of the incumbent population. The size of this transfer amounts to about 2 percent of the wage bills of both lower- and higher-skilled workers. *If* the labor market effect of the low-skilled immigration is proportionally the same for native low-skilled blacks and Hispanics as for low-skilled others (primarily whites), the net effect on the relative average earnings of blacks and Hispanics is fairly small (a reduction of about a half of 1 percent for the former and 1 percent for the latter). It can, however, be argued that the adverse impact of low-skilled immigration may be different for minorities than for nonminorities in the native, low-skilled population, and, in this case, the effect of low-skilled immigration on the ethnic distribution of income is much larger.

The policy experiment that underlies the results discussed later in this study is the absence of a drastic change in U.S. immigration policy. In the absence of such a change, there is likely to be an inflow of low-skilled immigrants during the next ten years of a magnitude roughly comparable to the inflow of the previous ten years. For the distributional effects not to occur, it would be necessary to impose and enforce measures that would (1) ban all legal immigration of potential low-skilled workers (but *not* of high-skilled workers) and (2) completely stop illegal immigration. Although I am not a political scientist, I doubt that such measures will be put in place.

MODELS OF THE EFFECTS OF IMMIGRATION
General Framework

It is useful to start by outlining the general features of a macroeconomic model that will permit us to make a set of reasonably informed guesses about the effects of immigration on the incomes of different groups in the population over intervals of time after that immigration occurs. This model will then be specialized in several alternative directions for purposes of tractability.

The labor force is assumed to be composed of I distinct groups that can be distinguished by "skill" (that is, what they do in the production process). The effective aggregate labor supply of each of these groups is N_i (person-hours of labor services per unit of time). The production function for the economy relates aggregate output (Y) to the quantities of labor services and capital input (K), that is

(1.1) $Y = F(N_1, ..., N_P, K)$.

I assume that F is linear homogeneous in its $I + 1$ arguments (that is, an x percent increase in each factors causes an x percent increase in Y).

Given competitive product and factor markets, the real wage rate of each labor group is

(1.2) $W_i = \dfrac{\partial Y}{\partial N_i} = F_i(N_1, ..., N_I, K),$

and the real rental price of a unit of capital is

(1.3) $r = \dfrac{\partial Y}{\partial K} = F_k(N_1, ..., N_I, K).$

Because of the assumed linear homogeneity of F, payments to factors exhaust Y, that is, $Y = \sum_i W_i N_i + rK$.

The hypothetical effects of a change in immigration policy on the distribution of income can be examined initially in the context of this framework. Suppose the particular policy would result in a rapid increase in the number of immigrants employed in group 1 jobs equal to dM_1. This would, by equations (1.2) and (1.3), change the values of the W_i's r. Assuming that there are no supply effects in the short run (that is, that the initial employment rates of each the initial population of each labor group, including the N_i's, as well as K did not change), the change in aggregate output per new immigrant is $dY/dM_1 = F_1 = W_1$. The changes per new immigrant in the aggregate income of the incumbent group 1 workers, the incomes of each of the other labor groups, and of the owners of capital are

(1.4) $\dfrac{d(W_i N_i)}{dM_1} = W_1 \gamma_i C_{1i}$

and

Figure 1.1   Effect of Immigration on the Labor Market for
Group 1 Workers

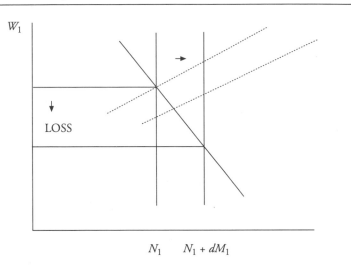

N_1 $N_1 + dM_1$

(1.5) $\dfrac{d(rK)}{dM_1} = W_1 \gamma_k C_{1k}$,

where γ_i is the output elasticity of labor group I, γ_k the same for capital, and C_{ij} is the partial elasticity of complementarity between factors i and j.[1]

An important implication of the theory of distribution in this case is that the marginal migrant receives the increase in Y attributable to him/her, W_1, the incumbent N_1's lose a certain amount, and all other factors gain by exactly the amount that the N_1's lose. The last two conclusions follow from the facts that $C_{1i} < 0$ (diminishing returns in each factor) and that each F_i is homogeneous of degree zero. The result is illustrated geometrically in figure 1.1. The new immigrants receive ΔY, and there is a transfer of earnings from the incumbent N_1's to the aggregate of all other factors equal to LOSS. (The area of the triangle in figure 1.1 goes to zero as dM_1/N_1 gets small.)

The aggregate of the other factors must gain from dM_1, but this is not necessarily true of each other factor. Labor group i benefits or loses from the policy as C_{1i} is positive or negative. Those groups that are substitutes for group 1 workers ($C_{1i} < 0$) lose, and their losses are part of an increased transfer to those groups that are complementary to group 1 ($C_{1i} > 0$).

This points to the importance of the nature of the aggregation of labor inputs in the assessment of the distributional impact of immigration. As will be pointed out later in this paper, we do not know enough about the empirical details of substitution to be very sure about very disaggregated questions.

A second issue concerns the effect of changes in factor prices on factor supplies. An important recent line of research points to the possibility that the effective supplies of some labor groups (especially those at the low end of the wage distribution) are subject to a fairly large positive wage elasticity. If this is true of the incumbent N_1's in the above example, the effects of dM_1 on Y and the aggregate income of the other factors will be smaller, for the immigrants displace some incumbent N_1's from employment (as is shown in figure 1.1 with a positive labor supply elasticity, ε_1). An extreme version of the upward sloping labor supply model is the case of real wage inflexibility. If this describes the labor market for group 1 workers, the "labor supply function" is horizontal at the initial wage, and dM_1 results in *complete* displacement of incumbent N_1's.

A similar question concerns the supply of capital. If $C_{1k} > 0$, the rental price of the existing stock of capital increases. K would tend to rise over time, above what it would have been otherwise—either because investment is attracted from international sources by the relatively high rate of return or because domestic saving rises as a result of the increase in Y/K. By either scenario, K changes until r returns to its initial (equilibrium) value. In the "long run" (the period necessary for the complete adjustment of K), the effect of immigration on the supply of capital is $dK/dM_1 = -\gamma_1 C_{1k} K/\gamma_k C_{kk} N_1$. Since $C_{kk} < 0$, this is positive or negative as group 1 labor is complementary with or substitutable for capital. It then follows that the change in the aggregate earnings of the ith labor group is

$$(1.6) \quad \frac{d(W_i N_i)}{dM_1} = W_1 \gamma_i \left[C_{1i} - \frac{C_{ik} C_{1k}}{C_{kk}^2} \right].$$

For group 1, this long run value is smaller than the short-run value given by equation 1.5 so long as $C_{1k} \neq 0$.

In addition to the effects of immigration on the labor supply decisions of each of the I skill groups of the incumbent population, there are other longer-run issues concerning labor supply. First, the dM_1 immigrants may be confined to working at a lower skill level than they were working in their source country because of poor language skills and other barriers to immediate assimilation. As time since the point of emigration passes, one would expect that some of the initial dM_1 immigrants would leave work in that skill level and move on to higher skill levels.[2] In this case, the initial distributional effects of immigration would shift over time.

A second set of long-run supply issues concerns the effect of immigration on human capital accumulation decisions by the native population. To the extent that low-skilled immigration increases the relative wages of skilled workers, younger cohorts in the nonimmigrant population will be more likely to obtain high levels of education. This would dampen the distributional effects of immigration.

The Effect of Immigration on the Incomes of Population Subgroups

The general framework discussed thus far indicates how in principle one assesses the impact of a particular immigration policy on the distribution of income across different labor groups and the owners of the initial capital stock. For some purposes it is useful to know how the policy affects the distribution of income across other dimensions (by, for example, gender, age, and ethnicity).

This is, in principle, fairly straightforward. The aggregate income of the population with characteristics p is given by:

$$(1.7) \quad Y_p = \sum_{i=1}^{I} \left(\frac{N_{pi}}{N_i} \right) W_i N_i + rK_p = W_p N_p + \left(\frac{K_p}{K} \right) rK,$$

where N_{pi} is the employment of the p population in labor group i, K_p is the amount of the capital stock owned by the p population, and W_p is the average wage across all jobs earned by p workers. In the short run, a particular immigration policy causes an increase in immigrant employment in group 1 jobs of dM_1. This, in turn, causes changes in all factor prices and (perhaps) the values of some of the N_{pi}'s. The short-run change in Y_p due to dM_1 is thus

$$(1.8) \quad \frac{dY_p}{dM_1} = \frac{d(W_p N_p)}{dM_1} + K_p \frac{dr}{dM_1}.$$

The first term on the right-hand side of equation (1.8) is the more likely to be positive if the skill distribution of the group p is skewed toward labor groups that are complementary with N_1.

In the long run, the changes in the W_i's are different from their short-run values (and thus so too are possible changes in the N_{pi}'s). In addition, short- and medium-run changes in $W_p N_p$ cause changes in the rate at which the p population accumulates assets (K_p). Given a constant saving rate out of gross income of each segment of the population (s_p), the time derivative of assets is

$$(1.9) \quad \dot{K}_p = s_p Y_p - \delta K_p = s_p [W_p N_p + r K_p] - \delta K_p,$$

where δ is the rate at which capital depreciates. In the long run, $W_p N_p$ goes to its long-run value and r returns to its long-run equilibrium value, and the long-run value of assets owned by the p population goes to

$$(1.10) \quad K_p = \frac{s_p}{\delta - r s_p} W_p N_p.$$

Now assume that all the investment is financed through domestic saving. The rate of change of the aggregate capital stock is $\dot{K} = sY - \delta K$, where $s = \sum_p s_p (Y_p / Y)$ is the average saving rate in the economy. In the long run the rate of growth of the capital stock is equal to the rate of economic growth, g_{Y^*}. This means that the long-run output/capital ratio is $Y/K = (g_{Y^*} + \delta)/s$.

Consumption per time unit by the p population is $C_p = (1 - s_p) Y_p$. Substituting equation (1.10) for K_p in 1.7, this consumption level becomes

$$(1.11) \quad \frac{C_p = (1 - s_p)\delta}{\delta - r s_p} W_p N_p.$$

From the results concerning the equilibrium rate of economic growth, we know that $r = F_k = \gamma_k Y/K = \gamma_k (g_{Y^*} + \delta)/s$. Equation (1.11) can then be rewritten as

$$(1.12) \quad C_p = \frac{(1 - s_p)\delta}{\delta - \dfrac{s_p}{s} \gamma_k (g_{Y^*} + \delta)} W_p N_p.$$

If the aggregate saving rate in the economy, s, is approximately equal to capital's share, γ_k, which is a necessary condition for the saving rate to be optimal in a Golden Rule sense, the coefficient on $W_p N_p$ reduces to $\delta (1 - s_p) / (\delta (1 - s_p) - s_p g_{Y^*})$. Since the value of δ is about .10 and the value g_{Y^*} is about .03, the value of this coefficient is only slightly greater than one over the relevant range of s_p. Thus, the long-run effect of an immigration policy on the welfare of population p is approximated by the value of $d(W_p N_p) / dM_1$

It is, of course, also true that a full welfare analysis of immigration must also take account of public finance issues. The analysis to this point has ignored taxes and government spending, for it has been cast entirely in terms of gross incomes. Taxes, government spending, and the distribution of social services across different groups could, in principle, be added to the model.

LABOR GROUP AGGREGATION ALTERNATIVES

The production function given by equation (1.1) is the most general specification, but any empirical application of the model must make some simplifying assumptions. These simplifications all include the assumption that capital is equally substitutable with all labor groups, and they also contain various specifications of the way in which workers with different skills should be aggregated in the production function.[3]

A common feature of many recent applications of labor demand models is to assume explicitly that labor and capital services can be treated as separable in the aggregate production function. In this case equation (1.1) is replaced by the two-level function

(1.13) $Y = F(G(N_1, ..., N_I), K),$

where G is the effective flow of aggregate labor services. F is linear homogeneous in G and K, and G is homogeneous in the I values of the different labor inputs. The output elasticity of G is $1 - \gamma_k$, and the output elasticity of capital is γ_k. The partial elasticity of complementarity between labor and capital services is now the reciprocal of the elasticity of substitution between them, σ, for

(1.14) $\hat{r} = \hat{F}_k = \dfrac{1 - \gamma_k}{\sigma}(\hat{G} - \hat{K}),$

where $\hat{r} = dr/r = d(\log r)$, and so on. The marginal condition for each labor group is

(1.15) $W_i = F_G(G, K)\, G_i(N_1, ..., N_I).$

The proportional change version of this equation is

(1.16) $\hat{W}_i = \dfrac{\gamma_k}{\sigma}[\hat{K} - \hat{G}] + \sum_{j=1}^{I} \beta_j D_{ij} \hat{N}_j = \sum_{j=1}^{I} \beta_j \left[D_{ij} - \dfrac{\gamma_k}{\sigma} \right] \hat{N}_j + \dfrac{\gamma_k}{\sigma} \hat{K}.$

$\beta_i = G_i N_i / G$ is the share of G attributable to group i, and $D_{ij} = G_{ij} G / G_i G_j$ is the partial elasticity of complementarity between i and j workers with K/G held constant.

The effects of the immigration policy allowing N_1 to increase by dM_1 (with all incumbent labor supplies unchanged) can be examined in the context of this special case. First, the change in aggregate output is $dY = F_G G_1 dM_1 = W_1 dM_1$, which is also the income of the immigrants. Second, the short-run change in the income of the owners of capital changes by $Kdr = (\gamma_k/\sigma) W_1 dM_1$. The negative value of this is also the change in the wage bill of all incumbent workers. Third, the short-run change in the aggregate earnings of the ith labor group is $\beta_i (D_{1i} - \gamma_k/\sigma) W_1 dM_1$. Since $D_{1i} < 0$, the earnings of the incumbent group 1 workers must fall as a result of the immigration policy. The earnings of each of the $I-1$ labor groups will either fall by (proportionally) less than the decline in the earnings of group 1 workers or increase. Since $\Sigma \beta_i D_{1i} = 0$, the change in aggregate labor earnings is $-(\gamma_k/\sigma) W_1 dM_1$, the transfer to the owners of capital.

Further simplification of the specification of the production process is necessary in order to apply the framework empirically. The simplest approach (one that has been used in the immigration context by Borjas, Freeman, and Katz [1997]) is to assume that the N_i's can be aggregated to form skilled and unskilled labor aggregates (S and U, respectively) that in turn form a labor aggregate (G).[4] The aggregate production function is in this case

$$(1.17) \quad Y = F(G(U,S), K = f\left(\frac{g(S/U)U}{K}\right)K,$$

where both the F and G functions are linear homogeneous. Labor's share of output is $1 - \gamma_k = f'gU/fK$, and skilled labor's share of the labor aggregate is $\beta = g'S/gU$. The elasticity of substitution between the labor aggregate and capital is σ; the elasticity of substitution between skilled and unskilled labor is τ.

The competitively determined prices of the two types of labor and of capital are $W_s = f'g'$, $W_U = f'(g - (S/U)g')$, and $r = f - (gU/K)f'$. It is useful to specify that the aggregate supply of skilled labor is $S = S_d + M_s$, where S_d and M_s are, respectively, the domestic and immigrant effective supplies of skilled labor; similarly, $U = U_d + M_u$.

A particular immigration policy allows the entry of dS_m and dU_m immigrants into the country. Assuming no effects on the labor supply of either group, the proportionate change in output associated with the immigration policy in the short run (capital held constant) is

$$(1.18) \quad \hat{Y} = (1 - \gamma_k)\, \beta\, \frac{dM_s}{S} + (1 - \gamma_k)\,(1 - \beta)\, \frac{dM_u}{U}.$$

The short-run proportional changes in the three factor prices are

$$(1.19) \quad \hat{W}_s = - \left[\frac{\gamma_k}{\sigma}\, \beta + \frac{1 - \beta}{\tau} \right] \frac{dM_s}{S} - (1 - \beta) \left[\frac{\gamma_k}{\sigma} - \frac{1}{\tau} \right] \frac{dM_u}{U},$$

$$(1.20) \quad \hat{W}_u = - \beta \left[\frac{\gamma_k}{\sigma} - \frac{1}{\tau} \right] \frac{DM_s}{S} - \left[\frac{\gamma_k(1 - \beta)}{\sigma} + \frac{\beta}{\tau} \right] \frac{dM_u}{U},$$

$$(1.21) \quad \hat{r} = \frac{(1 - \gamma_k)}{\sigma}\, [\beta\, \hat{S} + (1 - \beta)\, \hat{U}].$$

The short-run partial elasticity of substitution between the two labor groups is positive if $\sigma > \tau \gamma_k$. Otherwise, an increase in M_s lowers W_u (and an increase in M_u lowers W_s), because the reduction in the marginal product of the labor aggregate outweighs the effect increase in the relative scarcity of unskilled labor.

In the long run K adjusts so that r is equal to its equilibrium value, and $\hat{K} = \beta\,(dM_s\,/\,S) + (1 - \beta)(dM_u\,/\,U)$. The long-run proportional changes in the two wage rates are

$$(1.22) \quad \hat{W}_s = - \frac{1 - \beta}{\tau} \left(\frac{dM_s}{S} - \frac{dM_u}{U} \right),$$

$$(1.23) \quad \hat{W}_u = \frac{\beta}{\tau} \left(\frac{dM_s}{S} - \frac{dM_u}{U} \right).$$

From equations (1.22) and (1.23) it is clear that an immigration policy can be characterized as *skill-neutral* in the long run if the skill distribution of immigrants is equal to the skill distribution of the incumbent labor force, that is, if $dM_s/dM_u = S/U$. The policy favors skilled labor (it makes W_s rise at the expense of W_u) if $dM_s/dM_u < S/U$, and it favors unskilled workers if this inequality goes in the other direction.

A particular advantage of this approach to labor aggregation is that it facilitates the analysis of the effects of immigration across demographic distinctions. It is straightforward, in terms of the discussion later in this section, to determine whether the employment in group p workers is more or less skilled than the average of the incumbent population and then to see whether the immigration policy was relatively favorable to the skilled or the unskilled.

A limitation of this "linear synthesis" approach to labor aggregation is that it surely imposes too much structure on the problem. For example, there is ample evidence that men and women *tend* to perform different jobs in the labor market—especially below the highest tail of the skill distribution.[5] Aggregation of the labor force into S and U units would include the assumption that male and female high school graduates are perfect substitutes for each other, but this is not entirely plausible. There are similar questions with respect to aggregation by age, education, and other demographic characteristics.[6]

To illustrate this in the context of immigration policy, consider the case in which there are two types of unskilled jobs, U_1 and U_2, that are not perfect substitutes in production. U_1 is the quantity of labor employed in "bad" unskilled jobs, and U_2 is the quantity of labor employed in "good" unskilled jobs. I hypothesize that low-skilled immigrants flow into the 1 rather than the 2 jobs. The aggregate flow of labor services in this case is

(1.24) $G = G(H(U_1, U_2), S)$.

H is the flow of unskilled labor services, with U_1's share equal to $\alpha = H_1 U_1 / H$ and the elasticity of substitution between U_1 and U_2 in the production of H of θ. β is, as above, skilled labor's output share and τ the elasticity of substitution between H and S.

The wage rate of each of the three types of labor is F_G times the derivative of G with respect to that factor. We will consider an immigration policy that results in an increase in U_1 of dM_u, but we continue to assume that this does not affect the supply of incumbents employed in job 1. The long-run increase in the aggregate wage bill is $W_{U_1} dM_u$, which is the gross earnings of the immigrants. The changes in the earnings of incumbent workers in the three are given by

(1.25) $d(W_{U_1} U_1) = -\left(\dfrac{1-\alpha}{\theta} + \dfrac{\alpha\beta}{\tau}\right) W_{U_1} dM_u$,

(1.26) $d(W_{U_2} U_2) = -(1-\alpha)\left(\dfrac{1}{\theta} - \dfrac{\beta}{\tau}\right) W_{U_1} dM_u$,

(1.27) $d(W_S U) = -(1-\alpha)\left(\dfrac{1}{\theta} + \dfrac{\beta}{\tau}\right) W_{U_1} dM_u$.

The sum of these distributional effects is, of course, zero. The immigration has an unambiguously negative effect on the group that is directly competitive with the new immigrants, and it has an unambiguously positive effect on the earnings of skilled workers. The effect on the incumbent U_2's is positive if $\tau > \beta\theta$, but negative otherwise.

Short-Run Labor Supply Effects

As pointed out earlier in this section, some recent work on labor supply has argued that low-wage male workers appear to have been subject to a fairly high wage elasticity with respect to labor force participation. In order to close the model and make conclusions concerning the effect of immigration on the distribution of welfare it is necessary to treat this explicitly.

The simplest way to do this is to assume that the utility of each of the L_i members of the population in the ith skill group has the following utility function:

(1.28) $ut = W_i - v$, *employed; $ut = b$, not employed.*

W_i is, as above, the real wage of the skill group. V is the disutility of work, which is distributed according to $z(v)$ between v_0 and v_1; b is the pecuniary benefit associated with not working (a transfer payment from the government or some other part of society).

The labor supply function associated with this simple specification of preferences (assuming that $v_0 < W_i - b < v_1$) is

(1.29) $N_i = \left[1 - \int_{W_i - b}^{v_1} z(v)dv \right] L_i = Z(W_i - b, u_i)L_i.$

$\partial N_i / \partial W_i = z\ (W_i - b,\ u_i)L_i > 0$, and the taste parameter refers to the distribution of preferences (reflecting the parameters of the distribution of v) is defined such that $\partial N_i / \partial \mu_i > 0$. The real wage elasticity of labor supply for group i is $\varepsilon_i = z_i W_i / Z_i$, which is larger the larger the value of the marginal frequency z_i.

The aggregate utility of the group i population (net of that due to asset income) is

(1.30) $UT_i = \left[\int_{v_0}^{W_i - b} (W_i - v)g(v)dv + \int_{W_i - b}^{v_1} bg(v)dv \right] L_1.$

Differentiating equation (1.30) with respect to W_i and b, the change in the aggregate utility of the group 1 population is

(1.31) $dUT_i = N_i dW_i + (L_i - N_i)db.$

Thus, this simple specification implies that the effect of a change in the wage rate of a group on the utility level of that population is equal to the effect of the wage change on that group's earnings.[7]

The more important implications of a nonzero labor supply elasticity in the analysis of immigration policy can be illustrated in the context of the skill aggregation model. Attention will be confined to the long run (in which K is proportional to G), and I assume for simplicity that all immigrants are unskilled workers. The aggregate real wage bill is

(1.32) $Y - rK = F_G[G_U[U_d + M_u] = G_S S] = W_U[U_d + M_u] + W_S S,$

where U_d is the domestic supply of unskilled labor and M_u is the size of the immigrant population (all of whom are unskilled). From equation (1.29) the domestic supply of unskilled labor is

(1.33) $U_d = Z^u(W_u - b, \mu_{ui}) L_u,$

and it assumed that $\varepsilon_u > 0$. Both skilled labor and immigrants are assumed to supply labor services inelastically.

The marginal condition for unskilled labor is

(1.34) $W_U = F_G G_U(U_d + M_u, S).$

Since the long-run supply of K is proportional to G, F_G is constant. U_d and W_U are then determined in equations (1.33) and (1.34). Differentiating these equations totally, the change in the domestic supply of unskilled labor with respect to an unskilled immigrant is seen to be

(1.35) $\dfrac{\partial U_d}{\partial M_d} = -\lambda_u = -\dfrac{\beta(1 - m_u)\varepsilon_u}{\tau + \beta(1 - m_u)\varepsilon_u},$

where $m_u = M_u/U$ is the fraction of unskilled labor input that is composed of immigrants. The *displacement effect* of immigration on domestic unskilled employment is λ_u; λ_u is zero when $\varepsilon_u = 0$ and approaches one as ε_u gets large.

The proportional change in the unskilled wage rate associated with a change in the number of immigrants is, in terms of the value of the displacement effect,

$$(1.36) \quad \hat{W}_u = -\frac{\beta(1-\lambda_u)}{\tau}\frac{dM_u}{U}.$$

Similarly, the proportional wage change of skilled workers is

$$(1.37) \quad \hat{W}_s = \frac{(1-\beta)(1-\lambda_u)}{\tau}\frac{dM_u}{U}.$$

These results permit an accounting of the long-run effects of the immigration of unskilled labor on the level and distribution of output. Differentiating equation (1.32) with respect to M_u, we obtain the following expression for the change in $Y - \delta K$ and its distribution per new immigrant:

$$(1.38) \quad W_U(1-\lambda_u) = W_U - \frac{\beta(1-\lambda_u)m_u}{\tau}W_U - \left[\lambda_u + \frac{\beta(1-\lambda_u)(1-m_u)}{\tau}\right]W_U + \frac{\beta(1-\lambda_u)}{\tau}W_U.$$

| change in aggregate labor earnings | earnings of new immigrants | change in earnings of old immigrants | change in earnings of domestic unskilled | change in earnings of skilled |

To adjust equation (1.38) for the change in the monetary value of the increased nonmarket time of the domestic unskilled population, $\lambda_u W_u$ is added to both sides of the equation. Thus, the larger is the value of ε_u the smaller is the loss due to immigration on the part of both the domestic unskilled and incumbent unskilled immigrants and the smaller is the gain received by skilled workers.

Immigration with Structural Unemployment

The results to this point are based on the assumption that both skilled and unskilled labor markets clear over the relevant period of time of the analysis. An alternative assumption, which is more applicable to Western Europe than to the United States, is that W_u is institutionally fixed at too high a level to permit the full employment of the unskilled population.

In this case, both the domestic unskilled population and unskilled immigrants are subject to structural unemployment. The aggregate level of unskilled employment, U, is determined by W_u (as well as by S and K), and the employment rate of unskilled labor is $U/(L_u + M_u)$. The wage bills of the domestic unskilled and of immigrants are, respectively, $W_u UL_u / (L_u + M_u)$ and $W_u UM_u / (L_u + M_u)$. Since U is fixed (and independent of the aggregate supply of unskilled labor), an additional *employed* immigrant causes domestic unskilled unemployment to fall by one. This is equivalent to a displacement effect (λ_u) of one in the context of the labor supply model above.

Effect of Immigration on Net Incomes

An important qualification of all the preceding theoretical conclusions is that the model has concentrated solely on the potential effects of immigration on the *gross incomes* of immigrants and of various groups of natives. A more complete analysis would focus on the effect of immigration on the *net incomes* (both financial and nonpecuniary) of different groups. It would be straightforward to do this, but, as mentioned above, my goal is to focus on the first order labor market effects.

A focus on net rather than gross incomes would include the effects of a given amount and type of immigration on the level and distribution of government expenditures, tax revenues, and transfer payments. A first question would be the extent to which the additional immigration caused an increase in public expenditure (on health, police, education, and so on) that was greater or less than the increase in aggregate tax revenue. It would then have to be determined at what level of government additional (or lowered) taxes occurred as well as the degree to which state and local taxes are less progressive than federal taxes.

The results reported by Borjas (1996) suggest that the geographic distribution of low-skilled immigrants may be very sensitive to state welfare benefit levels. This has an important implication for the equilibrium determination of welfare benefits. If states perceive that relatively high benefit levels, which they may want to offer to their domestic citizens, attract a large immigrant population, they will obviously lower them. This would obviously lower the average net income of the domestic low-skilled population.

The presence of a large immigrant population can also affect the average amount and quality of public services that are supplied to the domestic population. In particular, one would imagine that this would apply to public expenditure on K-12 schooling. Julian R. Betts in this volume suggests that there is some indication that such an effect has occurred.

The Effects of Immigration in an Open Economy Setting

All of the results in this section have depended on the traditional macroeconomic assumption that the various goods produced in the economy can be meaningfully aggregated into a single good (Y). If this is true, the composition of aggregate output between consumption, investment, and net exports makes no difference, and the analysis of the effects of immigration on output and its distribution can proceed as above.

An alternative approach is the model underlying "classical" trade theory (see, for example, section 2.3 of Jones and Neary [1984]). Suppose that the economy consists of two industries: industry A, which is relatively intensive in skilled labor, and industry B, which is relatively intensive in unskilled labor and that both goods A and B are traded internationally. Assuming that the foreign and domestic versions of these goods are perfect substitutes for each other and that the home country (in our case the United States) is too small to have a perceptible effect on the world prices of these goods, the model then is quite different. We have a *much* different set of implications concerning the effect of changes in relative factor supplies in general (S/U) and of the immigration of unskilled labor in particular.

The reason for this is that the marginal conditions for the two types of labor are now $W_S = P_A \partial Q_A / \partial S_A = P_B \partial Q_B / \partial S_B$ and $W_U = P_A \partial Q_A / \partial U_A = P_B \partial Q_B / \partial U_B$, where P_j, Q_j, S_j, and U_j are the values of, respectively, the world price, the domestic output level, and the inputs of each type of labor in industry $j = A,B$. (Capital is assumed away—although its presence would not alter the conclusions.) Given the full employment conditions, $S_A + S_B = S$ and $U_A + U_B = U$, one can solve the model for W_S and W_U in terms of the exogenous variables of the model. Given that both goods A and B are produced (in the jargon of trade theory, the economy is within the "cone of diversification"), the equilibrium values of W_S and W_U each depend on the exogenous values of P_A and P_B as well as on various technology parameters associated with the industry production functions. Real and relative wages do not depend in any way on the relative supply of labor, that is, $\partial W_i / \partial (S/U) = 0$.

This means that, in the classical trade model, an increase in the value of U due to immigration, which, ceteris paribus, lowers the value of S/U, *has no effect on domestic wage rates*. Instead, the composition of output is shifted from the skill-intensive good A to the unskilled-intensive good B. The typical labor demand function (like figure 1.1 earlier) is horizontal rather than downward-sloping, and there are no transfers among domestic labor groups associated with immigration. Immigrants receive the increase in domestic output, and that is that.

That every economy has a large sector that produces goods and services that are not traded (say, Q_c) in no way alters the conclusion of the classical trade model with respect to the distributional effects of immigration. As long as the two tradable goods A and B can still be produced profitably, the existence of an additional good whose price is determined domestically does not alter the result that W_S and W_U are determined by the exogenous values of P_A and P_B. All that is different is that some S's and U's are employed in the service sector rather than exclusively in the tradable goods sector.

The implications of the classical trade model concerning the effects of relative factor supplies (and hence of immigration) on wages are upset if a few conditions are not met. First, if one of the two tradable goods industries (A or B) disappears because it is no longer profitable (the economy is outside the cone of divergence), the behavior of the economy is like that of the closed economy discussed before this section. Second, if one or both of the factors are not completely mobile between industries (such that, for example, the wage rates of unskilled workers are not equal across industries), the effect of a change on relative factor supplies on wages is represented by a model that is a blend of the closed model and the classical trade model. It is unlikely that labor is anything but completely mobile in the long run, but this long run may be twenty years.

A third qualification of the classical trade model is based on the likelihood that foreign and domestic versions of particular products may be imperfect substitutes. (For example, at given relative prices, some consumers in the United States prefer to purchase Buicks while others prefer Volvos.) This can be represented by assuming that the values of the elasticity of substitution between the foreign and domestic versions of each of the tradable goods in the aggregate utility function are finite. As these elasticities approach infinity, the resultant model approaches the classical trade model; as they approach one (from above), the model becomes essentially the closed, single-good model set out in this paper.

For the intermediate case (substitution elasticities between one and infinity), the model of the equilibrium of the labor market is, not surprisingly, a blend of the closed and classic trade models.[8] For values of the relevant substitution elasticities inferred from estimates of the price elasticities of imports and exports, the weight given the closed model versus the classical trade model in the context of the United States is in the range of 0.7 to 0.8. In small open countries (like Belgium), on the other hand, the weight on the closed model is much smaller, a range of 0.4 to 0.5.[9]

In terms of the empirical analysis of the effects of immigration, an increase in the degree to which an economy is open to international competition—such has occurred in the United States over the past twenty-five years—may be represented by an increase in the value of τ in equation (1.38). In the classical trade model (in which there is no perceived difference between the foreign and domestic versions of tradable goods), τ is effectively infinite, and unskilled immigrants have no long-run effects on the distribution of earnings among native workers.

In the more general approach, increased openness raises τ, from (perhaps) 1.25 to 1.75 in the U.S. context.

RANGE ESTIMATES OF THE QUANTITATIVE EFFECTS OF IMMIGRATION

The interesting set of questions in this paper revolve around *how large* the likely effects of immigration policy are on the distribution of income. In this section parameterized versions of some of the models set out earlier provide a range of estimates of the potential effects of immigration on the incomes of various groups in the economy—by skill, ethnicity, gender, and age and, in the short run, between labor and capital. I then ask: *What would have been the likely effects on the level and distribution of income of a ten-million increase as of 1993 in the number of unskilled immigrants in the United States?*

The Skill Composition of the Work Force

The first task is to disaggregate the labor force in 1993 by skill, gender, and ethnicity. In order to do this, it is necessary to make an assumption about the translation of observable characteristics of workers into different labor inputs. Initially, it is assumed that there are four relevant labor groups: male high school equivalents (the effective input of which is U_1), female high school equivalents (U_2), male college equivalents (S_1), and female college equivalents (S_2). The two-level CES variant of the aggregate production function, equation (1.13), is

$$(1.39) \quad Y = a \left[\mu G^{\frac{\sigma-1}{\sigma}} + (1-\mu) K^{\frac{\sigma-1}{\sigma}} \right]^{\frac{\sigma}{\sigma-1}}$$

$$G = b \left[\delta_1 U_{1e}^{\frac{\tau-1}{\tau}} + \delta_2 U_2^{\frac{\tau-1}{\tau}} + \delta_3 S_1^{\frac{\tau-1}{\tau}} + \delta_4 S_2^{\frac{\tau-1}{\tau}} \right]^{\frac{\tau}{\tau-1}},$$

where $\Sigma\delta_i = 1$. High school equivalent labor for each gender is defined as the sum of labor input for the following groups (appropriately weighted in terms of part-time versus full-time status and their year-round, full-time earnings relative to whites aged thirty-five to forty-four with a high school degree): (a) All eighteen- to twenty-four-year-olds and twenty-five- to sixty-four-year-olds, (b) with less than high school, (c) with only a high school degree, and (d) half of those with some college. College-equivalent labor is defined as the sum of all twenty-five- to sixty-four-year-olds in the following two groups (with supply adjustment and adjustment of inputs as a ratio of thirty-five- to forty-four-year-old white college graduates): (a) Half of those with some college, and (b) all college graduates.

Using published data from the CPS for 1983 and 1993, the population and employment of four separate demographic groups can be identified: blacks, Hispanics who were in the United States in 1983, Hispanics who immigrated between 1983 and 1992, and "others" (the difference between the total population and the three other groups). The aggregate populations (aged eighteen to sixty-five), employment levels (converted into full-time units but *not* adjusted for age-gender-ethnic wage differences), and the estimated aggregate wage bills of each of these four groups by gender in 1993 are reported in table 1.1.

The one aspect of the figures in table 1.1 that is not straightforward is the breakdown of the Hispanic population between those who resided in the United States in 1983 and those who immigrated into the United States between 1983 and 1992. To do this, the 1983 Hispanic population by gender was separated into groups with the following age ranges: eight to fourteen, fifteen to twenty-four, twenty-five to thirty-four, thirty-five to forty-four, and forty-five to fifty-four. On the assumption that the survival rate of domestic Hispanics by age and gender was the same as for all whites, the aggregate 1993 Hispanic population in the United States can be broken down into immigrants and nonimmigrants (since 1983). I further assume that (1) domestic Hispanics aged fifteen to twenty-four had the same educational distribution as blacks in that age interval and (2) that the shift from 1983 to 1993 in the educational distribution of domestic Hispanics aged twenty-five to fifty-four in 1983 was proportional to the shift for non-Hispanics. Finally, I assume that the ratio of full-time equivalent employment to population is the same, age/education/gender held constant, for domestic Hispanics and immigrants and that immigrants earn, ceteris paribus, 20 percent less than non-immigrant Hispanics.[10]

As seen from table 1.1, this estimation algorithm yields the (not very surprising) conclusion that Hispanic immigrants are more likely to be both male and less educated than the Hispanics who were in the United States prior to 1983. They are also much younger than the domestic population (64 percent of the eighteen- to sixty-four-year-old immigrants are under age thirty-five, compared to 48 percent of both blacks and the domestic Hispanic population and 41 percent of whites). Thus, while Hispanic immigrants compose 2.1 percent of the adult population, their estimated earnings constitute just 1.1 percent of the total wage bill.

Table 1.1 Population Aged Eighteen to Sixty-Four (Millions), Full-Time Equivalent Employment (Millions), and Labor Earnings (Billions of Dollars) for High School Equivalents (U) and College Equivalents (S) by Gender and Ethnicity, 1993

	U (High School)			S (College)		
	Population (a)	Employment (b)	Wages (c)	Population (d)	Employment (e)	Wages (f)
Black						
Men	6.85	4.63	106.1	1.70	1.35	60.0
Women	7.88	3.80	83.9	2.23	1.62	62.4
Other						
Men	39.15	28.23	989.9	22.25	19.16	1155.4
Women	42.31	23.25	544.0	28.20	13.82	586.6
Hispanic (domestic)						
Men	4.11	2.76	76.8	0.88	0.74	35.3
Women	4.42	1.95	44.0	0.91	0.58	22.8
Hispanic (immigrant)						
Men	1.77	1.28	25.2	0.15	0.13	5.5
Women	1.37	0.51	10.1	0.08	0.05	1.5
Aggregate	104.7	64.1	1879.9	48.2	37.3	1929.5

Given the assumption that the economy was in equilibrium with respect to the supply of capital in 1993, it is straightforward to fill in the parameters of equation (1.39). The marginal products of capital and a unit of effective labor services are

$$(1.40) \quad r = \frac{\partial Y}{\partial K} = MP_K = (1 - \mu)a^{1-1/\sigma} \left(\frac{Y}{K} \right)^{1/\sigma}$$

and

$$(1.41) \quad MP_N = \frac{\partial Y}{\partial G} = \mu a^{1-1/\sigma} \left(\frac{Y}{G} \right)^{1/\sigma}.$$

Further, the marginal product of each labor group is

$$(1.42) \quad \frac{\partial Y}{\partial N_i} = MP_N \, \delta_i b^{1-1/\tau} \left(\frac{G}{N_i} \right)^{1/\tau} , \quad N_i = U_1, U_2, S_1, S_2.$$

Given the observed wages and effective employment levels of each of the labor groups and the arbitrary assumption that in equilibrium MP_N equals one, the values of b and the δ_i's are determined in the four equations in (1.42) for an *assumed* value of τ. Given information on labor's share of output (.582 in 1993) and the assumption that r was at its equilibrium value in 1993, say r_o, the value of μ is determined from equations (1.40) and (1.41) for an assumed value of σ.

For the simulations to follow I assume that the distribution of characteristics (with respect to gender, age, education, and relative marginal products) of the hypothetical ten million additional immigrants is identical to that of the unskilled end of the existing 1983 to 1992 Hispanic immigrants. This means, given the characteristics of the 3.14 million "HS-Imm." U's category in table 1.1, the immigration scenario would cause the aggregate employment of unskilled labor to rise by 4.07 million men and 1.62 million women. In terms of efficiency units of labor this represents an increase in U_1 of $3.18 \times 25.3/1198.0 = 6.7$ percent and in U_2 of $3.18 \times 10.1/681.0 = 4.7$ percent.

The Impact of Immigration in the Short and Long Runs

We first examine the implications of a sudden increase in the number of unskilled immigrants under the assumption that the employment levels of all incumbent groups are unaffected. This means that the substitution and income elasticities of labor supply of each demographic group are of equal and opposite sign and that the level and structure of real wages are free to adjust such that there is continuous full employment of all labor groups.[11]

If the increases in U_1 and U_2 had no effect on the marginal products of each of the four types of labor and of capital, the new immigrants would receive the increase in aggregate output, 112.4 billion dollars (in 1993 dollars), and the earnings of each of the groups of incumbent workers would be unaffected. The models discussed earlier, however, suggest that the increases in U_1 and U_2 will lower W_1 and raise the relative wage rates of skilled workers, W_3 and W_4. In the short run the increase in G due to the immigration raises the marginal product of capital and lowers the marginal product of the labor aggregate, MP_N, so the qualitative effect of unskilled immigration on the earnings of skilled workers is ambiguous.

This is illustrated in the two sets of results, which are based on alternative values of the elasticity of capital/labor substitution (σ) of 0.5 and 1.0, for the short run in table 1.2. The elasticity of substitution between the four labor groups (τ) is assumed to equal 1.5, and the supplies of all the labor groups are fixed. The level of aggregate output satisfies:

$$(1.43) \quad Y = r_o K + (MP_K - r_o)K + MP_N \sum_i G_i .$$

output	capital	excess	labor
	cost	profit	earnings

As argued earlier, in the long run K adjusts such that there are zero excess products (because $r = MP_K \rightarrow r_o$). It is assumed that in the absence of the hypothetical immigration the value of K would have been in long-run equilibrium in 1993.

The short-run change in aggregate output due to the additional ten million immigrants in 1993 is, as seen in columns (a) and (c) of table 1.2, between 109.9 and 110.5 billion dollars for σ equal to, respectively, 0.5 and 1.0. The income received by the new immigrants, between 108.4 dollars and 108.8 dollars, is only slightly smaller than the increase in GDP. The degree to which labor and capital are substitutable, the value of σ, is important in the short-run reduction in the total wage bill of domestic labor, which is roughly equal to the short-run increase in aggregate profits, for the magnitude of this transfer is approximately twice as large with σ equal to 0.5 versus 1.0. The aggregate earnings of skilled workers fall slightly (by 0.5 percent) for $\sigma = 0.5$, but rise slightly (by 0.7 percent) for $\sigma = 1.0$.

Because the skill distribution of the different ethnic groups varies rather considerably, the short-run proportional impact of the assumed ten million unskilled immigrants varies across the four groups. Workers

Table 1.2 Absolute and Percentage Changes in Aggregate Output and Its Distribution Due to Hypothetical Increase in Unskilled Immigrants of Ten Million Persons, with and Without Capital Adjustment*

	Short Run (K fixed)				Long Run $(r \rightarrow r_o)$	
	$\sigma = 0.5$		$\sigma s = 1.0$			
	Δ (a)	% (b)	Δ (c)	% (d)	Δ (e)	% (f)
Output	109.9	2.9	110.5	2.9	191.2	2.9
Capital cost	0.0	0.0	0.0	0.0	80.0	2.9
Excess profit	92.7		46.2		0.0	
Domestic labor	−90.2	−2.4	−44.5	−1.2	1.1	0.0
U men	−56.5	4.8	−42.5	−3.6	−28.5	−2.4
U women	−23.9	−3.6	−15.8	−2.4	−7.8	−1.1
S men	−6.4	−0.5	9.0	0.7	24.3	1.9
S women	−3.4	−0.5	4.8	0.7	13.1	1.9
Blacks	−8.6	−2.8	−4.8	−1.6	−1.1	−0.4
Others	−74.7	−2.3	−35.2	−1.1	4.0	0.7
Hispanic (domestic)	−5.5	−3.1	−3.3	−1.9	−1.2	−0.7
Hispanic (immigrant)	−1.6	−3.8	−1.1	−2.6	−0.6	−1.4
Immigrants	108.4		108.8		110.1	

*Elasticity of intraskill substitution (τ) assumed to equal 1.5. All labor supply elasticities are assumed equal to zero.

in the "others" group, which has the highest average skill level, incur a loss of between 1.1 and 2.3 percent for, respectively, the higher and the lower value of σ. The reductions in the labor incomes of the other groups are considerably higher.

In the long run the supply of capital is assumed to increase such that the rental price of capital, r, returns to it equilibrium value, r_o, that is, excess profits return to zero. This increase in K shifts the demand function for the labor aggregate to the right and thus causes all wage rates to rise above their values in the short run after the increased immigration. As seen in columns (e) and (f) of table 1.2, the long-run effects of the immigration on the earnings of unskilled workers are less negative than in the short run, and the long-run effect on the earnings of skilled workers is unambiguously positive. In the long run the aggregate increase in GDP less capital cost is 111.2 dollars (equal to 191.2 − 80.0), 110.1 dollars of which goes to the immigrants and 1.1 dollars of which goes to the aggregate of domestic labor. There is, however, still a large transfer of earnings from the unskilled to the skilled workers, the amount of which is independent of the value of σ but is greater the larger the value of τ.

The long-run effects on the earnings of the domestic population of the hypothetical ten million additional immigrants are examined more closely in table 1.3. This gives the absolute (in billions of 1993 dollars) and percentage changes in wage rates for the four ethnic groups (blacks, others, pre-1983 Hispanics and post-1983 Hispanics) by skill and gender for three different values of the intralabor elasticity of substitution (τ), 1.0 (which is probably too small), 1.5, and 2.0 (which is probably too large).

There are two important points in this table. First, because males were overrepresented relative to the population as a whole in the Hispanic immigration of the 1983 to 1993 period, the proportional reduction in the wages of unskilled men is considerably greater than the reduction in the wages of unskilled women. Indeed, W_1, the wage rate of unskilled men, falls by approximately twice the drop in W_2, the wage of unskilled women. The hypothetical figure of ten million immigrants in this exercise was *assumed* to reflect the earlier Hispanic immigration. To the extent that a future immigration wave is more balanced with respect to gender, W_1 and W_2 would fall more equally.

Second, the long-run effect of immigration on the aggregate incomes of blacks and domestic Hispanics is fairly small. This obscures the fact that the hypothetical immigration causes a much more significant fall (of between 2 and 4 percent, depending on the value of τ) in the earnings of low-skilled minorities. To the extent that one feels that the economic status of *poor* minorities (rather than the status of minority groups as a whole) is a serious problem, the effect of immigration on the distribution of labor earnings is not trivial.

Labor Supply Effects

A model was set out earlier in which the labor supply of some groups depended positively on the wage rate received by these groups. It is, accordingly, straightforward to modify the simulation model to take account of this possibility in the analysis of the effects of a hypothetical ten million additional immigrants in 1993.

The largest supply elasticity I have seen in the recent literature is the estimate of ε of 0.4 reported by Juhn, Murphy, and Topel (1991). This applies to those male workers at the lowest end of the earnings distribution, and their estimated elasticity trails off to zero as earnings increase toward the top of the distribution. For the purpose of seeing what difference a positive labor supply elasticity makes, I simply assume that $\varepsilon = 0.4$ applies to all domestic unskilled workers (the U's) of both genders, with the exception of the Hispanic immigrants during the 1983 to 1992 period, for whom ε is assumed to equal zero. Skilled

Table 1.3   Absolute (Billions of Dollars) and Percentage Changes in Labor Earnings of Native Population by Ethnicity, Gender, and Skill in the Long Run Due to Immigration of an Additional Ten Million Persons

	U (High School)		S (College)		Total
	Men (a)	Women (b)	Men (c)	Women (d)	(e)
$\tau = 1$					
Black					
Δ	−3.8	−1.4	1.7	1.8	−1.7
					0.5%
Other					
Δ	−35.2	−9.4	33.6	17.0	6.0
					0.2%
Hispanic (domestic)					
Δ	−2.7	−0.8	1.0	0.7	−1.8
					−1.0%
Hispanic (immigrant)					
Δ	−.09	−0.2	0.2	0.0	−0.9
					−2.1%
%	−3.6	−1.7	2.9	2.9	
$\tau = 1.5$					
Black					
Δ	−2.5	−1.0	1.2	1.2	−1.1
					−0.4%
Other					
Δ	−23.5	−6.2	22.4	11.4	4.0
					0.1%
Hispanic (domestic)					
Δ	−1.8	−0.5	0.7	0.4	−1.2
					−0.7%
Hispanic (immigrant)					
Δ	−0.6	−0.1	0.1	0.0	−0.6
					−1.4%
%	−2.4	−1.1	1.9	1.9	
$\tau = 2$					
Black	−1.9	−0.7	0.9	0.9	−0.8
					−0.3%
Other					
Δ	−17.7	−4.6	16.8	8.5	3.0
					0.1%

(*Table continues on p. 42.*)

Table 1.3   *Continued*

	U (High School)		S (College)		Total
	Men (a)	Women (b)	Men (c)	Women (d)	(e)
Hispanic (domestic) Δ	−1.4	−0.4	0.5	0.3	−0.9 −0.5%
Hispanic (immigrant) Δ	−0.5	−0.1	0.1	0.0	−0.4 −1.0%
%	−1.8	−0.9	1.4	1.4	

1983 to 1992 period, for whom ε is assumed to equal zero. Skilled workers (the S's) are also assumed to supply labor inelastically ($\varepsilon = 0$).

One way to consider the quantitative effect of immigration on the labor supply of unskilled labor is to apply the relevant empirical parameters to the displacement effect given by equation 1.34. The displacement effect, the long-run (after adjustment of K to its equilibrium value) reduction in the supply of efficiency units of domestic unskilled labor per efficiency unit of immigrant unskilled labor, is given by

$$(1.44) \quad Displacement\ Effect = \lambda_u = \frac{\beta(1-m_u)\varepsilon_u}{\tau + \beta(1-m_u)\varepsilon_u}.$$

Skilled labor's share of the aggregate wage bill (β), is equal to .506, and the Hispanic immigrants' share of the unskilled wage bill is $m_u = .019$. Assuming that ε_u is equal to 0.4, the value of λ_u is equal to .16, .12, and .09 for, respectively, values of the elasticity of intrafactor substitution of 1.0, 1.5, and 2.0. This means that, after appropriate adjustment for relative productivity, 100 new immigrants cause between 9 and 16 incumbent unskilled workers to leave their jobs. If one had assumed (against all available evidence) that ε_u was equal to 1.5, this displacement effect would be between 27 and 42 percent. It should be pointed out that $\varepsilon_u = 0.4$ is at the extreme end of the estimates found in Juhn et al. (1991). A more reasonable characterization of their results would be an ε_u of .10, which yields displacement effects of between 2 and 5 percent.

The absolute and percentage long-run changes in the level and distribution of output due to the hypothetical ten million increase in the number of immigrants are reported in table 1.4 for $\tau = 1.5$ and for ε_u equal to, respectively, zero and 0.4. With the large positive labor supply

Table 1.4   Long-Run Effects of Immigration Scenario in 1993 with and Without Unskilled Labor Supply Adjustment ($\tau = 1.5$)

	Zero Elasticity ($\varepsilon = 0$)		Large Elasticity ($\varepsilon = .4$)	
	Δ (a)	% (b)	Δ (c)	% (d)
Output	191.2	2.9	169.7	2.6
Capital cost	80.0	2.9	71.0	2.6
Immigrants	110.1		110.3	
Domestic labor	1.1	0.0	−11.6	−0.3
U	−36.3	−1.9	−44.8	−2.4
S	37.4	1.9	33.2	1.7
Blacks	−1.1	−0.4	−2.2	−0.7
U	−3.5	−1.8	−4.3	−2.3
S	2.4	1.9	2.1	1.7
Others	4.0	0.1	−7.0	−0.2
U	−29.7	−2.0	−36.9	−2.4
S	33.7	1.9	29.9	1.7
Hispanic (domestic)	−1.2	−0.7	−1.9	−1.1
U	−2.3	−1.9	−2.9	−2.4
S	1.1	1.9	1.0	1.7
Hispanic (immigrants)	−0.6	−1.4	−0.5	−1.2
U	−0.7	−2.0	−0.6	−1.8
S	0.1	1.9	0.1	1.7
Percentage changes				
W_1 (male U)		−2.4		−2.1
W_2 (female U)		−1.1		−1.0
W_3, W_4 (S)		1.9		1.7
Domestic U supply		0.0		−0.7

elasticity the supply of domestic unskilled labor falls by 0.7 percent. The presence of a positive labor supply elasticity results in slightly smaller decreases in unskilled wage rates and a smaller increase in skilled wage rates. The long-run change in the aggregate wage bill is thus smaller (2.9 percent with $\varepsilon_u = 0$ versus 2.6 percent with $\varepsilon_u = 0.4$).

It should be stressed that the assumption of ε_u equal to 0.4 is purposely extreme. Its average value over the relevant U population is surely closer to zero than 0.4. Nevertheless, the effects of immigration on the distribution of income are relatively insensitive to the extreme assumption.

Alternative Labor Aggregation Specifications

The simulations presented thus far in this section are based on the assumption, embodied in (1.39), that all male unskilled workers (Others, blacks, Hispanics, and the hypothetical new immigrants) are perfect substitutes for each other in the sense that they compose a labor aggregate U_1. The same assumption applies to female unskilled labor. With this assumption of perfect substitutability, an additional unskilled male immigrant, for example, causes a fall in the male unskilled real wage (W_1), and this decline applies proportionally to all ethnic groups.

Following the discussion earlier in this study, it is possible that this assumption is not correct. To take an extreme view, we will assume instead that unskilled blacks and Hispanics (both the pre-1983 and post-1983) are employed in entirely different groups of jobs than unskilled Others. One way to represent this is to assume that the labor aggregate depends on the effective inputs of six different groups of jobs: unskilled male Others (the quantity, in terms of efficiency units, of which is U_{1a}); unskilled male minorities (U_{1b}), unskilled female Other and minorities (U_{2a} and U_{2b}); and male and female skilled labor (S_1 and S_2). The flow of labor services is thus $G = G(U_{1a}, U_{1b}, U_{2a}, U_{2b}, S_1, S_2)$, and it is assumed that this is CES with an elasticity of intrafactor substitution τ.[12]

A justification for making this (extreme) assumption is that, because of a combination of housing and labor market discrimination, unskilled blacks and Hispanics form a labor pool for a set of jobs (the U_{gb} jobs) and that they simply cannot transfer to other (U_{ga}) jobs.[13] Unskilled Others, on the other hand, do not want and do not have to take these "bad" jobs.

To see what difference this specification makes, table 1.5 reports the long-run distributional impact of the hypothetical immigration scenario for both the "Equally Competitive" case, which has been the working assumption to this point, and the "Complete Segregation" case, in which unskilled blacks and Hispanics are perfectly substitutable with immigrants, while unskilled Others are complementary with immigrants. In both sets of results the elasticity of intrafactor substitution (τ) is set equal to 1.5.

The results with respect to the effects of immigration on output and average skilled/unskilled relative wages are qualitatively similar in the two cases. The only difference is that the magnitude of the changes in these variables is slightly smaller in the Segregation case, reflecting the fact that the new immigrants are confined to a smaller set of jobs such that diminishing returns are more important. The important difference in the results is that in the Segregation case unskilled minorities bear the full burden of the labor market effects of

Table 1.5   Long-Run Effects of Immigration Scenario in 1993 for Equally Competitive and Complete Segregation Cases ($\tau = 1.5$)

	Equally Competitive		Complete Segregation	
	Δ (a)	% (b)	Δ (c)	% (d)
Output	191.2	2.9	176.2	2.7
Capital cost	80.0	2.9	73.7	2.7
Immigrants	110.1		94.1	
Domestic labor	1.1	0.0	8.4	0.2
U	−36.3	−1.9	−26.1	−1.4
S	37.4	1.9	34.5	1.8
Blacks	−1.1	−0.4	−26.6	−8.9
U	−3.5	−1.8	−28.8	−16.5
S	2.4	1.9	2.2	1.8
Others	4.0	0.1	58.5	1.8
U	−29.7	−2.0	27.4	1.8
S	33.7	1.9	31.1	1.8
Hispanic (domestic)	−1.2	−0.7	−17.9	−10.6
U	−2.3	−1.9	−19.0	−17.1
S	1.1	1.9	1.1	1.8
Hispanic (immigrant)	−0.6	−1.4	−5.6	−14.2
U	−0.7	−2.0	−5.7	−17.7
S	0.1	1.9	0.1	1.8
Domestic minorities	−2.9	−0.5	−50.1	−9.9
U	−6.5	−1.9	−53.5	−16.8
S	3.6	1.9	3.4	1.8

the immigration, whereas the burden is spread across all U's in the Equally Competitive case.

Another way to compare the distributional effects of immigration in the two cases is to aggregate the domestic population across groups into two classes, those *favorably affected* by the immigration under the Segregation case (all S's and Other U's) and those *unfavorably affected* (all minority U's). In the Equally Competitive case the aggregate income of the favorably affected segment rises by .07 per unit of earnings of the immigrants versus a fall of .06 for the unfavorably affected segment. In the Complete Segregation case, on the other hand, the changes in earnings per unit of immigrant earnings for the two segments are +.66 and −.57. Because, in the Complete Segregation case, the decline in the earnings of unskilled minorities swamps the increase in skilled minorities, the unskilled immigration causes substantial declines in the relative earnings of both African Americans and Hispanic Americans.

The relevance of each of the above two extreme specifications of the labor market status of minorities is an empirical matter. A first step in such an empirical investigation would be to calculate an Index of Occupational Dissimilarity (D) for low-skilled jobs. Suppose that we could observe the level of unskilled employment by ethnicity ($e = m$ for minorities and $= o$ for Others) across J correctly defined "jobs," N_{je}. The Index of Occupational Dissimilarity is given by

$$(1.45) \quad D = \frac{1}{2} \sum_{j=1}^{J} \left| \frac{N_{jm}}{\sum_j N_{jm}} - \frac{N_{jo}}{\sum_j N_{jo}} \right|.$$

Under the Complete Segregation case, all unskilled minority workers are confined to one set of jobs and all unskilled Others are employed in the remaining set of jobs. This implies, measurement errors aside, that D would be equal to one. Under the Equally Competitive case, the proportions of minorities and Others in each job would tend toward equality, so the value of D would tend toward zero.

Using published aggregate occupational data for eighty-six blue collar, nonfarm occupations in 1995, the value of D for blacks and Hispanics versus Others (nonblack, non-Hispanic) is .212. The value of D between blacks versus Others is .238, Hispanics versus Others .217, and blacks versus Hispanics .163. These aggregated data are obviously much less than perfect with respect to the underlying hypothesis, but they do suggest that the occupational distributions of blue-collar blacks and Hispanics are more similar to each other than either is to that of Others. Occupational distributions at a moment of time also do not say anything about changes in these distributions in response to a shock like the influx of ten million low-skilled immigrants.

It is obvious that the results using the Perfect Segregation model exaggerate the effect of immigration on the earnings of low-skilled minorities. On the other hand, to the extent that minorities and immigrants perform similar functions in the labor market, the "true" potential impact of low-skilled immigration on the earnings of minorities may be greater than that implied by the Equally Competitive model.

CONCLUSIONS

A fairly consistent result of the model throughout the previous section is that a very large inflow of low-skilled immigrants would be expected to have a negative effect on the absolute real and relative earnings of the

African American population. However, *the quantitative magnitude of this effect*, like its effect on the wages of the low-skilled population in general, *would most likely be quite small*. While this conclusion is modified under certain extreme assumptions (like the job segregation model on page 43, I believe that it is unlikely to be much changed within the range of plausible specifications of labor-market behavior.

There have been many empirical studies that have attempted to estimate the effects of immigration on relative wage levels by skill using variation in residence of immigrants across regions (for example, Grossman [1982] and Altonji and Card [1991]). Further, Butcher and Reimers, both in this volume, have attempted to use this methodology to estimate directly the effect on the wages of low-skilled workers by ethnic characteristics. Apart from the existence of several challenging econometric problems (including the serious one, pointed out by Borjas [1994], of the endogeneity of domestic labor supply, which is subject to potential interregional mobility), the results here point to another problem: Immigration of the scale that has been observed in the United States during the past two decades is likely to have had such a small effect on the relevant dependent variables as to prevent its estimation with any precision.

NOTES

1. $\gamma_i = F_i N_i / F$ is the output elasticity of group i, and their sum plus γ_k is equal to one. Each partial elasticity of complementarity is defined as $C_{ij} = F_{ij}F/F_iF_j$. See Johnson (1980) and Hamermesh (1993) for extensive discussion of the properties of PECs. The most relevant property for the present problem is that the demand function for each factor is homogeneous of degree zero, that is,

$$\sum_{j=1}^{I} \gamma_j C_{ij} + \gamma_k C_{kk} = 0.$$

2. This issue is the focus of perhaps the most acrimonious dispute in modern labor economics, that between Barry Chiswick and George Borjas (see Chiswick [1978] and Borjas [1985] for the beginnings of the controversy). My various simulation results [see page 34] do not allow for the possibility of Chiswick-style skill upgrading, but they could easily be extended to do so.

3. With this assumption, one would assert that, for example, the entry of five unskilled workers to work in laundries at ten thousand dollars per year would have exactly the same short-run effect on profits (that is, F_k) as the entry of a fifty thousand dollars-per-year computer technician. The alternative hypothesis (Griliches [1969]) is that F_k would rise more with the immigration of the computer geek than of the laundry workers.

4. The aggregation procedure assumes that group i workers contribute a_i units of unskilled labor services and b_i units of skilled labor services. Thus, $U = \Sigma a_i N_i$ and $S = \Sigma b_i N_i$, and the average wage of group i workers is $W_i = a_i W_U + b_i W_S$. A group is relatively skilled if $b_i / a_i > S/U$ and relatively unskilled if the inequality is reversed. For groups exactly in the middle of the skill distribution, the long run own and cross elasticities of complementarity, the D_{ij}'s, are all zero. Each relatively skilled group is substitutable for all other relatively skilled groups and complentary with all relatively unskilled groups.

5. See Johnson and Stafford (1996) for a discussion of this in a production function context.

6. For example, in the recent literature on the causes of changes in the wage structure in the United States during the 1980s, several different approaches to labor aggregation were employed. These include the S-U aggregation discussed earlier (Katz and Murphy [1992]), the assumption of a CES version of G in several age-education-gender groups (Bound and Johnson [1992]), a very general version (Murphy and Welch [1992]) with relatively freely estimated D_{ij}'s. A consensus result in these papers is that during this period G function shifted toward relatively skilled workers. However, the different approaches would have at least slightly different implications concerning the distributional effects of immigration. Incidentally, given the high likelihood that the G function has been subject to structural change, the empirical resolution of this question is at least very difficult.

7. This result applies strictly only to a small change in W_i. For a large influx of immigrants such that the negative value of ΔW_i is fairly large, the decline in UT_i is somewhat smaller than the initial value of (N_i/L_i) times $-\Delta W_i$, for the decrease in the aggregate disutility of employment must be subtracted from the gross loss. However, unless ε_i is very large, the net loss is fairly well approximated by the initial value of (N_i/L_i) times $-\Delta W_i$. See Borjas (1995) for a discussion of a somewhat similar model.

8. For a formal demonstration of this see Johnson and Stafford (1997). Such an approach is used as a justification by Borjas, Freeman, and Katz (1997) for using the "factor content method" in assessing the relative wage impact of trade and immigration.

9. It is possible that these substitution elasticities for unskilled intensive products are larger than for skilled intensive products, in which case the relative importance of closed economy versus open economy analysis is different for the two factors. I have not yet been able to find sufficiently disaggregated estimates of import/export elasticities to make a judgment on this issue.

10. This figure is in rough accord with the results reported in Funkhouser and Trejo (1995).

11. It is probably unreasonable to assume that if ten million additional immigrants had unexpectedly shown up in the United States in 1993 nominal wages would have adjusted *immediately* such that unemployment did not rise in 1993. The definition of the "short run" in this paper, however, is the period in which there is no adjustment of K in response to higher profitability, probably two or three years. None of the results apply to the "very short run" in which nominal wage rigidity could lead to unemployment. A major source of difficulty in analyzing very short run effects are the role of adjustment costs and lags, which are, thus far, not well understood (see Hamermesh and Pfann [1996]).

12. In terms of (I.39), the total flow of unskilled labor of each gender ($g-1,2$) may be written as:

$$U_g = \left[\kappa U_{ga}^{1-1/\theta} + (1-\kappa) U_{gb}^{1-1/\theta} \right]^{\frac{\theta}{\theta-1}},$$

where θ is the elasticity of substitution between Others and minorities within each gender. The assumption described above, that all six groups are equally substitutable for each other, is that $\theta = \tau$.

13. An example of this is Wilson's description of the labor market situation of African Americans in inner city Chicago (Wilson, 1996).

REFERENCES

Altonji, Joseph, and David Card. 1991. "The Effects of Immigration on the Labor Market Outcomes of Less-Skilled Natives." In *Immigration, Trade, and Labor Markets*, edited by J. Abowd and R. Freeman. Chicago: University of Chicago Press, 407–21.

Borjas, George. 1985. "Assimilation, Changes in Cohort Quality, and the Earnings of Immigrants." *Journal of Labor Economics* 4 (October): 463–89.

———. 1994. "The Economics of Immigration." *Journal of Economic Literature* 32 (December): 1667–1717.

———. 1995. "The Economic Benefits from Immigration." *Journal of Economic Perspectives* (Spring).

———. 1996. "Immigration and Welfare Magnets." Mimeo (October).

Borjas, George, Richard Freeman, and Lawrence Katz. 1997. "How Much Do Immigration and Trade Affect Labor Market Outcomes?" *Brookings Papers on Economic Activity* 1.

Bound, John, and George Johnson. 1992. "Changes in the Structure of Wages in the 1980's: An Evaluation of Alternative Explanations." *American Economic Review* 82 (June): 371–92.

Chiswick, Barry. 1978. "The Effects of Americanization on the Earnings of Foreign-Born Men." *Journal of Political Economy* 86 (October): 897–921.

Funkhouser, Edward, and Stephen Trejo. 1995. "The Labor Market Skills of Recent Male Immigrants: Evidence from the Current Population Survey." *Industrial and Labor Relations Review* 48: 792–811.

Griliches, Zvi. 1969. "Capital-Skill Complementarity." *Review of Economics and Statistics* 51 (November): 465–68.

Grossman, Jean. 1982. "The Substitutability of Natives and Immigrants in Production." *Review of Economics and Statistics* 64 (November): 596–603.

Hamermesh, Daniel. 1993. *Labor Demand.* Princeton, N.J.: Princeton University Press.

Hamermesh, Daniel, and Gerard Pfann. 1996. "Adjustment Costs in Factor Demand." *Journal of Economic Literature* 34 (September): 1264–92.

Johnson, George. 1980. "The Theory of Labour Market Intervention." *Economica* 47 (July): 309–30.

Johnson, George, and Frank Stafford. 1996. "Occupational Exclusion and the Distribution of Earnings." Mimeo, University of Michigan (January).

———. 1997. "International Trade and the Labor Market." Mimeo, Conference for Volumes III–IV of *Handbook of Labor Economics* (August).

Jones, Ronald W., and J. Peter Neary. 1984. "The Positive Theory of International Trade." In R. W. Jones and P. B. Kenen, *Handbook of International Economics.* Amsterdam: Elsevier Science Publishers.

Juhn, Chinhui, Kevin Murphy, and Robert Topel. 1991. "Why Has the Natural Unemployment Rate Increased Over Time?" *Brookings Papers on Economic Activity* 2: 75–142.

Katz, Lawrence F., and Kevin M. Murphy. 1992. "Changes in Relative Wages, 1963–1987: Supply and Demand Factors." *Quarterly Journal of Economics* 107 (February): 35–78.

Murphy, Kevin M., and Finis Welch. 1992. "The Structure of Wages." *Quarterly Journal of Economics* 107 (February): 215–306.

U.S. Bureau of the Census, Current Population Reports. *Educational Attainment in the United States: March 1982 to March 1985,* series P20-415.

———. *Educational Attainment in the United States: March 1993 and March 1992,* series P20-476.

———. *School Enrollment—Social and Economic Characteristics of Students: October 1983,* series P20-413.

Wilson, William Julius. 1996. "Work." *New York Times Magazine,* August 18, 1996, p. 26.

CHAPTER 2

Do Blacks Gain or Lose From Immigration?

George J. Borjas

The past two decades have witnessed both the rebirth of the debate over immigration policy in the United States as well as a resurgence of academic interest in studying the economic impact of immigration. How does immigration alter the skill composition of the work force? Do the "new" immigrants find it hard to adapt to their new country? What is the impact of immigration on the earnings and employment opportunities of native-born workers? Do immigrants "pay their way" in the welfare state? A large and rapidly growing number of studies investigate each of these questions in detail (see the recent surveys of Borjas 1994; Friedberg and Hunt 1995; and Rothman and Espenshade 1992). The empirical evidence indicates that more recent immigrant waves will remain economically disadvantaged throughout their working lives; that recent immigrants are more likely to participate in welfare programs than natives; and that immigration may have contributed to the increase in wage inequality observed during the 1980s.

Surprisingly, there has been little study of an equally important set of issues: Does the native population of the United States benefit from immigration, and how are these gains and losses distributed among natives?[1] This paper describes why natives benefit and lose from immigration, provides a simple methodology for assessing the "incidence" of these benefits and losses on particular segments of the native population, and evaluates the net impact that immigration has had on the population of black natives in the United States.

Perhaps the main insight that economic theory provides about the economic impact of immigration is that, on net, natives in the United States *do* benefit from immigration.[2] This paper will show, however, that this key result does not "carry over" to the black population for two distinct reasons. First, many of the benefits from immigration are received by firms. Blacks probably own a relatively small proportion of the capital stock of the nation. As a result, blacks have less to gain from immigration than whites. Moreover, although immigrants and natives exhibit different skill distributions, these differences are smaller when one compares immigrants and black natives. The similarity between the skill endowments of black natives and immigrants suggests that any adverse impacts of immigration on competing workers will fall hardest on black natives.

The analysis presented in this paper suggests that even though immigration benefits the typical native residing in the United States, the typical black native suffers a loss. This finding is not sensitive to the underlying assumptions of the model and will likely persist regardless of whether immigration policy encourages the admission of skilled workers or of unskilled workers.

THE IMPACT OF IMMIGRATION ON BLACKS IN A MODEL WITH HOMOGENEOUS LABOR

To isolate the reasons for the disproportionately adverse impact that immigration has on black natives, it is instructive to begin with the simplest theoretical framework.[3] The aggregate production function for the United States has two inputs, capital (K) and labor (L), and is given by:

$$(2.1) \quad Q = f(K, L).$$

The work force is composed of N native workers and M immigrant workers, and a given fraction of the native work force is black. Assume that capital is owned by natives. As we will see, any calculation of the economic impact of immigration on black natives will hinge crucially on the share of the capital stock that is owned by blacks, and I will provide a more detailed discussion of this parameter below. Finally, note that the model ignores skill differentials among workers and essentially assumes that all workers (whether immigrant or native, black or white) are perfect substitutes in production. We can then write $L = N + M$. Finally, assume that the supplies of capital and of both native- and foreign-born labor are perfectly inelastic.

The aggregate production function exhibits constant returns to scale, and the entire output in this one-good economy is distributed to the owners of capital and to workers. The equilibrium prior to the admission of M immigrants requires that each factor price equals the respective value of marginal product. Suppose that the rental price of capital is initially r_0 and the price of labor is w_0. The price of the output is the numeraire (so that the input prices are measured in units of output). In the pre-immigration regime, therefore, the national income accruing to natives is given by:

$$(2.2) \quad Q_N = r_0 K + w_0 N.$$

Figure 2.1   The Immigration Surplus

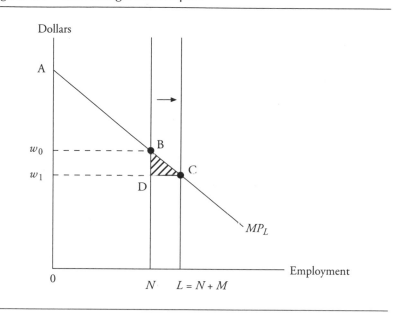

Figure 2.1 illustrates this initial equilibrium in the labor market. Because the supply of capital is inelastic, the area under the marginal product of labor curve (MP_L) gives the economy's total output. Prior to the entry of immigrants, therefore, the national income accruing to natives Q_N is given by the trapezoid ABN0.

When immigrants enter the country the supply curve shifts to the right and the wage falls to w_1. National income is now given by the area in the trapezoid ACL0. Part of the increase in national income is distributed directly to immigrants (who get $w_1 M$ in return for their labor services). Inspection of Figure 2.1 reveals that the increase in national income accruing to natives, or the "immigration surplus," is given by the triangle BCD. Because the market wage equals the productivity of the last immigrant hired, immigrants increase national income by more than what it costs to employ them.

The immigration surplus is given approximately by the area of the triangle BCD, which can be calculated as $\frac{1}{2} \times (w_0 - w_1) \times M$. We can write the immigration surplus, as a fraction of national income, as:[4]

$$(2.3) \quad \frac{\Delta Q_N}{Q} = -\frac{1}{2} s \, e \, m^2,$$

where s is labor's share of national income; e is the elasticity of factor price for labor (that is, the percentage change in the wage resulting from a 1 percent change in the size of the labor force holding marginal cost constant, or $\partial \log w / \partial \log L$); and m is the fraction of the work force that is foreign born ($m = M/L$).

The share of labor income in the United States is about 70 percent, and the fraction of immigrants in the work force is slightly less than 10 percent. Hamermesh's (1993) survey of the empirical evidence on labor demand suggests that the elasticity of factor price for labor is on the order of $-.3$, so that a 10 percent increase in the number of workers reduces the wage by 3 percent.[5] The immigration surplus, therefore, is on the order of .1 percent of GDP (that is, one-tenth of 1 percent). The economic gains from immigration in a 7 trillion dollar economy, therefore, are relatively small, about 7 billion dollars per year or 30 dollars per native-born person in the United States.

Even though the immigration surplus is small, immigration has a substantial economic impact. In particular, immigration causes a large redistribution of wealth from labor to capital. In terms of figure 2.1, native workers lose the area in the rectangle $w_0 BD w_1$, and this quantity plus the immigration surplus accrues to the owners of the capital stock. Expressed as a fraction of GDP, the net change in the incomes of native workers and capitalists are approximately given by:[6]

$$(2.4) \quad \frac{\text{Change in Native Labor Earnings}}{Q} = s\,e\,m\,(1-m),$$

$$(2.5) \quad \frac{\text{Change in Income of Capitalists}}{Q} = -s\,e\,m\left(1 - \frac{1}{2}m\right).$$

If the elasticity of factor price is $-.3$, native workers lose about 1.9 percent of GDP, or 133 billion dollars in a 7 trillion dollar economy, while native capital gains 2.0 percent of GDP, or 140 billion dollars. The small immigration surplus of 7 billion dollars thus disguises a sizable redistribution of wealth from workers to the users of immigrant labor.

Allocation of the Costs and Benefits to Black Natives

I now adapt this framework to allocate the gains and losses between black and white natives. The 1990 Census reports that blacks make up about 10 percent of the work force in the United States. If blacks also owned 10 percent of the productive resources of the country, the losses to black labor, the gains to black-owned firms, and the immigration surplus accruing to black natives would all be 10 percent of the respective magnitudes for the entire country.

However, blacks do not own 10 percent of the capital in the country. A growing number of studies attempt to estimate the share of wealth (or assets) that are owned by blacks. These studies conclude that the black-white gap in assets or wealth is far greater than the black-white wage gap that has been the focus of so much attention. For instance, using data drawn from the National Longitudinal Surveys in 1976 and 1978, Blau and Graham (1990) estimate a black-white wealth ratio of .18. Similarly, Smith (1995) uses data from the Health and Retirement Survey and finds that the black-white net worth ratio is about .27. Moreover, these studies suggest that the black-white gap in wealth rises if the calculation is restricted to business assets. The data, therefore, reveal that blacks own somewhere between 2 to 3 percent of the capital stock in the United States, far below their population representation. My calculations will assume that blacks own 2.5 percent of the capital stock. As we shall see below, this substantial racial gap in the ownership of the productive resources of the United States can play a crucial role in reducing the gains from immigration for the black population.[7]

Equation (2.4) indicated that immigration lowered workers' incomes by about 133 billion dollars (1.9 percent of GDP in a 7 trillion dollar economy). Because blacks make up about 10 percent of the native work force, black workers lose 13.3 billion dollars. Equation (2.5) indicated that native-owned firms gained about 140 billion dollars. If blacks own only about 2.5 percent of the country's capital stock, the gains accruing to black-owned firms would be roughly 3.5 billion dollars. As a group, therefore, black natives lose about 9.8 billion dollars. In 1990, there were almost 30 million black natives residing in the United States (U.S. Bureau of the Census 1992, 17). The calculations presented above suggest that immigration lowered the income of the average black native in the United States by about 300 dollars per year.

This standard economic model, therefore, isolates an important reason for a qualitative difference in the way that immigration affects the economic status of black and white natives. The adverse impact of immigration falls on "labor," the group of natives who compete with the resources brought in by immigrants. The gains from immigration are accrued by "capital," the group of natives whose resources become more productive as the size of the work force increases. Blacks, as a group, are well-represented in the labor category, and are greatly underrepresented in the capital category. It is no surprise, therefore, that immigration will have a net adverse impact on black natives.

It is also worth emphasizing that the native black population is simply one of many native groups that is "labor-intensive." If we were to conduct this same type of cost-benefit analysis for other native groups that are labor-intensive (and that would presumably include most subgroups of native workers), we would obtain the same general finding: Immigration is not beneficial for groups that are long on labor and short on capital.

The back-of-the-envelope calculation presented here uses a number of assumptions that might not accurately reflect the operation of the U.S. economy. For example, many of the gains from immigration that initially go to capitalists are eventually redistributed to consumers (in the form of lower prices for the goods that immigrants produce). As a result, black natives get additional gains because they profit from these lower prices. However, we do not have any direct evidence on the magnitude of these "price effects." Moreover, if many of the goods and services produced by immigrants cater to the demands of high-income native workers, the price effects will tend to disproportionately favor the white native population.

The calculations assume that immigrants have an adverse impact on the earnings of native workers. There is a great deal of debate over whether immigration reduces the earnings of natives *at all* (Borjas, Freeman, and Katz 1997; and Card 1997).[8] Regardless of the exact outcome of this debate, it is important to point out that unless immigrants bring in skills that are completely different from those of natives, there is bound to be some job competition between immigrant and native workers. Moreover, the theoretical discussion clearly indicates that the gains from immigration are intimately linked to the wage reduction that natives suffer: the smaller the wage reduction, the smaller the gains from immigration.

The derivation of the immigration surplus in equation (2.3) assumed that the capital stock in the United States is fixed. Obviously, immigrants may themselves add to the capital stock of the country, and the rise in the return to capital will encourage additional capital flows from both foreign and domestic investors.[9] It can be easily shown that these capital flows will tend to dissipate the gains from immigration to the United States (Borjas 1998). As a result, the immigration surplus in a model where the capital stock fully adjusts to the immigrant supply shock is zero. Put differently, the immigration-induced capital flows reestablish the capital/labor ratio that existed in the United States prior to immigration, and the native wage remains unchanged. In the end, natives neither gain nor lose from immigration, and the fact that blacks own relatively little capital does not matter at all.

The calculation also ignores the possibility of external effects. A number of recent studies have argued that an increase in trade generates increasing returns in the aggregate economy (see, for example, Helpman and Krugman 1985). Immigration expands the size of the market. It can introduce many new interactions among workers and firms, so that both workers and firms might "pick up" knowledge without paying for it. As a result, the external effects resulting from immigration might lead to increasing returns on the aggregate. Although models that incorporate external effects in the aggregate economy are used frequently in *theoretical* discussions of the gains from trade, there is little empirical evidence supporting the existence, let alone measuring the magnitude, of the external effects.

In the end, however, perhaps the main problem with the simple model presented in this section arises from the assumption of a homogeneous work force. Both immigrant and black native workers tend to be relatively unskilled. The adverse impact of immigration will likely fall on the natives whose skills most resemble those of immigrants. This fact introduces an additional factor that might explain why black natives may not gain from immigration, even though the country as a whole gains.

THE IMPACT OF IMMIGRATION IN A MODEL WITH HETEROGENEOUS SKILLS

The previous section illustrated how and why the gains from immigration arise in a competitive market. As I noted, the most restrictive aspect of the model is that it ignores the skill differentials that exist both within and across the native and immigrant populations. Before evaluating how these skill differences affect the costs and benefits from immigration differentially for black and white natives, it is instructive to consider a simple model where there are two skill classes in the work force, skilled workers (L_S) and unskilled workers (L_U), and we ignore the presence of capital in the production process. Suppose also that the fraction of skilled workers in the native population is b, and the respective fraction among immigrants is β, and that the supply of workers to the labor market is perfectly inelastic. Finally, the aggregate production function is linear homogeneous and there are no external effects, so that $Q = f(L_S, L_U)$.

Borjas (1995) has shown that this framework generates an immigration surplus (as a fraction of GDP) equal to:

(2.6) $\quad \dfrac{\Delta Q_N}{Q} = -\dfrac{1}{2}\dfrac{s_S\, e_{SS}\,(\beta-b)^2}{p^2{}_S\,(1-p_S)^2}\,(1-m)^2\, m^2,$

where s_S is the share of national income accruing to skilled workers; e_{SS} is the elasticity of factor price for skilled workers (that is, $e_{SS} = \partial \log w_S/\partial \log L_S$, holding marginal cost constant); and p_S is the fraction of the labor force that is composed of skilled workers. Equation (2.6) shows that the immigration surplus is positive as long as the skill composition of the immigrant flow differs from that of native workers (that is, as long as β is not equal to b). If the skill composition of immigrants were the same as that of natives, the constant returns to scale production function implies that the wages of skilled and unskilled workers are unaffected by immigration, and hence natives have nothing to gain from immigration. A key lesson of economic theory is that natives benefit from immigration only if immigrants are different from natives.

If the skill composition of immigrants differs from that of natives, the size of the immigration surplus depends on how different immigrants are. Suppose that 50 percent of the native work force is skilled. Figure 2.2 illustrates the relationship between the immigration surplus and the skill composition of the immigrant flow (as measured by the parameter β).[10] If the skill composition of immigrants was identical to that of natives ($\beta = .5$), native workers have nothing to gain from immigration. Equation (2.6) implies that the immigration surplus is maximized when the immigrant flow is composed of exclusively unskilled or exclusively skilled workers. Either policy choice generates an immigrant flow that is *very* different from the native work force, and hence maximizes the immigration surplus. Because I assumed that half of the natives are skilled, there is no particular economic advantage to admitting either an all-skilled or an all-unskilled immigrant flow. The United States presumably has a relatively skilled work force, particularly when compared with most other countries. *In the absence of capital*, therefore, our discussion would imply that the immigration surplus is largest if we pursue an immigration policy which admits *only* unskilled workers! This type of immigration policy maximizes the economic gains to natives by exploiting fully the production complementarities between immigrant and native workers.

This conclusion, however, hinges crucially on the assumption that capital plays no role in the production process. Suppose that the aggregate production function is linear homogeneous, that the capital stock is native-owned, that there are no external effects, and that all factors of production are supplied inelastically to the economy. The production function is then given by:

Figure 2.2.   The Immigration Surplus and Immigrant Skills, in a Model
Without Capital (Assuming 50 Percent of Natives Are
Skilled)

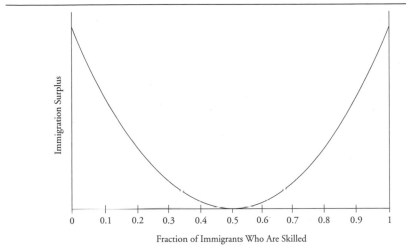

Fraction of Immigrants Who Are Skilled

(2.7) $Q = f(K, L_S, L_U) = f(K, bN + \beta M, (1 - b)N + (1 - \beta)M),$

where N is the number of native workers, and M is the number of immigrant workers. The wage of each factor of production (w_K for capital, w_S for skilled workers, and w_U for unskilled workers) is determined by the respective marginal productivity condition. The total increase in national income accruing to *natives* when the United States admits M immigrants (starting from a zero-immigration equilibrium) equals:

(2.8) $\Delta Q_N = \left(K \dfrac{\partial w_K}{\partial M} + bN \dfrac{\partial w_S}{\partial M} + (1 - b)N \dfrac{\partial w_U}{\delta M} \right) M.$

Define the elasticity of factor price $e_{ij} = \partial \log w_i / \partial \log X_j$ (where $X_j = K$, L_S, L_U).

If we convert equation (2.9) into percentage terms and use the condition that a weighted average of elasticities of factor price equals zero, we can write the income change (as a fraction of GDP) accruing to each of the factors of production as:[11]

(2.9)   Percent Change in Income of Capitalists =

$$-\left[\frac{s_U \varepsilon_{US}\,\beta m}{2p_S}+\frac{s_S \varepsilon_{SS}\,\beta m}{2p_S}+\frac{s_U \varepsilon_{UU}\,(1-\beta)m}{2p_U}+\frac{s_S \varepsilon_U\,(1-\beta)m}{2p_U}\right],$$

(2.10) Percent Change in Income of Skilled Workers =

$$\left[\frac{s_S \varepsilon_{SS}\beta^2 m}{2p_S}-\frac{s_S \varepsilon_{SS}\,\beta^2 m^2}{2p_S^2}+\frac{s_S \varepsilon_{SU}\,(1-\beta)m}{2p_U}-\frac{s_S \varepsilon_{SU}\,(1-\beta)m^2}{2p_S p_U}\right],$$

(2.11)   Percent Change in Income of Unskilled Workers =

$$\left[\frac{s_U \varepsilon_{US}\,\beta m}{2p_S}-\frac{s_U \varepsilon_{US}\,\beta(1-\beta)m^2}{2p_S p_U}+\frac{s_U \varepsilon_{UU}\,(1-\beta)m}{2p_U}-\frac{s_U \varepsilon_{UU}\,(1-\beta)^2 m^2}{2p_U^2}\right],$$

where s_S and s_U are the shares of national income accruing to skilled and unskilled workers, respectively; and p_S and p_U are the shares of the work force that are skilled and unskilled. The immigration surplus in this more general model equals the sum of equations (2.9), (2.10), and (2.11). Borjas (1995) shows that this immigration surplus is positive. On net, the United States benefits from immigration.[12]

Before proceeding to a discussion of the impact of immigration on black natives, it is instructive to compare the sensitivity of the immigration surplus to alternative policy choices. In particular, suppose that the United States is willing to increase its population by 10 percent through immigration, but that it is considering alternative values for β, the skill composition of the immigrant flow.

The net gains for each of the three groups in the economy depends on the relevant own- and cross-elasticities of factor price. Although there is a great deal of uncertainty about the "true" value of these elasticities (Hamermesh 1993, chapter 3), many studies report that the elasticity of factor price is greater (in absolute value) for skilled workers than for unskilled workers (that is, $\varepsilon_{SS} < \varepsilon_{UU}$).

Suppose that the fraction of skilled workers in the native work force is one-half. Our earlier discussion indicated that as long as we ignored capital, the immigration surplus was maximized whenever the immigrant flow was either exclusively skilled or unskilled. It turns out, however, that the presence of capital "breaks the tie" and the United States is better off admitting an exclusively skilled immigrant flow as long as $\varepsilon_{SS} < \varepsilon_{UU}$.

A skilled immigrant flow generates a larger immigration surplus partly because of the production complementarities that exist between skilled labor and capital. A very negative elasticity of factor price for skilled workers implies that skilled workers are highly complementary with other factors of production. In contrast, a numerically small elasticity of factor price for unskilled workers implies that unskilled workers are not highly complementary with other factors of production. Because the complementarities across factors play a central role in generating the gains from immigration, the immigration surplus is maximized when the immigrant flow is skilled.

Of course, the inference that the United States is better off admitting an exclusively skilled immigrant flow might change if the native work force were predominantly skilled. There then exist two sets of conflicting incentives. On the one hand, native workers gain most when the United States admits immigrants who are most complementary with the skilled native workers; that is, an unskilled immigrant flow. On the other hand, capital gains most when the United States admits immigrants who are most complementary with native-owned capital; that is, a skilled immigrant flow.

The Impact on Black Natives

We can now apply equations (2.9), (2.10), and (2.11) to calculate the overall impact of immigration on the black native population. The discussion suggests that in order to make these calculations, we must make assumptions about a relatively large number of parameters: the skill distribution of the immigrant and native populations; the matrix of factor price elasticities that represent the production technology; and the factor shares.

To provide an empirical foundation for this simulation, I made various calculations using the 1990 Public Use Sample of the U.S. Census. Table 2.1 illustrates the skill distribution of immigrants, of natives, and of black natives. One straightforward way of measuring the skills of the various groups uses the distribution of educational attainment. Table 2.1 reports the fraction of the population in each of the relevant groups that belongs to one of four educational categories: people with less than twelve years of schooling; people with twelve years of schooling; people with thirteen to fifteen years of schooling; and people with at least sixteen years of schooling. The data clearly illustrate that immigrants and natives have very different skill distributions and that both immigrants and black natives tend to be relatively unskilled.

Because the theoretical discussion used a three-factor model (capital, and two types of labor), I need to aggregate the educational distribution into two groups: the relative shares of unskilled and skilled workers.

Table 2.1   Skill Distributions of Natives, Immigrants, and Black
             Natives

	Group		
	Natives	Immigrants	Black Natives
Educational distribution			
% with less than 12 years	16.2	37.7	27.6
% with 12 years	30.4	17.6	33.1
% with 13 to 15 years	29.4	20.3	27.3
% with 16 or more years	24.0	24.4	12.0
% of skilled workers who are black	—	—	6.7
% of unskilled workers who are black	—	—	11.8
Wage distribution			
% below native median	50.0	58.6	62.4
% above native median	50.0	41.4	37.6
% of skilled workers who are black	—	—	6.9
% of unskilled workers who are black	—	—	11.8

Source: Tabulations from the Public Use Sample of the 1990 Census.

Notes: The statistics are calculated in the sample of men aged eighteen to sixty-four who did not live in group quarters and who worked in the civilian sector at some point in the 1989 calendar year. The "skilled" group based on the educational distribution refers to workers who have more than twelve years of schooling.

One simple breakdown defines the group of skilled workers to include people who have more than a high school education and the group of unskilled workers to include those who have at most a high school education. If we use this definition, the data suggest that skilled workers make up 53.4 percent of the native population, 44.7 percent of the immigrant population, and 39.3 percent of the black native population. In addition, the data indicate that blacks make up 6.7 percent of the skilled work force and 11.8 percent of the unskilled work force.

An alternative way of defining the two skill groups uses the distribution of hourly wage rates. I used the hourly wage rate to rank workers in the *native* population, and classified workers whose wage exceeded the median as "skilled" workers and workers with wages below the median as unskilled workers. By this definition, 50 percent of the native work force is skilled, 41.4 percent of the immigrant work force is skilled (in the sense that 41.4 percent of the immigrants have a wage rate that exceeds the median in the native population), and 37.6 percent of black natives are skilled. In addition, the data show that blacks make up 6.9 percent of the skilled work force and 11.8 percent of the unskilled work force.

The two alternative methods of classifying workers into skilled and unskilled groups lead to relatively similar results. In view of this similarity, I will simulate the model using a simple set of assumptions (based roughly on the data): 50 percent of the native work force is skilled; immigrants make up 10 percent of the work force and 40 percent of the immigrants are skilled; and blacks make up 7 percent of the skilled work force and 12 percent of the unskilled work force. This simple parameterization of the skill distributions "builds in" the fact that immigrants and black natives have roughly similar skills.

In addition to defining the skill groups, I must also assign numerical values to the elements in the matrix of factor price elasticities that underlie the labor market responses to immigration. As noted earlier, the own-factor price elasticity for skilled workers probably exceeds that of unskilled workers (in absolute value). The evidence also suggests some weak complementarity between skilled workers and unskilled workers. The calculations reported below will be conducted using four alternative sets of assumptions for the vector (ε_{SS}, ε_{UU}, ε_{SU}): ($-.2$, $-.4$, x), ($-.3$, $-.5$, x), ($-.5$, $-.7$, x), and ($-.8$, -1.5, x).[13] The range bracketed by these alternatives reflects the underlying uncertainty about the actual values of these elasticities. It is worth emphasizing, however, that this range covers most of the estimates that are reported in the literature (Hamermesh, 1993). The simulations will also use three alternative values for the cross-price elasticity ε_{SU}: 0, .05, and .1.[14]

Finally, the calculations require an assumption about factor shares. We maintain our earlier (and well-documented) assumption that the factor share of capital is about .3 . The 1990 Census reveals that the average wage of people in the skilled group (when the skilled group is defined in terms of the median wage) is about three times larger than the wage of people in the unskilled group. This fact implies that the factor share of less skilled people would be .175, and that the factor share of skilled workers is .525 (thus the two add up to a factor share for labor of .7). I also maintain the assumption that blacks own about 2.5 percent of the capital stock.

Table 2.2 reports the results of the simulation. I used equations (2.9), (2.10), and (2.11) to calculate the impact of immigration on the incomes of each of the three factors of production (assuming that the economy has a 7 trillion dollar GDP). The table also reports the national immigration surplus and the immigration surplus that accrues to black natives. One result is immediately evident: Regardless of the set of assumptions that we make about the matrix of factor price elasticities, the immigration surplus that accrues to the black population is

Table 2.2 Estimates of the Immigration Surplus (in Billions of Dollars)

	$\varepsilon_{SU} = 0$		$\varepsilon_{SU} = .05$		$\varepsilon_{SU} = .1$	
	All Natives	Black Natives	All Natives	Black Natives	All Natives	Black Natives
Panel A: $\varepsilon_{UU} = -.2$, $\varepsilon_{SS} = -.4$						
Capital	73.50	1.84	55.13	1.38	36.75	0.92
Skilled workers	−54.10	−3.79	−43.95	−3.08	−33.81	−2.37
Unskilled workers	−12.94	−1.55	−5.81	−0.70	1.32	0.16
Immigration surplus	6.46	−3.50	5.37	−2.40	4.26	−1.29
Panel B: $\varepsilon_{UU} = -.3$, $\varepsilon_{SS} = -.5$						
Capital	95.55	2.39	77.18	1.93	58.80	1.47
Skilled workers	−67.62	−4.73	−57.48	−4.02	−47.33	−3.31
Unskilled workers	−19.40	−2.33	−12.27	−1.47	−5.15	−0.62
Immigration surplus	8.53	−4.67	7.43	−3.57	6.32	−2.46
Panel C: $\varepsilon_{UU} = -.6$, $\varepsilon_{SS} = -.9$						
Capital	176.40	4.41	158.03	3.95	139.65	3.49
Skilled workers	−121.72	−8.52	−111.57	−7.81	−101.43	−7.10
Unskilled workers	−38.81	−4.66	−31.68	−3.80	−24.55	−2.95
Immigration surplus	15.87	−8.77	14.78	−7.66	13.67	−6.55
Panel C: $\varepsilon_{UU} = -.8$, $\varepsilon_{SS} = -1.5$						
Capital	279.30	6.98	260.93	6.52	242.55	6.06
Skilled workers	−202.86	−14.20	−192.72	−13.49	−182.57	−12.78
Unskilled workers	−51.74	−6.21	−44.61	−5.35	−37.49	−4.50
Immigration surplus	24.70	−13.43	23.60	−12.32	22.49	−11.21

Notes: The simulations make the following assumptions: the GDP in the United States equals seven trillion dollars; immigrants make up 10 percent of the work force; 50 percent of the native and 40 percent of the immigrant work force is skilled; the share of income going to capital is .3, the share going to skilled labor is .525, and the share going to unskilled labor is .175; and blacks own 2.5 percent of the capital stock, make up 12 percent of the unskilled work force, and 7 percent of the skilled work force.

negative (although it is, of course positive for the United States as a whole). If we assume some complementarity between skilled and un-skilled workers ($\varepsilon_{SU} = .05$), the net immigration "deficit" for blacks can be as low as 2.4 billion dollars or as high as 12.3 billion dollars, with the deficit being larger the greater the own-price elasticities. If we convert these calculations into a per-capita loss, the adverse effect on the black population varies between eighty and four hundred dollars per person.

It is of interest to examine why black natives, as a group, lose from immigration. The simulations indicate that, as in the two-factor model presented earlier, the loss can typically be traced to the fact that blacks are underrepresented in the capital sector of the economy, so that the gains from immigration are disproportionately lower for blacks. At the same time, because immigrants depress the wages of competing work-ers, black workers—whether skilled or not—have much to lose from immigration.

The simulations also show that the immigration surplus for the country as a whole falls as the cross-elasticity of factor price (ε_{SU}) rises. It turns out, however, that blacks are better off when this cross-elastic-ity is large (although blacks still suffer a loss even if the elasticity is .1). The reason for this striking difference is that a larger amount of com-plementarity between skilled and unskilled labor implies that there is relatively less complementarity between capital and skilled workers.[15] Since blacks are greatly underrepresented in the pool of people who own the capital stock, the country as a whole does worse when there is a great deal of complementarity between skilled and unskilled workers, but blacks do better.

The theoretical framework allows us to simulate how specific changes in immigration policy affect both the immigration surplus and the share of the surplus accruing to black natives. In particular, we can examine how the costs and benefits change when immigration policy either discourages or favors the entry of skilled workers. Table 2.3 re-ports the results from this simulation by considering three alternative policy choices, $\beta = 0$, .4, and 1, where the value of β indicates the frac-tion of skilled workers in the immigrant population. Recall that the value of $\beta = .4$ represents our current immigration policy. To simplify the discussion, I only report the results for the case where $\varepsilon_{SU} = .05$.

The results from this simulation are intriguing and surprising. As we noted earlier, the country as a whole is better off when the immigrant flow is composed exclusively of skilled workers. If the own-price elastic-ities $\varepsilon_{SS} = -.5$ and $\varepsilon_{UU} = -.3$, we find that the immigration surplus is 7.4 billion dollars when immigrants are exclusively unskilled and rises to 36.8 billion dollars when immigrants are exclusively skilled.

Table 2.3 The Immigration Surplus and the Skill Composition of the Immigrant Flow (in Billions of Dollars)

	$\beta = 0$		$\beta = .4$		$\beta = 1$	
	All Natives	Black Natives	All Natives	Black Natives	All Natives	Black Natives
Panel A: $\varepsilon_{UU} = -.2$, $\varepsilon_{SS} = -.4$						
Capital	6.13	0.15	55.13	1.38	128.63	3.22
Skilled workers	18.38	1.29	−43.95	−3.08	−117.60	−8.23
Unskilled workers	−19.60	−2.35	−5.81	−0.70	18.38	2.21
Immigration surplus	4.91	−0.91	5.37	−2.40	29.41	−2.81
Panel B: $\varepsilon_{UU} = -.3$, $\varepsilon_{SS} = -.5$						
Capital	18.38	0.46	77.18	1.93	165.38	4.13
Skilled workers	18.38	1.29	−57.48	−4.02	−147.00	−10.29
Unskilled workers	−29.40	−3.53	−12.27	−1.47	18.38	2.21
Immigration surplus	7.36	−1.78	7.43	−3.57	36.76	−3.95
Panel C: $\varepsilon_{UU} = -.6$, $\varepsilon_{SS} = .9$						
Capital	55.13	1.38	158.03	3.95	312.38	7.81
Skilled workers	18.38	1.29	−111.57	−7.81	−264.60	−18.52
Unskilled workers	−58.80	−7.06	−31.68	−3.80	18.38	2.21
Immigration surplus	14.71	−4.39	14.78	−7.66	66.16	−8.51
Panel C: $\varepsilon_{UU} = -.8$, $\varepsilon_{SS} = -1.5$						
Capital	79.63	1.99	260.93	6.52	532.88	13.32
Skilled workers	18.38	1.29	−192.72	−13.49	−441.00	−30.87
Unskilled workers	−78.40	−9.41	−44.61	−5.35	18.38	2.21
Immigration surplus	19.61	−6.13	23.60	−12.32	110.26	−15.34

Notes: All simulations set $\varepsilon_{SU} = .05$. The simulations make the following assumptions: the GDP in the United States equals seven trillion dollars; immigrants make up 10 percent of the work force; 50 percent of the native work force is skilled; the share of income going to capital is .3, the share going to skilled labor is .525, and the share going to unskilled labor is .175; and blacks own 2.5 percent of the capital stock, make up 12 percent of the unskilled work force, and 7 percent of the skilled work force.

The size of the immigration surplus accruing to black natives, however, is maximized when the immigrant flow is exclusively *unskilled*. This seems like a very odd result since, by assumption, about 60 percent of the black work force is unskilled. Nevertheless, the simulations reported in table 2.3 illustrate the intuition behind this result. The black *deficit* when the skilled composition of the immigrant flow is exactly that of blacks ($\beta = .4$) is 3.6 billion dollars. A change in immigration policy that admitted only skilled immigrants would increase the black deficit to four billion dollars, while a change in immigration policy that admitted only unskilled immigrants would reduce the black deficit to less than two billion dollars. The simulations thus reveal that if we wished to improve black economic status, the United States would have to pursue what would seem to be an odd immigration policy (in terms of its ultimate purpose): Admit only unskilled immigrants. This type of policy would minimize the adverse impact of immigration on the black population but would make the country as a whole worse off.

This result arises because an exclusively skilled flow has a very harmful impact on skilled blacks (who make up about 40 percent of the black work force in this exercise). At the same time, because blacks are grossly underrepresented among the owners of capital, these sizable losses are not offset by the gains to black capitalists. The parameters used to simulate the model then suggest that blacks would actually be better off with an exclusively unskilled flow, where the unskilled blacks would lose somewhat (but not as much because the wage of unskilled workers is less responsive to immigration than that of skilled workers).

Note also that despite the wide range of parameter values used to simulate the model, table 2.3 does not report a single instance where blacks as a group *gain* from immigration. The smallest black deficit occurs when the immigrant flow is exclusively unskilled and the own-elasticities of factor price are small. In particular, the black deficit falls to 910 million dollars when $\varepsilon_{SS} = -.4$ and $\varepsilon_{UU} = -.2$. If the own-elasticities are relatively high, however, the admission of an exclusively unskilled work force would generate a sizable loss for the black population, on the order of four to six billion dollars.

In the end, the model teaches us two valuable lessons. Although the fact that black natives and immigrants have roughly the same skill distribution contributes to the black deficit from immigration, this fact alone cannot explain why the deficit exists in the first place. Much of the deficit arises because the big "winners" from immigration are the natives who own the productive resources of the economy, and blacks are greatly underrepresented in this group of capitalists. As a result, the seemingly obvious solution of pursuing an immigration policy that restricts entry only to skilled immigrants might actually worsen the economic status of blacks (when contrasted to a policy that admits only unskilled immigrants). A second, and perhaps more important lesson, is that the simulations strongly suggest that when it comes to immigration, there is a high probability that the black native population comes out on the losing end, regardless of what policy choices are made about the skill distribution of the immigrant flow.

These results, of course, hinge crucially on the assumption that the capital stock is fixed and does not respond to immigration. As we have seen, however, immigration increases the return to capital and there are increased incentives for investors to invest in the United States. In addition, immigrants themselves might add to the nation's capital stock. Earlier I showed that in the simpler model with homogeneous labor, the presence of capital flows dissipates the immigration surplus and neither black nor white natives gain or lose from immigration. In the more general model considered here, the immigration surplus will not generally disappear as a result of the immigration-induced capital flows as long as the skill distribution of immigrants differs from that of native workers.

Borjas (1998) rederives the model in equations (2.8) through (2.11) in the case where the supply of capital is perfectly elastic so that the rental rate of capital, r, is unchanged by immigration. The immigration surplus in this model is given by:

$$(2.12) \quad \Delta Q_N \big|_{dr=0} = \left(bN \frac{\partial w_S}{\partial M} + (1-b)N \frac{\partial w_U}{\partial M} \right) M,$$

where the notation "$dr = 0$" indicates that capital flows keep the rental rate of capital constant. The wage changes experienced by skilled and unskilled workers are given by:

$$(2.13) \quad \frac{d \log w_S}{d \log M} \bigg|_{dr=0} = \frac{S_S}{c_{KK}} [c_{SS} c_{KK} - c_{SK}^2] \frac{(\beta - b)}{p_S p_U} (1 - m)m,$$

$$(2.14) \quad \frac{d \log w_U}{d \log M} \bigg|_{dr=0} = -\frac{S_U}{c_{KK}} [c_{UU} c_{KK} - c_{UK}^2] \frac{(\beta - b)}{p_S p_U} (1 - m)m,$$

where c_{ij} gives the elasticities of complementarity between inputs i and j. Table 2.4 simulates this model to estimate the gains and losses experienced by the United States as a result of current immigration policy.[16] The fact that the immigration-induced capital flows keep the rental price of capital constant dissipates most of the gains from immigration, and the immigration surplus in table 2.4 is much smaller than the corresponding estimates in table 2.2 (which keep the capital stock constant).

Some gains remain, however, because the skills of immigrants differ from those of natives. Note, however, that black natives still lose from immigration because black workers tend to resemble the unskilled immigrant population—although these losses, of course, are small. If we use the factor price elasticities at the upper end of the range reported in table 2.4, immigration increases the income accruing to all natives by between one and two billion dollars annually but decreases the income accruing to black workers by about six hundred million dollars per year.

CONCLUSION

The family of economic models analyzed in this paper provides the conceptual foundation for evaluating how immigration affects the economic status of the native population in the host country, as well as of particular subgroups of the native population. A key lesson of the analysis is that, on aggregate, immigration benefits natives in the host country—but this does not mean that every native subgroup benefits. In fact, the application of the analysis to the black native population in the United States suggests that blacks are likely to be on the losing end of immigration for two distinct reasons:

1. The gains from immigration—which dominate the calculations at the national level when we aggregate over all native groups—are largest for those groups who own resources that complement immigrant labor. Native employers who hire immigrants are likely to be among the biggest "winners" from immigration. Black natives, however, own little of the capital stock, and the gains from immigration are disproportionately lower for blacks.

2. Immigration will be most harmful to groups that "look like" the immigrants in terms of their skill distribution. The gains from immigration accruing to black natives would increase if the skills of immigrants were different from those of blacks. It turns out, however, that the losses suffered by blacks may well be minimized when the immigrant flow is composed exclusively of unskilled workers.

In the end, the analysis suggests that even though immigration raises the per capita income of U.S. natives, it has an adverse impact on the per capita income of black natives. A variety of alternative assumptions suggests that immigration has probably reduced the income of the typical black native in the United States by perhaps more than one hundred dollars annually. Moreover, a simulation of the model suggested that, under a

Table 2.4 Estimates of the Immigration Surplus Assuming the Rental Rate of Capital Is Constant (in Billions of Dollars)

	$\varepsilon_{SU}=0$		$\varepsilon_{SU}=.05$		$\varepsilon_{SU}=.1$	
	All Natives	Black Natives	All Natives	Black Natives	All Natives	Black Natives
Panel A: $\varepsilon_{UU}=-.2$, $\varepsilon_{SS}=.4$						
Skilled workers	3.86	.27	4.46	.31	4.23	.36
Unskilled workers	−3.70	−.44	−3.60	−.43	−2.72	−.33
Immigration surplus	.16	−.17	.86	−.12	1.51	−.03
Panel B: $\varepsilon_{UU}=-.3$, $\varepsilon_{SS}=-.5$						
Skilled workers	5.63	.39	6.42	.45	6.76	.47
Unskilled workers	−5.39	−.65	−5.48	−.66	−5.15	−.62
Immigration surplus	.24	−.26	.94	−.21	1.61	−.15
Panel C: $\varepsilon_{UU}=-.6$, $\varepsilon_{SS}=-.9$						
Skilled workers	11.07	.77	12.00	.84	12.77	.89
Unskilled workers	−10.58	−1.27	−10.82	−1.30	−10.89	−1.31
Immigration surplus	.49	−.50	1.18	−.46	1.88	−.42
Panel C: $\varepsilon_{UU}=-.8$, $\varepsilon_{SS}=-1.5$						
Skilled workers	15.31	1.07	16.13	1.13	16.83	1.18
Unskilled workers	−14.64	−1.76	−14.76	−1.77	−14.78	−1.78
Immigration surplus	.67	−.69	1.37	−.64	2.05	−.60

Notes: The simulations make the following assumptions: the GDP in the United States equals seven trillion dollars; immigrants make up 10 percent of the work force; 50 percent of the native and 40 percent of the immigrant work force is skilled; the share of income going to skilled is .3, the share going to skilled labor is .525, and the share going to unskilled labor is .175; and blacks own 2.5 percent of the capital stock, make up 12 percent of the unskilled work force, and 7 percent of the skilled work force.

wide range of reasonable parameter values, it would be difficult to devise an immigration policy that would restrict the immigration of certain skill groups and would generate a net benefit for the black population. The reason for this fact is provocative: Because of capital-skill complementarity, the gains from skilled immigration go mainly to natives who own the capital stock in the economy—and blacks are underrepresented in this group. Skilled immigration, therefore, is unlikely to benefit blacks. Similarly, unskilled immigration would disproportionately hurt blacks because a larger fraction of the black population is composed of less skilled workers. Unskilled immigration, therefore, is also unlikely to benefit blacks.

The social and economic conflicts introduced by the possibility that immigration creates a net gain for the United States as a whole, but a net loss for an important demographic group raises a number of interesting questions that have received little attention in the policy debate. It is important to add, however, that the analysis presented in this paper focuses solely on the economic ramifications of alternative immigration policies and ignores the cultural and social impacts that immigration imparts on many native groups.

NOTES

1. Borjas (1995), Johnson in this volume, and Borjas, Freeman, and Katz (1997) present recent studies of the costs and benefits of immigration. A number of theoretical models in the international trade literature also explore how immigrants affect the welfare of natives; see, for example, Bhagwati and Srinivasan (1983) and Ethier (1985). A rare empirical analysis is given by Svorny (1991), who estimates the gains to American consumers from the immigration of physicians.

2. This statement abstracts from the fiscal impacts of immigration through expenditures on welfare programs and other public services.

3. Borjas (1995) presents a more detailed discussion of the costs and benefits from immigration based on this framework.

4. In particular, note that if we let $(w_1 - w_0) \approx (\Delta w/\Delta L) \times M$, the immigration surplus can be rewritten as:

$$\frac{\Delta Q_N}{Q} = -\frac{1}{2}\left(\frac{\Delta w}{\Delta L} \cdot M\right)\frac{M}{Q} = -\frac{1}{2} \cdot \frac{wL}{Q}\left(\frac{\Delta w}{\Delta L} \cdot \frac{L}{w}\right) \cdot \frac{M}{L} \cdot \frac{M}{L}.$$

5. If there are only two factors of production, the elasticity of factor price for labor must equal $(1-s)^2/\eta$, where η is the output-constant elasticity of la-

bor demand (Hamermesh 1993, 26–29). There is some consensus that η is about $-.3$. Because the share of labor income is .7, the elasticity of factor price is also $-.3$.

6. To calculate the total losses accruing to native workers, again let $(w_1 - w_0)$ $\approx (\Delta w / \Delta L) \times M$. The reduction in total labor income, as a fraction of GDP, can then be written as:

$$\frac{(w_1 - w_0)N}{Q} = \left(\frac{\Delta w}{\Delta L} \cdot M\right)\frac{N}{Q} = \frac{wL}{Q}\left(\frac{\Delta w}{\Delta L}\frac{L}{w}\right) \cdot \frac{M}{L} \cdot \frac{N}{L}.$$

The gains accruing to capitalists are calculated by adding the absolute value of this expression to the immigration surplus (that is, to the area of the triangle).

7. The very large racial gap in self-employment rates provides tangential evidence that blacks own a relatively small part of the capital stock. In 1990, only 4 percent of self-employed workers were black. Recent studies of the racial difference in self-employment are given by Borjas and Bronars (1989) and Fairlie and Meyer (1996).

8. Much of this debate hinges on the possibility that the local labor market impacts of immigration (*if* they exist) are diffused to the national labor market by interregional flows of labor, capital, or goods. Borjas (1994) summarizes the theoretical issues and the empirical evidence.

9. The empirical evidence, however, suggests that capital is somewhat immobile across countries (see Feldstein and Horioka 1980).

10. Figure 2.2 is obtained by differentiating equation (2.6) with respect to β and assuming that immigration is "small" so that the fraction of the work force that is skilled is not affected by immigration (that is, $\partial p_S / \partial \beta = 0$).

11. The derivatives in (2.8) are evaluated at the "average" point. It is well known (Bhagwati and Srinivasan 1983, 294) that when the derivatives are evaluated at the initial equilibrium (where $L = N$, the infinitesimal increase in national income accruing to natives is zero. To calculate finite changes, therefore, we evaluate the immigration surplus using an "average" rate for $\partial w_i / \partial M$, where the average is defined by:

$$\frac{1}{2}\left(\left.\frac{\partial w_i}{\partial M}\right|_{L=N} + \left.\frac{\partial w_i}{\partial M}\right|_{L=N+M}\right).$$

12. Note that the immigration surplus is positive even when $b = \beta$ because the capital stock remains fixed even though immigration increases the quantity of the two labor inputs proportionately.

13. Once these elasticities are defined, the fact that a weighted average of fac-

tor price elasticities must add up to zero (where the weights are the factor shares) implicitly defines the own-elasticity for capital and the cross-elasticities between capital and the two labor inputs.

14. The assumption about the numerical value of ε_{US} determines the value of ε_{SU}. In particular, it can be shown that $s_U\, \varepsilon_{US} = s_S\, \varepsilon_{SU}$. In view of our assumptions about factor shares, the implied range for ε_{US} is (0, .15, .3).

15. This fact is again related to the mathematical property that a weighted average of the elasticities must add up to zero.

16. It is analytically convenient to conduct the simulations by assuming that the additional capital originates abroad and is owned by foreigners (or immigrants). The calculation can then ignore the income changes that might occur in the native population as some natives transfer resources to the capital market.

REFERENCES

Bhagwati, Jagdish N., and T. N. Srinivasan. 1983. *Lectures on International Trade.* Cambridge, Mass.: MIT Press.

Blau, Francine D., and John W. Graham. 1990. "Black-White Differences in Wealth and Asset Composition." *Quarterly Journal of Economics* 105 (May): 321–39.

Borjas, George J. 1994. "The Economics of Immigration." *Journal of Economic Literature* 32 (December): 1667–1717.

———. 1995. "The Economic Benefits from Immigration." *Journal of Economic Perspectives* 9 (Spring): 3–22.

———. 1998. "The Economic Analysis of Immigration." *Handbook of Labor Economics*, volume 3, edited by Orley Ashenfelter and David Card. Amsterdam: North-Holland, forthcoming.

Borjas, George J., and Stephen G. Bronars. 1989. "Consumer Discrimination and Self-Employment." *Journal of Political Economy* 97 (June): 581–605.

Borjas, George J., Richard B. Freeman, and Lawrence F. Katz. 1997. "How Much Do Immigration and Trade Affect Labor Market Outcomes." *Brookings Papers on Economic Activity*: 1–67.

Card, David. 1997. "Immigrant Inflows, Native Outflows, and the Local Labor Market Impacts of Higher Immigration." NBER Working Paper No. 5927 (February).

Ethier, Wilfred J. 1985. "International Trade and Labor Migration." *American Economic Review* 75 (September): 691–707.

Fairlie, Robert W., and Bruce D. Meyer. 1996. "Ethnic and Racial Self-Employment Differences and Possible Explanations." *Journal of Human Resources* 31 (Fall): 757–93.

Feldstein, Martin S., and Charles Horioka. 1980. "Domestic Savings and International Capital Flows." *Economic Journal* 90 (June): 314–29.

Friedberg, Rachel, and Jennifer Hunt. 1995. "The Impact of Immigration on Host County Wages, Employment and Growth." *Journal of Economic Perspectives* 3 (Spring): 23–44.

Hamermesh, Daniel S. 1993. *Labor Demand.* Princeton, N.J.: Princeton University Press.

Helpman, Elhanan, and Paul R. Krugman. 1985. *Market Structure and Foreign Trade.* Cambridge, Mass.: MIT Press.

Rothman, Eric S., and Thomas J. Espenshade. 1992. "Fiscal Impacts of Immigration to the United States." *Population Index* 58 (Fall): 381–415.

Smith, James P. 1995. "Racial and Ethnic Differences in Wealth in the Health and Retirement Survey." *Journal of Human Resources* 30 (Supplement): S158–S183.

Svorny, Shirley. 1991. "Consumer Gains from Physician Immigration to the U.S.: 1966–1971." *Applied Economics* 23 (February): 331–37.

U.S. Bureau of the Census. 1992. *Statistical Abstract of the United States.* Washington: U.S. Government Printing Office.

CHAPTER 3

Immigration and the Quality of Jobs

Daniel S. Hamermesh

"I can't hire all legal people. Who wants to work in this dirty job? American people? No." —JANE LEE, whose Manhattan firm, Jane Productions, was raided by the Immigration and Naturalization Service.[1]

Perhaps the most common argument in favor of immigration is that "immigrant workers are in jobs rejected by indigenous workers" (Castles and Kosack 1973, 112). This idea, that immigrants are welcome because they take jobs that natives would not take, and thus that would otherwise not be performed, underlies some academic discussion (Piore 1979). It is also much in (at least part of) the popular mind. For example, in discussing their migration to Germany from the former Soviet Union, the ethnic German returnees stated that, "their children wanted to work, even with jobs other Germans will not look at."[2]

It is not clear from either the academic discussion or popular sentiment what mechanism underlies the behavior implicit in these views. I do not believe that it is simply that immigrants will work for lower wages than otherwise identical natives. If that were the case, however, it would be difficult to see how the displacement of at least some very low-wage native workers could be avoided, especially in the presence of a binding minimum wage. It might be, as Piore (1979) implies, that employers create special "immigrant jobs" that would not otherwise exist; but without the immigrants themselves having preferences about jobs, and without some underlying supply behavior, treating them as passive tools of exploitative employers is both belittling and probably wrong.

I interpret the popular and academic suggestions as implying that immigrants are not simply workers who are willing to accept lower wages than natives. They may even have the same skills as natives; but they are more willing to take jobs that offer nonpecuniary aspects of work that natives find unacceptable. This view allows us to explore the extent of workplace disamenities faced by immigrants, as opposed to natives, particularly low-skilled and minority natives.

Examining workplace amenities faced by immigrants, low-skilled and minority natives, and other natives can provide the basis for evaluating the burgeoning literature on employment substitution between immigrants and natives. While a number of studies suggested that the extent of substitution is small (see the summary in Hamermesh 1993, table 3.10), more recent work (Borjas et al. 1996; Haisken-De New and Zimmerman 1996; Reimers, this volume) is increasingly conflicted on this issue. All of these studies categorize workers by location of birth and/or ethnicity and assume that workers in these categories form different groups in the labor market. While this artificial distinction, so prevalent in the literature, is convenient and may make sense, it is quite arbitrary and perhaps inconsistent with a more appropriate aggregation based on the skills embodied in the groups.[3] By studying how amenities differ among these groups, we can go beyond the standard approach and discover to what extent it is logically possible for the different groups to compete in the labor market.

This study should be viewed as a belated precursor to the large literature on immigrant-native labor-market competition, since it lays out the mechanism by which such substitution might arise and presents a variety of evidence on whether that mechanism is important in the United States. I first consider how an influx of immigrants might affect the workplace disamenities enjoyed by low-skilled workers and the effect on the average level of amenities faced by all low-skilled workers, immigrants included. I then describe the several sets of data used to examine these issues and the particular amenities on which this study focuses and compare the average extent of various amenities enjoyed by immigrant and native workers. Next, I test the model provided earlier directly by examining how a greater presence of immigrants affects the degree of two of the disamenities I consider that are experienced by workers in the native population: working at unpleasant times and the risk of on-the-job injury.

INFERRING THE EFFECT OF IMMIGRATION ON WORKPLACE DISAMENITIES

We wish to infer how the addition of a group of immigrants will affect the average level of workplace amenities and, even more important, the amenities enjoyed by native workers, particularly low-skilled workers. Building a model that imposes substitution possibilities directly in a production function would have the same faults—mainly that of arbitrarily assuming that substitution will exist—that are present in the literature on job competition between immigrants and natives. I specify instead a very simple model that allows no direct substitution between natives and workers in production. Rather, it relies on product-market clearing and the entry and exit of firms to generate results on both im-

migrant-native substitution and on the pattern of workplace disamenities in the economy. The general idea in the model is to examine the
implications for the amenities enjoyed by natives if the willingness of
immigrants to accept disamenities differs from that of natives. Thus it
captures the underlying behavior that seems implicit in the notion of
immigrants accepting jobs that natives will not take.

Consider first what wages and the distribution of disamenities will
look like in the absence of immigrants whose tastes differ from those of
natives. Assume that native workers are homogeneous and derive utility
from their jobs depending on the wage rate w^j received at firm j and on
θ^j, the level of the disamenity associated with work at firm j. The typical worker's indirect utility is then:

(3.1)　　$V = V(w^j, \theta^j)$

where $V_1 > 0$, $V_2 < 0$, and $V_{11} < 0$, $V_{22} < 0$. The signs of the first and
second derivatives are based on the notion that workers have increasing
marginal rates of substitution of wages for workplace disamenities as
the degree of the disamenities increases. I also assume that native workers have some reservation utility, V^N, below which they will not work
in the labor market. Presumably this reservation utility is supported by
the value of their household production (or perhaps too by the magnitude of governmental or other income transfers).

Assume that all firms sell the same product at a price P. Firms and
potential firms are distinguished from each other by a fixed θ^j associated with the firm, which is its particular immutable level of the disamenity. A firm is organized by one person, who is either running a
firm or not economically active. Workers cannot organize firms, and
entrepreneurs cannot be workers. Each firm employs either one worker,
if it produces, or no workers, if it does not produce. If firm j produces,
its profits are:

(3.2)　　$\pi = P\theta_j - w^j.$

Firms with higher values of the disamenity can produce more goods at
the same wage rate as those whose workplaces are safer, cleaner, and so
forth. Firms and potential firms can be viewed as being arrayed from
the lowest value of θ, at firm 1, to its highest value, at firm J.

Workers spend their entire incomes (which by assumption equal
their earnings) on the product of these firms, as do active entrepreneurs, so that:

$$(3.3) \quad \sum_{j=1}^{J^N} [w^j + \pi^j] = P \sum_{j=1}^{J^N} \theta^j.$$

The marginal firm, J^N, is making zero profits in equilibrium in the product market, so that:

$$(3.4) \quad \pi^{J^N} = P\theta^{J^N} - w^{J^N} = 0.$$

In labor-market equilibrium the worker at this firm is enjoying utility:

$$(3.5) \quad V^{J^N} = V(w^{J^N}, \theta^{J^N}) = V^N.$$

Because of the assumptions about the nature of workers' preferences, V, any firm indexed $j > J^N$ would earn negative profits if it produced, since the cost savings that it could obtain from having a higher value of θ would be more than offset by the higher wage that it would have to pay to induce a worker to accept the level of the disamenity that it offers, $\theta^j > \theta^{J^N}$. Taken together equations (3.3), (3.4), and (3.5) determine the endogenous variables in this system: J^N, the identity of the marginal firm; P^*, the equilibrium product price; and w^{J^N}, the wage rate at the marginal firm (and hence wage rates at each firm, since all workers receive utility equal to their reservation utility v^N).

In the absence of immigrants, native workers will be employed at all firms that provide a level of disamenities no worse than some endogenously determined amount. The number of active entrepreneurs is determined by the distribution of amenities and the workers' reservation utility. Among native workers those employed at firms offering a worse set of disamenities will receive a compensating wage differential for the risk of the potential suffering that they face.

Consider what happens in this economy if a fixed number, I, of immigrants enters the labor market. I assume that immigrants are homogeneous and have the identical skills (same education, and so on, as natives), but that unlike natives they are unconcerned about the presence of disamenities.[4] Thus each immigrant will work if he or she can obtain indirect utility:

$$(3.6) \quad V = V(w^j) \geq V^I,$$

a condition that defines the wage of immigrants, w^I. This assumption about immigrants' utility is extreme, but the difference between (3.1) and (3.6) does capture the notion, implicit in the epigraph to this study, that immigrants might take jobs that have such severe disamenities that no native would accept them.

The assumption that avoiding reductions in workplace disamenities enables a firm to produce more cheaply with workers of the same cost guarantees that immigrants will take jobs at those firms with the highest θ^j, since the potential entrepreneurs who enter the market in response to immigration can offer the immigrants a higher w^I and still make larger profits than potential firms with a lower index j. The first immigrant worker will thus be matched with the entrepreneur who opens firm J, the establishment with the worst disamenities; as more immigrants enter, more firms open up with successively lower indexes j $< J$. There is some firm type J^I that is the marginal one among those employing immigrants. (Even this firm is making positive profits: In this model sweatshops are quite profitable.) The marginal (zero-profit) firm is the highest-θ surviving firm that employs native workers.

With the influx of immigrant workers the spending-revenue equality becomes (since we must add the immigrants' production and the demand for output by them and by the entrepreneurs who "accommodated" them):

$$(3.7) \quad \sum_{J=1}^{J^N} [w^j + \pi^j] + \sum_{j=J^I}^{J} [Iw^I + \pi^j] = P \sum_{J=1}^{J^N} \theta^j + P \sum_{j=J^I}^{J} \theta^j.$$

Conditions (3.4) and (3.5) must also be satisfied at the new equilibrium, as must (3.6). This set of conditions generates a new set of equilibrium values of the product price, P^*, the marginal firm, J^N, the wage rate of the native worker at firm J^N, w^{J^N}, and J^I. This last, the identity of the lowest-θ firm employing immigrants, is trivially determined by the exogenous number of immigrants who have entered the labor market. What happens to P^* and J^N depends on the assumptions that we make about how the new (sweatshop-owning) entrepreneurs spend the large profits that they make. If we make the reasonable assumption that immigrants consume less than native workers, but assume that the profits of sweatshop owners disappear into a black hole, the sweatshops' output then competes with that of firms employing native workers. It drives down the product price and reduces the number of profitable firms that employ native workers. In this case the level of disamenities suffered by native workers decreases on average, as does their wage, along with the decrease in native employment.

More sensibly, at the very least it seems reasonable to assume that spending by the new entrepreneurs does not reduce P^*, so that J^N, and thus the wage rate and the disamenities faced by the marginal native worker remain unchanged. Thus the influx of immigrants raises the overall standard of living among natives by allowing the scope for some entrepreneurs to open up new firms.

Going even further, an alternative assumption is that, with higher average entrepreneurial incomes, the consumption demand of entrepreneurs increases, leading to an increase in P^*. That in turn makes it profitable for firm J^{N+1} to open up, implying an increase in native employment, a higher native wage, and worse amenities at the marginal firm (and worse amenities on average among native workers). The average level of disamenities economywide rises: Immigration has allowed the opening of jobs offering a higher rate of disamenities, both in sweatshops and in the marginal firms employing natives whose operations have become profitable.

This simple general-equilibrium model has led to two surprising conclusions: (1) Immigrants who do not mind disamenities will take jobs offering the worst possible set of disamenities; and (2) the average disamenity level in jobs filled by natives may be increased by immigration. Also, even though I assume there is no possibility for substituting immigrants for natives, the dynamics of the product market may make it appear that the influx of immigrants changes the job opportunities of natives.

This entire discussion has treated the native group as homogeneous, which is clearly an oversimplification. In particular, low-skilled workers, and those minorities who face labor-market discrimination, are more likely to be located in the firms that were offering the worst package of amenities before the immigration occurred. With an influx of immigrants the low-skilled (and/or minority) natives who are in jobs with the most severe disamenities may face competition from immigrants who are more willing to take jobs in firms that can be profitable only if they offer still worse disamenities. To the extent that the influx of immigrants does reduce native employment, it will do so especially among low-skilled workers. Alternatively, if it generates positive spillovers onto native workers' employment, those too will be greatest among less-skilled native workers.

HYPOTHESES ABOUT AMENITIES, AND THE DATA TO TEST THEM

The theory in the previous section makes it clear that an influx of migrants can affect the wages and amenities of native workers even if there is no direct substitution in the labor market, for the immigration may alter the identity of the marginal firm employing native workers through its effects on product demand. Employment opportunities of natives may change even though we have assumed that there is no labor-market competition. But is that assumption of no labor-market competition correct? Do we really need to go beyond the labor market to provide an explanation for the possibility that immigrants affect natives' wages and employment, or can we find labor-market evidence that demonstrates that the essential assumption of the model—that "immigrants take jobs that natives won't take"—is incorrect?

If immigrants are not competing directly with natives for jobs, we will observe that the immigrants are in jobs that offer distinctly inferior amenities to those offered in jobs held by otherwise identical natives. Both groups face the same market-determined trade-off between wages and amenities, so that it would make little sense to examine whether compensating wage differentials facing the two groups differ; but if immigrants' willingness to accept disamenities differs from that of natives, we will observe immigrants working in jobs that offer a worse package of amenities given the workers' characteristics. Thus the main order of business is to examine whether some identifiable amenities differ between immigrant and native workers, and, in particular, between immigrants and otherwise identical low-skilled or minority workers. This could be done using household data on amenities related to workers' characteristics (as I do later); or, if we had establishment data, we could test that and the additional implication of the model that workers would be segregated by immigrant status due to employers' inability to assign different amenities to different workers in the same workplace.[5]

Even if the amenities enjoyed by otherwise identical natives and immigrants differ, such differences say nothing about causation. Thus the second question is whether an influx of immigrants itself generates any change in the amenities in natives' jobs. The appropriate test of this issue should involve examining how natives' amenities, especially those of minorities, differ depending on the importance of the immigrant population in the labor force.

The main difficulty in performing these tests is the paucity of sets of data that contain information on large arrays of workplace amenities, that do so for large samples of workers (so that a reasonably large number of immigrants is present in the sample), and that identify workers' nativity. This problem severely restricts our ability to examine these ideas empirically and confines the analyses for the United States to three sets of micro data.

The first and best source of data for testing the ideas on this issue results from a fortuitous coincidence. In May 1991 the Current Population Survey (CPS) Multiple Jobholder Supplement obtained information on the starting and ending times of a worker's main job. In June 1991 the CPS contained a supplement on immigrants, including questions on date of migration and country of nativity. Because three-fourths of the respondents were in both the May and June 1991 surveys, I can combine the two surveys to form a data set that has information on immigrant status and, with some manipulation, on whether each respondent is at work at each particular hour. I have shown elsewhere (Hamermesh 1996) that work in the evening and at night is a disamenity: Workers with lower full incomes, other things equal, are more likely to be at work at those times. Since we can identify evening and night work as a disamenity, examining differences between immigrants and natives in the propensity to work at those times provides a test of whether the preconditions for immigrant-native labor-labor substitution are absent. The usual CPS demographic measures, including variables representing age, education, marital status, presence of a child under age six, location in the "Rust Belt" (the New England, mid-Atlantic or East North Central states), and metropolitan area size (greater than 2.5 million people, between 0.5 and 2.5 million people, less than 0.5 million people, with nonmetropolitan location the excluded group), can also be generated.[6]

The second source of data is the June 1991 CPS itself. Taking the entire sample we can merge workers using their industrial affiliation (three-digit Census code, linked to the 1987 SIC codes) with published information on injury rates per one hundred employees and the number of lost workdays per one hundred employees (U.S. Bureau of Labor Statistics 1990). Dividing the latter by the former yields the average duration (in days) of lost workday injuries. All the control variables that were generated for the study of work timing using the May 1991 CPS are generated for the examination of injuries. The link between the injury data and the June CPS industry code is not always clear, so that to avoid introducing errors in the crucial variable I discard nearly 10 percent of workers from the original June 1991 CPS sample.[7]

The 1971 and 1978 Quality of American Life (QAL) surveys identify immigrants (country of birth, actually) and provide information on the nativity of the respondents' parents. Pooling the samples for the two years yields a sufficiently large number of usable observations and thus provides a third sample that offers some hope of identifying differences between natives and immigrants. From the survey information I generate indicator variables for educational attainment, race, the size of the metropolitan area (whether among the largest twelve), main Census region, and marital status, and create continuous variables for the worker's age and hourly wage.[8] Most important, the QAL surveys also offer data on respondents' satisfaction with various nonwage characteristics of their jobs. While the sample elicits a large number of these subjective responses, I restrict the analyses to workers' feelings about the following questions: (1) How interesting is the job? (2) Does it offer opportunities to make friends? (3) Are the physical surroundings pleasant? (4) How good is the job security? (5) Can the worker develop his or her abilities? (6) Does the job use the worker's skills? (7) Is there enough time to finish work? The responses are on a four-point scale. I treat those workers who stated that they were very or somewhat satisfied with the particular aspect of the job as being satisfied, and the others as being dissatisfied. These measures have the disadvantage that they are subjective and thus liable to biases that arise because the workers' responses are partly affected directly by the wage they are paid (see Brown 1980).

In order to examine whether amenities differ among natives depending on the importance of the immigrant population in the work force, I obtained from the 1990 Census for each MSA the fraction of the labor force, IMMPCT, that are immigrants. Merging this fraction with the May 1991 CPS Supplement for the timing study, and with the June 1991 CPS for the injury study, generates a very large sample of non-Hispanic white native workers, and usefully large subsamples of native minorities, on which to test how work timing and injuries are affected by the presence of immigrants in the labor market. Because the data needed to construct IMMPCT are only available for metropolitan areas, however, all the analysis of this question is necessarily performed excluding the roughly one-third of workers who reside outside metropolitan areas.

DO NATIVES AND IMMIGRANTS ENJOY DIFFERENT AMENITIES?

Work at Unpleasant Times

I now examine the first of the two questions dealing with the relation of immigration to native workers' on-the-job amenities, namely whether the packages of amenities received by natives differ from those received by otherwise identical immigrants. Consider first the objective information from the May 1991 CPS Supplement on the disamenity, working in the evening or at night. In table 3.1 I list the means and their standard deviations of several economic and demographic measures and also the probability of work in the evenings or nights separately by sex and for native non-Hispanic whites, blacks and Hispanics, and for immigrants. Immigrants constitute around 10 percent of the workers in this sample, perhaps very slightly above what other studies have indicated was the immigrant proportion of the labor force in the early

Table 3.1 Means and Their Standard Errors, May 1991 CPS

	Men				Women			
	Non-Hispanic White	Native Black	Hispanic	Immigrant	Non-Hispanic White	Native Black	Hispanic	Immigrant
Weekly wages ($)	584.4 (6.30)	415.7 (12.9)	424.2 (18.3)	524.5 (18.6)	377.1 (4.40)	344.4 (11.7)	340.2 (21.4)	388.0 (12.8)
Education	13.39 (.020)	12.32 (.070)	11.28 (.122)	11.98 (.091)	13.35 (.019)	12.71 (.054)	11.96 (.104)	12.43 (.086)
Age	38.50 (.097)	38.32 (.326)	34.36 (.395)	37.18 (.262)	37.99 (.102)	37.47 (.282)	34.46 (.412)	37.56 (.292)
Working at								
8 P.M.–9 P.M.	.148 (.003)	.199 (.010)	.165 (.013)	.175 (.008)	.136 (.003)	.144 (.008)	.114 (.012)	.137 (.008)
9 P.M.–10 P.M.	.126 (.003)	.179 (.010)	.151 (.013)	.153 (.008)	.113 (.003)	.125 (.008)	.100 (.011)	.112 (.007)
10 P.M.–11 P.M.	.109 (.002)	.160 (.010)	.135 (.012)	.128 (.007)	.092 (.002)	.114 (.007)	.079 (.010)	.095 (.007)
11 P.M.–midnight	.098 (.002)	.128 (.009)	.118 (.011)	.107 (.006)	.077 (.002)	.091 (.007)	.062 (.009)	.079 (.006)
Midnight–1 A.M.	.079 (.002)	.107 (.008)	.095 (.010)	.082 (.006)	.060 (.002)	.079 (.006)	.053 (.008)	.060 (.006)
1 A.M.–2 A.M.	.074 (.002)	.095 (.008)	.089 (.010)	.077 (.006)	.056 (.002)	.073 (.006)	.050 (.008)	.058 (.005)
2 A.M.–3 A.M.	.071 (.002)	.092 (.008)	.077 (.009)	.069 (.005)	.054 (.002)	.069 (.006)	.047 (.008)	.054 (.005)
3 A.M.–4 A.M.	.070 (.002)	.090 (.007)	.074 (.009)	.068 (.005)	.052 (.002)	.065 (.006)	.047 (.008)	.051 (.005)
4 A.M.–5 A.M.	.073 (.002)	.084 (.007)	.079 (.010)	.070 (.005)	.053 (.002)	.066 (.006)	.050 (.008)	.050 (.005)
5 A.M.–6 A.M.	.085 (.002)	.099 (.008)	.092 (.010)	.093 (.006)	.058 (.002)	.073 (.006)	.063 (.009)	.053 (.005)
N	17272	1471	807	2269	15532	1913	761	1857

1990s.[9] The weekly wages of immigrant men are below those of native whites, and their education is substantially below that of whites.

The first thing to note about the timing of work is that for all groups a not-inconsiderable proportion of workers reports that the starting and ending times of their jobs bracket evening or night work. Nonetheless, these fractions are small compared to the nearly 90 percent of workers who are on the job at the peak work time, 3 P.M. (Hamermesh forthcoming). There are no significant differences between immigrants and native non-Hispanic white women in the probability of working evenings or nights. Male immigrants are, however, more likely than native non-Hispanic whites to work evenings, but their propensities to work nights are the same. The main intergroup difference in these data is that blacks, especially men, are significantly more likely than other workers to be at work at these times.

The same calculations as those underlying table 3.1 were made with the samples broken down by educational attainment (high school graduation or more, and others). This decomposition of the sample allows us to examine whether segmentation by the taste for amenities might exist only among less-educated Americans and immigrants. The conclusion from table 3.1, that there is little difference between immigrants and native non-Hispanic whites but that native blacks have substantially higher propensities to work evenings and nights, holds true for each education group.

Work timing is an especially crucial job disamenity, since the timing of work is inherent in one's choice of labor supply, which in turn depends on all the demographic and economic factors that have become standard in the literature. For that reason one cannot simply look at differences in means; instead, we need to adjust for as many observable differences among workers as is possible in order to infer whether workers with the same full income who differ by immigrant status enjoy different amounts of the particular amenity. The results of one such test are shown in table 3.2, which presents for each sex the adjusted excess probability of working at the particular time by immigrants, black natives, and Hispanic natives compared to non-Hispanic white natives. The derivatives from the probits in the top panel reflect adjustments for education, age, size of metropolitan area, marital status, presence of young children and region, all of which have been shown (Hamermesh 1996, chapter 3) to have independent effects on the timing of work. The probits also hold constant for total daily work hours, since those people who work longer hours are perforce more likely to be at work at any particular hour of the day.

Immigrant men are significantly more likely than demographically

Table 3.2 Effects of Immigrant Status and Ethnicity on the Timing of Work, May 1991 CPS

Dependent Variable	Men (N = 22230)				Women (N = 20431)			
	Mean at Work	Immigrant	Black Native	Hispanic Native	Mean at Work	Immigrant	Black Native	Hispanic Native
Without industry								
Working at								
8 P.M.–9 P.M.	.155	.029 (.009)	.057 (.010)	−.012 (.010)	.136	.011 (.009)	−.004 (.007)	−.033 (.009)
9 P.M.–10 P.M.	.134	.024 (.008)	.058 (.009)	−.005 (.009)	.114	.003 (.008)	.003 (.007)	−.019 (.008)
10 P.M.–11 P.M.	.115	.016 (.008)	.056 (.008)	−.004 (.008)	.095	.005 (.007)	.015 (.006)	−.010 (.008)
11 P.M.–midnight	.102	.008 (.007)	.035 (.008)	−.003 (.008)	.079	.003 (.006)	.010 (.005)	−.013 (.006)
Midnight–1 A.M.	.083	.005 (.006)	.035 (.007)	.000 (.007)	.062	−.001 (.004)	.016 (.004)	−.006 (.005)
1 A.M.–2 A.M.	.077	.005 (.006)	.029 (.006)	.000 (.006)	.058	.001 (.004)	.017 (.004)	−.005 (.005)
2 A.M.–3 A.M.	.073	.004 (.006)	.029 (.006)	−.003 (.006)	.055	−.001 (.004)	.016 (.004)	−.003 (.005)
3 A.M.–4 A.M.	.072	.003 (.005)	.027 (.006)	−.004 (.006)	.054	−.003 (.004)	.014 (.004)	−.000 (.004)
4 A.M.–5 A.M.	.074	.002 (.006)	.018 (.006)	−.001 (.006)	.054	−.004 (.004)	.015 (.004)	.001 (.005)
5 A.M.–6 A.M.	.088	.008 (.006)	.019 (.007)	−.003 (.007)	.060	−.004 (.004)	.016 (.004)	−.001 (.005)

With industry						
8 P.M.–9 P.M.	.012	.039	−.014	.001	−.005	−.028
	(.008)	(.009)	(.010)	(.008)	(.008)	(.010)
9 P.M.–10 P.M.	.010	.039	−.003	−.005	−.002	−.015
	(.008)	(.008)	(.009)	(.007)	(.007)	(.009)
10 P.M.–11 P.M.	.007	.037	−.004	−.001	.007	−.009
	(.007)	(.008)	(.008)	(.007)	(.006)	(.008)
11 P.M.–midnight	.002	.021	−.001	−.001	.003	−.014
	(.007)	(.007)	(.008)	(.006)	(.006)	(.007)
Midnight–1 A.M.	.003	.021	−.000	−.002	.010	−.007
	(.006)	(.006)	(.007)	(.005)	(.005)	(.006)
1 A.M.–2 A.M.	.005	.016	−.001	−.000	.010	−.006
	(.006)	(.006)	(.007)	(.005)	(.005)	(.006)
2 A.M.–3 A.M.	.005	.017	−.003	−.002	.009	−.003
	(.006)	(.006)	(.007)	(.005)	(.005)	(.006)
3 A.M.–4 A.M.	.005	.016	−.004	−.005	.007	−.001
	(.006)	(.006)	(.007)	(.005)	(.004)	(.006)
4 A.M.–5 A.M.	.005	.008	−.000	−.007	.008	.000
	(.006)	(.006)	(.007)	(.005)	(.005)	(.006)
5 A.M.–6 A.M.	.011	.005	−.001	−.008	.009	.002
	(.006)	(.007)	(.007)	(.005)	(.005)	(.006)

Notes: Other variables included in the probits in the upper panel are years of schooling, a quadratic in age, a vector of variables for the size of the metropolitan area, marital status, presence of children under age six, residence in the "Rust Belt," and total hours worked. The same variables are included in the fixed-effects least-squares regressions reported in the bottom part of the panel.

identical native non-Hispanic whites to be at work in the evenings, but their propensity for night work is no different. Immigrant women are no more likely than native non-Hispanic whites to be at work after 7 P.M. and before 6 A.M. African American workers of both sexes, on the other hand, are significantly more likely than native non-Hispanic whites to be at work at most of these unusual times and also significantly more likely than immigrants or native Hispanics to be at work at these times. Among men this is especially true for evening work, while among women the effect is strongest for night work (which is much less frequent than evening work). Among Hispanic natives the propensity to work at these times differs little from that of native non-Hispanic whites; if anything, they are less likely than non-Hispanic white natives to accept this particular disamenity. Comparing the relative impacts of race and immigrant status, it is clear that otherwise identical black men are significantly more likely than immigrant or other men to be at work in the evening or at night, while black women are more likely than immigrant or other women to be at work at night.[10]

The estimates in the top panel ignore interindustry differences in workplace amenities. I believe those estimates are the appropriate ones to use in comparing the amenities enjoyed by different groups, since interindustry differences that are correlated with race or immigrant status may reflect exactly the intergroup differences in preferences, and thus location on the risk-rewards locus, that we are trying to isolate. These estimates indicate differences among groups in workers' well-being rather than merely their possibly voluntary matching to particular technologies. Nonetheless, to examine whether these intergroup differences merely reflect differences in industrial affiliation by ethnicity or national origin, I estimate linear probability models for work at each hour that include the same variables as the probits, but that also add large vectors of indicator variables (over two hundred) that represent presence in each three- or four-digit SIC industry.

The results from the top panel of table 3.2 become somewhat attenuated in the results presented in the bottom panel, especially for immigrant men, for whom the difference in evening work compared to native white men is no longer significant. Among native black men, however, we still find a significantly greater propensity to work evenings and most night hours than among non-Hispanic white natives, and among native black women the propensity to work nights exceeds that of non-Hispanic white natives. Moreover, native black men are more likely than immigrants (in a few cases significantly so) to work in the evening and most night hours, while black women are significantly more likely than immigrant women to work nights.

Nearly three-fourths of the immigrants in the June 1991 CPS arrived in the United States after 1969. Since much of the attention of specialists in immigration has been devoted to demonstrating how the behavior of these more recent immigrant groups has differed from that of their earlier counterparts (see, for example, Borjas 1995), it is worth examining whether their tastes for work are implicitly such as to lead them to obtain a different, and presumably inferior, set of workplace disamenities. Accordingly, I reestimated the probits underlying table 3.2 by replacing the immigration indicator with separate indicators for whether the immigrant arrived before 1970 or after 1969. Among women the results look very much like those in the table: neither early nor recent immigrants differ from native non-Hispanic whites in their adjusted propensities to work hours between 8 P.M. and 6 A.M. The same is true for immigrant men working after midnight. Before midnight, however, while recent immigrants' propensities to work differ little from those of native whites, immigrants who arrived *before* 1970 are significantly more likely than native whites to be at work. This is the only piece of evidence I find in this study of any group of immigrants experiencing objectively inferior amenities to those enjoyed by native non-Hispanic whites. That it occurs among earlier immigrants to the United States seems to run counter to the notions of immigrant isolation that underlay the model discussed earlier.

Yet another possibility is that it is not immigrant status per se that matters but rather the immigrant's country of origin. Perhaps those who emigrated from countries where workers experience workplace amenities similar to those in the United States do compete with observationally identical natives, but that immigrants from less-developed countries are willing to take jobs with disamenities that natives will not accept. To examine this I divided the sample into immigrants from Canada, Oceania, and Europe versus others and included two separate indicator variables instead of one. The results for men differed little from those in the table. Among women, at a few of the work times immigrants from non-European, non–English-speaking countries had inferior experiences, but most of the differences were quite small and insignificant statistically.

The results in table 3.2 are not adjusted for workers' wages. Essentially they fail to account for the unobservables that contribute to determining both wages and disamenities. The reason for this failure is that information on earnings by immigrant status is available only for the one-fourth of the sample who were in the outgoing rotation groups of the June 1991 CPS. Reestimating the probits on this much smaller set of data, and including all the variables in table 3.2 plus weekly earnings, does not alter the conclusions that the timing of work by immigrants differs little from that of native whites and is somewhat more favorable than that of otherwise identical native blacks.[11]

Risk of Injury

The June 1991 CPS merged with industry aggregate risks of occupational injury/illness provides the opportunity to examine yet another nonpecuniary aspect of the job. Ideally we would like to obtain matched worker-firm data that shows the risk of injury on the job at the worker's firm. (That would be analogous to the information used earlier in our discussion.) Failing that, we fall back on information on the incidence per hundred employees and the duration in days of injuries that result in lost workdays from the set of mainly three-digit industries matched to the June 1991 CPS data.

The means and standard errors of these two measures of injury risk in the workplace are presented by sex for each of the four demographic groups in table 3.3. The results are striking. Among native non-Hispanic white, native Hispanic, and immigrant females there are no significant differences in the incidence or duration of workplace injuries. Black females, however, are somewhat more likely to be in a (narrowly defined) industry where the risk of workplace injury is higher. Among males there are no significant differences between native whites and Hispanics in the incidence or duration of injuries; but immigrants are much more likely to be in industries where the incidence *and* duration of workplace injuries are low. African Americans, on the other hand, are more likely than other groups to be in industries where the incidence of workplace injuries is high. That the duration of workplace injuries in industries that disproportionately employ immigrant workers is lower than elsewhere suggests that the burden on immigrants of this particular disamenity is even less severe than one might infer at first glance, since it is lengthened duration rather than a greater incidence of injury that workers implicitly view as the more severe disamenity (Hamermesh and Wolfe 1990).[12]

Given the evidence in table 3.1 on the education and age of immigrants compared to natives, adjusting the injury rates and duration for demographic differences is likely to increase our estimates of the relative advantage of immigrants over native whites. It might, however, reduce the apparent differences between African Americans and others in the incidence of job-related injuries. Table 3.4 presents regression estimates designed to adjust for these demographic differences. The variables included as controls in the top panel here are identical to those included in the top panel of table 3.2, except that I have excluded total work hours. Adjusting for demographic differences does not change the conclusions based on the means shown in table 3.3: The duration and incidence of injuries among immigrant men are lower, although not significantly so, than among native men. Even after adjustment for dem-

Table 3.3 Means and Standard Errors, June 1991 CPS

	Men				Women			
	Non-Hispanic White	Native Black	Hispanic	Immigrant	Non-Hispanic White	Native Black	Hispanic	Immigrant
Injury rate /100 employees	4.55 (2.70)	4.88 (2.87)	4.64 (2.59)	4.35 (2.52)	3.35 (2.29)	3.78 (2.53)	3.43 (2.31)	3.49 (2.31)
Injury duration in days	19.20 (3.52)	19.22 (3.45)	19.31 (3.58)	18.68 (2.95)	18.12 (2.87)	18.05 (2.52)	18.10 (2.79)	18.26 (2.58)
N	22312	2062	904	2628	19965	2529	850	1853

Table 3.4 Effects of Immigrant Status and Ethnicity on Injury Rates and Duration, June 1991 CPS

	Men (N = 27918)			Women (N = 25209)		
Dependent Variable	Immigrant	Black Native	Hispanic Native	Immigrant	Black Native	Hispanic Native
Without occupation						
Injury rate/100 employees	−.264	.115	−.129	.144	.360	−.082
	(.158)	(.175)	(.103)	(.112)	(.192)	(.132)
Injury duration in days	−.630	.006	−.128	.043	−.129	−.170
	(.280)	(.195)	(.168)	(.156)	(.162)	(.195)
With occupation						
Injury rate/100 employees	−.072	.062	−.041	−.092	.092	−.024
	(.134)	(.147)	(.088)	(.097)	(.164)	(.112)
Injury duration in days	−.195	−.010	.022	−.022	−.160	−.032
	(.238)	(.167)	(.142)	(.143)	(.148)	(.176)

Notes: Other variables included in the regressions in the upper panel are years of schooling, a quadratic in age, a vector of variables for the size of the metropolitan area, marital status, presence of children under age six, and residence in the "Rust Belt." The same variables are included in the occupation fixed-effects least-squares regressions reported in the bottom part of the panel. The standard errors of the coefficient estimates are robust to clustering of observations within three- and four-digit industries.

ographics, native black men and women are still in industries with higher risks of injury.

The difficulty with these estimates is that, unlike the estimates used earlier, the disamenities reflect solely the worker's industry, not anything unique to the worker. Because the injury data are industry-specific, we cannot hold constant for the industry the worker is located in. We can, however, adjust for the narrow occupation of each worker, and thus ask whether within particular occupations, and after adjustment for demographic differences, immigrants or African Americans are in industries where injury risks differ from those of native non-Hispanic whites. The results of estimates in which indicator variables for over 450 occupations are included are presented in the bottom panel of table 3.4. Even after this adjustment, immigrant men are less subject to the risk of workplace injury than other groups; and with these further adjustments the same is true for immigrant women. None of these differences is significant, but they still are in the same direction as before this very extensive adjustment was made.

I have already demonstrated a substantial difference in some cases between the disamenities experienced by recent immigrants and those of earlier immigrants. Such differences are not apparent in the distribution of the risks of workplace injuries. If we aggregate dates of immigration using the same indicator of pre- or post-1970 arrival, we find roughly the same negative coefficients for both groups and for both injury rates and duration. Not only are immigrants located in industries where the risk of injury is somewhat lower than that of native whites; that is equally true for recent and for earlier immigrants.

Subjective Satisfaction with Job Characteristics

Clearly the most useful analyses are of the actual distribution of amenities experienced by immigrants, African Americans, and others. Nonetheless, it is worth examining their subjective responses to the disamenities they face, in part merely to obtain more information on the phenomena, in part because the subjective information covers a wider range of disamenities. Table 3.5 presents the means and their standard deviations for these and the demographic variables separately for white and black natives and for immigrants ages sixteen to sixty-nine inclusive. Remembering that the QAL data are from the 1970s, it is not surprising that the immigrants are actually slightly older on average than natives. So too, it is unsurprising that they are also slightly better educated than natives. Interestingly, and also quite consistent with results using other samples, the QAL immigrants' hourly wages are below those of white natives despite their higher educational attainment (ob-

Table 3.5 Means and Their Standard Errors, Pooled QAL 1971, 1978

	White Natives	Black Natives	Immigrants
Hourly wage ($)	5.30	3.85	5.22
	(.153)	(.177)	(.351)
Years of Schooling			
≤ 12	.563	.701	.494
	(.009)	(.025)	(.040)
13–15	.246	.184	.212
	(.008)	(.021)	(.032)
16 +	.186	.109	.262
	(.007)	(.017)	(.035)
Age	38.46	38.98	39.24
	(.258)	(.695)	(.941)
Interesting job	.911	.886	.887
	(.005)	(.017)	(.025)
Chance to make friends	.895	.870	.792
	(.006)	(.018)	(.032)
Nice surroundings	.824	.830	.881
	(.007)	(.020)	(.026)
Job security	.840	.796	.849
	(.007)	(.022)	(.028)
Can develop skills	.785	.731	.719
	(.008)	(.024)	(.036)
Can use skills	.800	.752	.761
	(.008)	(.023)	(.034)
Enough time to do work	.820	.847	.856
	(.007)	(.019)	(.028
N =	2798	34	160

tained no doubt at least in part in foreign educational institutions). Blacks' wages are 73 and 81 percent of those of white natives of the same sex, roughly comparable to what is shown in more comprehensive surveys (for example, March CPS data) for these periods and these age groups.

The bottom part of table 3.5 presents the means of workers' satisfaction along each of the seven criteria we use to reflect subjective views of workplace amenities. Only three significant differences exist between immigrants and either white or black native workers in the QAL: (1) Immigrants are distinctly *less likely* than natives of either race to respond that their jobs offer them the chance to make friends; (2) they are significantly *more likely* than natives of either race to state that their workplace surroundings are more pleasant; and (3) they are significantly *less likely* than white natives to state that their job provides them with opportunities for development. While these differences are significant, the lack of other significant differences, and the implication from these that immigrants view at least some of these amenities as distinctly better than do natives, hints that these data too provide little evidence that immigrants experience inferior workplace amenities.

A formal test for intergroup differences in amenities requires that we hold constant for the demographic characteristics that might reflect tastes for amenities *and* for differences in workers' earnings that might indicate differences in their full incomes that allow them to "purchase" better working conditions.[13] The results of estimating probits on the seven job characteristics are reflected in the estimated derivatives with respect to immigrant status and race, and their standard errors, that are presented in table 3.6. The left-hand columns define immigrant status in the conventional manner; the right-hand columns define it more broadly to include as immigrants also those workers whose parents were both born outside the United States.

Some of the differences in the means that we observed in table 3.5 remain, in particular, the fact that immigrants view their jobs as offering fewer chances to develop their skills and fewer chances to make friends than do white natives. While immigrants view their surroundings as more appealing than do otherwise identical white natives, the difference is insignificant. They do, however, claim that they are less able to use their skills than do white natives. Thus along three of the seven nonwage dimensions of work, immigrants are significantly less satisfied with nonwage aspects of their jobs than are native whites with identical demographic characteristics who earn the same hourly wage.

Blacks respond very similarly to immigrants: The effect of race on the responses is the same sign as that of immigrant status along six out of the seven dimensions, although never so large. This finding suggests that, surely for different reasons, subjective views of workplace amenities by immigrants and blacks may be somewhat different from those enjoyed by similarly endowed white natives. What is particularly interesting, however, is that the results for immigrants change when we include second-generation Americans in the immigrant category. All of the derivatives in column (3) of table 3.2 are attenuated from their values in column (1), where only workers who are themselves immigrants

Table 3.6   Effects of Immigrant Status and Race on Job
Characteristics, Pooled 1971, 1978 QAL (N = 2810)

Dependent Variable	Foreign Born		Foreign Born or Both Parents Foreign Born	
	Immigrant	Black	Immigrant	Black
Interesting job	−.040	−.026	−.023	−.026
	(.026)	(.018)	(.021)	(.018)
Chance to make friends	−.060	−.022	−.029	−.022
	(.029)	(.021)	(.023)	(.021)
Nice surroundings	.044	.019	.040	.020
	(.035)	(.025)	(.028)	(.025)
Job security	.029	−.036	.039	−.034
	(.031)	(.025)	(.025)	(.025)
Can develop skills	−.075	−.050	−.025	−.049
	(.039)	(.028)	(.031)	(.028)
Can use skills	−.084	−.078	−.066	−.080
	(.038)	(.027)	(.031)	(.027)
Enough time to do work	.035	.026	.053	.028
	(.034)	(.025)	(.027)	(.025)

Notes: Other variables included in the probits are indicators for sex, a quadratic in age, the hourly wage rate, vectors of indicators representing the size of the metropolitan area, the main Census regions, and educational attainment, marital status, and a separate intercept for 1971.

were included in the definition of the indicator variable. Taken together the results suggest that, while immigrants may enjoy slightly less desirable amenities than white natives on jobs paying identical wages, even those small differences are reduced after one generation and roughly equal the differences between blacks and native whites.[14]

This finding of some significant differences between native blacks and native whites, and between immigrants and native whites, does not necessarily imply the existence of workplace discrimination. Rather, given that we held hourly wages constant, it might mean that workers in these groups, whose family incomes are more uncertain than those of native whites, choose to spend their full earnings on jobs that are tilted toward offering more money income and fewer amenities. The differences are not great. At most they offer only a tiny bit of very tentative (because we are examining workers' subjective responses) evidence that immigrants do take jobs with different amenities from those of native whites, and thus that there may be noncompetition between immigrants and native whites. The results also imply, however, that those jobs are quite close or even superior in the quality of the amenities that they offer to the ones that otherwise identical native black workers are more likely to take.

A Synthesis

Immigrants and native non-Hispanic whites may have different job-related activities: There are, after all, many dimensions of work along which job characteristics might differ that we have not examined. A fair conclusion from all the investigations here, however, is that there are few important differences between immigrants and native non-Hispanic whites in work timing, the rate or duration of work-related injuries, or in satisfaction with most job-related characteristics once we account for differences in their demographics and their earnings. This conclusion implies that there is a strong basis for believing that immigrants and native whites will be competing directly at least to some extent in the labor market.

Even along those dimensions where immigrants do experience fewer amenities than native whites, their outcomes are similar to or perhaps more attractive than those of native blacks. That suggests that, to the extent that the differences in the willingness to accept disamenities might generate noncompetition in the labor market, immigrants and native whites seem quite similar and should be viewed as potentially competing groups. Indeed, the evidence here implies that, if any group of workers is willing to accept jobs that otherwise identical workers will not accept, it is native blacks. Viewed differently, labor-market discrimination is apparent against African Americans in the nonwage aspects of their jobs even after adjustment for the wages they are paid.

DO IMMIGRANTS AFFECT NATIVES' WORKPLACE AMENITIES?

If immigrants and natives differ little in the amenities they enjoy on jobs measured at a fixed wage and among workers who are demographically otherwise identical, we should not expect to see any effect of an influx of immigrants on the amenities enjoyed by natives. Nonetheless, to examine this possibility I analyze how the 1990 Census information on IMMPCT (the percentage immigrant in each MSA) linked to the May and June 1991 CPS data is related to the timing of work and the incidence and duration of workplace injuries among natives resident in metropolitan areas. Initial insight into this question can be obtained by examining how these outcomes are related to differences in the importance of immigrants in

Table 3.7   Natives' Probability of Working and Injury Outcomes, in High- or Low-Percentage Immigrant MSAs, May, June 1991 CPS

	Men				Women			
	All	Non-Hispanic White	Black	Hispanic	All	Non-Hispanic White	Black	Hispanic
Working at								
8 P.M.–9 P.M.	.135	.126	.168	.156	.116	.120	.120	.074
	(.159)	(.152)	(.221)	(.219)	(.141)	(.137)	(.157)	(.189)
9 P.M.–10 P.M.	.115	.104	.166	.147	.099	.100	.106	.070
	(.139)	(.132)	(.198)	(.200)	(.116)	(.112)	(.132)	(.152)
10 P.M.–11 P.M.	.099	.089	.155	.127	.083	.082	.100	.057
	(.121)	(.114)	(.174)	(.181)	(.096)	(.091)	(.127)	(.116)
11 P.M.–midnight	.085	.076	.125	.111	.068	.065	.091	.046
	(.108)	(.103)	(.145)	(.156)	(.079)	(.076)	(.095)	(.098)
Midnight–1 A.M.	.068	.058	.116	.087	.053	.047	.080	.046
	(.086)	(.082)	(.110)	(.125)	(.062)	(.060)	(.076)	(.073)
1 A.M.–2 A.M.	.062	.054	.100	.081	.049	.043	.075	.044
	(.080)	(.076)	(.103)	(.119)	(.058)	(.057)	(.069)	(.067)
2 A.M.–3 A.M.	.059	.051	.100	.067	.047	.042	.071	.044
	(.076)	(.072)	(.100)	(.119)	(.055)	(.054)	(.067)	(.061)

3 A.M.–4 A.M.	.058	.051	.098	.067	.047	.041	.071	.046
	(.075)	(.072)	(.100)	(.106)	(.053)	(.052)	(.062)	(.055)
4 A.M.–5 A.M.	.060	.054	.084	.071	.047	.041	.069	.048
	(.077)	(.074)	(.096)	(.113)	(.054)	(.052)	(.066)	(.061)
5 A.M.–6 A.M.	.073	.067	.098	.079	.050	.043	.072	.066
	(.088)	(.085)	(.112)	(.125)	(.058)	(.057)	(.070)	(.061)
N	12837	11044	1128	665	12064	9967	1476	621
Injury characteristics								
Injury rate/100 employees	4.61	4.58	4.90	4.60	3.43	3.39	3.83	3.34
	(4.54)	(4.50)	(4.86)	(4.76)	(3.36)	(3.30)	(3.71)	(3.74)
Injury duration in days	19.32	19.31	19.41	19.41	18.16	18.16	18.15	18.16
	(19.03)	(19.04)	(19.00)	(18.95)	(18.03)	(18.05)	(17.92)	(17.93)
N	25278	22312	2062	904	23344	19965	2529	850

Note: A high-percentage immigrant MSA has over 10 percent immigrants; a low-percentage immigrant MSA has ≤ 10 percent immigrants.

the labor market. Table 3.7 shows the means of these outcomes for all natives, and for non-Hispanic whites, blacks, and Hispanics, separately for men and women. The upper figure in each pair is the mean in those metropolitan areas where more than 10 percent of the work force are immigrants; the lower figure (in parentheses) is the mean in areas where 10 percent or less of the labor force consists of immigrants.

The results on the timing of work are striking and completely surprising: At each evening and night hour, and for each subgroup of natives except black women working at night, the probability of working is lower in the areas where immigrants exceed 10 percent of the population. Implicitly immigration appears to be raising the amenities enjoyed by native workers. In terms of our model, that would imply that the identity of the marginal firm is changing, which is inconsistent with the implications of the previous section. Given the standard deviations of these means that were shown in table 3.1, most of these differences are significant. Just the opposite is true for injury characteristics: among both men and women injury rates and durations are somewhat, although not statistically significantly, higher in areas where immigrants constitute more than 10 percent of the population.

Do the remarkable differences in the timing of work between natives distinguished by the native-immigrant composition of their area disappear once we account for demographic and economic differences among the ethnic groups? The top half of table 3.8 lists the derivatives and their standard errors calculated from probits relating the probability of working evening and night hours to the fraction of immigrants in the metropolitan area and to the same set of controls used in table 3.2. Among native non-Hispanic white men there is a bit of evidence that otherwise identical individuals are less likely to be working in the evenings and at night if they reside in metropolitan areas with a large concentration of immigrants, as we saw in the means in top panel of table 3.7. All of the effects are negative, but few approach statistical significance. Among women, regardless of ethnicity, we find that the propensity to work evening or night hours is lower, although never significantly so, in metropolitan areas where immigrants form a larger part of the labor force.[15]

The results of estimating regressions like those in table 3.4, but also including the immigrant percentage in the area, are presented in the bottom panel of table 3.8. Adjusting for demographic factors changes the inferences we drew from the bottom panel of table 3.7: other things equal, we now see that where immigrants are more heavily concentrated, natives work in industries where the incidence of injuries is lower, but where the duration of lost workday injuries is longer. Like the results on the timing of work, no strong picture emerges of consistent differences in outcomes between natives distinguished by the concentration of immigrants in the labor markets.

One possibility is that the results in table 3.8 mask a threshold effect, with the large impacts of immigrants on natives' amenities becoming visible only when immigrants account for a sufficiently large fraction of the labor force. Nearly 20 percent of the metropolitan U.S. work force lives in areas where immigrants account for over 20 percent of the labor force, and it is perhaps these areas where natives experience the most severe effects of the immigrants' presence. To examine this explanation I added a quadratic in IMMPCT to the probits and regressions in table 3.8. The quadratic terms in the probits on work timing were generally insignificant. Some of the quadratic terms in the regressions on injury characteristics were significant, although their inclusion did not change the conclusions of generally lower incidence but longer duration of injuries where immigration had been more prevalent.[16]

CONCLUSIONS, AND IMPLICATIONS FOR JOB COMPETITIOIN

Throughout American history the possibility that immigrants "take jobs away from natives" has probably been the biggest spur to nativist sentiment. Economists have addressed this issue during the last twenty years directly by treating immigrants and natives as separate inputs into production and measuring the extent to which they are substitutes, or indirectly by examining how natives' wages or earnings are related to the presence of immigrants. The results of the now myriad studies using these approaches are somewhat conflicting. Here I take an alternative tack, asking whether the preconditions for the absence of direct labor-market competition exist in the form of immigrants' willingness to accept working conditions, and thus find jobs, in fields where jobs would otherwise not exist. To the extent that immigrants will take jobs that natives refuse to accept, one might conclude that they and native workers might be noncompeting groups in American labor markets, with any substitution between them coming only through product-market competition between firms using native labor and those using immigrants.

I interpret the preconditions as implying that immigrants will accept a job that has amenities inferior to one that an otherwise identical native would accept. I examine objective data from the Current Population Survey of May 1991 describing the timing of work over the day and the June 1991 CPS data (which contained information on immigrant status) linked to industry workplace injury rates and duration. I also examine this possibility using a variety of subjective responses about job amenities in the Quality of American Life surveys conducted in 1971 and 1978. There is at most only very weak evidence of any dif-

Table 3.8 Effects of the Percentage Immigrant Population in the MSA on Natives' Work Timing and Injury Outcomes, May, June 1991 CPS

	Men				Women			
Dependent Variable	All	Non-Hispanic White	Black	Hispanic	All	Non-Hispanic White	Black	Hispanic
Working at								
8 P.M.–9 P.M.	−.040	−.043	−.102	−.176	−.068	−.023	−.051	−.153
	(.040)	(.045)	(.140)	(.137)	(.038)	(.045)	(.102)	(.100)
9 P.M.–10 P.M.	−.050	−.057	−.075	−.167	−.051	−.018	−.068	−.120
	(.037)	(.042)	(.134)	(.134)	(.035)	(.041)	(.097)	(.094)
10 P.M.–11 P.M.	−.010	−.013	.090	−.213	−.033	−.012	−.049	−.070
	(.033)	(.038)	(.123)	(.125)	(.030)	(.035)	(.093)	(.083)
11 P.M.–midnight	−.027	−.070	.141	−.012	−.034	−.030	−.005	−.099
	(.031)	(.036)	(.113)	(.114)	(.026)	(.030)	(.078)	(.064)
Midnight–1 A.M.	−.025	−.057	.043	−.008	−.028	−.030	−.046	−.050
	(.027)	(.031)	(.101)	(.102)	(.020)	(.023)	(.069)	(.055)
1 A.M.–2 A.M.	−.015	−.046	.031	.023	−.023	−.030	−.013	−.050
	(.025)	(.028)	(.094)	(.099)	(.018)	(.020)	(.064)	(.053)
2 A.M.–3 A.M.	−.012	−.031	.042	−.053	−.020	−.026	−.023	−.025
	(.024)	(.027)	(.093)	(.092)	(.017)	(.019)	(.061)	(.051)

	Men				Women			
	All	Non-Hispanic White	Black	Hispanic	All	Non-Hispanic White	Black	Hispanic
3 A.M.–4 A.M.	−.018	−.043	.043	−.004	−.016	−.027	−.010	−.004
	(.023)	(.027)	(.092)	(.089)	(.016)	(.019)	(.057)	(.048)
4 A.M.–5 A.M.	−.014	−.038	.072	.001	−.015	−.016	−.012	−.058
	(.024)	(.028)	(.084)	(.092)	(.017)	(.019)	(.060)	(.058)
5 A.M.–6 A.M.	.017	−.009	.115	.035	.000	−.016	.036	.045
	(.027)	(.031)	(.094)	(.097)	(.019)	(.022)	(.063)	(.071)
Injury characteristics								
Injury rate/100 employees	−1.83	−1.72	−2.50	−1.81	−1.05	−.90	−.52	−3.34
	(.74)	(.77)	(1.26)	(.95)	(.43)	(.42)	(.64)	(1.05)
Injury duration in days	1.29	1.03	2.65	1.62	.93	.87	1.32	.03
	(.81)	(.78)	(1.44)	(1.51)	(.59)	(.56)	(.96)	(1.56)

Notes: Other variables included in the probits are the same as those included in table 3.2. Other variables included in the regressions on injury outcomes are the same as those included in table 3.4. The standard errors on the coefficients in the injury regressions are robust to the clustering of observations within three- and four-digit industries.

ference between immigrants and natives generally in the amenities associated with the jobs they hold, given the observable characteristics that they bring to the labor market. It thus seems fair to conclude that the preconditions for the absence of direct labor-market competition between immigrants and natives do not exist. Despite occasional anecdotal evidence along a variety of nonwage outcomes I find no evidence that immigrants in general are willing to "take jobs that [observationally identical] natives don't want."

The one group that differs from the others is African Americans. They are more likely to work at distinctly inferior times (evenings and nights) than are immigrants or other natives; they work in industries where the risk of injury is greater and the duration of injuries is longer, and they are less likely to report a variety of job amenities than are members of other groups of native workers. If anything, therefore, the results of this study suggest that African Americans, possibly because they choose freely, possibly because of residual segregation and discrimination, appear to take jobs that otherwise similar native whites and Hispanics, *and immigrants too*, are unwilling to take.

NOTES

1. *New York Times*, June 3, 1996, p. A1.

2. *New York Times*, March 24, 1996, p. 3.

3. See Heckman and Sedlacek (1985) for an approach that aggregates workers based on the skills that they implicitly bring to the labor market.

4. The model could be expanded to include immigrants with skills different from those of natives, but that extra complexity would add nothing to the illustration of the mechanisms discussed here.

5. See Stafford (1980) for a very perceptive discussion of the problems of discriminating among workers in the provision of workplace amenities.

6. Only workers with at least 20 hours per week on their main job are included in this sample, so that we can be sure that work at night means presence at work on at least three days per week. The self-employed are excluded from this study.

7. Immigrants constituted 0.3 percentage points fewer of the discarded observations than they did of the observations included in the analysis. This tiny difference suggests that the industries on which the data could not be merged are not particularly immigrant- or native-labor intensive.

8. The hourly wage is calculated as the midpoint of the bracketed annual earnings divided by 52 × weekly hours. For the highest category I use 1.5 times the lower bound of the categorized annual earnings.

9. In defining the immigrant population in this sample those (very few) people who were born abroad, but whose parents were both Americans, are included as natives even if they indicated that they were immigrants.

10. While I do adjust for detailed industry in the bottom half of table 3.2, it is interesting to examine whether excluding agriculture, where evening work is difficult, affects the results. Also, the data report usual work schedules on the main job, so that they may be generating a false impression if immigrants' propensities to take second jobs differ from those of natives. The probits in the top half of the table were thus reestimated excluding the roughly 9 percent of the male sample and 5 percent of the female sample who worked in agriculture or who held more than one job. The results changed only slightly, with immigrants generally working at these hours in the same proportion as natives, and with African Americans being more likely to be at work at these times.

11. These conclusions are based on a comparison to the results of probits identical to those of table 3.2, but estimated only over those workers on whom wage data were available. Workers whose hourly earnings were below 2.75 dollars in 1991 were excluded from both of these sets of probits, since it is likely that their hours or weekly earnings were reported incorrectly.

12. One possibility is that establishments employing unusually high proportions of immigrants are more likely to underreport injuries. While this is possible, the quality of the injury data was much higher by 1991 after nearly twenty years of detailed surveys than it had been earlier. Also, these are lost-workday injuries, about which employees are probably quite aware and which are more difficult to hide from statistical surveys than the mere presence of potentially dangerous working conditions.

13. Individuals whose calculated hourly earnings were below one dollar or above one hundred dollars (1971 dollars) per hour are excluded from the probits.

14. This is consistent with Borjas's (1993) evidence of substantial, but by no means complete, regression of immigrants' earnings toward population averages over one generation.

15. This result is also not due to the exclusion of detailed measures of workers' industrial affiliation. When least-squares estimates like those in the bottom panel of table 3.2 are estimated on the same samples, and with the same other variables, as in table 3.8, the coefficients on IMMPCT change only slightly. Nor is it due to interarea differences in unemployment rates. When published unemployment rates by area are interacted with the indicator for immigrant status (and also included as a main effect), no significant changes in the basic results are produced.

16. In another approach along these lines I replaced IMMPCT by a vector of

indicator variables corresponding to a categorization of the percentage of immigrants in an area's work force. The results in that case too gave little indication of consistent nonlinearities in the relationship between the presence of immigrants in the work force and the propensities to work evenings or nights or in injury outcomes.

REFERENCES

Borjas, George. 1993. "The Intergenerational Mobility of Immigrants." *Journal of Labor Economics* 11 (January): 113–35.

———. 1995. "Assimilation and Changes in Cohort Quality Revisited." *Journal of Labor Economics* 13 (April): 201–45.

Borjas, George, Richard Freeman, and Lawrence Katz. 1996. "Searching for the Effect of Immigration on the Labor Market." American Economic Association, *Papers and Proceedings* 86 (May): 246–51.

Brown, Charles. 1980. "Equalizing Differences in the Labor Market." *Quarterly Journal of Economics* 94 (February): 113–34.

Castles, Stephen, and Godula Kosack. 1973. *Immigrant Workers and Class Structure in Western Europe*. London: Oxford.

Haisken-De New, John, and Klaus Zimmermann. 1996. "Wage and Mobility Effects of Trade and Migration." Centre for Economic Policy Research, Discussion Paper No. 1318.

Hamermesh, Daniel. 1993. *Labor Demand*. Princeton, N.J.: Princeton University Press.

———. 1996. *Workdays, Workhours, Work Schedules: Evidence for the United States and Germany*. Kalamazoo, Mich.: W.E Upjohn Institute.

———. Forthcoming. "The Timing of Work over Time." *Economic Journal*.

Hamermesh, Daniel, and John Wolfe. 1990. "Compensating Wage Differentials and the Duration of Wage Loss." *Journal of Labor Economics* 8 (January): S175–97.

Heckman, James, and Guilherme Sedlacek. 1985. "Heterogeneity, Aggregation, and Market Wage Functions: An Empirical Model of Self-Selection in the Labor Market." *Journal of Political Economy* 93 (December): 1077–1125.

Piore, Michael. 1979. *Birds of Passage*. Cambridge, England: Cambridge University Press.

Stafford, Frank. 1980. "Firm Size, Workplace Public Goods, and Worker Welfare." In *The Economics of Firm Size, Market Structure and Social Performance*, edited by John Siegfried. Washington, D.C.: Federal Trade Commission.

U.S. Department of Labor, U.S. Bureau of Labor Statistics. 1990. *Occupational Injuries and Illnesses in the United States by Industry, 1988. Bulletin 2366* Washington, D.C.: U.S. Government Printing Office.

CHAPTER 4

Unskilled Immigration and Changes in the Wage Distributions of Black, Mexican American, and Non-Hispanic White Male Dropouts

Cordelia W. Reimers

A persistent reason for opposition to immigration among the general public is the belief that immigrants take jobs from native workers and that the additional supply of immigrant labor depresses the wages of natives. Even individuals who are generally "pro-immigration," because they believe that immigration is good for the country as a whole, express concern about its effect on disadvantaged American workers. This study is part of a rapidly growing body of empirical research that has responded to this concern by trying to measure the effect of immigration on native wages. As such, it builds on the work of Grossman (1982), Bean, Lowell and Taylor (1988), Borjas (1987, 1990), Card (1990, 1996), Altonji and Card (1991), LaLonde and Topel (1991), Borjas, Freeman, and Katz (1992, 1996, 1997), Jaeger (1996), Schoeni (1997), Bratsberg (1996), Butcher in this volume, and others, much of which has been summarized in Borjas (1994) and Friedberg and Hunt (1995). As do other studies in this volume, the analysis takes what Borjas, Freeman, and Katz (1996) have called the "area approach," in which the uneven spatial distribution of immigrants is used to estimate the impact of immigration on wages in local labor markets. This approach depends crucially on the assumptions that immigrants' destination decisions are largely exogenous to contemporaneous wage movements, and that local wages adjust more quickly than workers migrate. A "changes on changes" estimation strategy is used here to limit the effects of reverse causation, in which immigrants' being attracted to high-wage destinations creates a positive correlation between immigration and wages that may obscure a negative impact. If labor mobility does not completely arbitrage interarea wage differences within a very few years, the "area approach" as applied in this study can detect an effect of immigration on wages.

This study focuses on two of the groups that we might expect to be most vulnerable to the labor-market effects of unskilled immigration in

107

recent years: Mexican American and African American male high school dropouts.[1] White non-Hispanic dropouts are also analyzed, for comparison. Because the foreign-born may be even more vulnerable than U.S. natives, these groups are analyzed separately. The large numbers of Mexican Americans and native-born African Americans and non-Hispanic whites enable one to estimate effects quite precisely. Other disadvantaged groups such as Puerto Ricans have smaller sample sizes in the Census, so that effects are more likely to be masked by random errors in the data.

This study differs from preceding ones because it examines the impact of immigration on the shape of the entire distribution of wages of a given group of low-skilled workers, not just their average wage, controlling for other factors. If factors observable in the data do not adequately identify the workers affected, estimates of the effect on the average wage of workers with given observed characteristics may not capture all relevant effects. This study addresses essentially the same methodological problem as DiNardo, Fortin, and Lemieux (1996), that of analyzing the effects of various factors on the shape of the wage distribution; but they use kernel density methods, whereas I use quantile regression techniques.

This is also the first study of which I am aware that considers the impact of immigration specifically on Mexican Americans in the 1980s. Given the great differences among groups of Hispanic origin, one might expect Mexican American workers to be most affected by the large inflow of low-skilled immigrants from Mexico, and the effect on other Hispanics to be more diffuse. Yet Bean, Lowell, and Taylor (1988) is the only other large-scale study of the effects of immigration that treats Mexican Americans without lumping them together with other Hispanics.

This study also differs from most earlier research in estimating the impact of immigration on average hourly earnings, rather than weekly or annual earnings. Although some "noise" is introduced due to errors in reported hours, this more closely approximates the impact on the price of labor, unmixed with changes in time worked. While immigration would be expected to affect both dimensions of earnings, it is useful to analyze them separately. It matters whether earnings are reduced because of reduced hours or reduced wages. Other innovations in this study are that the analysis includes all wage earners, not only full-time workers; that it covers the entire United States, not only a selected set of metropolitan areas; and that the impact of *unskilled* immigration in particular, not immigration overall, is estimated. This is an important consideration as the debate over criteria for visa preference continues.

I will now discuss the theoretical framework underlying this analysis and some issues involved in the estimation. I then explain the procedures used to select the samples and to construct the variables used in the analysis and describe the methods of analysis in detail. Finally, I discuss the results and their interpretation.

THEORETICAL FRAMEWORK AND ESTIMATION STRATEGY

If there were perfect mobility of goods, capital, or labor, there would be no lasting impact of immigration on wages. Any tendency for wages to deviate from those prevailing elsewhere would simply induce movements of goods, capital, or workers until the prevailing wage was restored. The view that immigration is bad for native workers is supported theoretically by a simple partial equilibrium model of demand and supply for homogeneous labor with imperfect mobility of goods and factors. So long as the supply and demand for labor are not perfectly elastic (and immigration does not shift the demand for labor by increasing the capital stock or consumption demand), an increase in the supply of labor will depress the wage rate.

When effects of immigration on wages are analyzed using a more complex model, however, offsetting effects are predicted, and the overall outcome is theoretically indeterminate. Complementarity and substitutability among capital and workers with different skills, additional capital provided by immigrants, the effect of additional consumers on demand for output, and the mobility of labor, capital, and goods mean that the effect of immigration on native wages depends on the mix of skills, capital, and entrepreneurship that the natives have and the immigrants bring with them, on the various elasticities involved, and on which group of native workers is the object of attention. Moreover, insofar as immigrants increase the net supply and therefore reduce the price of "local" goods and services, native workers benefit in their role as consumers (that is, their real wage is increased). These theoretical models do predict that in the short run, immigrants are most likely to depress the wages of native workers who are most like themselves in productive characteristics and who are producing goods mainly for the outside world, so that the immigrants as consumers have little effect on demand for the natives' output.

Empirical efforts to measure the effect of immigration on the U.S. labor market have had difficulty finding the predicted negative impact on native wages. Case studies of particular cities and industries, such as the Los Angeles hotel janitors described by Mines and Avina (1993), have revealed important effects in some situations, but broader statistical analyses of Census data have generally found only small negative effects, if any. In fact, the cross-sectional correlation between immigration and wages across cities is often found to be significantly positive. This is usually attributed to reverse causation, as immigrants are attracted to cities with high and rising wages. However, studies that have controlled for this endogeneity of immigration still have mostly found small negative effects on wages in local labor markets (Bean, Lowell, and Taylor 1988; LaLonde and Topel 1991; Borjas 1994). Because measured variables may be inadequate to control for reverse causation, city-specific fixed effects, or other unmeasured factors that mask the true impact of immigration on wages, some researchers have taken an indirect approach, first estimating the elasticity of substitution between immigrant and native labor of the same skill level, and then using estimates of the elasticity of demand to simulate the impact of an increase in immigrant labor supply on wages (for an example, see Jaeger 1996).

Studies that more straightforwardly compare wages across labor markets with high vs. low immigration, while attempting to control for confounding factors, have generally found little or no effect.[2] Either the effects are concentrated on particular groups of native workers who get lost in the overall average; or complementarities among immigrant capital and skills and native labor, and increased consumer demand for local goods and services, offset the direct negative effect of competition between immigrant and native workers; or labor is sufficiently mobile to dampen the effect of an increase in supply on wages. Evidence of native out-migration from high-immigration cities is provided by Filer (1992), Frey (1996), and Frey and Liaw (1996). Furthermore, Borjas, Freeman, and Katz (1996) find that, the larger the geographic area considered as a unit (that is, the more mobility is internalized), the more negative is the estimated impact of immigration on wages. However, Butcher in this volume finds that the size of the impact on the white-black annual earnings gap *declines* as the level of geographic aggregation increases; and Card (1996) finds that, even after migration of natives and earlier immigrants is accounted for, each new immigrant is a net addition to the local population of his or her skill group.

My strategy in this study is to ask whether, in labor markets that had larger inflows of less-educated immigrants during the 1980s, less-educated blacks, Mexican Americans, and non-Hispanic white workers had lower wages in 1990 than they would otherwise have had. Whereas others (for example, LaLonde and Topel 1991) divide the labor force into natives and separate immigrant cohorts, I divide it into three entry cohort/skill groups: (1) recent unskilled immigrants (entered in the past ten years); (2) other unskilled workers (earlier immigrants and natives); and (3) skilled workers (regardless of nativity). This relaxes the assumption that all members of an immigrant cohort are equally skilled but constrains natives and earlier immigrants with the same skill level to have the same elasticity of complementarity with dropouts of a given minority group.

To avoid confounding the effects of immigration and other wage-influencing factors that may vary across labor markets, I control for personal characteristics such as years of schooling and area characteristics such as the employment growth rate. This adjustment is done in two steps: First, the effects of education, experience, industry, and occupation are removed, using "prices" of these attributes derived from the native white males' wage structure. Then the effects of immigrants' human capital and local labor market characteristics are removed by regressing the residuals on these variables.[3]

After thus eliminating the effects of other wage-influencing factors, I compare the *changes* in the distributions of the wage residuals between 1980 and 1990 across areas that had different *changes* in unskilled immigration from the 1970s to the 1980s.[4] This "changes on changes" model deals with the problems of reverse causation (immigrants being attracted to high-wage labor markets) and fixed effects (an area happening to have both persistent high immigration and persistent high wages due to unobserved unchanging factors). To identify the impact of *current* immigration, as opposed to relocation of persons who had entered the United States in earlier decades, the change in unskilled immigration is measured by the change in the share of the labor force who entered the United States in the previous ten years and have less than a high school education. Thus, only deviations from the immigration flows of past decades and changes in the wage distributions after adjusting for other factors are used to identify the effect of immigration on wages. This eliminates fixed effects and any reverse causation that operates with a lag of several years. Only insofar as immigrant flows shifted among destinations *during the 1980s* in response to shifts in wages during the *same* decade will the results be affected by reverse causation.

DATA

The 1980 and 1990 U.S. Censuses of Population 5 percent A PUMS (Public-Use Microdata Samples) are the basis for this study. For the analysis of wages I selected those males age sixteen or older who identified themselves as black,[5] of Mexican origin, or white and not of Hispanic origin; who had less than a twelfth-grade education; and who had positive hours worked and earnings, but no income from self-employment, in the previous year. This last restriction eliminates the conceptual and practical problems of assigning a wage rate for the self-employed. The Census does not contain direct information on hourly wage rates; rather, they must be computed by dividing annual earnings by the product of weeks worked and usual hours worked per week during the year. Reported self-employment income comprises interest, rent, and profit as well as wages; and hours worked per week are reported even less accurately for the self-employed than for wage and salary earners.[6] Military personnel, students, unpaid family workers, and residents of group quarters were also excluded from the samples because their money earnings are a poor measure of their actual compensation.

Men born in the United States or outlying areas or abroad of American parents (that is, native-born citizens) were classified as U.S. natives; all others born abroad were classified as immigrants. As mentioned earlier, average hourly earnings were computed by dividing wage and salary income in 1979 or 1989 by the product of weeks and hours worked in that year.[7] Nominal average hourly earnings in 1979 were then adjusted using the Consumer Price Index (CPI-U) so that real wage rates for both years were expressed in terms of 1989 dollars. An individual's education was measured as highest grade of school completed,[8] and potential experience as the minimum of (age-education-six) and (age-sixteen), to adjust for compulsory schooling laws in the United States.[9] As listed in table 4.1, indicators for degree of English fluency and date of entry to the United States and citizenship status for immigrants were created by direct recoding of the Census variables. An indicator was also created for entry before (approximately) age eighteen, by subtracting the difference between the Census year and the midpoint of the year-of-entry bracket from the man's age. Finally, each man was assigned to a local labor-market area (LMA) based on his place of residence. For residents of metropolitan areas, these LMAs correspond closely to MSAs (or CMSAs, where they exist) with adjustments to match boundaries between 1980 and 1990 as closely as possible.[10] I assigned the nonmetropolitan parts of each state to their own separate LMAs—one for each state, with the exceptions of California and Texas, where the nonmetropolitan territory was divided into regional LMAs.[11] The United States was thus divided into a total of 205 LMAs (listed in table 4.2).

The local labor-market characteristics are also derived from the 1980 and 1990 Census PUMS 5 percent A samples. A data set was drawn from each Census PUMS file that included everyone who was in the labor force during the Census week. Each person was assigned to an

Table 4.1   Variable Definitions

LRWAGE	log(annual wage and salary earnings/weeks worked/usual hours worked per week), in 1989 dollars
ED	Highest grade completed
EXP	Min(age-ED-6, age-sixteen)
EXTRACT	= 1 if industry is agriculture, forestry, fisheries, or mining; otherwise = 0
CONSTR	= 1 if industry is construction; otherwise = 0
NDURMFG	= 1 if industry is nondurable goods manufacturing; otherwise = 0
DURMFG	= 1 if industry is durable goods manufacturing; otherwise = 0
UTIL	= 1 if industry is transportation, communications, or other public utilities; otherwise = 0
TRADE	= 1 if industry is wholesale or retail trade; otherwise = 0
FIRE	= 1 if industry is finance, insurance, or real estate; otherwise = 0
BUSSERV	= 1 if industry is business or repair services; otherwise = 0
PERSERV	= 1 if industry is personal services; otherwise = 0
PROFSERV	= 1 if industry is entertainment, recreation, or professional services; otherwise = 0
PUBADMIN	= 1 if industry is public administration; otherwise = 0
MGR	= 1 if occupation is executive, administrative, or managerial; otherwise = 0
PROF	= 1 if occupation is professional specialty; otherwise = 0
TECH	= 1 if occupation is is technician; otherwise = 0
SALES	= 1 if occupation is sales; otherwise = 0
CLER	= 1 if occupation is administrative support; otherwise = 0
SERVICE	= 1 if occupation is service; otherwise = 0
CRAFT	= 1 if occupation is precision production, craft, or repair; otherwise = 0
OP_LAB	= 1 if occupation is operator, fabricator, or laborer; otherwise = 0
F_F_F	= 1 if occupation is farming, forestry, or fishing; otherwise = 0
ENGONLY	= 1 if speaks English only; otherwise = 0
ENGVWELL	= 1 if speaks English very well; otherwise = 0
ENGWELL	= 1 if speaks English well; otherwise = 0
ENGNWELL	= 1 if speaks English not well; otherwise = 0
ENGNONE	= 1 if speaks English not at all; otherwise = 0
ENGNVW	= 1 if does not speak English only or very well; otherwise = 0
CITIZEN	= 1 if a citizen; otherwise = 0
IMM8790	= 1 if entered the U.S. in 1987–1990; otherwise = 0
IMM8586	= 1 if entered the U.S. in 1985–1986; otherwise = 0
IMM8284	= 1 if entered the U.S. in 1982–1984; otherwise = 0
IMM8081	= 1 if entered the U.S. in 1980–1981; otherwise = 0
IMM7579	= 1 if entered the U.S. in 1975–1979; otherwise = 0
IMM7074	= 1 if entered the U.S. in 1970–1974; otherwise = 0
IMM6569	= 1 if entered the U.S. in 1965–1969; otherwise = 0
IMM6064	= 1 if entered the U.S. in 1960–1964; otherwise = 0
IMM5059	= 1 if entered the U.S. in 1950–1959; otherwise = 0
IMM0049	= 1 if entered the U.S. before 1950; otherwise = 0
IMMCHILD	= 1 immigrated before age eighteen; otherwise = 0

(Table continues on p. 114.)

Table 4.1   *Continued*

EMPCHG	rate of change in total employment in LMA, 1980–1990
URATECHG	change in LMA unemployment rate for white males aged twenty-five to fifty-four, 1980–1990
RI11CHG	change in share of LMA labor force who have less than a twelfth-grade education and immigrated to the United States in the last ten years
NRI11CHG	change in share of LMA labor force who have less than a twelfth-grade education and did *not* immigrate in the last ten years
CATRI11	= LOW if RI11CHG < −0.00049 (68 LMAs), = MED if −0.00049 <= RI11CHG <= + 0.00080 (69 LMSs), = HIGH if RI11CHG > + 0.00080 (68 LMAs) (See figures 4.1a–4.6a for the number of group members in each category in 1980 and 1990.)
CATRI11E	LOW, MED, HIGH cutoffs were chosen to approximately equalize the number of members of the group being analyzed in each LMA in 1990. (See figures 4.1b–4.6b for the number of group members in each category in 1980 and 1990.)

The cutoffs vary by group as follows:

	LOW/MED	MED/HIGH
Black natives	−0.00051	0.00102
Mexican American natives	−0.00012	0.01012
White non-Hispanic natives	−0.00033	0.00053
Black immigrants	−0.00220	0.01414
Mexican immigrants (Fig. 4.5b)	0.00649	0.01012
Mexican immigrants (Fig. 4.5c)	0.00058	0.00946
White non-Hispanic immigrants	−0.00262	−0.00040

The number of LMAs in each category vary by group as follows:

	LOW	MED	HIGH
Black natives	67	75	63
Mexican American natives	107	84	14
White non-Hispanic natives	80	51	74
Black immigrants	30	167	8
Mexican immigrants (Fig. 4.5b)	182	10	13
Mexican immigrants (Fig. 4.5c)	133	58	14
White non-Hispanic immigrants	26	49	130

LMA as described above, an employment status (employed, unemployed), a nativity/time in the U.S. group (native-born, immigrated in the last ten years, immigrated more than ten years ago), and an education level (less than twelfth grade, twelfth grade, more than twelfth grade). These data sets were used to calculate four variables reflecting changes in the overall labor market that may affect dropouts' wages: (1) the growth rate of employment in each LMA between 1980 and 1990;

Table 4.2   Descriptive Statistics for Local Labor Market Areas (LMAs)

LMA	EMPCHG	URATECHG	NRI11CHG	RI11CHG	CATRI11
Abilene	0.057	0.0302	−0.123	−0.00553	1
Albany, NY	0.192	−0.0162	−0.091	−0.00132	1
Albuquerque	0.152	−0.0056	−0.088	0.00246	3
Allentown	0.159	−0.0048	−0.113	−0.00214	1
Amarillo	0.033	0.0365	−0.098	0.00217	3
Appleton	0.209	−0.0072	−0.092	−0.00031	2
Atlanta	0.437	−0.0008	−0.137	0.00349	3
Atlantic City	0.356	−0.0127	−0.146	0.00047	2
Augusta, GA	0.216	−0.0039	−0.153	−0.00085	1
Austin	0.527	0.0154	−0.106	0.00559	3
Bakersfield	0.302	0.0111	−0.099	0.01263	3
Baltimore	0.225	−0.0081	−0.147	−0.00060	1
Baton Rouge	0.093	0.0129	−0.110	0.00022	2
Beaumont	−0.056	0.0162	−0.122	0.00067	2
Binghamton	0.100	−0.0043	−0.092	−0.00040	2
Birmingham	0.117	−0.0059	−0.113	0.00037	2
Boston	0.165	0.0179	−0.085	0.00075	2
Brownsville	0.198	0.0039	−0.106	−0.01537	1
Buffalo	0.053	−0.0203	−0.120	−0.00081	1
Canton	0.011	0.0027	−0.093	−0.00064	1
Charleston, SC	0.316	−0.0040	−0.133	0.00055	2
Charleston, WV	−0.061	0.0059	−0.117	−0.00106	1
Charlotte, NC	0.261	−0.0003	−0.169	0.00109	3
Chattanooga	−0.089	−0.0116	−0.130	0.00058	2
Chicago	0.087	−0.0040	−0.109	−0.00538	1
Chico, CA	0.374	−0.0156	−0.078	0.00307	3
Cincinnati	0.162	−0.0151	−0.128	−0.00073	1
Cleveland	0.023	−0.0062	−0.107	−0.00148	1
Colorado Springs	0.416	−0.0024	−0.072	−0.00095	1
Columbia, SC	0.236	−0.0082	−0.118	−0.00056	1
Columbus, OH	0.188	−0.0091	−0.100	−0.00035	2
Corpus Christi	0.034	0.0174	−0.139	−0.00007	2
Dallas–Fort Worth	0.376	0.0212	−0.109	0.01051	3
Davenport	−0.264	0.0040	−0.105	0.00081	3
Dayton	0.131	−0.0204	−0.107	−0.00019	2
Daytona Beach	0.634	0.0064	−0.107	0.00583	3
Denver	0.182	0.0095	−0.073	−0.00090	1
Des Moines	0.123	−0.0086	−0.087	0.00052	2
Detroit	0.088	−0.0250	−0.111	−0.00273	1
El Paso	0.289	0.0066	−0.069	−0.01763	1
Erie	0.043	−0.0021	−0.089	−0.00045	2
Eugene	0.099	−0.0128	−0.064	0.00100	3
Evansville	0.028	−0.0043	−0.119	−0.00044	2
Fayetteville, NC	0.334	−0.0015	−0.130	−0.00410	1
Flint	0.044	−0.0107	−0.107	−0.00122	1
Ft Myers	0.843	0.0023	−0.129	0.00545	3
Ft Pierce, FL	0.244	0.0099	−0.117	0.00177	3

(Table continues on p. 116.)

Table 4.2   *Continued*

LMA	EMPCHG	URATECHG	NRI11CHG	RI11CHG	CATRI11
Ft Wayne	0.165	−0.0269	−0.086	0.00028	2
Fresno	0.282	−0.0020	−0.074	0.02292	3
Grand Rapids	1.327	−0.0057	−0.114	0.00170	3
Greeley, CO	0.150	0.0114	−0.069	0.00674	3
Greensboro, NC	0.195	−0.0028	−0.155	0.00123	3
Greenville, SC	0.223	−0.0032	−0.170	−0.00014	2
Harrisburg	0.147	−0.0091	−0.096	−0.00097	1
Hartford	0.122	0.0084	−0.108	−0.00373	1
Honolulu	0.205	−0.0099	−0.068	−0.01032	1
Houston	0.165	0.0156	−0.103	0.01021	3
Huntington, WV	0.023	0.0020	−0.116	−0.00017	2
Indianapolis	0.178	−0.0161	−0.116	−0.00055	1
Jackson, MS	0.120	0.0077	−0.124	−0.00014	2
Jacksonville, FL	0.427	0.0050	−0.114	−0.00004	2
Johnson City, TN	0.100	−0.0073	−0.149	−0.00013	2
Kansas City	0.146	0.0042	−0.099	−0.00022	2
Killeen, TX	0.207	0.0287	−0.152	−0.00310	1
Knoxville	0.070	0.0031	−0.122	0.00014	2
Lakeland, FL	0.287	0.0204	−0.107	−0.00033	2
Lancaster, PA	0.250	−0.0066	−0.101	−0.00017	2
Lansing	0.790	−0.0072	−0.114	−0.00043	2
Laredo, TX	0.416	0.0437	−0.116	0.00865	3
Las Cruces, NM	0.268	0.0323	−0.091	0.01350	3
Las Vegas	0.635	0.0044	−0.099	0.00727	3
Lexington, KY	0.204	−0.0064	−0.125	−0.00087	1
Little Rock	0.166	0.0073	−0.106	−0.00181	1
Los Angeles	0.308	0.0040	−0.057	0.01013	3
Louisville	0.133	−0.0052	−0.124	−0.00005	2
Lubbock, TX	0.061	0.0156	−0.097	−0.00166	1
Macon	0.213	−0.0009	−0.146	−0.00029	2
Madison, WI	0.216	−0.0049	−0.066	−0.00092	1
McAllen, TX	0.278	0.0283	−0.096	−0.00668	1
Melbourne, FL	0.629	0.0108	−0.089	−0.00085	1
Memphis	0.178	−0.0011	−0.132	0.00040	2
Merced, CA	0.366	−0.0138	−0.059	−0.00517	1
Miami	0.246	0.0115	−0.101	0.01676	3
Midland, TX	−0.269	0.0302	−0.139	0.00820	3
Milwaukee	0.069	−0.0034	−0.100	−0.00090	1
Minneapolis	0.229	0.0067	−0.084	−0.00026	2
Mobile	1.042	0.0000	−0.172	0.00169	3
Modesto, CA	0.431	−0.0240	−0.105	−0.00392	1
Montgomery	0.296	0.0018	−0.098	0.00000	2
Naples, FL	1.417	0.0049	−0.148	0.01646	3
Nashville	0.270	−0.0106	−0.121	0.00033	2
New Haven	0.238	0.0064	−0.100	−0.00267	1
New London	0.300	0.0160	−0.120	−0.00133	1
New Orleans	−0.010	0.0164	−0.124	−0.00127	1

Table 4.2 *Continued*

LMA	EMPCHG	URATECHG	NRI11CHG	RI11CHG	CATRI11
NY/NJ/CT	0.135	0.0036	−0.104	−0.00220	1
Norfolk	0.359	−0.0003	−0.142	−0.00065	1
Odessa, TX	−0.083	0.0419	−0.090	−0.00895	1
Oklahoma City	−0.058	0.0244	−0.091	0.00316	3
Omaha	0.121	−0.0069	−0.083	−0.00018	2
Orlando	0.744	0.0053	−0.117	0.00096	3
Pensacola	0.346	0.0020	−0.095	0.00043	2
Peoria	0.278	−0.0028	−0.111	−0.00100	1
Philadelphia	0.170	−0.0073	−0.114	−0.00013	2
Phoenix	0.519	0.0050	−0.087	0.00749	3
Pittsburgh	−0.013	0.0116	−0.106	−0.00085	1
Portland, OR	0.215	−0.0051	−0.079	0.00614	3
Providence	0.107	0.0046	−0.123	−0.01240	1
Provo	0.380	−0.0128	−0.044	0.00269	3
Pueblo	−0.016	0.0104	−0.096	−0.00229	1
Raleigh	0.413	0.0052	−0.135	0.00099	3
Reading	0.137	−0.0159	−0.128	0.00240	3
Reno	0.367	−0.0028	−0.080	0.00946	3
Richland, WA	0.001	0.0002	−0.055	0.01423	3
Richmond	0.293	0.0027	−0.145	0.00102	3
Rochester, NY	0.108	−0.0112	−0.097	−0.00042	2
Rockford, IL	0.220	−0.0158	−0.115	0.00053	2
Sacramento	0.478	−0.0253	−0.068	0.00131	3
Saginaw	0.258	−0.0253	−0.113	−0.00057	1
St. Louis	0.105	−0.0088	−0.133	−0.00050	1
Salinas, CA	0.296	−0.0095	−0.053	−0.00272	1
Salt Lake City	0.258	0.0022	−0.069	−0.00120	1
San Angelo, TX	0.075	0.0370	−0.107	−0.00364	1
San Antonio	0.320	0.0238	−0.118	−0.00287	1
San Diego	0.522	−0.0065	−0.069	0.00767	3
San Francisco	0.242	−0.0016	−0.070	0.00649	3
Santa Barbara	0.312	−0.0040	−0.048	0.02151	3
Santa Fe	0.650	0.0088	−0.075	0.00128	3
Sarasota	0.542	0.0108	−0.091	−0.00018	2
Scranton	0.139	−0.0285	−0.109	−0.00016	2
Seattle	0.337	−0.0101	−0.076	0.00073	2
Shreveport	−0.153	0.0238	−0.150	−0.00075	1
Spokane	1.171	−0.0069	−0.062	−0.00262	1
Springfield, MA	0.113	0.0104	−0.082	−0.00373	1
Stockton, CA	0.446	−0.0109	−0.104	0.01048	3
Syracuse	1.109	−0.0366	−0.142	−0.00133	1
Tampa	0.488	0.0079	−0.105	0.00289	3
Toledo	0.008	−0.0286	−0.106	−0.00096	1
Tucson	0.310	0.0046	−0.069	0.00384	3
Tulsa	0.040	0.0203	−0.098	0.00131	3
Utica	−0.081	−0.0028	−0.120	−0.00034	2
Victoria, TX	0.031	0.0095	−0.150	0.00414	3
Visalia, CA	0.237	0.0122	−0.098	0.02733	3

(Table continues on p. 118.)

Table 4.2   *Continued*

LMA	EMPCHG	URATECHG	NRI11CHG	RI11CHG	CATRI11
Waco	0.133	0.0190	−0.132	0.00438	3
Washington, DC	0.369	0.0000	−0.088	0.00893	3
West Palm Beach	0.637	0.0114	−0.122	0.01414	3
Wichita, KS	0.059	0.0108	−0.086	−0.00019	2
Worcester	0.131	0.0199	−0.124	−0.00048	2
Yakima, WA	0.102	0.0135	−0.085	0.02461	3
York, PA	0.200	−0.0046	−0.111	0.00170	3
Youngstown	−0.011	−0.0090	−0.103	−0.00014	2
Yuba City, CA	−0.052	−0.0157	−0.099	−0.01059	1
Yuma, AZ	0.509	−0.0113	−0.088	−0.01312	1
Bal of AL	0.051	−0.0049	−0.128	−0.00032	2
Alaska	0.492	−0.0051	−0.068	−0.00041	2
Bal of AZ	0.274	−0.0047	−0.102	0.00366	3
Bal of AR	0.134	−0.0088	−0.139	0.00148	3
Bal of N CA	0.355	−0.0383	−0.065	0.00765	3
Bal of S CA	0.555	−0.0195	−0.068	0.00291	3
Bal of CO	0.223	0.0035	−0.072	0.00047	2
Bal of CT	0.238	0.0130	−0.109	−0.00941	1
Bal of DE	0.276	−0.0148	−0.104	0.00178	3
Bal of FL	0.521	0.0030	−0.109	0.00321	3
Bal of GA	0.246	−0.0037	−0.162	0.00348	3
Bal of HI	0.480	−0.0364	−0.099	−0.00475	1
Idaho	0.139	−0.0178	−0.084	−0.00129	1
Bal of IL	0.017	−0.0079	−0.116	−0.00063	1
Bal of IN	0.085	−0.0243	−0.100	−0.00024	2
Bal of IA	0.007	0.0027	−0.098	0.00022	2
Bal of KS	0.025	0.0096	−0.086	0.00275	3
Bal of KY	0.115	−0.0100	−0.144	−0.00013	2
Bal of LA	0.004	0.0145	−0.142	−0.00012	2
Maine	0.250	0.0030	−0.112	−0.00018	2
Bal of MD	0.161	−0.0075	−0.144	0.00053	2
Bal of MA	0.249	0.0113	−0.102	−0.01115	1
Bal of MI	−0.089	−0.0107	−0.085	0.00003	2
Bal of MN	0.075	−0.0119	−0.106	0.00010	2
Bal of MS	0.080	0.0013	−0.131	−0.00051	1
Bal of MO	0.144	−0.0053	−0.103	−0.00024	2
Montana	0.063	−0.0216	−0.084	−0.00035	2
Bal of NE	0.031	−0.0047	−0.087	0.00066	2
Bal of NH	0.208	0.0192	−0.105	0.00016	2
Bal of NM	0.183	0.0212	−0.097	−0.00119	1
Bal of NY	−0.019	−0.0066	−0.087	−0.00003	2
Bal of NC	0.193	−0.0079	−0.169	0.00155	3
North Dakota	0.058	0.0060	−0.109	−0.00054	1
Bal of OH	0.080	−0.0015	−0.106	−0.00015	2
Bal of OK	0.159	0.0222	−0.115	−0.00022	2
Bal of OR	0.113	−0.0321	−0.080	0.00136	3
Bal of PA	0.060	−0.0119	−0.104	−0.00033	2
Bal of SC	0.154	−0.0017	−0.174	−0.00014	2

Table 4.2   *Continued*

LMA	EMPCHG	URATECHG	NRI11CHG	RI11CHG	CATRI11
South Dakota	0.093	−0.0048	−0.091	−0.00006	2
Bal of TN	0.313	−0.0164	−0.152	−0.00013	2
Bal of Border TX	0.063	0.0230	−0.101	−0.01565	1
Bal of Cent TX	0.289	0.0109	−0.159	0.00579	3
Bal of Gulf TX	−0.034	0.0231	−0.181	0.00335	3
Bal of East TX	0.128	0.0172	−0.137	0.00222	3
Bal of North TX	0.042	0.0329	−0.138	0.00312	3
Bal of West TX	0.011	0.0287	−0.120	0.00597	3
Bal of UT	0.188	0.0112	−0.080	−0.00223	1
Vermont	0.259	0.0091	−0.093	0.00010	2
Bal of VA	0.116	−0.0076	−0.162	−0.00038	2
Bal of WA	0.094	−0.0251	−0.078	0.00612	3
Bal of WV	−0.021	0.0145	−0.115	−0.00055	1
Bal of WI	0.150	−0.0231	−0.099	0.00039	2
Wyoming	−0.054	0.0154	−0.077	−0.00254	1

(2) the change in the unemployment rate for prime-aged (twenty-five to fifty-four) white males; (3) the change in the share of the labor force in entry cohort/skill group 1 (entered the U.S. in the last ten years with less than a twelfth-grade education); and (4) the change in the share of the labor force in group 2 (natives or earlier immigrants with less than twelfth-grade educations).[12]

Finally, to facilitate graphical depiction of the effect of recent unskilled immigration on the distribution of wage residuals, the LMAs were divided into three categories, based on the sign and size of the change from 1980 to 1990 in the share of the labor force who were unskilled recent immigrants. In one classification scheme, one third (68) of the LMAs were assigned to the "low" category, with a change in share less than −0.049 percentage points; one third (68) were assigned to the "high" category, with a change in share greater than +0.080 percentage points; and the other 69 were assigned to the "medium" category. This maximizes the variation in LMAs within each category, which should reduce the influence of unobserved LMA characteristics on the measured shift in the wage distribution due to unskilled recent immigration. Because the population groups are unevenly distributed across LMAs, this scheme produces unequal numbers of observations in each category. This unequal sample size reduces the precision of the estimated differences between categories in the shifts of the wage distribution. A second classification scheme therefore attempts to equalize the numbers of the particular group being analyzed who were in each category in 1990, by varying the numbers of LMAs assigned to each category.[13] This means that a given LMA may be in different categories for different groups. Descriptive statistics for the 205 LMAs are listed in table 4.2. A number of places that we think of as "immigrant" cities (New York, Chicago, and many in Texas, for example) turn out to be in the "low" category in the first classification scheme. These are places that had more low-skilled immigration in the 1970s than in the 1980s, so that the change in share of *recent* immigrant dropouts from 1980 to 1990 was actually negative.

METHODS OF ANALYSIS

Before estimating the effect of changes in unskilled immigration on changes in the entire wage distribution of male high school dropouts in a given race/ethnic group, the wage distributions in each year must first be adjusted for other influences that may be correlated with immigration. The analysis proceeds in four steps. First, I estimate the following wage equation for native white non-Hispanic males with fluent English, to determine the "prices" of education and experience and the interindustry and interoccupation differences in the wage structures of those years:

$$(4.1) \quad lnW_{iWt} = X_{iWt}\beta_{Wt} + \mu_{iWt}$$

where W_{iWt} is the real wage of white man i in year t, X is a vector of education, experience, industry, and occupation terms (including a constant), β_w is a vector of coefficients for native-born non-Hispanic white males with fluent English (that is, the "prices" of education, experience, industry, and occupation), and μ represents the unobservable factors influencing the individual's wage. To smooth somewhat while still using a very flexible functional form, quartics in years of schooling and potential experience were completely interacted with each other, and dummy variables for one-digit industry and occupation were included to shift the intercept.

Second, I use these "prices" to predict the wages in 1980 and 1990 of native-born and immigrant Mexican American, black, and non-Hispanic white men with less than a high school education, given their schooling, potential experience, industry, and occupation, and I express the person's actual wage as a deviation from this predicted wage. These deviations are due to such factors as fluency in English, time in the United States, age at entry, citizenship, conditions in their local labor market, and unobserved characteristics of the individual and the job (quality of schooling, job tenure, specialized training, specific job assignment, size of firm, union coverage, fringe benefits, working conditions, discrimination, ability, motivation). The deviations will not sum to zero if these factors differ between native whites and minorities or immigrants. The "prices" of the immigrant-specific characteristics could not be estimated in the first-stage equations for native-born white non-Hispanics, for obvious reasons. Because English fluency and changes in labor-market conditions affect the wages of minorities, immigrants, and white natives differently, these variables were not included in the first-stage regressions, either.[14] These observed and unobserved factors are reflected in the distributions of the wage deviations.

Third, I removed the effects of these additional personal characteristics and labor-market conditions by performing the following regression (using OLS) for 1980 and 1990 separately:

$$(4.2) \quad ln W_{ijct} - X_{ijct} \, \hat{\beta}_{Wt} = Z_{ijct} \, \gamma_{jt} + \Delta V_c \delta_{jt} + \Delta S_{2c} \, \theta_{2jt} + \varepsilon_{ijct}$$

The dependent variable is the wage deviation of individual i in race/ethnic-nativity-gender-skill group j in area c in year t from his predicted wage using the native whites' wage structure. Z is a set of dummy variables measuring command of English and (for immigrants only) entry cohort, arrival before age eighteen, and citizenship status. ΔV and ΔS_2 are vectors containing cubic functions of changes in labor-market conditions: ΔV includes the percentage change in total employment and the percentage point change in the unemployment rate of prime-age (twenty-five to fifty-four) white non-Hispanic males, and ΔS_2 includes the percentage point change in the labor-force share of immigrant cohort/skill group 2 (unskilled immigrants who entered more than ten years ago and unskilled natives). The symbols γ, δ, and θ_{2j} are vectors of coefficients to be estimated, where θ_{2j} represents the elasticity of complementarity between cohort/skill group 2 and group j workers. Finally, ε includes the change in labor-force share of cohort/skill group 1 (recent unskilled immigrants) as well as unobservable factors influencing the individual's wage (including those that cause returns to education and other characteristics to differ between native whites and the other groups).

The inclusion of ΔV and ΔS_2 adjusts for the effects of other changes in labor-market conditions during the 1980s that may be correlated with the change in labor-force share of recent immigrant dropouts and may affect the change in the wage distribution of dropouts. In the regression for 1980 the coefficients of these variables measure how much higher (or lower) a group's average wage was, ceteris paribus, in 1980 in LMAs that had, for example, a 1 percentage-point higher employment growth rate during the subsequent decade. In the regression for 1990, the coefficients measure how much higher (or lower) the average wage was, ceteris paribus, in 1990 in those same LMAs. Thus the residuals distributions for both 1980 and 1990 are adjusted for these inter-LMA differences, and any change in the adjusted distributions of residuals between 1980 and 1990 must then be due to factors other than these changes in labor-market conditions. The effect of recent unskilled im-migration can thus be separated from the effects of these other changes. Including these additional LMA characteristics in the regression also further reduces the problem of unobserved heterogeneity (that is, un-observed factors that create a correlation across places between changes in immigration and wages). Only insofar as these unobserved factors are uncorrelated with the included LMA characteristics will they still bias the final results.

Finally, graphical and quantile regression techniques are used to ana-lyze the influence of changes in unskilled recent immigration on the distribution of residuals from the third-step regressions. For the graph-ical analysis, the wage residuals from regression (4.2) are obtained:

$$(4.3) \quad \hat{\varepsilon}_{ijct} = lnW_{ijct} - X_{ijct}\,\hat{\beta}_{Wt} - Z_{ijct}\,\hat{\gamma}_{jt} - \Delta V_c\,\hat{\delta}_{jt} - \Delta S_{2c}\,\hat{\theta}_{2jt}$$

These $\hat{\varepsilon}_{ijct}$ are then sorted into three LMA categories, according to the change in share of the labor force who are unskilled recent immigrants, as described earlier. Within each category the difference between the 1990 and 1980 residual log-wage values at each percentile is plotted. The graphs are compared to determine whether this shift was smaller (more negative or less positive) in labor markets where there was a larger influx of unskilled immigrants during the decade (that is, a larger positive or smaller negative change in the labor-force share of high school dropouts who entered the United States in the last ten years). Because the grouping of LMAs is somewhat arbitrary, I use two classifi-cation schemes for the graphs, one that has equal numbers of LMAs in each category and one that attempts to equalize the number of individ-uals in the group being analyzed in 1990.

The graphs can show whether there appear to be systematic effects of immigration on the shape of the wage distribution. However, the grouping of the continuous variable into three categories is essentially arbitrary, and one cannot tell whether these effects are statistically sig-nificant. I therefore use quantile regression to estimate the effect of the continuous variable, change in the labor-force share of unskilled recent immigration, on the value of each decile of the distribution of wage residuals in 1980 and 1990.

$$(4.4) \quad \hat{\varepsilon}_{ijct} = \hat{R}^q_{jct} + \varepsilon^q_{ijct}, \qquad q = .1, .2, \ldots, .9; \, t = 1980, 1990$$

where $\hat{R}^q_{jct} = \hat{\lambda}^q_{0jt} + \hat{\lambda}^q_{1jt} \Delta S_{1c}$

so $\quad \Delta \hat{R}^q_{jc} = \Delta \hat{\lambda}^q_{0j} + \Delta \hat{\lambda}_{1j} \Delta S_{1c}$

Here, $\hat{\varepsilon}_{ijct}$ is individual i's third-step residual (defined in equation 4.3), $\hat{R}^q_{jct}$ is the value of the qth percentile of the distribution of log-wage residuals of group j in area c in year t, ε^q_{ijct} is the deviation of the individual's residual from this value, ΔS_{1c} is the change between 1980 and 1990 in the share of entry cohort/skill group 1 (unskilled immigrants who entered less than ten years ago) in the labor force of area c, and $\hat{\lambda}^q_{0jt}$ and $\hat{\lambda}^q_{1jt}$ are least absolute deviations (LAD) estimators of the intercept and coefficient, respectively, of the quantile regression. The change in $\hat{\lambda}^q_{0jt}$ between 1980 and 1990 tells how much that decile's value changed in LMAs where the share of unskilled recent immigration did not change during the decade. The change in $\hat{\lambda}^q_{1jt}$ between 1980 and 1990 (multiplied by .01) tells how much a 1 percentage-point increase in the share of unskilled recent immigrants in the local labor force (that is, switching 1 percent of the labor force from skilled workers to unskilled recent immigrants) changes the value of the qth percentile of the log-wage residuals distribution of male dropouts in group j.[15]

RESULTS

The results of the graphical analysis are summarized in figures 4.1 through 4.6. The results for native-born and immigrant black, Mexican American, and non-Hispanic white male dropouts are shown separately. The tenth to the ninetieth percentiles of the distributions of wage residuals are plotted on the horizontal axis, and the size of the 1980–1990 shift in the residual log-wage is plotted on the vertical axis.[16] The heights of the three lines in each figure show the size of the shift separately for labor markets with high, medium, and low increases in the labor force share of recent immigrants who did not complete high school. If substituting less-educated immigrants for better-educated workers in a labor market depresses the wages of native or foreign-born high school dropouts, the line for high share-increase LMAs

(Text continues on p. 137.)

Figure 4.1a   Impact of Recent Immigrant Dropouts on Wage Distribution of Native Black Male Dropouts
(One Third of LMAs in Each Category)

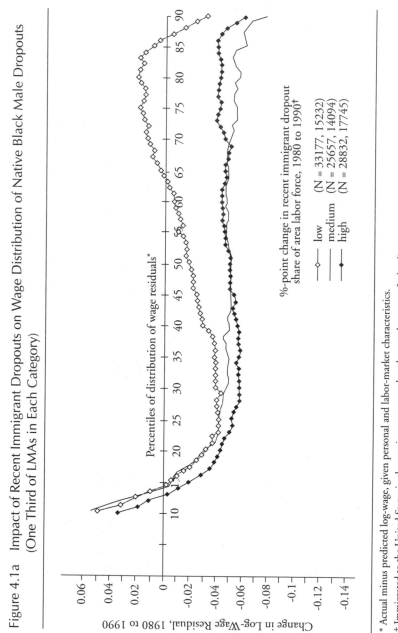

* Actual minus predicted log-wage, given personal and labor-market characteristics.
† Immigrated to the United States in the previous ten years, less than twelve years of schooling.

Figure 4.1b Impact of Recent Immigrant Dropouts on Wage Distribution of Native Black Male Dropouts (Approximately One Third of Group Members in Each Category in 1990)

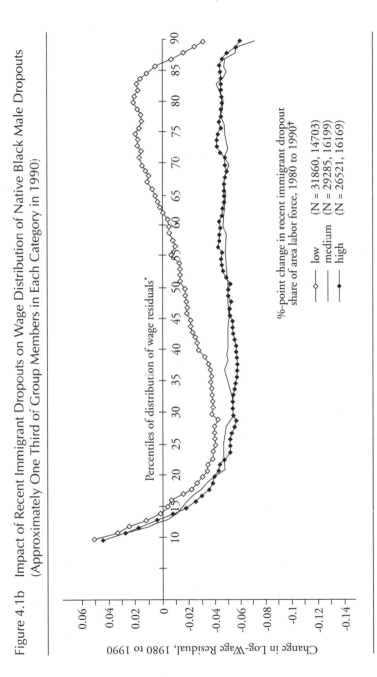

% -point change in recent immigrant dropout share of area labor force, 1980 to 1990†

low   (N = 31860, 14703)
medium (N = 29285, 16199)
high   (N = 26521, 16169)

* Actual minus predicted log-wage, given personal and labor-market characteristics.

† Immigrated to the United States in the previous ten years, less than twelve years of schooling.

Figure 4.2a   Impact of Recent Immigrant Dropouts on Wage Distribution of Native Mexican Male
Dropouts (One Third of LMAs in Each Category)

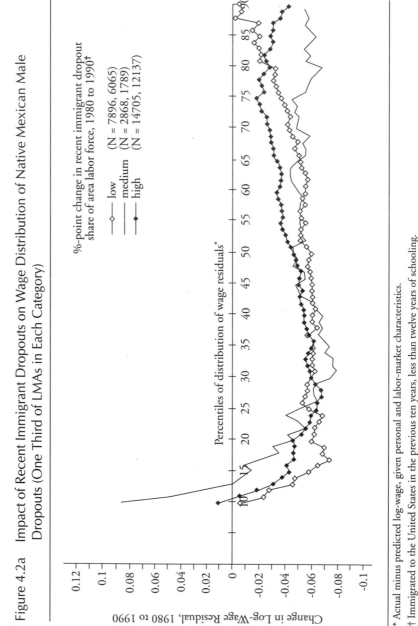

* Actual minus predicted log-wage, given personal and labor-market characteristics.

† Immigrated to the United States in the previous ten years, less than twelve years of schooling.

Figure 4.2b   Impact of Recent Immigrant Dropouts on Wage Distribution of Native Mexican Male Dropouts (Approximately One Third of Group Members in Each Category in 1990)

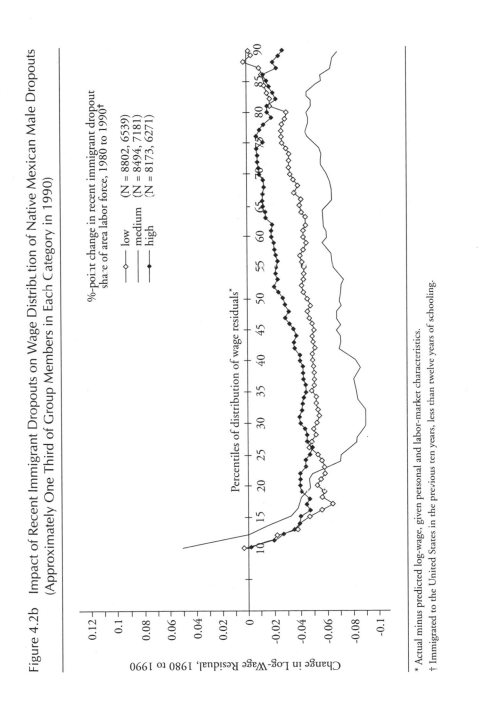

* Actual minus predicted log-wage, given personal and labor-market characteristics.

† Immigrated to the United States in the previous ten years, less than twelve years of schooling.

Figure 4.3a   Impact of Recent Immigrant Dropouts on Wage Distribution of Native Non-Hispanic White Male Dropouts (One Third of LMAs in Each Category)

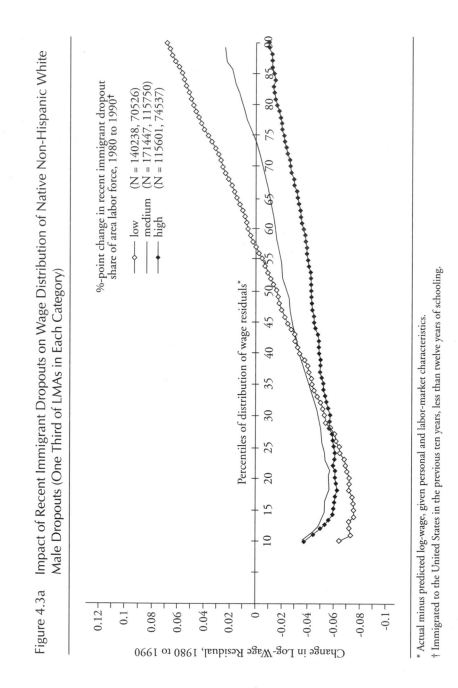

* Actual minus predicted log-wage, given personal and labor-market characteristics.

† Immigrated to the United States in the previous ten years, less than twelve years of schooling.

Figure 4.3b Impact of Recent Immigrant Dropouts on Wage Distribution of Native Non-Hispanic White Male Dropouts (Approximately One Third of Group Members in Each Category in 1990)

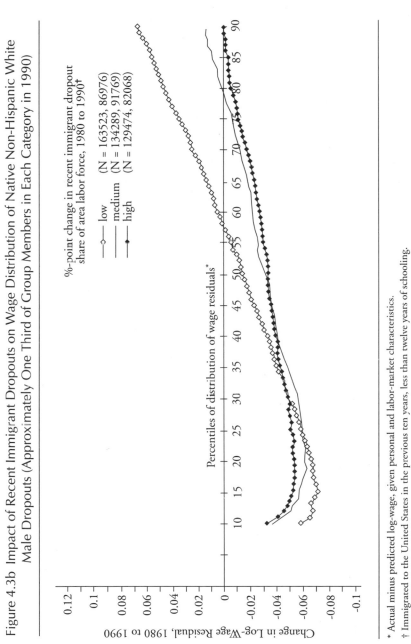

%-point change in recent immigrant dropout share of area labor force, 1980 to 1990†

low   (N = 163523, 86976)
medium   (N = 134289, 91769)
high   (N = 129474, 82068)

Percentiles of distribution of wage residuals*

Change in Log-Wage Residual, 1980 to 1990

* Actual minus predicted log-wage, given personal and labor-market characteristics.

† Immigrated to the United States in the previous ten years, less than twelve years of schooling.

Figure 4.4a   Impact of Recent Immigrant Dropouts on Wage Distribution of Black Immigrant Male
                Dropouts (One Third of LMAs in Each Category)

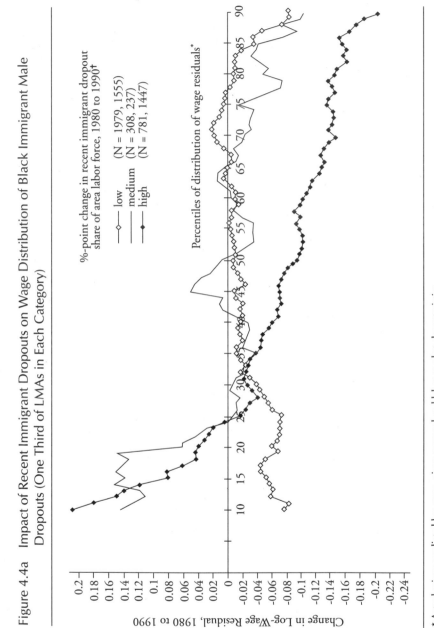

% -point change in recent immigrant dropout
share of area labor force, 1980 to 1990†

— ◇ — low   (N = 1979, 1555)
——— medium   (N = 308, 237)
— ◆ — high   (N = 781, 1447)

Percentiles of distribution of wage residuals*

Change in Log-Wage Residual, 1980 to 1990

* Actual minus predicted log-wage, given personal and labor-market characteristics.
† Immigrated to the United States in the previous ten years, less than twelve years of schooling.

Figure 4.4b   Impact of Recent Immigrant Dropouts on Wage Distribution of Black Immigrant Male Dropouts (Approximately One Third of Group Members in Each Category in 1990)

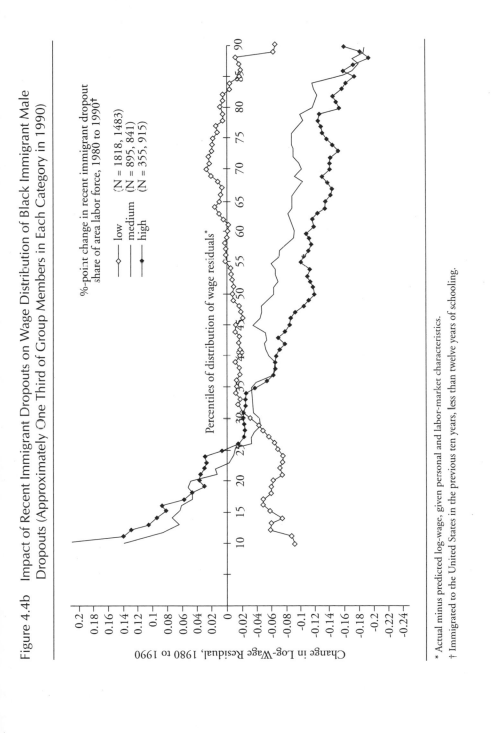

* Actual minus predicted log-wage, given personal and labor-market characteristics.
† Immigrated to the United States in the previous ten years, less than twelve years of schooling.

Figure 4.5a Impact of Recent Immigrant Dropouts on Wage Distribution of Mexican Immigrant Male Dropouts (One Third of LMAs in Each Category)

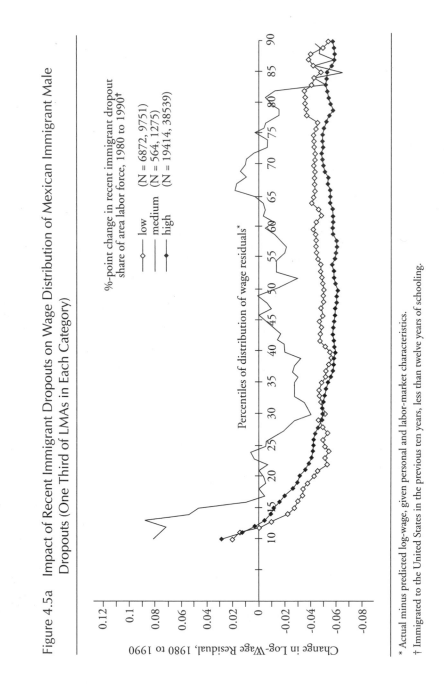

%-point change in recent immigrant dropout share of area labor force, 1980 to 1990†

— low   (N = 6872, 9751)
— medium   (N = 564, 1275)
—◆— high   (N = 19414, 38539)

Percentiles of distribution of wage residuals*

Change in Log-Wage Residual, 1980 to 1990

* Actual minus predicted log-wage, given personal and labor-market characteristics.
† Immigrated to the United States in the previous ten years, less than twelve years of schooling.

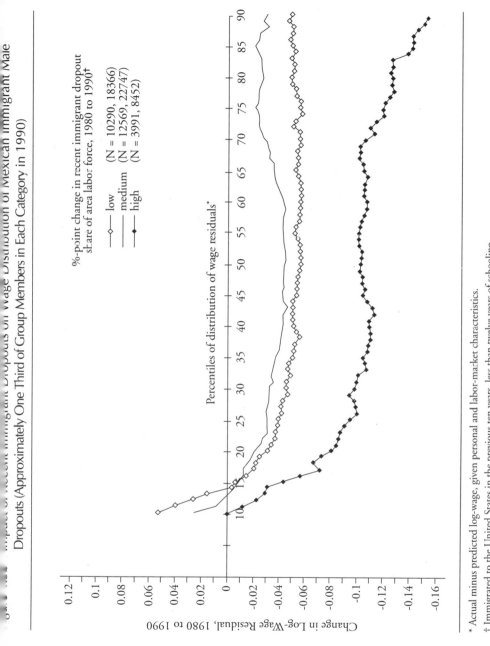

Impact of Recent Immigrant Dropouts on Wage Distribution of Mexican Immigrant Male Dropouts (Approximately One Third of Group Members in Each Category in 1990)

%-point change in recent immigrant dropout share of area labor force, 1980 to 1990†

- low   (N = 10290, 18366)
- medium (N = 12569, 22747)
- high   (N = 3991, 8452)

Percentiles of distribution of wage residuals*

Change in Log-Wage Residual, 1980 to 1990

* Actual minus predicted log-wage, given personal and labor-market characteristics.

† Immigrated to the United States in the previous ten years, less than twelve years of schooling.

Figure 4.5c   Impact of Recent Immigrant Dropouts on Wage Distribution of Mexican Immigrant Male Dropouts (Approximately One Third of Group Members in Each Category in 1990—Los Angeles in "High")

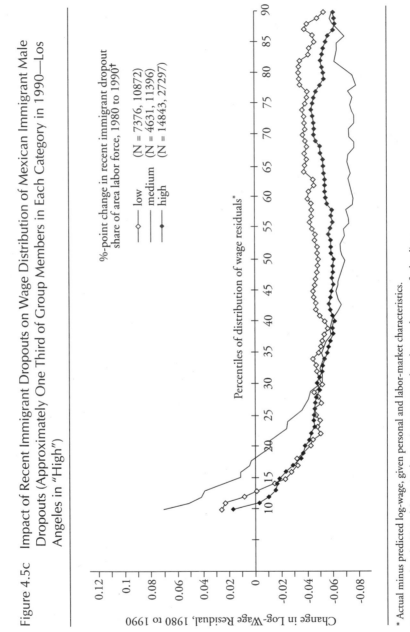

%-point change in recent immigrant dropout share of area labor force, 1980 to 1990†

—◇— low   (N = 7376, 10872)
—— medium   (N = 4631, 11396)
—◆— high   (N = 14843, 27297)

Percentiles of distribution of wage residuals*

Change in Log-Wage Residual, 1980 to 1990

* Actual minus predicted log-wage, given personal and labor-market characteristics.
† Immigrated to the United States in the previous ten years, less than twelve years of schooling.

Figure 4.6a   Impact of Recent Immigrant Dropouts on Wage Distribution of Non-Hispanic White
Immigrant Male Dropouts (One Third of LMAs in Each Category)

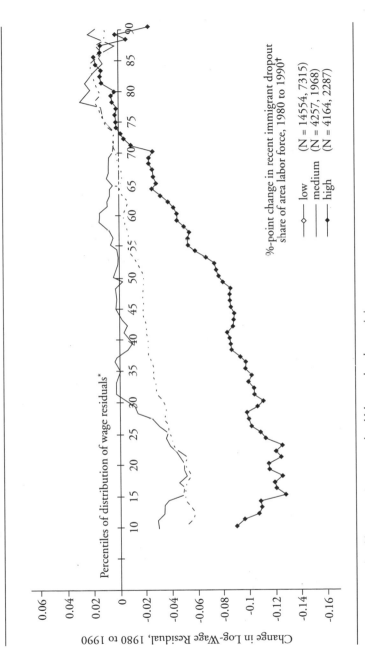

* Actual minus predicted log-wage, given personal and labor-market characteristics.

† Immigrated to the United States in the previous ten years, less than twelve years of schooling.

Figure 4.6b Impact of Recent Immigrant Dropouts on Wage Distribution of Non-Hispanic White
Immigrant Male Dropouts (Approximately One Third of Group Members in Each Category
in 1990)

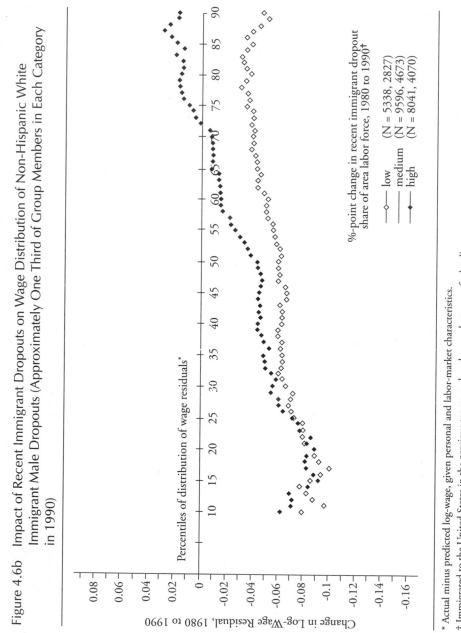

* Actual minus predicted log-wage, given personal and labor-market characteristics.
† Immigrated to the United States in the previous ten years, less than twelve years of schooling.

should be lowest, and the line for low share-increase LMAs should be highest.

The cutoffs between the "high," "medium," and "low" categories differ between the "a" and "b" figures for each group (and among figures 4.5a, 4.5b, and 4.5c for Mexican immigrants). In the "a" figures, each category has the same number of LMAs (68, 69, and 68). Because LMAs vary in size, the number of individual wage observations varies across categories—dramatically so for Mexicans and immigrants, who are unevenly distributed geographically. (On the figures, the two numbers following "*N=*" are the sample sizes in 1980 and 1990, respectively.) The unequal sample sizes result in wider confidence bands around the lines, on average. For the "b" figures, therefore, the cutoffs were chosen to try to equalize the numbers of the group being analyzed who are in each LMA category in 1990.[17] Thus, the numbers of individuals represented by the lines on a given "b" figure are less unequal than on the corresponding "a" figure, although considerable variation remains due to the very large concentrations of certain groups in a few large cities. However, inspection of the graphs shows that larger sample sizes produce smoother lines. The sample of black immigrants is so small that differences between the lines in figures 4.4a and 4.4b may not be significant. This also affects the "medium" category for Mexicans in figures 4.2a and 4.5a.

Where the lines are below the horizontal axis, it indicates that wages fell from 1980 to 1990 in that part of the distribution of residuals. This was the case for most groups in most LMA categories. Conversely, where the lines are above the axis, wages rose over the decade. A downward-sloping line indicates that wages rose more (or fell less) at the lower percentiles within the relevant range, and an upward-sloping line indicates that wages rose more (or fell less) at the higher percentiles. Thus, for black and Mexican dropouts, given observed characteristics, wages for those in the lower tail (up to the 10th or 15th percentile) increased in the 1980s. In the middle range most groups' wages declined rather evenly, indicating a fairly uniform shift downward of the wage distributions for dropouts, given observed characteristics.[18] This generalization applies best to Mexican immigrants (figure 4.5), to U.S.-born Mexicans in low and medium share-change areas (figure 4.2), and to native blacks in high and medium share-change areas (figure 4.1). The distributions for white non-Hispanics (figures 4.3 and 4.6), for native-born Mexican Americans in high share-change areas (figure 4.2), and for native blacks in low share-change areas (figure 4.1) became more unequal as wages fell more at lower than at higher percentiles (for the third through the eighth deciles, at least). In fact, in low share-change areas wages *rose* during the 1980s for native black dropouts between the sixty-fifth and eighty-fifth percentiles and for native white non-Hispanics above the sixtieth. For black immigrants in high share-change areas (for example, Miami) the graph indicates a great compression of the distribution, as wages rose most at the bottom and fell most at the top. This is, however, based on a very small sample.

Comparing the lines for the low and high share changes provides some evidence on the effects of an increase in the share of unskilled recent immigrants in the local labor force. This does appear to depress the wages of black and native non-Hispanic white dropouts in the upper two thirds of the distribution of residuals (see figures 4.1, 4.3, and 4.4). The size of this effect increases as wages do. For Mexican immigrants the lines are quite close together, indicating that a larger change in the share of unskilled recent immigrants in the local labor force has little effect on the wage distribution, except when Los Angeles is in the "medium" category (figure 4.5b). Apparently wages of unskilled Mexican male immigrants fell less in Los Angeles than in other LMAs that are in the "high" category. Thus, when Los Angeles is moved from "high" (figure 4.5c) to "medium" (figure 4.5b), the "high" line shifts down.[19] For U.S.-born Mexican Americans, however, a larger increase in unskilled immigration appears to have a *positive* effect on wages.

The graphs are suggestive, but not conclusive, because we cannot tell whether the distances between the lines for low and high change in labor-force share of unskilled recent immigrants are statistically significant, and the classification into three groups of LMAs is arbitrary. A better test of the influence of unskilled immigrants on dropouts' wages is provided by the results of the quantile regressions reported in table 4.3. These results confirm the tentative conclusions drawn from the evidence in the graphs. They show that an increase in the share of unskilled recent immigrants in the local labor force significantly reduced wages of native white non-Hispanic male dropouts at the twentieth percentile and above in the distribution of wage residuals. The effect of a 1 percentage-point increase in the unskilled recent immigrants' labor-force share (the size of the increase experienced by Los Angeles, Houston, and Dallas–Fort Worth in the 1980s) increases steadily as we move up in the native whites' distribution, ranging from a 1.5 percent wage reduction at the twentieth percentile to a 5.4 percent reduction at the ninetieth. The negative effect on native black dropouts' wages was smaller than for whites, but it was still significant at the median to the eightieth percentile of the distribution of residuals. This negative effect, too, increases as the residuals do, from a 2.2 percent reduction at the median to a 4.7 percent reduction at the eightieth percentile. The estimated reduction of unskilled black immigrants' wages was large enough

Table 4.3 Quantile Regression of Log-Wage Residuals on Change in Share of Recent Immigrants with Less Than HS Education in LMA Labor Force: Change in Coefficient of RI11CHG, 1980 to 1990

			Male High-School Dropouts			
Percentile	Native Black	Native Mexican American	Native White Non-Hispanic	Immigrant Black	Immigrant Mexican American	Immigrant White Non-Hispanic
0.1	-1.709	-0.101	0.106	15.946*	0.699	-3.467
	(1.979)	(1.683)	(0.762)	(4.804)	(1.263)	(2.284)
0.2	-1.321	1.554	-1.533*	4.306	0.935	-3.066
	(1.256)	(0.983)	(0.529)	(3.259)	(0.716)	(1.686)
0.3	-1.204	0.519	-2.503*	-0.450	1.120	-2.762
	(0.985)	(0.818)	(0.442)	(2.389)	(0.613)	(1.425)
0.4	-1.369	0.227	-2.656*	-2.822	0.707	-1.787
	(0.914)	(0.750)	(0.398)	(2.248)	(0.575)	(1.211)
0.5	-2.177*	1.141	-2.803*	-4.744*	0.581	-1.099
	(0.936)	(0.698)	(0.393)	(2.275)	(0.497)	(1.144)
0.6	-1.920*	2.027*	-3.220*	-3.823	0.080	-0.073
	(0.867)	(0.648)	(0.378)	(2.239)	(0.515)	(1.179)
0.7	-3.337*	2.572*	-3.778*	-7.319*	0.066	0.847
	(1.007)	(0.708)	(0.424)	(2.224)	(0.566)	(1.130)
0.8	-4.741*	1.487	-4.331*	-6.615*	-1.143	1.491
	(1.163)	(0.841)	(0.467)	(2.790)	(0.629)	(1.384)
0.9	-2.511	-0.136	-5.390*	-5.494	-1.781	-1.425
	(1.849)	(1.180)	(0.686)	(4.287)	(0.928)	(2.211)
N						
1980	87,666	25,469	341,829ᵃ	3,068	26,850	22,975
1990	47,071	19,991	260,813	3,239	49,565	11,570

Note: Dependent variable: second-stage regression residual (std errors in parentheses).
ᵃ80% random sample

(4.7 to 7.3 percent) at the median to the eightieth percentile of the distribution of residuals to be statistically significant despite the small samples and consequently large standard errors.

The quantile regression results are clearer than the graphs in revealing a significant *positive* impact of unskilled immigration on the wages of native-born Mexican American high school dropouts at the sixth and seventh deciles of the distribution of residuals. Increasing the labor-force share of unskilled recent immigrants by 1 percentage point is estimated to increase the wage of these better-paid (given their observed characteristics) U.S.-born Mexican Americans by 2.0 to 2.6 percent.[20] In the quantile regressions, no significant effects are found for Mexican or non-Hispanic white immigrants.[21]

The change in the intercepts of the quantile regression models estimates the change in the wage residual at each decile in LMAs where there was no change in the labor-force share of unskilled recent immigrants from 1980 to 1990, that is, where the influx of unskilled immigrants, relative to the size of the labor force, was the same in the 1980s as in the 1970s. This is an estimate of wage changes due to factors other than immigration of unskilled workers. Again, the graphical evidence is confirmed. Table 4.4 shows that, except at the first decile, wage residuals fell significantly over the decade for native blacks, Mexican Americans, and Mexican immigrants. For native white non-Hispanics, they fell significantly at all deciles except the eighth and ninth (where they rose significantly); and for white non-Hispanic immigrants, they fell significantly at the median and below. For black immigrants, the decline in wage residuals was small and not statistically significant (partly due to small sample sizes), except at the sixth and ninth deciles.

SUMMARY AND CONCLUSIONS

This study uses variation across labor markets in the United States to estimate the effect of unskilled immigration in the 1980s on the entire wage distributions of African American, Mexican American, and non-Hispanic white male high school dropouts. By disaggregating immigrants by skill level and entry cohort, it focuses on the group that is most likely to compete directly with disadvantaged American workers and is of most policy concern: unskilled recent immigrants. By analyzing changes in the labor force share of this group while controlling for overall growth of local employment, the "substitution" effect of additional unskilled immigration is estimated, excluding the "scale" effect due to the added population. To minimize the problems caused by unobserved city-specific fixed effects and reverse causation (that is, immigration induced by high wages), a "changes on changes" strategy is em-

Table 4.4   Quantile Regression of Log-Wage Residuals on Change in Share of Recent Immigrants with Less than HS Education in LMA Labor Force: Change in Intercept, 1980 to 1990

			Male High-School Dropouts			
Percentile	Native Black	Native Mexican American	Native White Non-Hispanic	Immigrant Black	Immigrant Mexican American	Immigrant White Non-Hispanic
0.1	0.048	0.007[b]	−0.059	−0.009[b]	0.017[b]	−0.054
	(0.009)	(0.015)	(0.003)	(0.036)	(0.012)	(0.013)
0.2	−0.043	−0.066	−0.075	−0.026[b]	−0.046	−0.060
	(0.006)	(0.009)	(0.002)	(0.024)	(0.007)	(0.010)
0.3	−0.057	−0.072	−0.065	−0.022[b]	−0.060	−0.038
	(0.004)	(0.007)	(0.002)	(0.019)	(0.006)	(0.008)
0.4	−0.057	−0.064	−0.052	−0.028[b]	−0.068	−0.028
	(0.004)	(0.007)	(0.002)	(0.017)	(0.006)	(0.007)
0.5	−0.049	−0.062	−0.039	−0.030[b]	−0.066	−0.023
	(0.004)	(0.006)	(0.002)	(0.018)	(0.005)	(0.007)
0.6	−0.042	−0.056	−0.028	−0.037	−0.059	−0.004[b]
	(0.004)	(0.006)	(0.002)	(0.017)	(0.005)	(0.007)
0.7	−0.032	−0.051	−0.012	−0.014[b]	−0.054	0.006[b]
	(0.004)	(0.007)	(0.002)	(0.018)	(0.006)	(0.007)
0.8	−0.020	−0.045	0.007	−0.023[b]	−0.047	0.019
	(0.005)	(0.008)	(0.002)	(0.022)	(0.007)	(0.009)
0.9	−0.053	−0.040	0.026	−0.108	−0.049	0.016[b]
	(0.008)	(0.011)	(0.003)	(0.033)	(0.010)	(0.013)
N						
1980	87,666	25,469	341,829[a]	3,068	26,850	22,975
1990	47,071	19,991	260,813	3,239	49,565	11,570

Note: Dependent variable: second-stage regression residual (std errors in parentheses)

[a] 80% random sample

[b] p > .05 (not significant at 5% level)

ployed, which relates the *change* in unskilled immigration to an area to *changes* in the shape and position of the wage distribution. Graphical and quantile regression techniques are used to analyze the distribution of wage residuals after adjusting for observed human capital, industry, occupation, and other labor market conditions. These methods can reveal impacts that are obscured when only within-group mean wages are analyzed.

The results vary by ethnicity. On the one hand, they reveal that an increase in unskilled immigration does depress the wages of native white non-Hispanic male high school dropouts and of black dropouts who earn more than would be expected, given their observed characteristics. The size of the estimated effect at certain deciles of the wage distribution is greater than has been found in other studies, which have focused on the effects on the mean of the distribution. For example, at the eightieth percentile of the wage residuals of native black and white non-Hispanic dropouts, a 1-percentage-point increase in the share of unskilled recent immigrants in the local labor force during the 1980s (such as that experienced by Los Angeles, Houston, and Dallas–Fort Worth) reduced wages by over 4 percent. Apparently, unskilled immigrants compete more directly with the better-paid than the lower-paid black and native white dropouts. Perhaps unionized blacks and native whites, or those earning seniority rents, lose those rents when nonunion immigrants are available to replace them.

On the other hand, this analysis finds that an increase in the share of unskilled recent immigrants in the local labor force has a *positive* effect on the wages of U.S.-born Mexican American male dropouts. This is consistent with the findings of Bean, Lowell, and Taylor (1988), who suggest that ethnic enclaves may shelter Mexican Americans from some of the competitive forces in the labor market. Alternatively, native-born Mexican American high school dropouts may be complements with unskilled new immigrants in the labor market, many of whom are Spanish-speaking, because their knowledge of both Spanish and English makes them capable of supervising the newcomers. The other side of this coin is that native black and white dropouts may have fewer opportunities to be supervisors than in the past, as the least-skilled workers are increasingly Spanish-speaking. This may contribute to the decline found in the upper part of the wage distributions of black and white dropouts.

Thus, despite the potential positive biases and the possibility that the effect on wages is attenuated by migration, this study finds larger negative impacts of immigration on some groups of native black and white male workers than other researchers have found. And whereas most theories expect unskilled immigrants to lower the wages of *all* unskilled natives, and especially those who are most similar to them, this study finds evidence that they may raise the wages of some groups of natives of the same ethnicity and similar skill level, such as better-paid native-born Mexican American dropouts, who appear to be complementary with unskilled immigrants from Mexico and Central America. The difference from others' findings may be due to this study's focus on the impact of *recent, unskilled* immigrants on the shape of the *entire hourly wage distribution* of *unskilled* members of *particular* ethnic groups, its exclusion of the "scale" effects of additional immigrants as consumers, or its other differences in sample selection, model specification, and estimation procedures.

APPENDIX

Table 4A.1   Mean of Natural Logarithm of Real Wage
Male High School Dropouts

	1980	1990	Difference
Blacks			
U.S. natives	2.074	1.975	−0.098
	(0.003)	(0.004)	(0.005)
Foreign-born	2.127	2.041	−0.086
	(0.016)	(0.012)	(0.020)
Mexican Americans			
U.S. natives	2.115	1.963	−0.151
	(0.005)	(0.005)	(0.007)
Foreign-born	2.001	1.867	−0.134
	(0.005)	(0.003)	(0.006)
Non-Hispanic Whites			
U.S. natives	2.286	2.123	−0.163
	(0.001)	(0.001)	(0.002)
Foreign-born	2.390	2.402	0.012
	(0.005)	(0.007)	(0.008)

Note: std. errors in parentheses

NOTES

1. Throughout this chapter, the term "high school dropout" includes anyone who did not complete at least twelve grades of school, including those who finished less than eight grades.

2. An exception is Altonji and Card (1991), who find, when they use the fraction of immigrants in an SMSA in 1970 as an instrument for the change in the fraction between 1970 and 1980, that a 1 percentage-point

increase in the fraction of immigrants in an SMSA reduces less-skilled native wages by 1.2 percent.

3. This procedure assumes, as do Juhn, Murphy, and Pierce (1991, 1993) and Blau and Kahn (1997), that one "price" of education, experience, industry, and occupation applies to all groups and is best measured by the dominant group's wage structure; and that differences in estimated returns between native white males and other groups and are due to omitted variables (including unobserved skill and discrimination). However, I allow the effects of immigrants' characteristics and labor market conditions to differ across groups.

4. It is implicitly assumed that, at each step of the analysis, the residuals are uncorrelated with the regressors. Thus, this final step analyzes the relationship between the variations in wages and unskilled recent immigration that are uncorrelated with the variables included in the previous steps. Because the overall growth of local employment is controlled for, the "substitution" effect of new unskilled immigration on wages is estimated, excluding the "scale" effect due to adding consumers and producers. This should tend to make my estimates more negative than if scale effects were included.

5. This includes black Hispanics; therefore, there is a very small overlap between the black and Mexican samples.

6. The errors in measuring hours worked probably increase the variance of the wage distribution. If this effect is similar in 1980 and 1990, it will cancel out when intertemporal comparisons are made. I did not delete "wild" wage values because any cutoff is arbitrary and would affect measured changes in the variance over time. Since "wild" values affect only the extreme tails of the wage distribution, this study will focus on shifts in the 10–90 percentile range.

7. To protect confidentiality, the Census Bureau top-coded wage and salary income at "75,000 dollars or more" in 1980 and "140,000 dollars or more" in 1990. In 1990, the Census Bureau replaced wage and salary incomes above 140,000 dollars with the state median of values above 140,000 dollars. To make wage computation consistent across years, I multiplied top-coded values of wage and salary income in 1980 by the state-specific ratio in 1990 of the median of values above the top-code to the top-code (140,000 dollars). Even with this imputation, the very highest earnings are understated. The small number (less than 0.2 percent) of male high school dropouts with top-coded values are concentrated in the top two percentiles of their wage residuals, however, and consequently do not seriously affect the analysis.

8. The 1980 Census measured education as highest grade attended and whether or not it was completed; the 1990 Census combined grades 1 to 4 and 5 to 8 and measured high school graduation and beyond in terms of degrees rather than years of schooling. I used the equivalents recommended by Jaeger (1997) to make the 1980 and 1990 codes commensurate. I am grateful to David Jaeger for sharing his unpublished results for grades 5-8. The equivalents for 12 years or less of schooling are:

1990 category	Highest grade completed
Grades 1–4	2.5
Grades 5–8	6.5
12th grade, no diploma	12
HS diploma or GED	12

9. Ignoring work experience before age 16 has little effect on predicted wages, since the wage-experience profile for dropouts is quite flat. Persons with negative potential experience were deleted from the samples.

10. I am greatly indebted to John Bound, who generously shared the codes used in Bound and Holzer (1996) to match 1990 PUMAs and 1980 COGRPs to 132 CMSAs/MSAs, and to Susanna Loeb, David A. Jaeger, Sarah E. Turner, and Lisa Lee, who created this code (see Jaeger [1996] for a description of the matching process). I added 15 MSAs with large numbers of Mexican Americans and 58 "balance of state" areas, making a total of 205 labor market areas that include the entire U.S. population.

11. The nonmetropolitan balance of California was divided between North and South; the balance of Texas was divided among North, East, West, Central, Gulf, and Border.

12. Note that the change in the share of the labor force with at least a twelfth-grade education is the sum of these two share changes, with the reverse sign. Thus the estimated effect of a change in the share of unskilled recent immigrants, holding constant the change in share of other unskilled workers, is the effect of substituting unskilled recent immigrants for workers with a high school education or beyond.

    The 1980 Census PUMS is a self-weighted sample; the 1990 Census is not. Throughout the analysis the 1990 data were weighted using the person weights; therefore the results represent the U.S. population.

13. Complete equalization is impossible to achieve because of varying LMA size. Moreover, because nearly 50 percent of black immigrant dropouts live in the New York/New Jersey/Connecticut CMSA and nearly 40 percent of Mexican immigrant dropouts live in the Los Angeles CMSA, it is impossible to produce three categories with even approximately equal numbers of individuals for these groups. Since Los Angeles is borderline

between "medium" and "high" for the Mexican immigrants, I classified it alternatively as "medium" and "high," adjusting the cutoff between "low" and "medium" to equalize the numbers in those two categories.

14. A few native white non-Hispanics are recorded as having less than fluent English but not enough to estimate the "price" of fluent English reliably.

15. Because the labor force is divided into three entry cohort/skill groups, their share changes sum to zero and one (ΔS_{3c}) is omitted from the model. Since ΔS_{2c} was already controlled for in step 3, a change in share of recent unskilled immigrants (ΔS_{1c}) implies an equal and opposite change in workers with at least a high-school education (group 3).

16. The shifts in the top and bottom deciles were so large that they could not be shown on the same figure with the rest of the distribution without drastically compressing the vertical scale and obscuring the differences elsewhere. As discussed in footnote 6, the tails of the distributions are affected by "wild" wage values produced by dividing annual earnings by annual hours, where both are measured with error. This study therefore focuses on shifts in the tenth to ninetieth percentile range.

17. As explained in note 13, Los Angeles is classified as "medium" in figure 4.5b and "high" in figure 4.5c, and the cutoff between "low" and "medium" is adjusted in each case to equalize (approximately) the numbers in those two categories.

18. This does not mean that the *average* residual fell; indeed, the average residual in each year is zero by construction. A pronounced "S" shape appears if the graphs are extended to the top and bottom deciles. This may reflect the presence of more extreme wage values due to reporting errors in hours and earnings in 1980 than 1990.

19. The only difference between the "high" categories in figures 4.5b and 4.5c is the absence or presence of Los Angeles. However, the composition of the "low" and "medium" categories differs considerably between the two figures.

20. The estimated effects on Mexican Americans' wage residuals were virtually the same when the quantile regressions were reestimated with the change in labor-force share of unskilled recent Hispanic immigrants as the regressor.

21. If immigrants' destinations shift rapidly enough in response to interarea shifts in Mexicans' relative wages, reverse causation may still be reflected in these results, despite my effort to reduce its influence by examining the correlation of changes in recent unskilled immigrant share with changes in the distribution of wage residuals during a single decade. Out-migration also may offset the wage-depressing effects of increased immigration. In addition, there may be unobserved area-specific factors (for example, ethnic enclaves) that are positively correlated with changes in both immi-

gration and wages, even after the changes in total employment, the unemployment rate, and the share of less-educated workers who are not recent immigrants are taken into account. Perhaps wages did in fact rise less or fall more than they would have in the absence of immigration, and this cannot be detected due to an inability to control for all the relevant factors. Nevertheless, the results of this analysis provide no support for the claim that an influx of unskilled immigrants seriously depresses the wages of disadvantaged Mexican American workers.

REFERENCES

Altonji, Joseph G., and David Card. 1991. "The Effects of Immigration on the Labor Market Outcomes of Less-Skilled Natives." In *Immigration, Trade, and the Labor Market*, edited by John M. Abowd and Richard B. Freeman. Chicago: University of Chicago Press.

Bean, Frank D., B. Lindsay Lowell, and Lowell J. Taylor. 1988. "Undocumented Mexican Immigrants and the Earnings of Other Workers in the United States." *Demography* 25(1): 35–52.

Blau, Francine D., and Lawrence M. Kahn. 1997. "Swimming Upstream: Trends in the Gender Wage Differential in the 1980s." *Journal of Labor Economics* 15(1, Part 1): 1–42.

Borjas, George J. 1987. "Immigrants, Minorities, and Labor Market Competition." *Industrial and Labor Relations Review* 40(3): 382–92.

———. 1990. *Friends or Strangers: The Impact of Immigrants on the U.S. Economy.* New York: Basic Books.

———. 1994. "The Economics of Immigration." *Journal of Economic Literature* 32(4): 1667–1717.

Borjas, George J., Richard B. Freeman, and Lawrence F. Katz. 1992. "On the Labor Market Effects of Immigration and Trade." In *Immigration and the Work Force*, edited by George J. Borjas and Richard B. Freeman. Chicago: University of Chicago Press.

———. 1996. "Searching for the Effect of Immigration on the Labor Market." *American Economic Review* 86(2): 246–51.

———. 1997. "How Much Do Immigration and Trade Affect Labor Market Outcomes?" *Brookings Papers on Economic Activity* 1: 1–90.

Bound, John and Harry J. Holzer. 1996. "Demand Shifts, Population Adjustments, and Labor Market Outcomes: 1980-1990." NBER Working Paper 5685 (July). Cambridge, Mass.: National Bureau of Economic Research.

Bratsberg, Bernt. 1996. "The Effect of Immigration on Domestic Wages: Evidence from Longitudinal Data." Kansas State University. (June). Unpublished paper.

Card, David. 1990. "The Impact of the Mariel Boatlift on the Miami Labor Market." *Industrial and Labor Relations Review* 43(2): 245–57.

————. 1996. "Immigrant Inflows, Native Outflows, and the Local Labor Market Impacts of Higher Immigration." Industrial Relations Section Working Paper no. 368, (November) Princeton, NJ: Princeton University.

DiNardo, John, Nicole M. Fortin, and Thomas Lemieux. 1996. "Labor Market Institutions and the Distribution of Wages, 1973–1992: A Semiparametric Approach." *Econometrica* 64(5): 1001–1044.

Filer, Randall K. 1992. "The Effect of Immigrant Arrivals on Migratory Patterns of Native Workers." In *Immigration and the Work Force*, edited by George J. Borjas and Richard B. Freeman. Chicago: University of Chicago Press.

Frey, William H. 1996. "Immigration, Domestic Migration, and Demographic Balkanization in America: New Evidence for the 1990s." *Population and Development Review* 22(4): 741–63.

Frey, William H., and Kao-Lee Liaw. 1996. "The Impact of Recent Immigration on Population Redistribution within the United States." Population Studies Center Research Report no. 96-376, University of Michigan (December).

Friedberg, Rachel M., and Jennifer Hunt. 1995. "The Impact of Immigrants on Host Country Wages, Employment and Growth." *Journal of Economic Perspectives* 9(2): 23–44.

Grossman, Jean B. 1982. "The Substitutability of Immigrants and Natives in Production." *Review of Economic and Statistics* 64(4): 596–603.

Jaeger, David A. 1996. "Skill Differences and the Effect of Immigrants on the Wages of Natives." U. S. Department of Labor. U.S. Bureau of Labor Statistics, Working Paper no. 273 (March). Washington: U.S. Department of Labor.

————. 1997. "Reconciling the Old and New Census Bureau Education Questions: Recommendations for Researchers." *Journal of Business and Economic Statistics* 15(3): 300–309.

Juhn, Chinhui, Kevin M. Murphy, and Brooks Pierce. 1991. "Accounting for the Slowdown in Black-White Wage Convergence." In *Workers and Their Wages*, edited by Marvin Kosters. Washington, D.C.: AEI Press.

————. 1993. "Wage Inequality and the Rise in Returns to Skill." *Journal of Political Economy* 101(3): 410–42.

LaLonde, Robert J., and Robert H. Topel. 1991. "Labor Market Adjustments to Increased Immigration." In *Immigration, Trade, and the Labor Market*, edited by John M. Abowd and Richard B. Freeman. Chicago: University of Chicago Press.

Mines, Richard, and Jeffrey Avina. 1993. "Immigrants and Labor Standards: The Case of California Janitors." In *U.S. Mexican Relations: Labor Market Interdependence*, edited by Jorge A. Bustamente, Clark W. Reynolds, and Raul A. Hinojosa-Ojeda. Stanford, Cal.: Stanford University Press.

Schoeni, Robert F. 1997. "The Effect of Immigrants on the Employment and Wages of Native Workers: Evidence from the 1970s and 1980s." RAND (March). Unpublished paper.

CHAPTER 5

An Investigation of the Effect of Immigration on the Labor-Market Outcomes of African Americans

Kristin F. Butcher

The effect of immigration on the labor-market outcomes of the native born has historically been the most contentious issue surrounding the debate about how many immigrants to allow into the United States. As Claudia Goldin (1993) remarks in her paper on the political economy of immigration restriction, "Almost all serious calls for . . . [immigration restriction] . . . were preceded by economic downturns, some of major proportions, and few economic downturns of the era were not accompanied by a call for restriction in the halls of Congress." Currently the United States is not experiencing an economic downturn, but the 1980s witnessed an unprecedented change in the wage distribution. Native-born workers with low skills have experienced a decline in real wages, and the gap between the wages of workers with high and low skills has expanded. Since African Americans are overrepresented among low-skilled workers, this led to increasing wage disparity between white non-Hispanic workers and African Americans.

The reasons for the increase in the wage gap between high- and low-skilled workers is hotly debated in labor economics. The explanations range from skill-based technological change to changes of the role of labor-market institutions to changes in labor supply. Since immigration levels in the 1980s were higher than in any decade since the turn of the century, immigration is potentially a key player in increasing the supply of labor.[1] Additionally, on average the characteristics of immigrants in the 1980s are different from those of native-born United States citizens. While the proportion of immigrants with college education is about the same as among the native born, there is a much higher fraction of immigrants with less than a high school diploma. Immigrants in the 1980s were also more likely to be Hispanic or Asian than earlier immigrants or the native born. These changes in immigrant characteristics imply that immigrants may have substantially increased the supply of low-skilled workers in some areas. The question this study investigates is whether an increase in the fraction immigrant in an area is correlated with adverse labor-market outcomes for African Americans.

This is a question that has been addressed in other research. Most of the literature using data from the 1970s and 1980s found few effects of immigration on the labor-market outcomes of the native born. However, there are several reasons why it is worth revisiting this issue here. First of all, things may have changed since the 1970s and 1980s. We know that immigration has increased and the compositional changes that began in the early 1970s continued. We also know that the labor market facing African Americans has changed. Thus updating earlier work with data from more recent time periods is a useful exercise.

Of course, there are also several current papers that use recent data to investigate these issues. I will present a brief overview of the current literature on the impact of immigration on the labor-market outcomes of African Americans and low-skilled, native-born workers, borrowing heavily from two recent and thorough reviews by Borjas (1994) and Friedberg and Hunt (1995).

The problem with comparing results across different studies is that all may use different techniques, different data, or focus on a different group of native-born workers. In studying the effect of immigration on labor-market outcomes of the native born, one has to make several decisions: which techniques to use, which group of native-born workers to focus on, whether to use nominal or relative outcomes, and so on. The results may be sensitive to each of these decisions. The goal here is to use a variety of techniques on the same data to see how sensitive the results are to these differences.

I analyze the effects of immigration on four different labor market outcomes: employment, weeks worked, log hourly wages, and total annual earnings. I start by investigating whether the estimated impact of immigration on the labor-market outcomes of the native born is sensitive to whether unadjusted or adjusted metropolitan level means are used to measure those outcomes. I then compare the estimated effect of immigration on the 1980 to 1990 change in black labor market outcomes to the effect of immigration on the 1980 to 1990 change in white-black *gaps* in labor market outcomes. I also examine whether the choice of comparison group affects these relative outcome measures. Since the African American community is heterogeneous, and the effects of immigration may differ across skill or demographic groups, I estimate the effects of immigration on the labor-market outcomes for six different groups of African Americans: all black men, young black men, black men with less than a high school degree as well as all black women, young black women, and black women with less than a high school degree. Immigrants are also a heterogeneous group and the "type" of immigrant who enters an area may affect labor-market outcomes. I investigate whether the impact of immigration differs according to whether the immigrants are young, Hispanic, or have less than a high school degree. Finally, I use two different techniques to try to control for estimation problems that arise because immigrant inflows, native-born inflows and outflows, and labor-market outcomes may all be simultaneously determined.

In general, the findings are consistent with the previous literature and with the studies in this volume by Meyer and Fairlie and by Reimers. I estimate small and imprecise effects of immigration on employment, weeks, and hourly wage rates of all groups of African Americans. On the other hand, I find a significant impact from an increase in the fraction immigrant in a geographic area on the change in the white-black gap in annual earnings. An increase in the immigrant share appears to increase the gap in annual earnings between white non-Hispanic men and all groups of African Americans considered. Depending on the group under study, the 3.3-percentage-point increase in the immigrant share in metropolitan areas between 1980 and 1990 increased the white-black annual earnings gap by between 275 dollars to 666 dollars. Although these changes are statistically significant, the response of the white-black gap to changes in the immigrant share is small. The implied elasticity ranges from 0.04 to 0.38 (depending on the group and estimation strategy considered).

PREVIOUS LITERATURE

The literature on the effect of immigration on the labor-market outcomes of the native born has been recently and ably reviewed by George Borjas (1994) and by Rachel Friedberg and Jennifer Hunt (1995). I will now briefly revisit some of the points made in those papers, and discuss more recent evidence. As both literature reviews point out, the study of the effect of immigration on the labor market outcomes of the native born has taken three approaches: production function studies, geographic area studies, and natural experiments. Each of these approaches has its own benefits and problems.

Production Functions

The production function approach computes elasticities of substitution between immigrants and the native born. The benefit of this approach is that it allows one to determine the effect of immigrants on other factor prices. The drawback is that it requires fairly restrictive assumptions about the form of the production function.

Using the production function approach and data from the 1980 Census, Borjas (1987) reports that black native-born men may have experienced an increase in their earnings due to the increase in immigrant labor. Elasticities calculated from his estimates range from -0.03 to 0.02. More recent work by David Jaeger (1996) finds much larger adverse effects on the wages of some native-born workers. While that work does not specifically investigate the impact of immigration on the wages of African Americans, it does investigate the effects by skill group. Not surprisingly, Jaeger finds immigration has a particularly detrimental effect on the wages of the native born for whom immigrants are most closely substitutable, that is, high school dropouts. Depending on the assumptions about the production function, Jaeger finds that immigration can account for approximately 1.5 to 3 percentage points of a 10-percentage-point decline in their real wages over the 1980s. To the extent that African Americans are overrepresented among high school dropouts, this work suggests that they may have suffered from the increase in immigration during the 1980s.

Geographic Area Studies

Geographic area studies exploit the fact that immigration is geographically concentrated. These studies usually investigate whether the native born who live in metropolitan areas with heavier concentrations of immigrants have worse labor-market outcomes. While this approach sounds straightforward, there are several problems that may make the results unreliable. First of all, using a cross section to investigate how the wage levels of the native born vary with the fraction immigrant in a metropolitan area yields large positive and significant effects. This is primarily because immigrants tend to locate in large cities with high costs of living and high wage rates.

A second approach to the metropolitan area data is to use data from two time periods and estimate first differences. This approach investigates whether the change in labor-market outcomes for the native born over time is affected by changes in the immigrant concentration. Using the change in metropolitan-level outcomes controls for any fixed differences between cities. If immigrants tend to locate in cities with permanently higher wage rates (due to permanent cost of living effects), then this will be controlled for using this approach.

However, further difficulties remain. If immigrants migrate to cities that are currently booming, then an increase in the fraction immigrant is correlated with transitory changes in the local labor market. This will tend to bias results away from finding an adverse effect of immigration on labor-market outcomes. Although labor-market outcomes may look fairly good in these metropolitan areas, the question one would like to answer is "what would the labor market have looked like if the immigrants had not come." If it would have looked even better, then one could say the immigrants had an adverse effect.

A related issue has to do with the fact that natives may respond quickly to labor-market conditions in their own or other metropolitan areas. If the native born move out as immigrants move in or fail to move into places they otherwise would have, then any adverse effects of immigration will be dampened by this "factor-price equalization."

One approach to both of these issues is to find a suitable instrument for the change in the fraction immigrant in an area. A suitable instrument would be something that is highly correlated with the change in the fraction immigrant but uncorrelated with the change in the labor-market outcome under study. Altonji and Card (1991) suggest using the initial stock of immigrants in a metropolitan area as an instrument for the change in the fraction foreign born. Altonji and Card study the impact of an increase in the immigrant concentration in Standard Metropolitan Statistical Areas (SMSAs) on the labor-market outcomes of low-skilled natives between 1970 and 1980 using the U.S. Census. The estimates control for average age, education, and total population in each metropolitan area. For black men with less than thirteen years of education, their approach yields a negative effect of immigration on the fraction employed in the previous year (although the effect is not statistically significant). They do find a negative and significant effect of an increase in the fraction immigrant on log earnings per week. Their estimate suggests that a 1-percentage-point increase in the fraction immigrant would reduce the earnings per week of black men with low levels of education by at most 1.9 percent. Their results for black women with less than thirteen years of education are similar: a negative but insignificant result for fraction employed and a negative and marginally significant effect on log earnings per week (-1.4 percent). On the other hand, they find that immigration unexpectedly improves the unemployment rate and has no significant effect on labor force participation.

Altonji and Card found small effects of immigration on the labor market outcomes of the less skilled. However, much may have changed since the 1970 and 1980 Census data were collected. A recent paper by Robert Schoeni (1996) uses similar techniques but includes data from the 1990 Census. This not only includes more recent data; it also allows for more efficient instrumental variables estimates, since the initial stock of immigrants in 1970 and 1980 can be used to predict the change in foreign born between 1980 and 1990. Additionally, Schoeni uses metropolitan area–specific cost-of-living adjustments in order to control for the fact that wages may increase more rapidly in areas where the foreign-born population increased, merely because the cost of living rose more quickly. The benefits of adjusting for cost of living using an appropriate city-specific price deflator are clear; however, there are problems with the price deflator used here (ACCRA index),[2] since it is difficult to gauge how accurate the data are, and because the data are only available for a small subset of the cities.[3]

For black male high school dropouts in the 1970s, Schoeni finds a negative and marginally significant effect of immigration on labor force participation, no effect on employment, a negative effect on weekly wages, and no effect on annual earnings. In the 1980s, these effects change. He reports no effect on participation, weekly wages, or annual earnings but a negative effect on employment. For black female high school dropouts, he finds negative effects on weekly wages and annual earnings and no effect on employment or participation in the 1970s. In the 1980s, he finds significant effects on participation and annual earnings but none for employment and (marginally significant) weekly wages.

The analysis for blacks with more education is different in the 1980s. Black male high school graduates experienced adverse effects on employment in the 1980s but no other effects. Black female high school graduates experienced negative effects on employment in the 1980s, but *positive* effects on weekly wages. Black males with more than a high school diploma experienced a tiny negative effect on employment and no other effects. Black women with more than a high school degree were not affected by immigration in the 1980s.

A recent paper by Bernt Bratsberg (1996) takes a different approach to the geographic area studies. This study uses data from the National Longitudinal Survey of Youth (NLSY) to get information on the wages and annual earnings of individuals. Data from the U.S. Censuses and from the Immigration and Naturalization Service are then used to calculate the fraction immigrant in an individual's county in each year. These data are then merged with the individual data. Bratsberg finds that the elasticity of black male wages with respect to the fraction immigrant in the county is -0.07. The elasticity for black male annual earnings is substantially higher, -0.14.

Natural Experiments

A final approach to estimating the impact of immigration on the labor market outcomes of the native born is to use a "natural experiment." Many of the problems cited with the above work stem from the fact that local labor-market conditions may influence both the wage and employment outcomes of the native born in those locations and the decision of immigrants to settle there (and possibly the decisions of the native born to move in or out of those areas). One way around this problem is to analyze the effect of an exogenous inflow of immigrants. An example of such a study is David Card's work (1990) on the impact of the Mariel boatlift on the wages and employment of the native born in Miami. Of particular interest here are Card's findings on the impact of the Mariel immigrants on the labor-market outcomes of blacks and blacks with low levels of education. The Mariel immigrants were on average low skilled and might have been expected to act as substitutes for black workers in Miami. Card uses Current Population Survey data to investigate employment and wages of blacks in Miami compared to cities that did not experience this exogenous increase in the size of the immigrant population. He finds few effects of this large inflow of immigrants on the labor-market outcomes of blacks in Miami. In 1979, for example, adjusted wages for black workers in Miami were 15 percent lower than in comparison cities. By 1985, this figure was only 1 percent. The outcomes for blacks with low levels of education are even more striking: the adjusted wage comparison went from 15 percent less in Miami in 1979 to 9 percent *higher* in 1985. The effects on employment-population ratios and unemployment rates were negligible. Although this type of study may also suffer from the factor price equalization problem—with the native born moving out of an area (or failing to move in) and offsetting the adverse effects of immigration—it is worth noting that factor price equalization is a long-run concept. Card uses year to year changes over a seven-year period and finds few effects. If natives are acting to offset the effects of immigration, the adjustment happens very quickly.

This brief summary of the literature suggests several things. First, there are many different approaches to addressing the effect of immigration on the labor-market outcomes of immigrants. These different approaches may yield different results. Second, the time period under study appears to matter. The studies focusing on immigration in the 1970s seem to find few effects. However, as the Schoeni study shows, the effects may be different in the 1980s.

DATA

I analyze the effects of an increase in the fraction immigrant in a metropolitan area on changes in the labor-market outcomes for African Americans. I use the 1 percent Public Use Microdata Samples of the

1980 and 1990 U.S. Census. In order to perform this analysis one needs to match metropolitan areas across the two Census years. Because of demographic changes over the decade, there have been substantial changes in the Census definitions of metropolitan regions between 1980 and 1990. In many cases, the Census Bureau tightened its definition of a metropolitan area, dropping some less-populated areas on the fringes. These types of changes could generate spurious correlations between changes in labor-market outcomes and immigrant concentrations. For example, low-wage areas on the fringe of a metropolitan area might be dropped from the Census definition of a particular area. If immigrants tend to locate in densely populated sections of metropolitan regions, this change will make both the wage rate and the fraction immigrant appear to increase, without any real underlying change in the labor market. A consistent matching of metropolitan areas between the two decades is very important.

Unfortunately, a consistent matching is a very difficult and time-consuming thing to create. In this analysis, I rely on the matching scheme employed in Bound and Holzer (1996) that uses the state and county group codes in 1980 and the state and PUMA (public use microdata area) codes in 1990 to create consistent geographic areas.[4] I will refer to these areas as "metropolitan areas."

Using these consistent definitions of metropolitan areas, I run regressions on the individual-level employment probabilities, weeks worked, log hourly wages, and annual earnings for various groups of African Americans. The employment variable is equal to 1 if the individual reports having worked a positive number of weeks in the previous year and has positive earnings. Log hourly wages are constructed from the information on total annual wage and salary earnings, total weeks worked, and usual hours worked per week. Number of weeks is the total number of weeks individuals report for a given year. Only those with positive weeks and valid wages are included here. The annual earnings variable is total wage and salary earnings reported in the Census. I use this variable to investigate the cumulative effect of immigration, whether through employment, wages, or weeks worked on the earnings of the native born. Therefore, zeros are included and I use this variable in levels, not logs.

The data used in these regressions include African American men and women between the ages of sixteen and sixty-four, inclusive. Individuals born in United States outlying areas (for example, Puerto Ricans) have been dropped from the analysis. The regressions include a dummy variable for each metropolitan area, and the constant has been suppressed. I use the coefficients from these fixed effects as the left-hand side variables in the subsequent analysis.

I also compute the demographic characteristics for each metropolitan area. The variable of most interest here is the fraction of the population that is foreign born. I also calculate the fraction of the population that is young and foreign born, Hispanic and foreign born, and foreign born with low levels of education. In order to capture demographic changes that are not related to immigration, I calculate changes in demographic composition of the metropolitan areas among the native born only. The data for these calculations include all individuals, including those born in the United States outlying areas who are counted among the native born. For the results presented here I include only the fifty largest metropolitan areas. Using only the larger metropolitan areas means that the labor-market outcomes under study and the demographic characteristics of the geographic areas are more reliably estimated. However, the results are not qualitatively different when I include all metropolitan areas.

Table 5.1 presents information on some of the demographic changes that took place between 1980 and 1990. The information is presented for three different geographic areas: metropolitan areas, states, and Census divisions. The first four columns of table 5.1 show the changes in the immigrant share for various groups of immigrant. The fraction of the population that is foreign born increased over the decade by an average of 3.3 percentage points in metropolitan areas. Since immigrants are more likely to settle in metropolitan areas than are the native born, the fraction immigrant increased more in these areas than at the state or division level. The changes in the fractions of subgroups of immigrants follow a similar pattern.

While immigration has been an important component of demographic change over the past decade, it is certainly not the only contributing factor. Demographic characteristics among the native born have changed as well. These changes in the native-born population may be correlated with changes in immigration and may also have effects on (and be influenced by) changes in the labor market. The last three columns of table 5.1 show the changes in the fraction black, Hispanic, and those with less than a high school degree among the native born. The fraction black and Hispanic have both increased. The fraction of the native born with very low levels of education has declined over the decade.

EMPIRICAL STRATEGY

As I indicated earlier, there are many different comparisons that one can make. Should one look at a straight cross-sectional comparison? Should one adjust the outcomes for individual level characteristics? Should one look at changes for one particular group, or relative

Table 5.1 Summary Statistics: Changes in Selected Demographic Variables, 1990 to 1980 (Standard Errors)

	Change in Fraction Immigrant	Change in Fraction Young Immigrant	Change in Fraction Hispanic Immigrant	Change in Fraction Immigrant with Low Education	Among Native-Born Only		
					Change in Fraction Black	Change in Fraction Hispanic	Change in Fraction with Low Education
Metro-level	0.033 (0.0068)	0.013 (0.0027)	0.017 (0.0046)	0.011 (0.0039)	0.007 (0.0091)	0.014 (0.0063)	−0.082 (0.0085)
State-level	0.023 (0.0033)	0.008 (0.0012)	0.010 (0.0020)	0.006 (0.0016)	0.007 (0.0016)	0.006 (0.0011)	−0.085 (0.0033)
Division-level	0.027 (0.0089)	0.010 (0.0032)	0.013 (0.0057)	0.009 (0.0047)	0.005 (0.0026)	0.007 (0.0041)	−0.082 (0.0054)

Sources: Data are from the 1980 and 1990 (1 percent) PUMS of the U.S. Census. Ages sixteen to sixty-four are included. Only the fifty largest metropolitan areas are included in the metropolitan-level results. The means are weighted in proportion to the sample size. "Low Education" means less than a high school degree.

changes? If one looks at relative wages, then relative to whom? Immigrants may have different effects on different groups, so which group should be the focus? Finally, does the effect of immigration depend on the characteristics of the immigrants? I analyze how robust the estimated effects of immigration are to differences in the analytical approach. All of the estimates rely on some form of geographic analysis, but I vary the group under inspection, the comparison group, the estimation strategy, and the level of aggregation. I will describe each comparison in turn.

Changes in Labor-Market Outcomes for Native-Born African American Men: Adjusted Versus Unadjusted Outcomes

As was discussed earlier, it is well known that a cross-sectional regression of wages, for example, on the fraction immigrant in a city yields a large positive coefficient. This is likely to be spurious because immigrants tend to locate in large cities with high costs of living. For this reason, I concentrate on investigating whether changes in the fraction immigrant in a geographic area can explain changes in labor-market outcomes between 1980 and 1990. This strategy controls for any area-level fixed effects that might affect immigration and labor-market outcomes. In effect, this answers whether the immigrant inflow during the 1980s adversely affected native-born labor-market outcomes. This is not the same thing as asking whether the stock of immigrants adversely affects labor-market outcomes. However, questions about the flow of immigrants are of policy import: the immigration policy under current debate revolves around restricting the future flow of immigrants, not around wide-scale deportation.

Consider table 5.2. In this table I limit the focus to the employment, weeks worked, log hourly wages, and annual earnings of native-born African American men.[5] The top panel shows the results when the left-hand-side variable is the change in the unadjusted metro-area mean. The bottom panel contains the results when the left-hand-side variable is the change in the adjusted metro-area mean. For example, in the first column, bottom panel, I first estimated a linear probability model for employment, controlling for age, age squared, marital status, and education for black native-born men in 1980 and 1990. A dummy variable for each metropolitan area was included. I took these fixed-effect coefficients and matched the metropolitan areas between the two years. The left-hand-side variable is the 1990 coefficient minus the 1980 coefficient. Because the amount of data for each metropolitan area varies, the precision of the estimate of the mean for each area will vary.[6] To take this into account, each of the regressions presented here uses the inverse

Table 5.2   Estimated Effect of a Change in Metropolitan-Level
Immigrant Share on the Change in African American
Men's Labor-Market Outcomes (Standard Errors)

	Employment	Weeks	Log Hourly Wages	Annual Earnings
	Unadjusted*			
1990 − 1980 change	0.098	2.291	0.817	14015.95
in fraction immigrant	(0.3643)	(7.507)	(0.5119)	(11084.67)
R-squared	0.0034	0.0020	0.0604	0.0382
	Adjusted*			
1990 − 1980 change	0.185	−6.182	0.401	6605.75
in fraction immigrant	(0.3608)	(5.872)	(0.4369)	(9738.25)
R-squared	0.0150	0.0241	0.0170	0.0132

Sources: Data are from the 1980 and 1990 (1 percent) PUMS of the U.S. Census. Ages sixteen to sixty-four are included. The results are from weighted ordinary least squares, where the inverse of the standard error of the left-hand-side variable is used as the weight. A constant is included, but not reported.
*The unadjusted left-hand-side variables are the changes in the mean of the metropolitan-area-level variable between 1990 and 1980. The adusted left-hand side-variables are the metropolitan area means adjusting for age, age^2, high school dropout, high school degree, some college education, and marital status. The data include only the fifty largest metropolitan areas.

of the standard errors of the left-hand-side variable as the weights.[7] The smaller the standard error, the greater the weight.

Table 5.2 presents evidence on whether native-born black men in areas where immigrant concentrations rose experienced less growth in nominal wages and smaller increases in employment, weeks worked, and nominal annual earnings. The first entry in column one shows a positive coefficient of 0.098. This implies that a 1-percentage-point increase in the immigrant share increases the fraction employed by 0.098 percentage points, although the effect is statistically insignificant. The difference between the top and bottom panels shows whether using adjusted or unadjusted metro-level outcomes affects the analysis. Adjusting the outcome variable for the underlying characteristics of the population roughly doubles the size of this coefficient, but it is still imprecisely estimated. The second column shows the effect of a change in the fraction immigrant on weeks worked. The unadjusted coefficient is positive and the adjusted coefficient is negative, but neither is significantly different from zero. The third column shows that an increase in the fraction immigrant was correlated with an increase in the growth of black men's wages during the 1980s. Again, however, the effect is very imprecisely estimated. Although the two estimates are not statistically significantly different from one another, the adjusted estimate is smaller than the unadjusted estimate. The last column presents results for annual earnings. A 1-percentage-point increase in the immigrant share is associated with a one hundred forty dollar increase in annual earnings, although the estimate is statistically insignificant. The adjusted estimate is roughly half the unadjusted estimate.

The fact that adjusting the left-hand-side variables for the underlying characteristics of the native born reduces the size of the estimates for wages and annual earnings suggests that immigration may be correlated with the characteristics of the native born that affect their earnings. Immigrants may be living in the same metropolitan areas as the native born who experienced more wage growth during the 1980s. In order to keep this effect from confounding the influence of immigration on labor-market outcomes, I will use the adjusted left-hand-side variables in the analyses that follow.

As discussed earlier, one may be skeptical of whether this analysis has any causal interpretation. Although the results are insignificant, they imply better outcomes for black men in areas with a larger immigrant inflow during the 1980s. This could come about for many reasons other than immigrants actually creating a better labor market environment for native-born blacks. One possible explanation is simply that immigrants moved to fast-growing regions with a larger increase in the cost of living during the 1980s. One approach to correcting this problem is to use a metropolitan area price deflator as in Schoeni (1996). However, this limits the number of metropolitan regions that can be used and is only as good as the price deflator. Another approach is to investigate whether immigration affected the relative changes in labor-market outcomes for blacks.

Relative Labor-Market Outcomes for Black and White Non-Hispanic Men

The ideal comparison group for this "differences-in-differences" analysis is one that experiences exactly the same labor market shocks as the group under study, except for the shock whose effect we are interested in. In other words, we would like a control group that is affected by precisely the same labor-market conditions as African Americans, except that they are not affected by the inflow of immigrants. Such a comparison group is difficult to find. Since immigrants may be substitutes or complements for different groups of workers, we cannot be sure that immigrants have no effect on any one group. Therefore, we cannot be sure that the estimates are telling us whether immigration is correlated with, for example, worse outcomes for black men or better outcomes for the comparison group. Second, if the comparison group is unaffected by the immigration shock, then it is less compelling to argue that they experience other labor-market changes in the same way. With those cautions in mind, I will use white non-Hispanic men as the comparison group. Much of the literature has found small effects on the labor-market outcomes of white non-Hispanic men. In some cases, the effects appear to be positive. In addition, since black-white wage differentials are of interest in and of themselves, white men seem a reasonable group against which to benchmark the changes in blacks' labor-market outcomes. Since immigrants are, on average, unlikely to be substitutes for those with high levels of education, and because we know that differences in labor-market outcomes between skill groups became particularly important during the 1980s, I show the results using two different comparison groups: all white non-Hispanic men[8] and white non-Hispanic men with at least some college education.

Table 5.3 presents the results. Recall that the left-hand-side variables have all been adjusted for the underlying human capital characteristics of the native born. The top panel reproduces the results from the previous table: these are nominal changes for all black men. The next two panels show the results for the change in the white-black gaps. The left-hand-side variables are defined as the white-black gap in 1990 minus the white-black gap in 1980. A positive coefficient, therefore, indicates that an increase in the fraction immigrant exacerbated the difference between whites and blacks over the decade.

The first column shows that the white-black gap in employment shrank in areas that experienced an increase in immigrant concentration. This effect is statistically insignificant, and the difference between the two comparison groups of whites has no effect on the analysis. The second column shows that an increase in the fraction immigrant was associated with an increase in the gap in number of weeks worked. Similarly, the gap in log hourly wages is positively correlated with the change in the fraction immigrant. Again, both the weeks and wages effects are very imprecisely estimated, and the difference between the comparison groups seems to have little effect on the point estimate.

The fourth column shows a different outcome: the white-black gap in annual earnings increased significantly in regions that experienced

Table 5.3   Estimated Effect of a Change in Metropolitan-Level
Immigrant Share on the Change in Labor-Market
Outcomes for All African American Men Using Different
Comparison Groups (Standard Errors)

	Employment	Weeks	Log Hourly Wages	Annual Earnings
	Change for All Black Men			
1990 − 1980 change	0.185	−6.182	0.401	6605.75
in fraction immigrant	(0.3608)	(5.872)	(0.4369)	(9738.25)
R-squared	0.0034	0.0241	0.0170	0.0132
	Change in the Gap Between All White Men and All Black Men			
1990 − 1980 change	−0.143	9.233	0.200	19339.16
in fraction immigrant	(0.3261)	(5.660)	(0.2065)	(6657.10)
R-squared	0.0105	0.0529	0.0084	0.133
	Change in the Gap Between White College Educated Men and All Black Men*			
1990 − 1980 change	−0.143	10.400	0.224	25379.97
in fraction immigrant	(0.3259)	(6.369)	(0.2306)	(8077.10)
R-squared	0.0104	0.0579	0.0094	0.1524

Sources: Data are from the 1980 and 1990 (1 percent) PUMS of the U.S. Census. Ages sixteen to sixty-four are included. The results are from weighted ordinary least squares, where the inverse of the standard error of the left-hand-side variable is used as the weight. A constant is included, but not reported. Only the fifty largest metropolitan areas are included here.

Notes:The left-hand-side variables have been adjusted for age, age^2, high school dropout, high school diploma, some college education, and marital status. The white-black gaps are defined as: (W90-B90)-(W80-B80).

*"College educated" refers to those with at least some college education.

an increase in immigrant share. This effect is significant whether we compare black men to all white men or to white men with some college education. As would be expected, the comparison to better-educated white men shows a larger increase in the gap. The estimates suggest that a 1-percentage-point increase in the fraction immigrant results in about a 193 dollar increase in the gap in annual earnings between African American men and white men. This figure for the gap between black men and white men with some college education is about 254 dollars. The implied elasticities at the mean are 0.16 and 0.13, respectively.[9]

This annual earnings figure is for all individuals in the data. A gap in annual earnings can result because of differences in labor force participation, employment, wages, weeks worked, and hours worked per week. Although there are no significant effects on any of these individual components, there is no necessary conflict with the fact that the annual earnings gap grows; this merely indicates that the covariances among the components are such that the total gap in annual earnings is significantly affected. The total weeks outcome does not add much information to the analysis and will be dropped in the subsequent tables.

Up to now I have only presented results for black men. There are several reasons why we might expect the results to vary by demographic and skill groups. Additionally, we might worry more if immigration adversely affects the labor-market outcomes of young black men or young black women, for example, more than other groups, since poor labor-market outcomes for these groups are thought to be connected with other adverse outcomes, for example, crime or welfare participation. I will now investigate the impact of immigration on several different groups of African Americans.

Relative Labor-Market Outcomes for Various Groups of African Americans

There are good reasons to suspect that the impact of immigration differs according to skill level and/or demographic group. In their analysis of immigrant concentrations by industry, Altonji and Card (1991) find that in 1980 the ten highest immigrant-share industries also employed a high proportion of native-born women, particularly black women.[10] In fact, Altonji and Card report that black men tended to be least concentrated in the ten most immigrant-intensive industries. Perhaps the negligible impact of immigrants on the employment and wages of black men reported in tables 5.2 and 5.3 simply indicates that this is not a group in direct competition with immigrants, and we might find larger effects if we analyze outcomes for other groups.

Table 5.4 presents the results for several different groups of African Americans. The first row repeats the results for all black men. The other groups are young black men (age sixteen to twenty-nine), black men with less than a high school diploma, all black women, young black women, and black women with less than a high school diploma. The left-hand-side variables here are the (adjusted) change in the white-black gap in the relevant outcome variable. All white men are used as the comparison group. One could imagine using white women, for ex-

Table 5.4 Estimated Effect of a Change in Metropolitan-Level
Immigrant Share on the White Male/African American
Gap in Labor-Market Outcomes for Various Groups of
African Americans (Standard Errors)

	Employment	Log Hourly Wages	Annual Earnings
All Black Men			
1990 − 1980 change in	−0.143	0.200	19339.16
fraction immigrant	(0.3261)	(0.2065)	(66571.1)
R-squared	0.0105	0.0084	0.1339
Young Black Men (16–29)			
1990 − 1980 change in	0.034	−0.527	15577.39
fraction immigrant	(0.4125)	(0.4104)	(7877.98)
R-squared	0.0003	0.0200	0.1118
Black Men with Less than a High School Diploma			
1990 − 1980 change in	−0.101	−0.233	20830.20
fraction immigrant	(0.5383)	(0.4730)	(10152.25)
R-squared	0.0021	0.0042	0.1297
All Black Women			
1990 − 1980 change in	−0.006	0.011	11590.74
fraction immigrant	(0.1625)	(0.3400)	(6090.57)
R-squared	0.0000	0.000	0.0867
Young Black Women (16–29)			
1990 − 1980 change in	0.555	0.546	8595.34
fraction immigrant	(0.3679)	(0.7848)	(8073.93)
R-squared	0.0534	0.0150	0.0354
Black Women with Less than a High School Diploma			
1990 − 1980 change in	0.077	0.234	24828.78
fraction immigrant	(0.4081)	(0.9669)	(8406.49)
R-squared	0.0007	0.0015	0.1496

Sources: Data are from the 1980 and 1990 (1 percent) PUMS of the U.S. Census. Ages sixteen to sixty-four are included. The results are from weighted ordinary least squares, where the inverse of the standard error of the left-hand-side variable is used as the weight. A constant is included, but not reported. The data include only the fifty largest metropolitan areas. The sample size is forty-nine for those with less than a high school degree, and fifty for all others.

Notes: The left-hand-side variables are metropolitan area means that have been adjusted for age, age^2, high school dropout, high school diploma, some college education, and marital status. White is actually white non-Hispanic here. The white-black gaps are defined as: (W90-B90)-(W80-B80).

ample, as the comparison group for black women, but it seems reasonable to use a consistent benchmark. This way any differences in the results must be due to differences in the effects on the group of black workers under study.

Once again, we see that an increase in the fraction immigrant in a metropolitan area has no effect on relative employment, regardless of the group of African Americans considered. Turning to log hourly wages, most of the coefficients are positive, except in the case of young black men and black men with less than a high school education. Once again, however, the results are statistically insignificant. This story changes in the last column: an increase in the immigrant share is associated with a statistically significant increase in the annual earnings gap between white males and all groups of African Americans except for young black women. For young black women, the effects are similarly positive but less precisely estimated. Although the estimates are not significantly different from one another, the results tend to indicate that the largest effect is on the relative annual earnings of poorly educated black men and women.

The results for black men with low levels of education are corroborated by Altonji and Card (1991), who report negative effects of an increase in immigrant concentrations on the change in log weeks worked for native-born black men with less than thirteen years of education between 1970 and 1980. Altonji and Card, however, report *positive* effects on the change in weeks worked for black women with low levels of education during this time period. It is, of course, possible that the effect of immigration changed for this group of women between 1980 and 1990. The results here suggest a larger impact on annual earnings than other labor market outcomes. This is consistent with Bratsberg (1996), who reports larger adverse effects of immigration on annual earnings than on hourly wages.

Two-Stage Least Squares

As discussed earlier, the estimates presented thus far may not have a causal interpretation. Estimating the equations in first differences will control for any area-level fixed effects, but if changes in immigrant concentrations are correlated with transitory labor-market conditions, then the coefficient estimates from the first differences will still be biased. For example, if immigrants and the native born both move to fast-growing areas with high wage growth, then population increases will be positively correlated with wage increases.[11] If the inflow of immigrants is proportionally larger than the inflow of the native born, then the fraction immigrant will rise and will appear to be positively related to growth in wages.

An appropriate technique for dealing with this type of bias is to find an instrument for the change in the fraction immigrant that is uncorrelated with the changes in labor-market outcomes under study. Altonji and Card (1991) suggest using the initial fraction immigrant as such an instrument. Immigrants tend to move where previous immigrants live, perhaps to live with relatives or friends until they find their own housing or to take advantage of labor-market contacts. In the data used here, the regression of change in the fraction immigrant on the initial stock of immigrants in 1980 has a coefficient of 0.405 with a t-statistic of about three. As long as the initial stock of immigrants does not belong in the regressions for changes in the labor-market outcomes, it is a suitable instrument. This technique should eliminate the bias associated with immigrants moving to fast-growing areas and with the bias toward zero that arises if the native born move to equalize factor prices across the country.

Table 5.5 presents the two-stage least squares results for all the different demographic and skill groups listed in table 5.4. The first column reports the two-stage least squares estimates for employment. Although all the coefficients are now positive, indicating that an increase in the fraction immigrant increases the white-black gap in employment, none are significant. The second column reports the estimates for relative log hourly wages. The results for less-educated black men, all black women, and young black women have changed sign from the ordinary least squares (OLS) results. For the results that are of the same sign as the OLS, the instrumental variables (IV) estimates tend to be larger in magnitude. However, none of the IV estimates is significant. The third column reports the IV estimates for the change in the gap in white-black annual earnings. Here there are substantial differences from the OLS estimates. All of the effects are much larger than the OLS, and most are at least marginally significantly different from zero. Like the OLS results, the biggest effects are for the change in the white-black earnings gap for black men and women with less than a high school diploma. The results indicate that a 1-percentage-point increase in the fraction immigrant leads to 637 dollars and 691 dollars increases in the gaps in annual earnings between white men and poorly educated black men and women, respectively. The implied elasticities are 0.38 and 0.31. These results suggest that the OLS results for the effect of an increase in immigration on the white-black earnings gap may be biased toward zero.

Table 5.5   Estimated Effect of a Change in Metropolitan-Level
Immigrant Share on the White Male/African American
Gap in Labor-Market Outcomes for Various Groups of
African Americans: Two Stage Least Squares* (Standard
Errors)

	Employment	Log Hourly Wages	Annual Earnings
All Black Men			
1990 − 1980 change in fraction immigrant	0.140 (0.3617)	0.276 (.05596)	45191.27 (26471.03)
Young Black Men (16–29)			
1990 − 1980 change in fraction immigrant	0.945 (0.5867)	−1.775 (1.209)	51362.99 (26503.96)
Black Men with Less than a High School Diploma			
1990 − 1980 change in fraction immigrant	0.801 (0.5200)	0.405 (1.242)	63734.66 (35979.73)
All Black Women			
1990 − 1980 change in fraction immigrant	0.261 (0.4533)	−0.347 (0.6777)	42332.5 (28376.14)
Young Black Women (16–29)			
1990 − 1980 change in fraction immigrant	1.881 (1.455)	−1.589 (1.560)	45324.96 (27375.92)
Black Women with Less than a High School Diploma			
1990 − 1980 change in fraction immigrant	0.373 (0.6639)	0.835 (1.546)	69162.36 (39775.00)

Sources: Data are from the 1980 and 1990 (1 percent) PUMS of the U.S. Census. Ages sixteen to sixty-four are included. The results are from weighted regressions, where the inverse of the standard error of the left-hand-side variable is used as the weight. A constant is included, but not reported. The data include only the fifty largest metropolitan areas. The sample size is forty-nine for those with less than a high school degree, and fifty for all others.

Notes: The left-hand-side variables are metropolitan area means that have been adjusted for age, age^2, high school dropout, high school diploma, some college education, and marital status. White is actually white non-Hispanic here. The white-black gaps are defined as: (W90-B90)-(W80-B80).

*Fraction immigrant in 1980 is used as an instrument for the change in the fraction immigrant.

Table 5.6   Estimated Effect of a Change in Metropolitan-Level
Immigrant Share on the White Male/African American
Male Gap in Various Labor-Market Outcomes (Standard
Errors)

	Employment	Log Hourly Wages	Annual Earnings
Change in the Gap Between All White Men and All Black Men			
1990 − 1980 change	−0.143	0.200	19339.16
in fraction immigrant	(0.3261)	(0.2065)	(6657.10)
R-squared	0.0105	0.0084	0.1339
Change in the Gap Between All White Men and All Black Men Other Changes Held Constant*			
1990 − 1980 change	−0.207	−0.108	9133.49
in fraction immigrant	(0.5677)	(0.2901)	(13263.12)
R-squared	0.0562	0.1926	0.3599

Sources: Data are from the 1980 and 1990 (1 percent) PUMS of the U.S. Census. Ages
sixteen to sixty-four are included. The results are from weighted ordinary least squares,
where the inverse of the standard error of the left-hand-side variable is used as the
weight. A constant is included, but not reported. Only the fifty largest metropolitan areas are included here.

Notes: The left-hand-side variables are metropolitan area means that have been adjusted
for age, age^2, high school dropout, high school diploma, some college education, and
marital status. White is actually white non-Hispanic here. The white-black gaps are defined as: (W90-B90)-(W80-B80).

*Changes in the native-born population are held constant: change in the fraction His-
panic, black, Asian, "other" race, high school dropout, high school graduate, and some
college, and the change in mean age.

Other Demographic Changes over the Decade

The regression specifications presented thus far are parsimonious. There
may be other changes in the demographic profile of metropolitan areas
that affect the labor-market outcomes of the native born. In order to investigate this, table 5.6 shows the effect of holding other demographic
changes constant. The top row repeats the results from table 5.4 for black
men. The second row shows the estimated impact of a change in the fraction immigrant holding constant changes in the *native-born* population:
change in the fraction Hispanic, fraction black, fraction Asian, and fraction "other" race. Also included are changes in the fractions of the native-
born population with less than high school, high school, and some college education. In addition, change in mean age is included.

Holding other demographic changes constant increases the estimated effect of a change in immigration on the white-black employment gap, but the effect is still insignificant. The effect on log hourly wages changes from being positive and insignificant to negative and insignificant. Finally, the effect on the annual earnings gap is positive and significant with no controls and falls to insignificance when other demographic changes are held constant.

Clearly these other demographic changes are correlated with labor-market outcomes. However, as with the change in the fraction immigrant, these changes are unlikely to be exogenous. The changes in the characteristics of the native-born population may be affected by labor-market outcomes, and, as some have argued, they may be affected by changes in the fraction immigrant. In fact, many of these coefficients have signs that we would not expect if we believed the variables to be capturing a pure supply increase. It would be appropriate to estimate the effects of these variables using a technique to handle this endogeneity. We could use the initial fraction of the population that is native born and Hispanic, for example, as an instrument for the change in fraction native-born Hispanics, as we did with the change in the fraction immigrant. The use of this variable as an instrument is less compelling: recall that the justification in the case of immigration is that immigrants have many reasons besides labor-market conditions to follow earlier waves of immigrants. The same reasoning does not apply for changes in the native-born population.[12] I will now present some results holding constant other demographic changes, but interpreting the relationships as causal should be done cautiously.

Changes in Fraction Young, Hispanic, and Poorly Educated Immigrants

In the preceding analysis, I investigated the effect of a change in the overall fraction immigrant on changes in labor-market outcomes for various groups of African Americans. This measure of the change in immigrant share may be too coarse to discern adverse effects of immigration. While it is true that immigrants on average have fewer years of schooling than the native born, the average masks a great deal of variation. Immigrants are extremely diverse (Butcher and DiNardo 1996). Some geographic areas may have received a large inflow of highly skilled immigrants (Silicon Valley), while other areas received large inflows of low-skilled immigrants (the San Joaquin Valley). In one area, the immigrants may be unlikely to compete for jobs with low-skilled African Americans, while in the other they may directly affect their labor-market outcomes.

I will now disaggregate the measure of immigration. I analyze the effect of a change in the fraction young immigrant, fraction Hispanic immigrant, and fraction immigrant with less than a high school diploma. I limit the analysis to changes in the gaps in labor-market outcomes between white men and African Americans with less than a high school diploma. This group of African Americans suffered the most with the increasing wage inequality during the 1980s and is the most likely to be in direct competition with these groups of immigrants.[13]

Table 5.7 reports the results for the change in the gap in log hourly wages and annual earnings. The disaggregation of the measure of immigrant inflows had no affect on the estimated effect on the employment gap, so this outcome is dropped from the analysis. The top panel reports the OLS results, the bottom panel the two-stage least square results, using the initial fraction immigrant (for each type) as the instrument. The first two columns report the results with no other control variables. The second set of columns include the controls for changes in the native-born population.

Consider the results for log hourly wages for men in the first column. Although insignificant, the OLS coefficients are all larger than in table 5.4, which shows the impact of the overall change in the fraction immigrant. Again, the two-stage least squares results are insignificant. When we turn to the third column, however, where other controls are included, there are several significant coefficients. The results show that the gap in hourly earnings between white men and poorly educated black men shrank significantly in areas that experienced an increase in the fraction young immigrants and fraction immigrants with low levels of education. The result for an increase in the fraction Hispanic immigrants is similar. Once instrumental variables are used to control for the potential endogeneity of the immigrant inflow, the results are no longer significant.

The results for poorly educated black women are also interesting. There is no significant effect on the gap in wages for an increase in any of these groups of immigrants until we control for demographic changes in the native-born population. Holding changes in the native-born population constant, it appears that the wage gap between poorly educated black women and white men expanded significantly in areas that experienced an increase in these immigrant groups. Using two-stage least squares increases the size of the coefficients. The effect of a change in the fraction young immigrant and fraction Hispanic immigrant remains significant, while a change in the fraction immigrant with low levels of education falls to insignificance. The two-stage least squares results indicated that a 1-percentage-point increase in the fraction Hispanic immigrant is correlated with a 4.8 percent increase in the

Table 5.7 Estimated Effect of a Change in the Share of Various Groups of Immigrants on the Change in Gap in Labor-Market Outcomes Between White Men and African Americans with Less than a High School Diploma (Standard Errors)

	Log Hourly Wages		Log Hourly Wages with Controls		Annual Earnings		Annual Earnings with Controls	
	Men	Women	Men	Women	Men	Women	Men	Women
OLS								
Change in fraction								
Young immigrant	−0.865	1.981	−1.450	4.967	50956.6	51803.2	31955.2	47193.1
	(1.140)	(2.561)	(0.775)	(2.397)	(24377.9)	(23507.1)	(23142.4)	(27203.8)
Hispanic immigrant	−0.547	0.415	−0.932	4.247	16595.5	19534.6	21435.3	33855.8
	(0.5743)	(1.949)	(0.5035)	(1.131)	(10812.3)	(14508.3)	(14651.1)	(16062.7)
Low-education immigrant	−0.742	0.799	−1.351	4.594	14362.8	16473.6	20684.2	33564.3
	(0.6830)	(2.522)	(0.698)	(1.699)	(13688.2)	(19351.6)	(21018.9)	(23469.4)
TSLS*								
Change in Fraction								
Young immigrant	0.397	0.666	−2.080	9.402	113181.9	139043	147594	189322.3
	(2.835)	(3.732)	(2.222)	(4.041)	(66954.3)	(74044.4)	(108805)	(136952)
Hispanic immigrant	−0.133	0.927	−0.820	4.813	40000.7	54973.5	57067.4	75768.2
	(1.119)	(1.564)	(0.7860)	(1.415)	(25273.5)	(28693.4)	(29655.9)	(39568.1)
Low-education immigrant	0.699	2.738	0.023	12.587	145555.4	180229.2	174348.1	246259.2
	(3.187)	(3.629)	(4.229)	(10.519)	(122140)	(145481)	(204158)	(283352)

Sources: Data are from the 1980 and 1990 (1 percent) PUMS of the U.S. Census. Ages sixteen to sixty-four are included. The results are from weighted regressions, where the inverse of the standard error of the left-hand-side variable is used as the weight. A constant is included, but not reported. Forty-nine metropolitan areas are included.

Notes: The left-hand-side variables are metropolitan area means that have been adjusted for age, age^2, high school dropout, high school diploma, some college education, and marital status. White is actually white non-Hispanic here. Other controls include change in the native-born population: change in the fraction Hispanic, black, Asian, "other" race, high school dropout, high school graduate, and some college, and the change in mean age.

The white-black gaps are defined as: (W90-B90)-(W80-B80).

*Fraction immigrant in 1980 is used as an instrument for the change in fraction immigrant.

wage gap between white men and poorly educated African American women, holding constant changes in the native-born population.

Turning to the results for the annual earnings gap for men, we see that the OLS results are larger for the increase in fraction young immigrant than for immigrants overall (table 5.4) and the other two subgroups of immigrants. The two-stage least squares coefficients are much larger, but the standard errors also increase substantially, so these results are insignificant. When demographic changes in the native-born population are held constant, both the OLS and instrumental variables results are insignificant. For women we see a similar pattern. The OLS results with no controls show a large and statistically significant impact of an increase in the fraction young immigrant, while the effect of an increase in either Hispanic immigrant share or the share of immigrants with less than a high school diploma has no effect. The two-stage least squares results are insignificant. When other controls are added, the effect of an increase in the share of Hispanic immigrants significantly increases the white-black gap in annual earnings, but all effects are insignificant in the two-stage least squares results.[14]

The results presented in table 5.7 are among the strongest in the paper. They suggest that it is not only overall immigration that matters but the characteristics of the immigrants. The results suggest that there is a correlation between increases in these groups of immigrants and an increasing gap between the hourly wages of poorly educated black women and white men. This is consistent with results in Altonji and Card (1991) that indicate a greater overlap in industry between black women and immigrants than between other groups.

One should keep in mind that these results only come out of the regressions that hold changes in the native-born demographic profile constant. Many of these changes have puzzling effects on the change in the white-black wage gap. For example, an increase in the share of native-born Hispanics and African Americans from 1980 to 1990 is predicted to *decrease* the white-black gap in log hourly earnings for this group of poorly educated women. If this were a purely exogenous supply shift, we would expect a positive effect. As discussed above, the change in fraction of the native-born population of a particular type is likely to be endogenous. This may simply mean that these are labor markets that are relatively attractive to blacks and Hispanics. Conditional on that, the immigrant share adversely affects the white-black gap.

Levels of Aggregation

As discussed earlier, most papers using area studies to evaluate the effects of immigration on the labor-market outcomes of the native born have found little or no effect. Borjas, Katz, and Freeman (1996) suggest that one reason for this is that the areas considered are too small. The metropolitan area studies essentially treat each area as its own, separate labor market. If workers can easily shift between metropolitan regions in response to changes in wages or employment, then these movements will offset the effects of immigration. Borjas, Katz, and Freeman suggest that there could be negative effects on the entire country that fail to materialize when we study small components of the country. Their paper suggests that using geographic regions that are wider in scope may show effects that the metropolitan area studies do not. They demonstrate that as they increase the size of the geographic region from metropolitan area to state to region the effect of an increase in the relative number of immigrants (within education group) on the change in native-born wages becomes larger.

Here I have found few effects of immigration on the labor-market outcomes of black men. If African American men are more mobile than the other groups considered here, they may move to offset the adverse effects of immigration. I will now investigate the effect of using larger geographic areas on the estimated impact of immigration on the labor-market outcomes for all black men.

Table 5.8 reports the results of this approach for the change in the gap in labor-market outcomes between white men and all black men. The first row repeats the results for the metropolitan area level. The second row shows how the change in immigrant share in a state affects the change in the state-level white-black gap. The third row reports results for a change in the fraction immigrant on the Census division-level change in the white-black gap in labor-market outcomes. The first set of columns gives the OLS coefficients. The second shows the results using the initial immigrant share as an instrument for the change in the immigrant share.

Consider the OLS results first. As has become familiar, the effects for the change in the employment gap and the change in the log hourly wage gap are insignificant. The second-to-last column again shows that an increase in the fraction immigrant in each geographic region has a positive effect on the change in the white-black gap in annual earnings. The effect is significant at both the metropolitan and state levels but insignificant at the division level. Contrary to the results in Borjas, Katz, and Freeman (1996), here we see that increasing the size of the area under study has no consistent impact on the size of the effect. The effect of a change in the fraction immigrant on the white-black annual earnings gap is approximately the same for the state and metropolitan levels and somewhat smaller (and insignificant) for the division level.[15]

Turning to the two-stage least squares results, again we see that an

Table 5.8   Estimates of the Effect of a Change in Immigrant Share on the Change in White Male/African American Male Gap in Labor-Market Outcomes Using Various Levels of Aggregation (Standard Errors)

	Employment		Log Hourly Wages		Annual Earnings	
	OLS	TSLS	OLS	TSLS	OLS	TSLS
Metro-level changes						
1990 – 1980 change in fraction immigrant	−0.143 (0.3261)	0.140 (0.3617)	0.200 (0.2065)	0.276 (0.5596)	19339.16 (66571.1)	451591 (26471.0)
State-level changes						
1990 – 1980 change in fraction immigrant	0.026 (0.2610)	−0.256 (0.2333)	−0.246 (0.4153)	0.253 (0.5443)	21985.79 (9308.9)	35086.1 (13827.3)
Division-level changes						
1990 – 1980 change in fraction immigrant	0.141 (0.2031)	−0.047 (0.2061)	−0.189 (0.5740)	−0.670 (0.3597)	14189.9 (12133.3)	18575.4 (15656.9)

Sources: Data are from the 1980 and 1990 (1 percent) PUMS of the U.S. Census. Ages sixteen to sixty-four are included. The results are from weighted regressions, where the inverse of the standard error of the left-hand-side variable is used as the weight. A constant is included, but not reported. Sample sizes are fifty, fifty, and ten, for the metro-level, state-level, and division-level results, respectively.

Notes: The left-hand-side variables are adjusted means for metropolitan areas, states and divisions. The means are adjusted for age, age^2, high school dropout, high school diploma, some college education, and marital status. The fraction immigrant in 1980 is used as an instrument for the change in the increase in the fraction immigrant has a positive and significant impact on the gap in annual earnings at the metropolitan and state levels. However, the size of the effect decreases as the level of aggregation increases. A 1-percentage-point increase in the immigrant share at the metropolitan level is predicted to increase the white-black earnings gap by 451 dollars (an elasticity of 0.38). The analogous figure for the state level is 351 dollars (elasticity of 0.27). At the division level, a 1-percentage-point increase in the immigrant share is predicted to increase the white-black annual earnings gap by 186 dollars (elasticity of 0.16).

There are several potential reasons for the difference in the results here and those of Borjas, Katz, and Freeman. First, the left-hand-side variables here are relative changes in the labor-market outcome variables. The maintained assumption in this paper is that white non-Hispanic men are unaffected by immigrant inflows, and thus one can use their labor-market outcomes as a benchmark against which to measure the impact of immigration on African Americans. If instead, white non-Hispanic men who are affected simply move quickly to other areas of the country, then the impact on them will only show up when we look at larger and larger geographic areas. If this were the case, the larger the area considered, the more *similar* the effects of immigration would be for African Americans and white men, and the gap in labor-market outcomes would appear less affected. Note that for this to be the case, white non-Hispanic men (but not African Americans) must move quickly in response to immigrant inflows. Card (1996) finds little evidence that native-born outflows offset immigrant inflows.

Second, the initial regressions used to estimate the area-level fixed effects for each education group in their paper only control for age and gender. The area-level outcomes used here are adjusted for age, age squared, education levels, and marital status. Third, they study the changes in wages for many different area-education groups, while the results in this paper only use the adjusted area-level wages for black and white men. Among other things, this means that the initial regressions used to create the left-hand-side variables here are less restrictive, since the area fixed effects come from regressions run separately for each group of interest. This allows the effect of age, for example, to vary by each group under study and could affect the adjusted mean for the area-level outcome. Finally, the right-hand-side variable that Borjas, Katz, and Freeman use is different: they use the change in the relative number of immigrants in each area-level education group to measure the supply impact of immigrants. Here the change in the total fraction immigrant is used.

Any one of the above differences could account for the difference in the results presented here and those in Borjas, Katz, and Freeman. These differences do, however, imply that the answer is fairly sensitive to the techniques used to address the question. Borjas, Katz, and Freeman, in more recent work (May 1997), show how sensitive these results can be. While they find that for the 1980s the size of the adverse effect of immigration on native-born labor-market outcomes increases with the size of the geographic area studied, the results do not hold for other decades.

SUMMARY AND CONCLUSION

The results here suggest that an increase in the metropolitan area fraction immigrant has no effect on the change in employment, weeks worked, hourly wages, or annual earnings for black men. When we look at the gap in labor-market outcomes between all white men and all black men, the story changes for one of these outcomes. The gap in annual earnings between white men and black men increased between 1980 and 1990 in areas that had an increase in the fraction immigrant. While the effect is statistically significant, it is small. For men, the elasticity of the white-black annual earnings gap with respect to the immigrant share is about 0.16.

The results here also show that although the effects of immigration are similar in sign for various groups of African Americans, there do appear to be some differences in the magnitude. As one might expect, the change in immigrant share had a larger adverse effect on the relative annual earnings of black men and women with low levels of education. Furthermore, the effect of an increase in the immigrant share depends on the characteristics of the immigrants. Depending on the specification, an increase in the share of young immigrants has the largest impact on the relative outcomes of poorly educated black men and women.

This paper uses two approaches to control for potential biases in the first-difference estimation. These biases could arise for many reasons, for example, if immigrants choose where they move based on wage growth, or if natives are quickly driven out of metropolitan regions by immigrants. First, I use the initial stock of immigrants to instrument for the change in the fraction immigrant in each metropolitan area. These results again show no effect for the change in the white-black employment and wage gaps, but the annual earnings gaps are even larger with this technique. Second, I show how the results are affected by aggregating over larger and larger areas. If the native born respond to immigrant inflows by moving out, then focusing on narrowly defined geographic regions may miss the negative effects of immigration, even if they exist for the country as a whole. If this is the case, then moving from metropolitan area level to state and to division should increase the size of the estimated effect of an increase in the fraction immigrant. In the framework employed in this paper, this effect would require that white men are completely unaffected by immigration, and that African Americans who are adversely affected by immigration move out of their metropolitan areas. The results here again show a significant positive effect of a change in fraction immigrant on the gap in annual earnings between white and black men, but, contrary to expectations, the size of the effect declines as the level of aggregation increases.

The one robust finding in this paper is that an increase in the immigrant share is positively correlated with an (small) increase in the white-black annual earnings gap. The extent to which we interpret that to mean that immigrants have harmful effects on African Americans depends on the extent to which we believe that white men are a good "control" group for the labor-market outcomes of African Americans. In other words, the extent to which we believe that the changes in annual earnings experienced by white men would have been experienced by African Americans if the immigrants had not arrived. Caution is in order before accepting that conclusion, since there were many changes over the 1980s that could be expected to affect these two groups differently.

NOTES

1. Note that despite the large inflows of immigrants during the 1980s, immigrants comprised only about 9 percent of the working-age population in 1990.

2. An index calculated by the American Chamber of Commerce Researchers Association.

3. The sample size for the estimates for blacks drops from about eighty metropolitan areas to about forty using the cost-of-living adjustment.

4. This matching scheme is the result of work by David Jaeger, Susanna Loeb, and Sarah Turner. I thank David Jaeger for making the computer code available to me.

5. I performed all these analyses for all the groups discussed in the study. The results were fairly similar across groups, and the tables became unwieldy when all permutations were included.

6. The underlying regressions for black men contain 28,834 and 22,937 observations for employment and annual earnings in 1980 and 1990, respectively, 20,050 and 17,142 for weeks and log wages in 1980 and 1990.

7. Since the left-hand-side variable here is the difference between two means, I use the inverse of the standard error for the difference between means as the weight. All weights are defined analogously.

8. From here on out I will refer to the comparison group as "white men," rather than "white non-Hispanic men."

9. These elasticities are calculated at the means. I first calculated the effect on the white-black gap of a 3.2-percentage-point increase in the immigrant share (the mean increase across the fifty largest MAs during this period) implied by the estimated coefficient. That is the change in the gap. I divided this change by the 1980 white-black annual earnings gap to get the percentage change in the gap. I next divided this number by the percentage change in the immigrant share (58.2 percent at the mean for the fifty largest MAs).

10. Butcher and Piehl (1997) find similar results in New Jersey in 1980 and 1990. Immigrants and native-born black women tend to be over-represented in the apparel and finished textiles industry.

11. The correlation between immigrant and native-born inflows into metropolitan areas is an important and unsettled question. Filer (1992) reports evidence that the native born both move out of and refrain from moving into high immigrant areas. On the other hand, Butcher and Card (1991) report positive correlations between immigrant and native-born inflows into metropolitan areas. Card (1996) also finds little evidence that native outflows offset immigrant inflows.

12. I tried TSLS instrumenting all the changes with their initial values. All coefficients are insignificant.

13. This is the only group for which the disaggregation in the immigration variable made a difference.

14. Again, there may appear to be some conflict between the results for the hourly wage gap and the results for annual earnings. However, in all cases presented here the effects of immigration on weeks worked and usual hours worked per week reconciles these differences.

15. The implied elasticity estimates of the white-black annual earnings gap to the changes in immigrant share at various levels of geographic aggregation are small: 0.16 for metropolitan areas, 0.17 for states, 0.13 for divisions.

REFERENCES

Altonji, Joseph, and David Card. 1991. "The Effects of Immigration on the Labor Market Outcomes of Less-Skilled Natives." In *Immigration, Trade and the Labor Market*, edited by J. Abowd and R. Freeman. Chicago: University of Chicago Press.

Borjas, George. 1987. "Immigrants, Minorities, and Labor Market Competition." *Industrial and Labor Relations Review* 40(3): 382–92.

———. 1994. "The Economics of Immigration." *Journal of Economic Literature* 32(4): 1667–1718.

Borjas, George, Richard Freeman, and Lawrence Katz. 1996. "Searching for the Effect of Immigration on the Labor Market." *American Economic Review* 86(2): 246–51.

———. 1997. "How Much Do Immigration and Trade Affect Labor Market Outcomes?" Mimeo, Harvard University (May).

Bratsberg, Bernt. 1996. "The Effect of Immigration on Domestic Wages: Evidence from Longitudinal Data." Mimeo, Department of Economics, Kansas State University (June).

Bound, John, and Harry Holzer. 1996. "Demand Shifts, Population Adjustments, and Labor Market Outcomes during the 1980s." NBER Working Paper no. 5685, National Bureau of Economic Research (July).

Butcher, Kristin F., and David Card. 1991. "Immigration and Wages: Evidence from the 1980s." *American Economic Review* 81(2): 292–96.

Butcher, Kristin F., and John DiNardo. 1996. "The Immigrant and Native-born Wage Distributions: Evidence from U.S. Censuses." Mimeo (October).

Butcher, Kristin F., and Anne Morrison Piehl. 1997. "Immigration and the Wages and Employment of U.S.-Born Workers in New Jersey." In *Keys to Successful Immigration: Implications of the New Jersey Experience*, edited by Thomas Espenshade. Washington, DC: Urban Institute Press, 1997.

Card, David. 1990. "The Impact of the Mariel Boatlift on the Miami Labor Market." *Industrial and Labor Relations Review* 43(2): 245–57.

———. 1996. "Immigrant Inflows, Native Outflows, and the Local Labor Market Impacts of Higher Immigration." Industrial Relations Section Working Paper no. 368, Princeton University, Princeton, N.J. (November).

Filer, Randall K. 1992. "The Effect of Immigrant Arrivals on Migratory Patterns of Native Workers." In *Immigration and the Workforce*, edited by George J. Borjas and Richard B. Freeman. Chicago: University of Chicago Press.

Friedberg, Rachel M., and Jennifer Hunt. 1995. "The Impact of Immigrants on Host Country Wages, Employment and Growth." *The Journal of Economic Perspectives* 9(2): 23–44.

Goldin, Claudia. 1993. "The Political Economy of Immigration Restriction in the United States, 1890 to 1921." NBER Working Paper no. 4345, National Bureau of Economic Research (April).

Jaeger, David A. 1996. "Skill Differences and the Effect of Immigrants on the Wages of Natives." Working Paper no. 273, BLS Working Paper Series, U.S. Department of Labor, U.S. Bureau of Labor Statistics, Office of Employment Research and Program Development (March).

LaLonde, Robert, and Robert Topel. 1991. "Labor Market Adjustments to Increased Immigration." In *Immigration, Trade, and the Labor Market*, edited by John Abowd and Richard Freeman. Chicago: University of Chicago Press.

Schoeni, Robert. 1996. "The Effect of Immigrants on the Employment and Wages of Native Workers: Evidence from the 1970s and 1980s." Mimeo, Rand Corporation (March).

PART II

ECONOMIC EFFECTS BEYOND THE LABOR MARKET

CHAPTER 6

Does Immigration Hurt African American Self-Employment?

Robert W. Fairlie and Bruce D. Meyer

A large number of studies examine the impact of immigration on the labor-market outcomes of native-born Americans.[1] These studies often focus on the effects of immigration on the wages and employment of African Americans and other groups with low average earnings.[2] This research, however, has neglected a large and growing segment of the labor force, the self-employed. The self-employed also contain a disproportionate number of immigrants, especially those from Asian countries.[3] We might expect that the propensity for immigrants to choose self-employment makes the displacement of self-employed natives more likely. In this study we examine whether immigration has a negative impact on the self-employment prospects of native-born blacks.[4] The potential effect of immigration on black self-employment is especially important given the already low rate of black self-employment in the United States.

Black business ownership in the United States is a topic of much interest. Several previous studies document and examine the causes of low rates of black self-employment.[5] The underlying causes of these low rates, however, remain largely undetermined. The low black self-employment rate is particularly troubling because self-employment has historically been a route of economic advancement for disadvantaged groups.[6] For example, the success of Chinese and Japanese immigrants in the United States is in large part due to their ownership of small businesses.[7] Overall, a high self-employment rate for an ethnic or racial group is strongly associated with a high average income for that group.[8] Furthermore, and despite likely underreporting, the self-employed earn more on average than wage and salary workers. The low black self-employment rate is also of immediate public policy interest because self-employment is viewed as a potential route out of poverty. It is currently being promoted by many states and the federal government as a way to leave the welfare and unemployment insurance rolls.[9] The low rate of business ownership among blacks also contributes to racial tensions in urban areas throughout the United States. The recent racial conflicts between Koreans and African Americans in many large cities are in large part due to the presence of Korean-owned businesses in black communities.[10] It has also been argued that political influence comes with success in small business.[11]

An examination of the impact of immigration on black self-employment is also of interest for the same reasons we are interested in the impact of immigration on the wages and employment of native-born wage and salary workers. The extent to which immigrants displace native workers from their jobs and bid down their wages determines one of the main costs of immigration and affects political support for U.S. immigration policies.

In this study, we use 1980 and 1990 Census microdata to study the impact of immigration on self-employed blacks. Specifically, we examine the relationship between levels of immigration and black self-employment across ninety-four of the largest metropolitan areas in the United States. We also examine the relationship between changes in immigration and changes in black self-employment in these metropolitan areas. We generally find that immigration has no effect or only a small negative but statistically insignificant effect on black male or female self-employment. Our findings are similar if we weight immigration rates by the propensity of immigrant groups to be self-employed or if we limit our sample of immigrants to those from only Asian countries. With only a few exceptions, our findings are robust to alternative estimation techniques and specifications.

An important advantage of this study over previous studies of the effect of immigration on the earnings and employment of natives is that our key explanatory variable is more likely to be exogenous to our outcome measure.[12] The likelihood that the black self-employment rate has a direct influence on the location decisions of immigrants who are potential business owners is small. Although the black self-employment rate varies across metropolitan areas, these rates are generally so low that blacks make up only a small share of the potential competitors for immigrants. Another advantage over previous studies that focus on wage/salary workers is that our estimates are less likely to suffer from the potential downward bias caused by native migration in response to immigration. We provide some evidence that self-employed blacks are less mobile than blacks who are wage and salary workers.

We first describe past work on the effects of immigration on the self-employment prospects of natives. Next, we describe a model that illustrates how an inflow of immigrants affects self-employment among native blacks. Following this analysis, we discuss the Census data used in the analyses and some of our descriptive results. Finally, we describe our regression methods and their results.

PREVIOUS RESEARCH

There exists an extensive literature in economics that examines the impact of immigration on the labor-market outcomes of native-born Americans.[13] Most of these studies look at the relationship between the level or change in immigration and the level or change in labor-market outcomes of natives across metropolitan areas.[14] This research generally finds that immigration has a weak negative effect on the employment and earnings of natives.

Although this literature does not examine the relationship between immigration and black self-employment, a few studies from outside economics do. Light and Rosenstein (1995) use aggregate data from 272 metropolitan areas from the 1980 Census to identify the effect of immigration on the self-employment rate and earnings of native-born workers.[15] In their metropolitan-area-level regressions, they find that the immigrant self-employment rate and the immigrant share of the total self-employed have essentially no effect on the self-employment rates or self-employment earnings of native whites or blacks.[16] They also do not find evidence of a large negative effect of the Korean self-employment rate or the Korean share of the total self-employed on the self-employment rate or self-employment earnings of native-born blacks. They argue that the interaction between these two groups is the most likely case in which to find a negative effect of immigration on native self-employment.[17]

Boyd (1990) also examines the effect of immigration on black self-employment. Instead of using metropolitan-area-level data, however, he estimates a regression for the probability of being self-employed among a sample of black workers from the 1980 Census. To test the hypothesis, he includes the percentage of the population who are Asian (in logarithms) and the growth rate in the Asian population in the SMSA in his individual-level self-employment regressions. He finds that the coefficients on these explanatory variables are negative but are very small and insignificant.

In several ways, we contribute to this scant literature on the impact of immigration on native black self-employment. First, we use the most recent Census data from 1990 as well as the 1980 data. The 1990 data follow a period of much higher immigration and are thus better suited to study the effects of immigration. It is also possible that more recent waves of immigrants have had different effects on blacks than earlier ones. Second, unlike the previous studies that rely on one year of data, we can account for differences across metropolitan areas that are not easily measured (unobserved metropolitan-area fixed effects) and that may be correlated with the level of black self-employment and the measure of immigration or immigrant self-employment. Previous estimates of the effect of immigration on black self-employment may be biased due to the presence of these unobserved fixed effects.[18] Third, we also go one step further by employing an instrumental variables technique to remove metropolitan-area transitory effects that are correlated with changes from 1980 to 1990 in black self-employment and immigration. Fourth, we include a measure of immigration that is weighted by the propensity of different immigrant groups to choose self-employment, thus addressing the concern that immigrant groups differ in their impact on black self-employment. Finally, we include an improved set of individual and metropolitan-area-level controls in our regressions.

A MODEL OF THE EFFECTS OF IMMIGRATION

We do not provide the details here, but a formal model is useful to assess the likely impact of immigration flows on the self-employment prospects of natives. In Fairlie and Meyer (1997a) we build upon past work such as Altonji and Card (1991) and Borjas (1994) to specify such a model. Similar to these previous studies, we allow immigration to have an effect on the derived demand for labor (through its effect on product demand) as well as on labor supply.

In our model, workers choose to supply their labor to one or more sectors (self-employment and wage/salary) based on the wage in the sectors and possibly other characteristics. Immigrants and natives are allowed to differ in these labor supply functions as well as their product demand functions. These differences in supply and demand functions can be due to differences in skill composition or to different preferences for job autonomy or other nonwage characteristics (such as hours of work).

An increase in the number of immigrants increases both the supply of self-employment labor and the demand for self-employment output. Holding demand constant, the increase in the supply of labor to the self-employment sector reduces the return to self-employment and consequently reduces the self-employment rate of native blacks. The inflow of immigrants, however, also increases the demand for the goods and services provided by the self-employed, thus increasing the return to self-employment and dampening or reversing any employment effect. We are interested in determining the net impact from these two offsetting effects. When the value of immigrant consumption of self-employment output is less than the value of its self-employment output, then increased immigration drives down the rate of self-employment among natives. The self-employment rate of natives rises in response to increased immigration when immigrant self-employment consumption exceeds its output.

Under some simplifying assumptions we can show that the decline in the number of natives who are self-employed when a self-employed immigrant arrives is less than ($\rho - 1$), where ρ is the ratio of immigrant self-employment output to consumption. If we assume that immigrant and native levels of self-employment consumption are approximately equal, then a rough estimate of ρ is the immigrant/native self-employment rate ratio.[19] Estimates of these self-employment rates indicate that ($\rho - 1$) < 0.20.[20] Thus, less than 0.20 self-employed natives would be displaced by each self-employed immigrant. Therefore, if even most or all of the native self-employment rate losses come from blacks, the effect would be fairly modest. Since it is likely that any losses will be more broadly shared, it would seem that the potential black losses are small. Contrary to some public perceptions, this analysis suggests that, overall, immigrant displacement of black businesses is likely to be limited. Nevertheless, in certain cities, neighborhoods, and industries, there may be noticeable displacement if that is where immigrants congregate.

THE 1980 AND 1990 CENSUS DATA

The data used in this study are from the Public Use Microdata 5-Percent Samples of the 1980 and 1990 Censuses of Population. These data sets are the only sources of national microdata that are large enough to allow comparisons of black self-employment rates across a large number of metropolitan areas. In addition, they are preferable to published aggregate data because they provide more flexibility in creating sample restrictions and definitions of key variables and because they allow us to directly control for individual-level characteristics in our regressions. Finally, the detailed geographical information in the Census makes it possible to create consistent metropolitan-area definitions across the decade.

Self-employed workers are defined as those individuals who identify themselves as mainly self-employed in their own not incorporated or incorporated business on the "class of worker" question.[21] In 1990, the relevant choices on the Census questionnaire were response 6, "SELF-EMPLOYED in own NOT INCORPORATED business, professional practice, or farm" and response 7, "SELF-EMPLOYED in own INCORPORATED business, professional practice, or farm" (U.S. Bureau of the Census, 1993, E-15).[22] We find using a 1/1000 random sample from the 1990 Census that 34.0 percent of all self-employed men and 24.2 percent of all self-employed women report having their own incorporated business.

We also note two additional characteristics of the self-employed. First, the majority of the self-employed do not hire other workers. Characteristics of Business Owners (CBO) data indicate that nearly 70 percent of businesses have no paid employees (U.S. Bureau of the Census 1992).[23] Second, only a small fraction of the total self-employed are accounted for by professional specialty occupations, which include lawyers, physicians, and dentists. Using the random sample from the 1990 Census, we find that professional occupations include 16.0 percent of self-employed men and 15.9 percent of self-employed women.

In our study, we include only individuals ages sixteen to sixty-four and impose additional sample restrictions depending on the measure of self-employment that we are using. Our first measure, the self-employment rate, is defined as the fraction of workers who are self-employed. We include only individuals who worked at least twenty weeks in the past year and usually worked at least fifteen hours per week during that year. As in most previous studies of self-employment, we include only workers in nonagricultural industries. Our second measure, the self-employment ratio, is defined as the fraction of the total population who are self-employed. The sample used to calculate this ratio is not restricted to include only workers. Instead, we exclude only individuals who are currently enrolled in school or who are institutionalized. Therefore, agricultural workers, the unemployed, and workers with few total annual hours are included in the sample. We provide estimates using both measures of self-employment in most of the following analyses.

The Industry Distribution of the Self-Employed

We first examine whether self-employed blacks are located in the same industries as self-employed immigrants. The similarity of the industry distributions for these two groups is a potential indicator of the amount of competition between them. We also examine whether industries with large concentrations of self-employed blacks are the industries for which immigrants also comprise a large share of the total self-employed.

In table 6.1, we report the industry distribution of the self-employed by immigrant status, race, and gender for the United States in 1990. We also report the fraction of the total self-employed in the industry who are immigrants or Asian immigrants. For all estimates, we use the same weeks, hours, and industry restrictions as those used to calculate the self-employment rate. We report separate columns for Asian immigrants because Asian business owners are commonly thought to be in direct competition with many black business owners.

The industry distribution of self-employed native black men is fairly similar to that of self-employed native white men. There appears to be less of a similarity, however, between the distribution of self-employed black men and those of either self-employed immigrants or Asian immigrants. Furthermore, the industries with the largest concentrations of self-employed black men generally do not have large immigrant or

Table 6.1 1990 Industry Distribution of the Self-Employed by Immigrant Status, Race, and Gender

| | Industry Distribution | | | | | | Immigrant Share of Self-Employed | |
| | Native Blacks | | Native Whites | | Immigrants | | | |
Industry Category	Males	Females	Males	Females	All	Asian	All	Asian
Mining	0.0014	0.0006	0.0058	0.0014	0.0009	0.0003	0.0254	0.0020
Construction	0.2180	0.0182	0.2171	0.0352	0.1107	0.0357	0.0756	0.0066
Manuf. (nondurables)	0.0200	0.0260	0.0251	0.0335	0.0366	0.0413	0.1371	0.0418
Manuf. (durables)	0.0402	0.0126	0.0539	0.0262	0.0418	0.0249	0.1002	0.0161
Trans., comm., and utils.	0.1063	0.0180	0.0485	0.0230	0.0490	0.0309	0.1211	0.0206
Wholesale trade (durables)	0.0163	0.0040	0.0294	0.0136	0.0189	0.0173	0.0861	0.0213
Wholesale (nondurables)	0.0129	0.0087	0.0257	0.0161	0.0320	0.0358	0.1463	0.0441
Retail trade	0.1120	0.1357	0.1509	0.1995	0.2532	0.3694	0.1550	0.0610
Fin., ins., and real estate	0.0573	0.0494	0.0817	0.0862	0.0552	0.0566	0.0747	0.0206
Busn. and repair services	0.1545	0.1271	0.1135	0.1073	0.1023	0.0556	0.0967	0.0142
Personal services	0.0564	0.1822	0.0282	0.1083	0.0718	0.1028	0.1334	0.0516
Enter. and rec. services	0.0251	0.0116	0.0188	0.0219	0.0153	0.0118	0.0842	0.0175
Professional services	0.1173	0.4019	0.1681	0.3166	0.1773	0.1996	0.0901	0.0274
Other	0.0623	0.0041	0.0333	0.0113	0.0351	0.0180	0.1295	0.017
Total	1.0000	1.0000	1.0000	1.0000	1.0000	1.0000	0.1062	0.0286

Note: For the entire United States, those aged sixteen to sixty-four working at least fifteen hours per week and at least twenty weeks last year and who are not in agriculture, weighted by Census sample weights.

Asian-immigrant shares of the self-employed. The main exception is Retail Trade, which contains a large share of the self-employed black men, immigrants, and Asian immigrants and in which immigrants and Asian immigrants are a large share of all self-employed.

One industry, Professional and Related Services, contains 40.2 percent of all self-employed black women in the United States.[24] This industry has a large concentration of self-employed immigrants and Asian immigrants, but has immigrant and Asian-immigrant shares of all self-employed comparable to those for the total. Other industries with large concentrations of black women, such as Personal Services and Retail Trade, however, have large immigrant or Asian-immigrant shares of the self-employed.

Overall, the industry distributions of self-employed blacks and immigrants are similar enough that we expect direct competition between the two groups in many cases. Our findings from an analysis of more narrowly defined industries do not cause us to change this conclusion. It is possible that immigrant and black businesses are geographically separated within metropolitan areas (MAs), but even in this case they may be potential competitors on the margin. On the other hand, these tabulations do indicate that immigrants are only a small share of the self-employed in most industries.

Metropolitan Area Definitions and Descriptive Statistics

In order to assess the effects of immigration on black self-employment we examine differences in immigration and self-employment across geographic areas. These geographic areas should approximate labor markets for the self-employed. We take the standard approach in the literature that uses MAs as the geographic areas. The specific MA definitions we use follow Jaeger (1996) and Bound and Holzer (1996). These definitions combine detailed geographical areas identified in the Censuses to provide consistent or nearly consistent definitions of 132 metropolitan areas in 1980 and 1990.

To create outcome measures for blacks, we use data from only the subset of these MAs that have a sufficient number of native-born black observations. Specifically, we include all individuals who live in MAs that have a total native black sample size (ages sixteen to sixty-four) greater than or equal to 600 in both Census years. This creates a sample of individuals who live in ninety-four MAs that represent 77.3 percent of the U.S. native black population (ages sixteen to sixty-four) in 1980 and 78.2 percent in 1990.[25]

In table 6.2, we report descriptive statistics for the MA-level variables used later in the chapter for the 1980 and 1990 cross-sections and for the change between the two Census years.[26] The self-employment rate and self-employment ratio for native-born blacks are defined as we did earlier. The low average black self-employment rates and ratios for black men and women in our sample accord with findings in other data sets. The average black self-employment rates for the ninety-four MAs are similar to estimates for blacks in the entire United States and are much lower than U.S. total rates for all races.[27] From 1980 to 1990, the mean self-employment rate and ratio increased substantially for black women, but only slightly for black men. The increase for black women agrees with other evidence on increases in female self-employment (see Devine 1994).

The immigrant, Asian immigrant, and black shares are defined as the fractions of the total population (ages sixteen to sixty-four) represented by each group.[28] Although the mean immigrant share and Asian-immigrant share in our sample of MAs are relatively low in both years, the increases in these two measures from 1980 to 1990 are notable. The average increase in the Asian-immigrant share is almost as large as the mean value in 1980. The mean black share in our sample is larger than the black share of the U.S. population due to our inclusion of the MAs with the largest black populations. The change in the mean value between 1980 and 1990 is small.

In table 6.2, we also report estimates for the weighted immigrant share. This measure addresses the concern that immigrant groups differ in their impact on black self-employment. For example, it is likely that an immigrant from a high self-employment rate group, such as Cubans, Koreans, or Russians, has a larger crowding-out effect on self-employed blacks than an immigrant from a low self-employment rate group, such as Cambodians, Filipinos, or Mexicans.[29] This observation suggests that we weight the immigrant share in an MA by the propensity of immigrants in that area to be self-employed.

We define the weighted immigrant share in MA m as:

$$(6.1) \quad I_m^W = \frac{1}{\alpha N_m^T} \sum_{g=1}^{G} S_{-mg} N_{mg},$$

where $g = 1, \ldots, G$ denotes immigrant groups, α is an adjustment factor defined below, S_{-mg} is the self-employment rate (or ratio) for group g using all MAs except MA m, N_{mg} is the number of immigrants of group g in MA m, and N_m^T is the total population in MA m. Using the self-employment rates (or ratios) as weights allows immigrants from high self-employment rate groups to count more than immigrants from low self-employment rate groups. There are a few things to note about equation (6.1). First, we exclude MA m when calculating the self-employment rate (or ratio) for each immigrant group to avoid the possibility that

Table 6.2 Descriptive Statistics for Metropolitan-Area Variables

Variable	Mean	Standard Deviation	Minimum	Maximum
1980				
Self-employment rate, black men	0.0367	0.0133	0.0107	0.0747
Self-employment rate, black women	0.0138	0.0072	0.0035	0.0526
Self-employment ratio, black men	0.0352	0.0124	0.0058	0.0690
Self-employment ratio, black women	0.0124	0.0055	0.0033	0.0313
Immigrant share of population	0.0529	0.0527	0.0102	0.2781
Weighted immigrant share using self-employment rate	0.0528	0.0440	0.0114	0.2615
Weighted immigrant share using self-employment ratio	0.0526	0.0442	0.0112	0.2699
Asian immigrant share	0.0100	0.0164	0.0007	0.1377
Black share of population	0.1369	0.0909	0.0184	0.3826
1990				
Self-employment rate, black men	0.0371	0.0145	0.0066	0.1036
Self-employment rate, black women	0.0220	0.0091	0.0033	0.0604
Self-employment ratio, black men	0.0384	0.0128	0.0156	0.0926
Self-employment ratio, black women	0.0221	0.0073	0.0046	0.0548
Immigrant share of population	0.0696	0.0752	0.0117	0.3930
Weighted immigrant share using self-employment rate	0.0706	0.0645	0.0144	0.3677
Weighted immigrant share using self-employment ratio	0.0701	0.0647	0.0144	0.3766
Asian immigrant share	0.0180	0.0230	0.0032	0.1678
Black share of population	0.1431	0.0937	0.0236	0.3988
1990 – 1980				
Self-employment rate, black men	0.0004	0.0157	−0.0527	0.0509
Self-employment rate, black women	0.0082	0.0098	−0.0249	0.0442
Self-employment ratio, black men	0.0032	0.0117	−0.0228	0.0470
Self-employment ratio, black women	0.0097	0.0079	−0.0195	0.0332
Immigrant share of population	0.0167	0.0261	−0.0073	0.1244
Weighted immigrant share using self-employment rate	0.0178	0.0238	−0.0078	0.1156
Weighted immigrant share using self-employment ratio	0.0175	0.0237	−0.0079	0.1161
Asian immigrant share	0.0080	0.0091	−0.0023	0.0529
Black share of population	0.0062	0.0116	−0.0278	0.0432

Notes: From ninety-four metropolitan area sample of those aged sixteen to sixty-four. The *self-employment rate* is the fraction of the employed that is self-employed. The *self-employment ratio* is the fraction of the noninstitutional, not-in-school population that is self-employed. The *immigrant, Asian immigrant, black,* and *weighted immigrant shares* are shares of the population of both genders. Census sample weights are used in 1990.

these rates (or ratios) depend on the level of black self-employment in the MA. Second, we classify immigrants into twenty-four different immigrant groups based on their responses to the place-of-birth question on the Census. In many cases, we group countries with relatively few immigrants into broader categories based on their geographical proximity and similarity in average propensities for self-employment. Third, the adjustment factor, α, is chosen to equate the total number of "weighted" immigrants and the total number of actual immigrants in the entire sample. Therefore, the weighted immigrant share variable has the same scale as the immigrant share. The weighted immigrant-share variables turn out to be very similar to the unweighted share variables. The main exception to this pattern is that MAs with many immigrants from Mexico tend to have lower weighted immigrant shares than unweighted immigrant shares, and MAs with many immigrants from Asian countries tend to have higher weighted immigrant shares.

Before discussing our probit results, it is useful to examine the relationship between the self-employment rate (or change in the self-employment rate) and the immigrant share (or change in the immigrant share) across our sample of MAs. In figures 6.1 through 6.6, we plot the relationship between these two variables. We use a two-letter code to indicate the data point for each of the ninety-four MAs. The size of these two-letter codes is proportional to the inverse of the variance of the corresponding self-employment rate. Appendix table 6a.1 lists these two-letter codes and their associated metropolitan areas.

We plot the relationship between the black male self-employment rate and the immigrant share for 1980 in figure 6.1 and for 1990 in figure 6.2. Most of the MAs are concentrated at the intersection of the means of the two variables in both Census years. The MAs with the highest rates of black male self-employment tend to be located in California or Florida, and the MAs with the largest shares of immigrants tend to be large MAs overall and located in California, Florida, and Texas. In both years, there appears to be a slightly positive relationship between the black male self-employment rate and the immigrant share.

In figure 6.3, we plot the relationship between the change from 1980 to 1990 in the black male self-employment rate and the change in the immigrant share. Again, most of the MAs in our sample are concentrated around the intersection of the mean values. The metropolitan areas with the largest increases in the immigrant share tend to be the same as those that have the largest immigrant share in 1980 and 1990. There does not appear to a be clear geographic pattern to the MAs that have the largest increases in black self-employment. In this figure, there appears to be a flat or slightly negative relationship between the two variables.

In figure 6.4, we plot the analogous relationship between the level of

(Text continues on p. 199.)

Figure 6.1   Black Male Self-Employment Rate Versus Immigrant Share, 1980

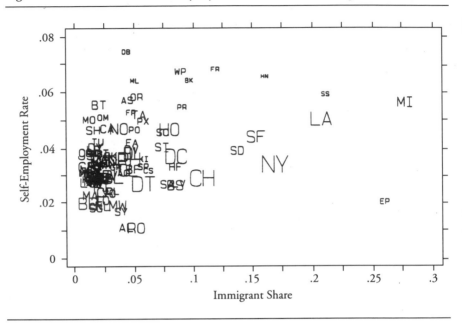

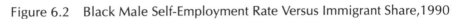

Figure 6.2   Black Male Self-Employment Rate Versus Immigrant Share, 1990

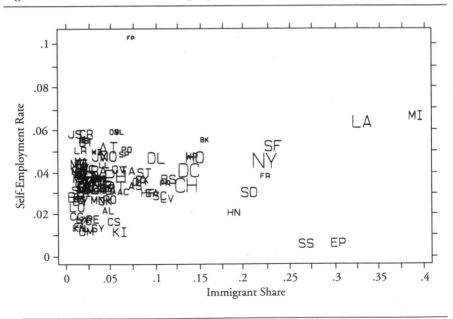

Figure 6.3 Black Male Self-Employment Rate Versus Immigrant Share, 1990 – 1980

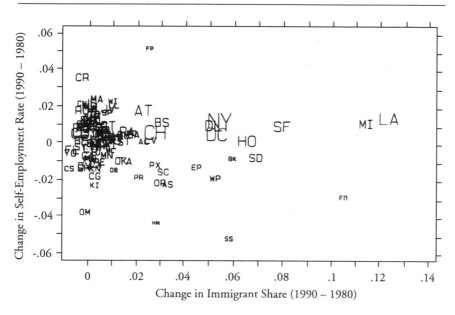

Figure 6.4 Black Female Self-Employment Rate Versus Immigrant Share, 1980

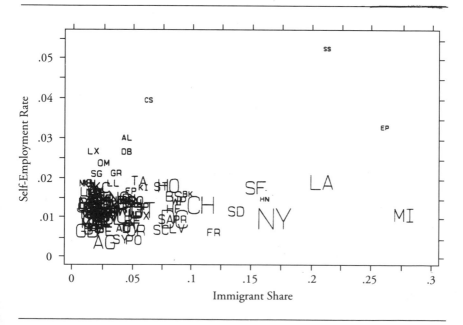

Figure 6.5   Black Female Self-Employment Rate Versus Immigrant Share, 1990

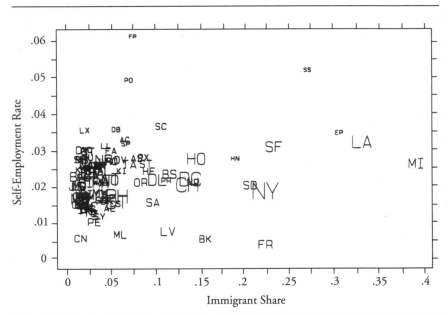

Figure 6.6   Black Female Self-Employment Rate Versus Immigrant Share, 1990 – 1980

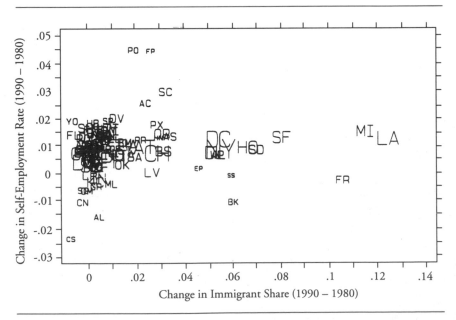

female self-employment and the immigrant share in 1980. In figure 6.5, we report the same relationship for 1990, and in figure 6.6 we report the relationship between the changes from 1980 and 1990 in the two variables for women. The plots have many of the same features as those for males, though a notable exception is the increase in the self-employment rate for women that is apparent for most MAs in figure 6.6. The 1980 plot appears to show a flat or slightly positive relationship between the level of immigration and the self-employment rate. The 1990 plot shows a slightly more positive relationship. The change between 1980 and 1990 again shows a flat or slightly positive relationship. In all cases, any relationship appears to be weak.

REGRESSION METHODS AND RESULTS

Although the plots are informative, we are interested in obtaining an estimate of the size of the effect of immigration on black self-employment and determining whether this effect is statistically different from zero. We accomplish these goals by estimating equations for the probability of self-employment using our sample of native blacks residing in one of the ninety-four MAs. In addition, these equations allow us to control for individual-level, as well as MA-level, characteristics that affect the self-employment decision. Formally, we assume that self-employment is determined by an unobserved latent variable,

$$(6.2) \quad Y_{im}^* = X_{im}'\beta + Z_m'\gamma + u_m + \epsilon_{im},$$

for person i, $i = 1, \ldots, N_m$, and MA m, $m = 1, \ldots, M$. We only observe Y_{im} which equals 1 if $Y_{im}^* \geq 0$, implying that person i chooses self-employment; Y_{im} equals 0 otherwise. X_{im} is a vector of individual-level characteristics, Z_m is a vector of MA-level characteristics that includes our measure of immigration, u_m is an MA-specific error term, and ϵ_{im} is an individual-specific error term. The MA-specific error term is included because we suspect that there are unmeasured MA characteristics that affect the self-employment probability of blacks. We allow for the presence of these omitted group-level determinants of the self-employment probability in our individual-level equations by using a two-stage estimation method.[30] If we take ϵ_{im} to be normally distributed, the assumptions imply that the data are described by a probit model. Although the normality assumption should only be taken as an approximation, the probit model provides a useful descriptive model for the binary event that a person is self-employed.

In the first stage, we estimate the probit regression:

$$(6.3) \quad Prob(Y_{im} = 1) = \Phi(X_{im}'\beta + \alpha_m),$$

where α_m is an MA fixed effect, and Φ is the cumulative normal distribution function. The second stage consists of a linear regression of the estimates of these fixed effects on the MA-level variables:

$$(6.4) \quad \hat{\alpha}_m = Z_m'\gamma + w_m.$$

The fixed effects in this equation are transformations of MA self-employment rates after controlling for differences in individual-level characteristics across MAs. Therefore, equation (6.4) is a regression of the adjusted self-employment tendency in an MA on MA-level variables. The second-stage coefficient estimates from equation (6.4) are in the same metric as the probit coefficients in equation (6.3) and their standard errors account for the group-level component in the error term.

As suggested in Borjas and Sueyoshi (1994), we estimate the second-stage regression using generalized least squares (GLS). Specifically, we use the weighting matrix $\Omega = \sigma_u^2 I_M + V_{\alpha\alpha}$, where $V_{\alpha\alpha}$ is the M × M block of the covariance matrix from equation (6.3) that is associated with the fixed effects.[31] The use of Ω places different weights on each MA that are related to the inverse of the precision of its fixed effect in the first-stage probit regression. We also use OLS to estimate our second-stage regressions as a sensitivity check.

We estimate several equations of the form (6.3) and (6.4). All of these regressions are estimated separately for our samples of native black men and native black women residing in the ninety-four MAs. We include individual-level controls for age, education level, marital status, number of children, disability status, and veteran status in the first-stage probit regressions.[32] We do not report these results, and instead focus on the results for the second-stage regressions.

In table 6.3, we report estimates of the second-stage regressions using GLS. We report separate estimates for our two measures of self-employment, the self-employment rate, and the self-employment ratio. Specifications 1 and 4 in the table use the 1980 cross-section, and specifications 2 and 5 use the 1990 cross-section. Specifications 3 and 6 report estimates from a different estimation technique that we discuss later in this section. All second-stage regressions include the reported immigration measure and several additional MA-level controls.[33] We do not discuss the coefficient estimates for these variables here, but a discussion can be found in Fairlie and Meyer (1997b). The inclusion of these variables has little effect on our immigration coefficients. We first present our cross-sectional results for the self-employment rate (specifications 1 and 2). The samples of native black men and women used in the first stage regressions are limited to the working population (ages sixteen to sixty-four).

Table 6.3 Two-Stage Probit Estimates of Self-Employment Rate and Self-Employment Ratio with Scaled Derivatives, GLS Second Stage

Sample and Immigration Measure	Self-Employment Rate			Self-Employment Ratio		
	1980	1990	1990 – 1980	1980	1990	1990 – 1980
	(1)	(2)	(3)	(4)	(5)	(6)
Native black men						
Immigrant share	1.0442	0.7865	−0.6809	0.7235	0.9156	−0.2878
	(0.2153)	(0.2127)	(0.6591)	(0.2968)	(0.1159)	(0.4955)
Scaled derivative	0.0470	0.0345	−0.0301	0.0367	0.0433	−0.0141
Weighted immigrant share	1.0462	0.8721	−0.7611	0.7401	0.9415	−0.3379
	(0.2358)	(0.2528)	(0.7239)	(0.3337)	(0.1450)	(0.5475)
Scaled derivative	0.0471	0.0332	−0.0337	0.0376	0.0445	−0.0165
Asian immigrant share	2.0118	0.9790	−0.1442	0.5872	1.9012	0.1007
	(0.9438)	(0.7230)	(2.1090)	(1.2197)	(0.4563)	(1.6215)
Scaled derivative	0.0887	0.0392	−0.0060	0.0297	0.0859	0.0048
Native black women						
Immigrant share	0.2553	0.5436	−0.0435	0.2217	0.5054	−0.5235
	(0.2028)	(0.1985)	(0.4150)	(0.1615)	(0.1300)	(0.5757)
Scaled derivative	0.0045	0.0148	−0.0010	0.0051	0.0166	−0.0150
Weighted immigrant share	−0.1153	0.5723	0.0701	−0.0993	0.4977	−0.4502
	(0.2262)	(0.2345)	(0.4529)	(0.1757)	(0.1473)	(0.6450)
Scaled derivative	−0.0021	0.0156	0.0016	−0.0023	0.0163	−0.0129
Asian immigrant share	2.9521	2.3253	−0.1580	1.7495	2.2937	0.7344
	(1.0305)	(0.7280)	(1.4159)	(0.8556)	(0.4583)	(1.8350)
Scaled derivative	0.0514	0.0578	−0.0034	0.0404	0.0718	0.0204

Notes: From ninety-four metropolitan area sample of those aged sixteen □ sixty-four. *Standard errors* are reported in parentheses. The *scaled derivative* approximates the change in the number of native self-employed blacks when the number of self-employed immigrants (or Asian immigrants) increases by one. The *self-employment rate* is the fraction of the employed that is self-employed. The *self-employment ratio* is the fraction of the noninstitutional, not-in-school population that is self-employed. The *immigrant, weighted immigrant,* and *Asian immigrant shares* are shares of the population of both genders. The *weighted immigrant share* weights immigrant groups by their self-employment rate (or ratio). All specifications include the following control variables: black share of the population, log average income of natives, black mayor, native unemployment rate, and log native population. The Asian immigrant share specifications also include the non-Asian immigrant

The second-stage equation that we report first for native black men includes the immigrant share as our measure of immigration. The coefficient on the immigrant share for both the 1980 and 1990 cross-sections is positive and statistically significant, suggesting that immigration increases the probability of self-employment among black men. In the second reported equation, we include the weighted immigrant share. The results for this measure are very similar to the those from the unweighted immigrant share. In the final equation reported for black men, we include the Asian-immigrant share. The coefficient on this variable is positive and larger than those on the immigrant share, though it is statistically significant only in 1980. Overall, our finding of a positive relationship between immigration and the probability of self-employment among black men is not sensitive to whether we weight immigration shares by the propensity for self-employment of the immigrant groups or to whether we focus on all immigrants or only Asian immigrants.

In our second-stage regressions using native black women, we find similar qualitative results for the effects of immigration on self-employment. The coefficients on the immigrant share and the Asian-immigrant share are positive in both the 1980 and 1990 cross-sections. An exception to the qualitative similarity between the results for black men and black women is the negative coefficient estimate on the weighted immigrant share in the 1980 cross-section for black women. This coefficient, however, is imprecisely measured and is not statistically different from zero at conventional levels.

Specifications 4 and 5 report estimates from the second-stage regressions for the self-employment ratio. The samples used to estimate the first-stage regressions include the entire nonschool, noninstitutionalized population (ages sixteen to sixty-four). The self-employment ratio is a much broader measure of self-employment than the self-employment rate, because it also includes individuals who, while primarily self-employed, worked few weeks or few hours per week last year. In addition, the use of this measure does not exclude from the sample someone who may have been displaced from self-employment into unemployment.[34] For black men, the use of this alternative sample and definition of self-employment does not change the conclusions substantially. The coefficient estimates on the immigrant share and weighted immigrant share are positive and mostly similar in magnitude and significance to those for the self-employment rate. For the Asian-immigrant share there are some differences, with the positive coefficient now being insignificant in 1980 but significant in 1990. For black women, the 1980 and 1990 estimates are even more similar to those for the self-employment rate. Apparently, our finding of a positive effect of immigration on black self-employment is not sensitive to our definition of self-employment and the sample restrictions used.

The general finding of a positive coefficient on the immigrant share and Asian-immigrant share in our regressions is surprising. Thus far, however, we have not determined if these positive coefficient estimates imply large or small effects of immigration on black self-employment. Recall that our second-stage coefficients are in the same metric as the probit coefficients, making them difficult to interpret. We convert these coefficients into derivatives, which are much easier to interpret. Let γ_I be the coefficient on the immigrant share. Then $\gamma_I \phi\,(\Phi^{-1}(S_B))$, is the derivative of the probability of self-employment with respect to the immigrant share, where S_B is the black self-employment rate (or ratio) for the relevant gender. An additional adjustment provides an expression (the scaled derivative) that can be interpreted as the change in the number of self-employed blacks in an MA when one more self-employed immigrant arrives. To make this adjustment we multiply the last expression by the number of people associated with a unit change in the black self-employment rate and divide by the number of self-employed people associated with a unit change in the immigrant share.[35] The resulting scaled derivative is $\gamma_I \phi(\Phi^{-1}(S_B))*LF_B/S_I$, where LF_B is the number of blacks in the labor force (or nonschool, noninstitutionalized population) of the appropriate gender divided by the total population of men and women, and S_I is the number of self-employed immigrants of either gender divided by the total number of immigrants.[36]

We report estimates of these derivatives in table 6.3. Standard errors are not reported but are simply equal to the coefficient standard error times the ratio of the derivative estimate to the coefficient estimate.[37] The derivative estimates indicate that the coefficients on the immigrant share imply small effects of immigration on black self-employment using either measure of self-employment. The derivative estimates imply that an additional self-employed immigrant results in an increase of 0.03 to 0.05 self-employed black men and an increase of about 0.01 self-employed black women. The derivative estimates for the weighted immigrant share are very similar for black men in both years and black women in 1990. For black women in 1980 the derivative estimates for the weighted immigrant share are negative but are very small and are based on coefficient estimates that are not significantly different from zero. The derivative estimates for the Asian-immigrant share imply somewhat larger effects, that is, that an additional self-employed Asian immigrant increases the number of self-employed black men by 0.03 to 0.09 and increases the number of self-employed black women by 0.04 to 0.07. We should emphasize that most of the estimates for both 1980 and 1990 have the opposite sign from what would be expected if immigrants displace self-employed blacks.

Potential Explanations for the Cross-Sectional Results

We now discuss two potential explanations for the unexpected positive coefficient and scaled derivative estimates presented above. First, the location decisions of immigrants may be directly related to MA levels of black self-employment, implying that the immigrant share is not an exogenous variable in our second-stage regressions. We argue, however, that this is unlikely because the level of black self-employment is generally so low that blacks make up only a small share of the potential competitors for immigrants. Further support of this argument is provided by the finding in Bartel (1989) that recent immigrants tend to locate in SMSAs that have large numbers of previous immigrants from the same country, and that economic factors have a relatively small effect on location decisions.

Another explanation is that the positive estimates are due to unobserved MA characteristics that are correlated with black self-employment and the immigrant share. In particular, our positive coefficient estimates may be due to an omitted MA fixed effect that both increases the level of black self-employment and is positively correlated with immigration. Examples of omitted MA fixed effects affecting black self-employment include the level of consumer discrimination against minority-owned businesses, local government business development policies, consumer demand for the goods and services produced by small businesses, and local economic conditions for small businesses. It is not unreasonable that immigrants may locate in the MAs with favorable values of these characteristics for self-employed blacks. At best, the MA-level controls currently included in our second-stage regressions serve as crude proxies for some of these factors.

1990 – 1980 Estimates

We address the issue of a bias in our results from unobservable MA fixed effects by estimating MA-level regressions for the change in self-employment between 1980 and 1990, again using a two-stage procedure. We first estimate a probit regression for the self-employment probability which uses pooled data from the 1980 and 1990 cross-sections. We rewrite equation (6.3) as:

$$(6.5) \quad Prob(Y_{imt} = 1) = \Phi(X_{imt}'\beta + \alpha_m + \delta_m D_{90}),$$

where $t = 80, 90$, and D_{90} is a dummy variable indicating whether the observation is from 1990. This equation controls for changes over time as well as differences across individuals in the values of characteristics such as education that are included in X_{imt}. In this equation, δ_m represents the change in the metropolitan-area-level determinants of self-employment for metropolitan area m. The estimates of these first-difference fixed effects become the dependent variable in the second-stage regression:

$$(6.6) \quad \hat{\delta}_m = \bar{Z}_m{'} \, \bar{\gamma} + \eta_m,$$

where $\bar{Z}_m = Z_{m90} - Z_{m80}$. This equation is a regression of the first-differences of the adjusted self-employment tendencies on the first-difference of the MA-level variables. Therefore, these estimates remove any unobserved MA characteristics that affect the self-employment probability and are constant over time.

Specifications 3 and 6 of table 6.3 provide estimates of the coefficients in equation (6.6). These regressions include first differences of all of the MA-level controls that we include in equation (6.2) for the 1980 and 1990 MA-level cross-sections. We first discuss the results for the self-employment rate, reported in specification 3. The coefficients on the immigrant share, weighted immigrant share, and Asian-immigrant share are now negative for black men. These coefficient estimates, however, are statistically insignificant and do not imply large effects. The scaled derivative estimates indicate that an additional self-employed immigrant displaces 0.03 self-employed blacks. In other words, it takes over thirty-three self-employed immigrants to reduce the number of self-employed black men by one. The effect of an additional self-employed Asian-immigrant is even smaller. Using our sample of black women, the first-difference coefficient estimates on the immigration variables are essentially equal to zero, implying that there is no effect of immigration on black female self-employment.

The results for the self-employment ratio, reported in specification 6 of table 6.3, differ little from the results for the self-employment rate. For black men, the negative coefficients on the immigrant, weighted, and Asian-immigrant shares are smaller in absolute value or become positive. For black women, some of the coefficients change sign, but all of them are still small. None of the coefficients for the self-employment ratio is statistically significant, and each one implies only a very small effect of immigration on black male or female self-employment.

In general, the point estimates of the derivatives from the first-difference regressions are negative and close to zero for black men and women. The standard errors on these derivative estimates, however, are substantial. We examine whether large negative effects can be ruled out by confidence intervals for these derivatives. Using the scaled derivative estimate on the weighted immigrant share reported in specification 3 for black men, the symmetric 95 percent confidence interval created by subtracting and adding 1.96 times the standard error is $[-0.096, 0.029]$. The confidence interval for the weighted immigrant share in specification 6 using black women is $[-0.049, 0.023]$. These intervals were calculated using the immigrant or weighted immigrant share derivative estimates for black men and women that have the largest (in absolute value) negative lower limits of their confidence intervals. Using the less precisely measured derivative estimates for the Asian-immigrant share, the confidence intervals are $[-0.178, 0.166]$ for black men (specification 3) and $[-0.080, 0.120]$ for black women (specification 6). These findings suggest that, although our coefficients are imprecisely measured, we can rule out that each self-employed immigrant displaces more than 0.09 self-employed black men and 0.05 black women. The corresponding numbers for Asian immigrants are about twice as large because of larger standard errors, even though the point estimates are much smaller.

Additional Second-Stage Regressions

We estimate several additional second-stage regressions to check the robustness of the estimates presented above. In table 6.4, we report the results from several of these regressions using our pooled sample.[38] The samples and explanatory variables used are the same as those used in table 6.3 unless noted otherwise. We first estimate the second-stage regressions using OLS.[39] These estimates are reported in specifications 1 and 4. For black men, the coefficients on the immigration measures are more negative than those using GLS, with the exception of the Asian-immigrant coefficient in the self-employment rate specification. The negative effects of immigration implied by these OLS coefficients, however, are not large and are far from being statistically significant. The comparison between the OLS and GLS coefficients for black women is similar (that is, the OLS coefficients are more negative except for Asian immigration), however, none of the coefficients is statistically significant or imply large negative effects. Overall, the findings from our second-stage regressions using OLS do not change our conclusions regarding the effect of immigration on black self-employment.

Our first-difference estimates eliminate the bias due to MA fixed effects that are correlated with black self-employment and the immigrant share. These estimates, however, do not eliminate potential biases due to MA-specific transitory effects that are correlated with changes in black

Table 6.4 Two-Stage Probit Estimates of Self-Employment Rate and Self-Employment Ratio with Scaled Derivatives, Alternative Specifications for 1990 – 1980

Sample and Immigration Measure	Self-Employment Rate			Self-Employment Ratio		
	OLS	IV	Segregation Included	OLS	IV	Segregation Included
	(1)	(2)	(3)	(4)	(5)	(6)
Native black men						
Immigrant share	-1.4465	-0.9558	-0.5303	-0.5414	-0.0865	-0.0294
	(0.8273)	(0.7510)	(0.7173)	(0.6555)	(0.5603)	(0.5005)
Scaled derivative	-0.0640	-0.0422	-0.0235	-0.0265	-0.0042	-0.0014
Weighted immigrant share	-1.6953	-1.0859	-0.5944	-0.5748	-0.2102	-0.0649
	(0.9217)	(0.8754)	(0.7826)	(0.7358)	(0.6554)	(0.5455)
Scaled derivative	-0.0750	-0.0482	-0.0263	-0.0281	-0.0103	-0.0032
Asian-immigrant share	0.9789	-4.6305	0.2332	-0.7670	0.5821	0.6077
	(2.7370)	(2.9009)	(2.1357)	(2.2404)	(2.1465)	(1.5253)
Scaled derivative	0.0408	-0.1929	0.0097	-0.0365	0.0277	0.0289
Native black women						
Immigrant share	-0.7200	0.0855	0.1483	-1.4537	-0.6471	-0.2902
	(1.1134)	(0.4657)	(0.4531)	(0.8581)	(0.6536)	(0.6385)
Scaled derivative	-0.0163	-0.0019	0.0034	-0.0416	-0.0185	-0.0083
Weighted immigrant share	-0.4844	0.0168	0.2935	-1.2352	-0.6122	-0.1805
	(1.1454)	(0.5615)	(0.4860)	(0.9326)	(0.7760)	(0.7038)
Scaled derivative	-0.0110	0.0004	0.0067	-0.0353	-0.0175	-0.0052
Asian-immigrant share	3.6749	-0.3316	-0.0267	1.4758	1.3280	0.8589
	(3.4483)	(1.6415)	(1.4395)	(2.9426)	(2.3031)	(1.9065)
Scaled derivative	0.0784	-0.0071	-0.0006	0.0411	0.0370	0.0239

Notes: See table 6.3. The *OLS* columns use OLS in the second stage. The *IV* columns use the 1980 immigration variable to instrument for the change between 1980 and 1990. The *segregation included* columns include the dissimilarity index to measure segregation and only include ninty-one metropolitan areas.

self-employment and changes in the immigrant share. In particular, immigrants may choose to live in MAs that are experiencing fast local economic growth. The MAs that are experiencing fast local economic growth are also likely to have increasing levels of black self-employment, thus causing a spurious correlation between changes in black self-employment and immigration. To address this problem, we apply the instrumental variables (IV) approach taken in Altonji and Card (1991). In particular, we use the 1980 value of our immigration measure as an instrument for the change in its value from 1980 to 1990.[40]

We report the IV results in specifications 2 and 5 of table 6.4.[41] For black men, the coefficients on the immigrant and weighted immigrant shares are now slightly more negative for the self-employment rate, but are slightly less negative for the self-employment ratio. All of these coefficients imply small negative and statistically insignificant effects of immigration on black male self-employment. For black women, the IV coefficient estimates are generally more negative for the immigrant and weighted immigrant shares, but they remain small and statistically insignificant.

The IV estimates on the Asian-immigrant share differ from the GLS coefficients. For black men, the coefficient in specification 2 implies a substantial negative effect of Asian immigration on black male self-employment. The derivative estimate indicates that an additional self-employed immigrant displaces 0.19 self-employed black men. This result, however, is sensitive to the definition of self-employment, as the coefficient on the Asian-immigrant share in specification 5 is now positive (although very small). For black women, the coefficient in specification 2 remains negative and small, whereas the coefficient in specification 5 is still positive but is now larger. In nearly all cases, the IV estimates do not differ substantially from our original estimates and thus do not provide evidence of a negative effect of immigration on black self-employment. The one possible exception is the finding of a substantial negative but insignificant coefficient estimate on the Asian-immigrant share for black men in the self-employment rate specification.

We next estimate second-stage regressions that include a measure of black residential segregation as an additional control (reported in specifications 3 and 6). To measure segregation, we use the dissimilarity index which is defined for a given MA as:

$$(6.7) \quad D = 0.5 \sum_{j=1}^{J} \left| \frac{B_j}{B} - \frac{W_j}{W} \right|,$$

where $j = 1, \ldots, J$ denotes census tracts, B_j and W_j are the black and white populations in census tract j, and B and W are the total black and white populations in the MA.[42] The dissimilarity index provides a measure of the unevenness of the distribution of blacks and whites in an MA and provides an estimate of what percentage of blacks would have to be resettled to achieve complete integration (that is, equal black/white population ratios in all census tracts in the MA). The index ranges from 0 indicating complete residential integration of blacks and whites to 1 indicating complete segregation. Descriptive statistics for this variable are reported in appendix table 6a.2. We are limited to including only ninety-one MAs because the dissimilarity index is not available for a few of our original MAs. The coefficient estimates on the dissimilarity index range from 0.180 to 0.337 for black men and from 0.171 to 0.566 for black women, however, none of these coefficient estimates is statistically significant. These results provide some evidence that segregation may increase black self-employment by creating a "captive" market of black consumers who presumably do not discriminate against other blacks. Some of the coefficients on the immigrant measures change with the inclusion of the dissimilarity index, but these changes do not affect our general conclusions regarding the effect of immigration on black self-employment. We do not find substantial negative coefficient estimates on our immigration measures in any of the specifications.

As a final check, we estimate regressions that include interactions between our measures of immigration and the dissimilarity index. It is possible that the effect of immigration on black self-employment in a local labor market depends on the level of residential segregation in that market. To explore this possibility, we first divide our sample of MAs into two groups: those with dissimilarity indices at or below the median in 1980 (low-segregation MAs) and those with dissimilarity indices above the median (high-segregation MAs). We then allow the effect of immigration on black self-employment to differ between the two groups.

In table 6.5, we report the results for regressions that include separate immigrant and Asian-immigrant share coefficients for low-segregation MAs and high-segregation MAs. For black men, the immigrant-share coefficients are positive and small for the high-segregation MAs and are negative for the low-segregation MAs. The Asian-immigrant share coefficients show a similar pattern, except the positive coefficients for the high-segregation MAs are much larger and Asian immigration increases self-employment in low-segregation MAs. For each specification, we test whether the immigration coefficients are statistically different for the two groups of MAs. The coefficients are never statistically different even at the $\alpha = .10$ significance level. Overall, these results do not provide evidence that immigration has a larger negative effect on black self-employment in MAs with lower levels of residential segregation.

Table 6.5   Two-Stage Probit Estimates of Self-Employment Rate and Self-Employment Ratio with Scaled Derivatives, 1990 – 1980, GLS with Segregation Interactions

Sample and Immigration Measure	SE Rate (1)	SE Ratio (2)
Native black men		
Immigrant share * high segregation	0.1433	0.1505
	(0.8220)	(0.5678)
Scaled derivative	0.0063	0.0074
Immigrant share * low segregation	−1.8771	−0.5552
	(1.0774)	(0.7772)
Scaled derivative	−0.0831	−0.0271
Asian-immigrant share * high segregation	3.5461	3.4537
	(3.5486)	(2.4034)
Scaled derivative	0.1477	0.1644
Asian-immigrant share * low segregation	0.3048	−0.4774
	(2.5437)	(1.8473)
Scaled derivative	0.0127	−0.0227
Native black women		
Immigrant share * high segregation	0.3640	0.0080
	(0.4828)	(0.7126)
Scaled derivative	0.0082	0.0002
Immigrant share * low segregation	0.4249	−1.1204
	(0.7976)	(1.0025)
Scaled derivative	0.0096	−0.0320
Asian-immigrant share * high segregation	−2.7640	−0.2354
	(2.2280)	(2.9560)
Scaled derivative	−0.0589	−0.0066
Asian-immigrant share * low segregation	0.4558	2.5819
	(1.8696)	(2.2057)
Scaled derivative	0.0097	0.0719

Notes: See table 6.3. *High segregation* and *low segregation* are indicators for a metropolitan area being above or below median in the dissimilarity index, respectively. The Asian-immigrant share specifications also include non-Asian–immigrant share interactions with the segregation indicators as additional control variables. Only ninty-one metropolitan areas are included in these specifications.

The Migration of Self-Employed Blacks

An important issue in our analysis and in previous studies that use variation across MAs to identify the effect of immigration on native outcomes is whether natives move in response to immigration. Borjas (1994) suggests that native migration may be partly responsible for the general finding of a weak negative effect of immigration on the wages and employment of natives.[43] He argues that if native workers respond to the entry of immigrants by moving to metropolitan areas that provide better opportunities, then the correlation between immigration and the outcomes of native workers will naturally be small. He cites evidence by Filer (1992) and Frey (1995) of a negative correlation between immigration and native out-migration across MAs in the United States. This issue, however, is potentially much less of a problem for our study. Because of the difficulties in transporting physical capital and established clientele, we expect the self-employed to be less mobile than wage/salary workers.

We check this hypothesis using a question on the 1990 Census that asks where the respondent lived in 1985. We calculate migration rates for self-employed and wage/salary blacks in each of the ninety-four MAs identified in our sample. We define the self-employed (wage/salary) migration rate as the percent of self-employed (wage/salary) blacks who lived in a different MA in 1985. Individuals are classified as self-employed or as a wage/salary worker based on their work status in 1990. The average migration rates across our ninety-four MAs are 0.090 for self-employed black men and 0.140 for wage/salary black men. For black women, the average migration rates for the self-employed and wage/salary workers are 0.078 and 0.106, respectively. These estimates suggest that there is less geographical mobility among the self-employed. Although this finding is only suggestive, it implies that our estimates are less likely to suffer from the potential bias of native migration than previous studies.

SUMMARY AND CONCLUSIONS

We analyze immigration and black self-employment in ninety-four of the largest U.S. metropolitan areas using 1980 and 1990 Census microdata. We first examine the relationship between immigration and self-employment at a point in time, either 1980 or 1990. In these cross-sectional analyses, we find a statistically significant positive relationship in most cases between immigration and black self-employment. These results contradict the hypothesis that self-employed immigrants crowd out self-employed blacks. We suspect that this counterintuitive result is due to omitted metropolitan-area characteristics that we cannot measure well, such as the local economic conditions for small business and the extent of consumer discrimination. When we examine changes in immigration and changes in self-employment using fixed-effects estimates, we generally find a weak negative and statistically insignificant relationship. Therefore, our estimates using data on changes between 1980 and 1990 do not provide strong evidence of crowding out of black self-employment by self-employed immigrants. These findings do not change if we if use an immigration measure that weights immigrant groups by their propensity to be self-employed to account for the marked differences in self-employment between groups such as Cubans, Koreans, and Mexicans. Our results are also similar if we limit our sample of immigrants to those from only Asian countries.

Our fixed-effects estimates indicate that approximately 0.02 self-employed black men and 0.01 black women are displaced by each self-employed immigrant. Calculating confidence intervals for these estimates, we can rule out the possibility that each self-employed immigrant displaces more than 0.09 self-employed black men and 0.05 black women. When we limit our sample of immigrants to those from Asian countries, our estimates suggest that immigration leads to increases in black self-employment about as often as decreases. Primarily due to the larger standard errors on these last estimates, we can only rule out reductions in black self-employment greater than 0.18 men and 0.08 women for each self-employed Asian immigrant.

Our results are similar using a number of alternative estimation techniques and specifications. To address the concern that MA differences in local levels of economic growth are causing a spurious correlation between changes in immigration and black self-employment, we estimate instrumental variables regressions. We use the 1980 level of immigration as an instrument for the change in immigration between 1980 and 1990, since later immigrants tend to locate in areas that have a large number of earlier immigrants. We try a number of different methods to ensure that our results are not sensitive to particular definitions of self-employment or particular control variables. We try controls for population growth, changes in unemployment and in income, and the election of a black mayor. We should also note that migration is less likely to disguise immigration effects on natives in the case of self-employment because the self-employed have lower migration rates than wage/salary workers.

The results of our empirical analyses are consistent with the earlier predictions of our theoretical model that immigration would, at most, have a small negative effect on native black self-employment. An alternative explanation for our finding is that recent immigrants may primarily displace the self-employed among earlier immigrant cohorts or native whites. It may also be the case that self-employed immigrants crowd out self-employed blacks in certain cities, industries, or neighborhoods where they congregate, but we find no evidence of a substantial overall effect.

APPENDIX

Appendix Table 6A.1   Metropolitan Areas with Their Two-Letter Codes

AL	Albany-Schenectady-Troy, NY	GB	Greensboro-Winston-Salem-
AT	Atlanta, GA		High Pt., NC
AC	Atlantic City, NJ	GV	Greenville-Spartanburg, SC
AG	Augusta, GA-SC	HB	Harrisburg-Lebanon-Carlisle,
AS	Austin, TX		PA
BK	Bakersfield, CA	HF	Hartford-New Britain-Middle-
BL	Baltimore, MD		town-Bristol, CT (N)
BT	Baton Rouge, LA	HN	Honolulu, HI
BM	Beaumont-Port Arthur, TX	HO	Houston-Galveston-Brazoria,
BR	Birmingham, AL		TX (C)
BS	Boston-Lawrnce-Salem-	IN	Indianapolis, IN
	Lowell-Brockton, MA (N)	JS	Jackson, MS
BF	Buffalo-Niagara Falls, NY (C)	JV	Jacksonville, FL
CN	Canton, OH	KC	Kansas City, MO-KS
CR	Charleston, SC	KL	Killeen-Temple, TX
CT	Charlotte-Gastonia-Rock Hill,	KN	Knoxville, TN
	NC-SC	LL	Lakeland-Winter Haven, FL
CG	Chattanooga, TN-GA	LV	Las Vegas, NV
CH	Chicago-Gary-Lake Cnty, IL-	LX	Lexington-Fayette, KY
	IN-WI (C)	LR	Little Rock-North Little Rock,
CI	Cincinnati-Hamilton, OH-		AR
	KY-IN (C)	LA	Los Angeles-Anaheim-
CL	Cleveland-Akron-Lorain,		Riverside, CA (C)
	OH (C)	LO	Louisville, KY-IN
CS	Colorado Springs, CO	MA	Macon-Warner Robins, GA
CA	Columbia, SC	ML	Melbourne-Titusville-Palm
CU	Columbus, OH		Bay, FL
DL	Dallas-Fort Worth, TX (C)	ME	Memphis, TN-AR-MS
DY	Dayton-Springfield, OH	MI	Miami-Fort Lauderdale, FL (C)
DB	Daytona Beach, FL	MW	Milwaukee-Racine, WI (C)
DV	Denver-Boulder, CO (C)	MN	Minneapolis-St. Paul, MN-WI
DT	Detroit-Ann Arbor, MI (C)	MB	Mobile, AL
EP	El Paso, TX	MO	Montgomery, AL
FA	Fayetteville, NC	NA	Nashville, TN
FL	Flint, MI	NO	New Orleans, LA
FP	Fort Pierce, FL	NR	Norfolk-Va. Beach-Newport
FW	Fort Wayne, IN		News, VA
FR	Fresno, CA	NY	NY-Northern NJ-Long Island,
GR	Grand Rapids, MI		NY-NJ-CT (C)

(Table continues on p. 214.)

Appendix Table 6A.1   *Continued*

OK	Oklahoma City, OK	SS	Salinas-Seaside-Monterey, CA
OM	Omaha, NE-IA	SA	San Antonio, TX
OR	Orlando, FL	SD	San Diego, CA
PE	Pensacola, FL	SF	San Francisco-Oakland-San
PH	Philly-Wilmington-Trenton,		Jose, CA (C)
	PA-NJ-DE-MD (C)	ST	Seattle-Tacoma, WA (C)
PX	Phoenix, AZ	SH	Shreveport, LA
PI	Pittsburgh-Beaver Valley, PA	SP	Springfield, MA
	(C)	SL	St. Louis, MO-IL
PO	Portland-Vancouver, OR-WA	SY	Syracuse, NY
	(C)	TA	Tampa-St. Petersburg-
PR	Providence-Pawtucket-		Clearwater, FL
	Woonsocket, RI (N)	TO	Toledo, OH
RA	Raleigh-Durham, NC	TU	Tulsa, OK
RI	Richmond-Petersburg, VA	WP	W. Palm Beach-Boca Raton-
RO	Rochester, NY		Delray Beach, FL
SC	Sacramento, CA	DC	Washington, DC-MD-VA
SG	Saginaw-Bay City-Midland,	WI	Wichita, KS
	MI	YO	Youngstown-Warren, OH

Notes: Metropolitan area groupings are from U.S. Bureau of the Census (1993). Those listed with (C) are consolidated metropolitan statistical areas, and those listed with (N) are New England county metropolitan areas.

Appendix Table 6A.2   Descriptive Statistics for Additional Metropolitan-Area Variables

Variable	Mean	Standard Deviation	Minimum	Maximum
1980				
Log average income of natives	9.8282	0.1125	9.5618	10.1137
Black mayor	0.0957	0.2958	0.0000	1.0000
Native unemployment rate	0.0641	0.0205	0.0300	0.1382
Log native population	13.2215	0.9156	11.6335	16.0749
Dissimilarity index ($N=91$)	0.6864	0.1168	0.3270	0.8970
1990				
Log average income of natives	9.8906	0.1344	9.6088	10.2624
Black mayor	0.2128	0.4115	0.0000	1.0000
Native unemployment rate	0.0616	0.0152	0.0339	0.1057
Log native population	13.3373	0.8866	11.8004	16.0625
Dissimilarity index ($N=91$)	0.6358	0.1229	0.2270	0.8760
1990 to 1980				
Log average income of natives	0.0623	0.0827	−0.1602	0.2501
Black mayor	0.1170	0.3549	−1.0000	1.0000
Native unemployment rate	−0.0024	0.0173	−0.0417	0.0440
Log native population	0.1159	0.1527	−0.1752	0.7239
Dissimilarity index ($N=91$)	−0.0506	0.0388	−0.1560	0.0370

Note: From ninety-four metropolitan area sample of those aged sixteen to sixty-four.

NOTES

1. See Borjas (1994) and Friedberg and Hunt (1995) for thoughtful reviews of this literature.

2. For brevity, we use the term *blacks* in the remainder of the study.

3. See Borjas (1986) and Yuengert (1995) for evidence of higher rates of self-employment among immigrants than natives, and see Fairlie and Meyer (1996) for evidence of high self-employment rates among some Asian ethnic groups.

4. The perceived threat of immigration to black business opportunities has been the topic of articles in national newspapers (see "For Immigrants, Tough Customers," *New York Times*, November 25, 1990) and black magazines (see "The Korean Invasion: A New Threat to Black Business," *Metro Atlanta*, March 1989).

5. Earlier studies include Myrdal (1944), Cayton and Drake (1946), Frazier (1957), Kinzer and Sagarin (1950), and Glazer and Moynihan (1970). Recent work includes Bates (1989), Borjas and Bronars (1989), Meyer (1990), and Fairlie (1997).

6. Glazer and Moynihan (1970, p. 36) argue that "business is in America the most effective form of social mobility for those who meet prejudice."

7. See Light (1972) for a description of the history of the Chinese and Japanese in the United States and Loewen (1971) for a description of the Chinese in Mississippi.

8. See section six of Fairlie and Meyer (1996).

9. See Guy et al. (1991) for a description of the program promoting self-employment among AFDC recipients and Benus et al. (1992) for a description of the program promoting self-employment among unemployment insurance recipients.

10. See In-Jin Yoon (1991b) for a description of the causes and character of the racial tensions between Koreans and African Americans in Chicago, and see Min (1996) for a summary of the numerous black boycotts of Korean merchants in New York and Los Angeles in the past two decades.

11. See Brown, Hamilton, and Medoff (1990).

12. We should note, however, that some support for this assumption in previous studies is provided by Bartel (1989). She finds that recent immigrants tend to locate in SMSAs that have large numbers of previous immigrants from the same country, and that economic factors have a relatively small effect on location decisions.

13. Besides Borjas (1994) and Friedberg and Hunt (1995), see also Borjas,

Freeman, and Katz (1996) and Butcher (this volume) for discussions of the main approaches taken in this literature.

14. Recent examples include Altonji and Card (1991), LaLonde and Topel (1991), Butcher and Card (1991), Butcher (this volume) and Reimers (this volume).

15. The results from an earlier study by Light and Sanchez (1987) which uses the same data are similar.

16. These two explanatory variables may be endogenous, however, as it is likely that they are partly determined by the level of native self-employment in the metropolitan area.

17. There exists a large literature in sociology that attempts to identify the factors leading to both the high level of business ownership among Asians (especially among Koreans) and the low rates among blacks. See Aldrich and Waldinger (1990) and Light (1984, 1994) for reviews of this literature.

18. Examples of unobserved metropolitan-area fixed effects include the level of consumer discrimination against minority-owned businesses, local government business-development policies, consumer demand for the goods and services produced by small businesses, and local economic conditions for small businesses.

19. This assumption is probably conservative given the special demands of many immigrant groups for ethnic products that are often provided by the self-employed.

20. The 1990 self-employment rate of male immigrants is 12.1 percent, while that of male natives is 10.4 percent. For women, the numbers are 7.2 and 5.6 percent, respectively.

21. Unpaid family workers are not counted as self-employed.

22. The "class of worker" question refers to the individual's "chief job activity or business last week." Individuals who hold more than one job are asked to refer to the one at which they worked the most hours. The "class of worker" question on the 1980 Census is nearly identical.

23. The Census does not record the existence or number of employees for the self-employed.

24. These self-employed black women are mainly in health and social services.

25. These samples represent 60.6 and 61.2 percent of the native white population (ages sixteen to sixty-four) and 85.4 and 87.3 percent of the immigrant population (ages sixteen to sixty-four) in 1980 and 1990, respectively.

26. These statistics weight each of the ninety-four MAs in our sample equally.

In our regressions discussed later we use GLS weights. Means and standard deviations calculated using these weights are similar for the self-employment measures but are considerably larger for the immigration measures.

27. Fairlie and Meyer (1996) report black self-employment rates of 0.044 for men and 0.020 for women for the entire United States in 1990. The total self-employment rates are 0.108 for men and 0.058 for women.

28. The immigrant share includes Asian and black immigrants as well as other immigrants, and the black share includes black immigrants as well as other blacks.

29. Even within the Asian category there exist large differences across groups. See Fairlie and Meyer (1996) for evidence on this point.

30. See Borgas and Sueyoshi (1994) for a complete description of the issues.

31. We estimate σ_u^2 following Borjas (1987).

32. The coefficient estimates on these variables are consistent with previous work. We find that the self-employment probability is higher for those who are older, more educated, married, and nonveterans. These tendencies generally hold for both genders, Census years, and measures of self-employment. The estimates for the number of children and disability status are not easily summarized as they differ more by sample and gender.

33. We include the black share of the population, the log average income of natives, a black mayor indicator variable, the native unemployment rate, and the log native population as controls in all specifications and the non-Asian–immigrant share as an additional control in the specifications with the Asian-immigrant share.

34. A simple calculation shows that this second difference is probably of less importance. A self-employed worker displaced into unemployment reduces the numerator of both the self-employment rate and ratio by one, reduces the denominator of the ratio by one, but leaves the denominator of the rate unchanged. However, since the denominator is so much larger than the numerator, the resulting difference between the rate and ratio measures will be small.

35. This formula relies on the implicit assumption that the number of immigrants who are self-employed in an MA is proportional to the number of immigrants in that MA. While crowding out or enclave effects (which work in different directions) would make this assumption not strictly correct, it is unlikely to be far from the truth.

36. We use the appropriate self-employment definition (rate or ratio) to count the number of self-employed immigrants.

37. We assume that LF_B, S_B and S_I are nonstochastic for this calculation.

38. Although they are not reported, we also estimate a set of second-stage regressions that include the nonblack self-employment rate as an additional control. The coefficient estimates on the immigrant and weighted immigrant shares are very similar to those reported in specifications 3 and 6 of table 6.3 for black men and women. A few of the coefficient estimates on the Asian-immigrant share are larger in absolute value, however, none of these imply large negative effects. In addition, the nonblack self-employment rate is statistically insignificant in all of the regressions.

39. A potential problem with the GLS estimates occurs if there is an important omitted variable that is specific to one or a few of the MAs with large regression weights. Because OLS places the same weight on each observation, the effect of such an omitted variable on the coefficient estimates is lessened.

40. Given Bartel's (1989) finding that recent immigrants tend to locate in SMSAs that have large numbers of previous immigrants from the same country, the 1980 immigrant share should be strongly correlated with the 1980 to 1990 change in the immigrant share. In fact, the weighted correlation between the two variables is .87.

41. The formula for the vector of second-stage coefficient estimates is: $(\check{Z}'\Omega^{-1}W(W'\Omega^{-1}W)^{-1}W'\Omega^{-1}\check{Z})^{-1}\check{Z}'\Omega^{-1}W(W'\Omega^{-1}W)^{-1}W'\Omega^{-1}\hat{\delta}$, where $\check{Z}$, Ω, $\hat{\delta}$ are as defined above, and W includes the 1980 immigration measure and first differences of the MA-level controls.

42. Estimates of the dissimilarity index were taken from Harrison and Weinberg (1992). See Zax in this volume for a further discussion of the construction of this variable and other measures of residential segregation.

43. Also see Borjas, Freeman, and Katz (1997). Card (1997) provides an alternative view.

REFERENCES

Aldrich, Howard E., and Roger Waldinger. 1990. "Ethnicity and Entrepreneurship." *Annual Review of Sociology* 16(1): 111–35.

Altonji, Joseph G. and David Card. 1991. "The Effects of Immigration on the Labor Market Outcomes of Less-Skilled Natives." In *Immigration, Trade, and the Labor Market*, edited by John M. Abowd and Richard B. Freeman. Chicago: University of Chicago Press.

Bartel, Ann P. 1989. "Where Do the New U.S. Immigrants Live?" *Journal of Labor Economics* 7(4): 371–91.

Bates, Timothy. 1989. "The Changing Nature of Minority Business: A Comparative Analysis of Asian, Nonminority, and Black-Owned Businesses." *The Review of Black Political Economy* 18(2): 25–42.

Benus, Jacob M., Michelle L. Wood, Christopher J. Napierala, and Terry R. Johnson. 1992. "Massachusetts UI Self-Employment Demonstration." In *Self-Employment Programs for Unemployed Workers.* Unemployment Insurance Occasional Paper 92-2, U.S. Department of Labor, Employment and Training Administration, Unemployment Insurance Service.

Borjas, George J. 1986. "The Self-Employment Experience of Immigrants." *Journal of Human Resources* 21(4): 487–506.

———. 1987. "Self-Selection and the Earnings of Immigrants." *American Economic Review* 77(4): 531–53.

———. 1994. "The Economics of Immigration." *Journal of Economic Literature* 32(4): 1667–1717.

Borjas, George, and Stephen Bronars. 1989. "Consumer Discrimination and Self-Employment." *Journal of Political Economy* 97(3): 581–605.

Borjas, George J., Richard B. Freeman, and Lawrence F. Katz. 1996. "Searching for the Effect of Immigration on the Labor Market." *American Economic Review Papers and Proceedings* 86(2): 246–51.

———. 1997. "How Much Do Immigration and Trade Affect Labor Market Outcomes?" *Brookings Papers on Economic Activity* (1): 1–90.

Borjas, George, and Glen Sueyoshi. 1994. "A Two-Stage Estimator for Probit Models with Structural Group Effects." *Journal of Econometrics* 64(1-2): 165–82.

Bound, John, and Harry J. Holzer. 1996. "Demand Shifts, Population Adjustments, and Labor Market Outcomes during the 1980s." National Bureau of Economic Research, Working Paper 5685.

Boyd, Robert L. 1990. "Black and Asian Self-Employment in Large Metropolitan Areas: A Comparative Analysis." *Social Problems* 37: 258–73.

Brown, Charles, James Hamilton, and James Medoff. 1990. *Employers Large and Small.* Cambridge: Harvard University Press.

Butcher, Kristin F., and David Card. 1991. "Immigration and Wages: Evidence from the 1980s." *American Economic Review Papers and Proceedings* 81(2): 292–96.

Card, David. 1997. "Immigrant Inflows, Native Outflows, and the Local Labor Market Impacts of Higher Immigration." NBER Working Paper no. 5927.

Cayton, Horace R., and St. Clair Drake. 1946. *Black Metropolis.* London: Jonathan Cape.

Devine, Theresa J. 1994, "Changes in Wage-and-Salary Returns to Skill and the Recent Rise in Female Self-Employment." *American Economic Review* 84(2): 108–13.

Fairlie, Robert W. 1997. "The Absence of the African-American Owned Business: An Analysis of the Dynamics of Self-Employment." *Journal of Labor Economics* (forthcoming).

Fairlie, Robert W., and Bruce D. Meyer. 1996. "Ethnic and Racial Self-Employment Differences and Possible Explanations." *Journal of Human Resources* 31(4): 757–93.

———. 1997a. "The Effect of Immigration on Native Self-Employment." Working Paper, Northwestern University.

———. 1997b. "Does Immigration Hurt African-American Self-Employment?" Institute for Policy Research, Northwestern University, Working Paper WP-97-1 and Department of Economics, University of California, Santa Cruz Working Paper no. 380.

———. 1997c. "Trends in Self-Employment among Black and White Men: 1910–1990." Working Paper, University of California, Santa Cruz.

Filer, Randall K. 1992. "The Effect of Immigrant Arrivals on Migratory Patterns of Native Workers." In *Immigration and the Work Force: Economic Consequences for the United States and Source Areas*, edited by George J. Borjas and Richard B. Freeman. Chicago: University of Chicago Press.

Frazier, E. Franklin. 1957. *The Negro in the United States*, 2nd ed. New York: Macmillan.

Frey, William H. 1995. "Immigration and Internal Migration 'Flight' from U.S. Metropolitan Areas: Toward a New Demographic Balkanisation," *Urban Studies*, 32(4-5): 733–57.

Friedberg, Rachel M., and Jennifer Hunt. 1995. "The Impact of Immigrants on Host Country Wages, Employment and Growth." *Journal of Economic Perspectives* 9(2): 23–44.

Glazer, Nathan, and Daniel P. Moynihan. 1970. *Beyond the Melting Pot: The Negroes, Puerto Ricans, Jews, Italians, and Irish of New York City*, 2nd ed. Cambridge, Mass.: MIT Press.

Guy, Cynthia, Fred Doolittle, and Barbara Fink. 1991. *Self-Employment for Welfare Recipients: Implementation of the SEID Program*. New York: Manpower Demonstration Research Corporation.

Harrison, Roderick J., and Daniel H. Weinberg. 1992. "Changes in Racial and Ethnic Residential Segregation, 1980–1990," Working Paper. Washington, D.C.: U.S. Bureau of the Census.

Jaeger, David A. 1996. "Regional and Local Area Impacts of Immigration on Natives' Wages," U.S. Department of Labor, U.S. Bureau of Labor Statistics Working Paper.

Joint Center for Political Studies. 1981. *National Roster of Black Elected Officials 1980*. Vol. 10, Washington, D.C.: JCPS.

———. 1991. *Black Elected Officials: A National Roster 1990*. Washington, D.C.: JCPS and Economic Studies Press.

Kinzer, Robert H., and Edward Sagarin. 1950. *The Negro in American Business: the Conflict between Separatism and Integration*. New York: Greenberg.

LaLonde, Robert J., and Robert H. Topel. 1991. "Labor Market Adjustments to Increased Immigration." In *Immigration, Trade, and the Labor Market*, edited by John M. Abowd and Richard B. Freeman. Chicago: University of Chicago Press.

Light, Ivan. 1972. *Ethnic Enterprise in America.* Berkeley: University of California Press.

———. 1984. "Immigrant and Ethnic Enterprise in North America." *Ethnic and Racial Studies* 7(2): 195–216.

———. "The Ethnic Economy." In *Handbook of Economic Sociology*, edited by Neil J. Smelser and Richard Swedberg. Princeton, N.J.: Princeton University Press.

Light, Ivan, and Carolyn Rosenstein. 1995. *Race, Ethnicity, and Entrepreneurship in Urban America.* New York: Aldine De Gruyter.

Light, Ivan, and Angel A. Sanchez. 1987. "Immigrant Entrepreneurs in 272 SMSAs." *Sociological Perspectives* 30: 373–99.

Loewen, James W. (1971). *The Mississippi Chinese: Between Black and White.* Cambridge: Harvard University Press.

Meyer, Bruce. 1990. "Why Are There So Few Black Entrepreneurs?" National Bureau of Economic Research, Working Paper no. 3537.

Min, Pyong Gap. 1996. *Caught in the Middle: Korean Merchants in America's Multiethnic Cities.* Berkeley: University of California Press.

Myrdal, Gunnar. 1944. *An American Dilemma: the Negro Problem and Modern Democracy.* New York: Harper and Brothers.

U.S. Bureau of the Census. 1992. *Characteristics of Business Owners.* Washington, D.C.: U.S. Government Printing Office.

———. 1993a. *Census of Population and Housing, 1990: Public Use Microdata Sample U.S. Technical Documentation.* Washington, D.C.: U.S. Government Printing Office.

———. 1993b. *1990 Census of Population and Housing: Population and Housing Unit Counts, United States, 1990 CPH-2-1.* Washington: U.S. Department of Commerce, Economics and Statistics Administration, Bureau of the Census.

Yoon, In-Jin. 1991. "Immigrant Entrepreneurship: Korean Business in Chicago." Working Paper, University of Chicago.

Yuengert, Andrew M. 1995. "Testing Hypotheses of Immigrant Self-Employment." *Journal of Human Resources* 30(1): 194–204.

CHAPTER 7

Immigration, Race, and Space

Jeffrey S. Zax

R esidential segregation is perhaps the predominant characteristic of
black urban populations in the United States. Segregation restricts
black choices in housing markets (Yinger 1995) and, more generally, in
the market for household assets (Kain and Quigley 1975). It is responsible for segregation in public schools (Harding 1983) and black under-
representation on city councils elected by districts (Zax 1990). Incomes
of metropolitan blacks may depend on the nature of segregation and
more generally on metropolitan spatial organization through both spatial mismatches and neighborhood effects.

The spatial mismatch hypothesis asserts that segregation can restrict
blacks to neighborhoods that are remote from many workplaces. In
consequence, blacks endure extended commutes and limited labor-
market opportunities. These difficulties may be exacerbated where segregation confines blacks to central city residences and when workplaces
are decentralizing.[1]

Segregation must also restrict the economic externalities available in
black neighborhoods. Neighbors reinforce each other's social and economic behavior (Jencks and Mayer 1990b) and contribute to the flow
of labor-market information (Montgomery 1991). Furthermore,
neighborhood levels of human capital and wealth may affect both individual human capital investments (Benabou 1993) and their productivity (de Bartolome 1990). Segregation concentrates blacks in neighborhoods that may be isolated from the broader ranges of economic and
social experiences.

Competition between blacks and immigrants in metropolitan housing markets may change the extent and nature of residential segregation. If so, immigration may alter both neighborhood and spatial mismatch effects. Immigrants may further change the terms of the spatial
mismatch by competing with blacks in metropolitan labor markets.

I offer a preliminary assessment of these possibilities by examining
aggregate relationships among immigration, segregation, commuting
time, and black labor-market outcomes across metropolitan areas. The
association between immigration and segregation suggests the possibility of an important spatial interaction between immigrants and blacks.
Variations in the relationship between segregation and commuting

time associated with variations in levels of immigration suggest that this interaction may alter the spatial mismatch. This suggestion is reinforced by variations in the relationship between segregation and black economic welfare associated with variations in immigration.

The analysis here relies on a data set that contains both an unusually large number of metropolitan areas and an unusually comprehensive description of each. It matches Harrison and Weinberg's (1992) detailed measures of segregation to economic and social data in the STF3C files of the 1980 and 1990 *Censuses of Housing and Population.* The sample includes 242 Metropolitan Statistical Areas (MSAs), all those that appear in the 1980 STF3C file, and whose populations as reported in the 1980 and 1990 Census files are both within 10 percent of the populations tabulated by Harrison and Weinberg.[2]

Despite the richness of these data, they do not contain the spatial detail necessary to identify "structural" effects. Any examination of the spatial mismatch hypothesis relying on data from the decennial *Censuses* must be indirect because of the absence of data describing the spatial distribution of employment. Data for Census tracts would reveal the distribution of immigrant residences within any MSA, but no known source provides aggregate measures of these distributions that are comparable across metropolitan areas. Therefore, the evidence here must consist of effects that are consistent with interactions between immigration and segregation, rather than explicit evidence of these interactions, themselves.

Furthermore, both segregation and immigration arise out of processes with long histories specific to each metropolitan area. Cross-sectional relationships between contemporaneous levels of the two are unlikely to be informative about causal interactions. Relationships between contemporaneous changes in the two would be free of contamination from underlying MSA-specific fixed effects, but again the direction of any causation would be unclear. Relationships between sequential changes might purge fixed effects and establish a presumption of causality through temporal ordering but would also require data from three different points in time.

Therefore, the analytical strategy here takes as "dependent" metropolitan characteristics measured in 1990 and examines their relationships with "explanatory" characteristics measured as of 1980. At a minimum, this strategy ensures that the explanatory characteristics are predetermined. This may at least obviate some forms of endogeneity among the variables at issue, if not capture all elements of causality. However, the results of this strategy must be interpreted from the perspective that apparent associations may be attributable to persistent, underlying, but unmeasured metropolitan characteristics upon which both segregation and immigration depend.

INTERMETROPOLITAN VARIATION IN IN-MIGRATION AND IMMIGRATION

Generally, the inflow of foreign-born residents into American MSAs appears to be relatively steady. Table 7.1 demonstrates that foreign-born individuals entering the United States in the four years between 1987 and 1990 comprise, on average, less than 40 percent of all foreign-born MSA residents entering between 1980 and 1990, a share roughly proportional to the ratio of the lengths of the two periods. On average, nearly 60 percent of the foreign-born MSA residents in 1990 arrived in the United States prior to 1980.[3]

Table 7.1   MSA-Level Measures of In-migration and Immigration

Year	Measure	Mean	Standard Deviation	Minimum	Maximum
1980	% of persons foreign born	.0449	.0458	.00527	.356
1980	% of persons aged greater than four abroad in 1975	.0173	.0158	.00181	.0878
1980	% of persons aged greater than four not in MSA of 1980 residence in 1975	.223	.0949	.0690	.504
1990	% of persons foreign born	.0524	.0613	.00394	.451
1990	% of persons aged greater than four abroad in 1985	.0180	.0173	.00143	.0942
1990	% of persons aged greater than four not in MSA of 1980 residence in 1985	.208	.0823	.0693	.544
1990	% of persons foreign born and entering between 1987–1990	.00825	.0101	.000147	.0626
1990	% of persons foreign born and entering between 1980–1990	.0217	.0289	.000791	.198

Note: The sample consists of 242 MSAs.

Despite this steady flow, most MSAs contain relatively few immigrants. Foreign-born individuals entering the United States between 1987 and 1990 and between 1980 and 1990 comprise, respectively, slightly less than 1 percent and slightly more than 2 percent of 1990 MSA populations. All foreign-born persons constitute approximately 5 percent of the average MSA population in both 1980 and 1990.

Furthermore, immigration typically represents a relatively small fraction of the mobility in MSA populations. In both 1980 and 1990, as much as one-half, and on average between one-fifth and one-quarter, of an MSA's population lived elsewhere five years prior to the Census day. Of that proportion, slightly less than one-tenth would have been abroad.[4]

At the same time, MSAs vary widely in the international character of their populations. In 1980, the proportions of MSA populations born abroad ranged from below 1 percent to more than one-third. The range in 1990 extended to nearly half of the population in at least one MSA.

These variations are persistent: the correlation between the proportions foreign-born in 1980 and 1990 is .973. MSAs with large stocks of foreign-born residents receive systematically higher flows of immigrants: the correlations between the proportions foreign-born and abroad five years previously are .706 in 1980 and .773 in 1990. Moreover, the correlation between the proportion foreign-born in 1980 and the proportion entering the United States between 1980 and 1990 is .905.

These variations suggest that the impact of immigration on black welfare, and particularly on the spatial aspects of black welfare, may vary substantially across MSAs. However, MSAs that are attractive to migrants from without the United States may also be attractive to migrants within: the correlation between the proportions of the Census year MSA population living elsewhere and living abroad five years prior to the Census are .538 for 1980 and .542 for 1990.[5] These correlations imply that any effects of mobility, in general, on black welfare must be identified in order to accurately assign any effects to immigration.

BLACK RESIDENTIAL SEGREGATION

Black residential segregation has been a perdurable characteristic of American metropolitan areas. This section describes five dimensions of segregation and the indices that represent them. It reviews the historical evidence regarding segregation and segregation levels in the sample analyzed here. Lastly, it examines the relationship between population characteristics, and particularly in-migration and immigration, and the different segregation dimensions.

The Measurement of Segregation

Massey and Denton (1988b) identify five indices that appear to capture five important dimensions of segregation.[6] "Evenness" is represented by the dissimilarity index, which measures the proportion of the black population that must be relocated from disproportionately black tracts to tracts that are disproportionately white in order to achieve complete integration. It indicates complete integration with a value of zero and complete segregation with a value of one.

The interaction index, the average of the white share in tract populations weighted by the tract share of the MSA black population, measures "exposure." It estimates the expected population share of whites in tracts inhabited by blacks. This index yields a value of zero when each tract is completely segregated. It is equal to the white proportion in the MSA population when all tracts have the same racial composition and therefore has a limiting value of one in an MSA with no blacks.

Relative concentration compares the relative tendencies of blacks and whites to reside in physically small Census tracts. A value of zero indicates complete integration. Positive values indicate that the black population resides in disproportionately small tracts. Negative values indicate that it resides in disproportionately large tracts.[7]

The absolute centralization index compares the cumulative proportions of blacks and metropolitan land area at increasing distances from the MSA center. Again, a value of zero indicates "integration" or no tendency for blacks to have more or less decentralized residences than whites. The minimum value of negative one indicates that all blacks reside in the single Census tract farthest from the center. It approaches a maximum asymptote of positive one if all blacks reside in the single tract closest to the center.

The spatial proximity index measures "clustering," whether tracts inhabited by blacks tend to be "near" each other or surrounded by tracts inhabited by whites. Values greater than one, as in the metropolitan areas examined here, identify the first case. Values less than one identify the second case.

The Extent of Segregation

The severity of black residential segregation in American metropolises has fluctuated over the past fifty years. However, it has always been extreme. The average dissimilarity index for 109 cities in 1940 was .852, indicating the need to relocate approximately 85.2 percent of black residents in order to achieve complete integration. The average dissimilarity indices for the same cities in 1950 and 1960 were .873 and .861, respectively (Taeuber and Taeuber 1965).

Dissimilarity indices for metropolitan areas yield slightly lower values. Van Valey, Roof, and Wilcox (1977) report average values of .754 among 144 SMSAs in 1960 and .695 among 237 SMSAs in 1970. The average dissimilarity index in 60 SMSAs declined from .792 to .694 between 1970 and 1980 (Massey and Denton 1987). It also declined between 1980 and 1990 across all 318 SMSAs defined after the 1980 Census, from .736 to .694 (Harrison and Weinberg 1992). Nevertheless, complete integration would still require enormous relocations.

Interaction indices for blacks and whites also indicate extreme levels of segregation but much less improvement over time. Schnare (1980) estimates average indices of .304 in 1960 and .333 in 1970 across 130 SMSAs. McKinney and Schnare (1989) estimate average values of .335 in 1960, .310 in 1970, and .345 in 1980 for 64 SMSAs. Massey and Denton (1987) estimate average values for 1970 and 1980 of .333 and .376, respectively. For all SMSAs, Harrison and Weinberg (1992) report average values of .341 in 1980 and .379 in 1990. Even in the most recent years, estimated black residential interactions with whites are equivalent to those that would be experienced if all blacks lived in Census tracts that were no more than one-third white.

Black residential segregation remains far greater than that measured for any other ethnic or racial group. In the 60 SMSAs of Massey and Denton (1987), average dissimilarity indices for Hispanics and whites are .444 in 1970 and .434 in 1980. Average dissimilarity indices for Hispanics and whites across all SMSAs in 1980 and 1990 are .500 and .504, respectively (Harrison and Weinberg 1992).

Average dissimilarity indices for Asians and whites in 1970 and 1980 are .437 and .342, respectively (Massey and Denton 1987). Average dissimilarity indices for Asians and Pacific Islanders and whites are .397 in 1980 and .409 in 1990 (Harrison and Weinberg 1992). Average dissimilarity indices for American Indians, Eskimos, and Aleuts and whites are .363 and .349 in the same two years (Harrison and Weinberg 1992).[8]

Lastly, black residential segregation is much less susceptible to either assimilationist or market forces than is that of other minorities. Improvements in black socioeconomic characteristics are much less likely to be associated with reductions in interaction indices than are improvements in Hispanic socioeconomic characteristics in 1960 and 1970 (Massey and Mullen 1984). Black dissimilarity indices in 1970 are largely invariant to black educational attainments, incomes, or occupations (Farley 1977). While Asian and Hispanic dissimilarity indices in 1980 decline with socioeconomic status, those of blacks do not (Denton and Massey 1988).

The Dimensions of Black Segregation in 1980 and 1990

Table 7.2 presents summary statistics of the five indices defined above for the 242 MSAs examined here, based on the MSA-specific indices of Harrison and Weinberg (1992).[9] While average levels of black segregation are high, variations across MSAs can also be quite large. Extreme values for the five indices are consistent with both complete segregation and virtually complete integration.

Table 7.3 demonstrates that average changes in segregation indices between 1980 and 1990 were small, with the exception of the relative concentration measure. The third column demonstrates that MSA-specific changes did not greatly alter relative degrees of segregation across MSAs: values for all indices in 1990 are nearly proportional to those in 1980.

Nevertheless, segregation in this sample is multidimensional. Table 7.4 presents simple contemporaneous correlations among the five segregation measures. The dissimilarity, interaction, and spatial proximity indicies are intimately related, with correlations that exceed .66 in absolute value in both years. Absolute centralization and relative concentration are also related in both years, though less strongly. However,

Table 7.2   Segregation Measures for 1980 and 1990

1980 Segregation Measure	Mean	Standard Deviation	Minimum	Maximum
Evenness (dissimilarity)	.591	.143	.250	.908
Exposure (interaction)	.650	.245	.162	.999
Concentration (relative)	.555	.396	−1.68	1.08
Centralization (absolute)	.737	.261	−.769	.977
Clustering (spatial proximity)	1.16	.166	1.00	1.85
1990 Segregation Measure				
Evenness (dissimilarity)	.540	.139	.227	.899
Exposure (interaction)	.677	.226	.158	.999
Concentration (relative)	.573	.371	−1.37	.942
Centralization (absolute)	.733	.254	−.588	.969
Clustering (spatial proximity)	1.15	.156	1.00	1.86

Note: Averages are unweighted.

Table 7.3   Comparisons, 1980 and 1990 Segregation Measures

Segregation Measure	Average Absolute Change in Mean Values, 1980 to 1990	Average Relative Change in Mean Values, 1980 to 1990	Correlation, Values in 1980 and 1990
Evenness (dissimilarity)	−.0512	−.0853	.941
Exposure (interaction)	.0261	.0639	.981
Concentration (relative)	.0188	.311	.911
Centralization (absolute)	−.00337	−.00880	.976
Clustering (spatial proximity)	−.0103	−.00733	.959

Notes: Averages are unweighted. Absolute difference is $X_{90} - X_{80}$, where X indicates the mean value for the segregation measure and the subscript indicates the year. Relative difference is is $[X_{90} - X_{80}]/X_{80}$. All correlations are significant at 1 percent.

half of the ten correlations for each of the years are less than .2 in ab-solute value. The differences among these indices again suggest that each may capture a separate dimension of black segregation. Therefore, I will now address all five.

Table 7.4   Correlations Between Contemporaneous Segregation Measures

	Evenness (Dissimilarity Index)	Exposure (Interaction)	Concentration (Relative)	Centralization (Absolute)
1980 segregation measures				
Exposure (interaction)	−.734*			
Concentration (relative)	.319*	−.0750		
Centralization (absolute)	.175*	−.0960	.391*	
Clustering (spatial proximity)	.668*	−.823*	.0109	.0937
1990 segregation measures				
Exposure (interaction)	−.734*			
Concentration (relative)	.317*	−.0908		
Centralization (absolute)	.130†	−.0829	.359*	
Clustering (spatial proximity)	.701*	−.837*	.00691	.0819

Note: * and † indicate significance at 1 percent and 5 percent, respectively.

Causes of Segregation

Attempts to explain black residential segregation are less numerous than attempts to measure it, but they are plentiful nevertheless. These explanations rely principally on three mechanisms (Mieszkowski and Syron 1979): differences between blacks and whites in socioeconomic characteristics, differences in preferences regarding the racial composition of residential neighborhoods, and overt discrimination in housing markets. The balance among these components is controversial (Clark 1986, 1988; Galster 1988, 1989).

Evidence supports the claims of some role for all three mechanisms. Interaction indices are substantially lower in MSAs with lower black incomes, especially lower incomes in the bottom half of the black income distribution (Cloutier 1982). Blacks generally prefer integrated neighborhoods (Davis and Casetti 1978; and the references in Galster (1982), but whites prefer neighborhoods with smaller proportions of black residents (see references in Clark 1986). Real estate agents and mortgage lenders may reinforce white preferences through subtle but deliberate discrimination (Munnell et al. 1986; Yinger 1986, 1995; Newburger 1989).

Other mechanisms have received less attention. Surprisingly, the effects of local fair housing legislation have been largely ignored, though they may be salutary (Smith 1989). Black segregation is apparently not attributable to black misperceptions of housing market conditions (Farley and Colasanto 1980).

Immigration may increase segregation if, for example, strong ethnic identification within immigrant white communities reinforces preferences for neighbors with similar backgrounds and characteristics (McKinney 1989). These same sorts of preferences may lead to increased segregation when black inmigration rates are high (Ottensmann, Good, and Gleeson 1990). However, immigration could reduce segregation if in-migrants compete for the same housing stock as blacks, or if increased liquidity in the housing market provides more opportunities for market forces to erode the effects of discrimination.

MSA-level data are not very informative about microeconomic mechanisms such as prejudice and discrimination. Nevertheless, these mechanisms should manifest themselves in aggregate differences in segregation. Therefore, inter-MSA variations in segregation might at least indicate some of the circumstances in which these mechanisms are most active.

However, these variations have been subjected to surprisingly few multivariate analyses. Marshall and Jiobu (1975) and Galster (1987) find that segregation depends on, among other things, the relative status of blacks and the size of the black population. Cloutier (1982) reports that segregation declines most noticeably in response to increases in income among the poorest blacks.[10] Table 7.5 provides a new exploration of the relationships between black residential segregation, differences in black and white socioeconomic characteristics, and immigration.

Each column reports regressions of one of the 1990 segregation indices on a large number of 1980 explanatory variables. These equations explain large proportions of the variances in the dissimilarity, interaction, and spatial proximity indexes but are less successful for the relative concentration and absolute centralization index. Nevertheless, as a whole they demonstrate that previous socioeconomic characteristics are strongly associated with subsequent segregation.[11]

The specification in table 7.5 attempts to capture both aggregate MSA characteristics and differences in the characteristics of the white and black populations. The first category includes size, the age and rate of turnover in the housing stock. The second includes black and white income distributions, schooling attainment, and housing characteristics.

Segregation in 1990 is significantly associated with aggregate 1980 MSA characteristics. Larger MSAs tend to be more heavily segregated in all dimensions except relative concentration. Holding constant MSA population, larger black proportions reduce interaction and increase spatial proximity but reduce relative concentration.

The first two effects associated with the proportion black are to some extent definitional. The interaction index is likely to decline algebraically with increases in the proportion black regardless of behavioral changes. Similarly, if the average proximity between blacks exceeds that between whites, spatial proximity increases with the proportion black even if these average proximities do not change.

However the relationship between the proportion black and relative concentration does not appear to be algebraically imposed. Instead, it suggests that increases in the proportion black tend to be associated with shifts of the black population into physically larger and presumably more suburban census tracts.

Housing market conditions also demonstrate a complicated association with segregation. In principle, the competitive mechanisms that would tend to reduce segregation should be more effective in markets with greater liquidity. This characteristic is not explicitly represented in table 7.5. However, it may be the source of the estimated effects of the housing variables there.

For example, the flow of new housing is significantly associated only with relative concentration. New building is associated with relative increases in the proportions of blacks who live in physically larger tracts. If these tracts are both suburban and the sites of most new residential

Table 7.5   Regressions of 1990 Segregation Measures on 1980 MSA Characteristics

			Dependent Variables		
Explanatory Variables	1990 Evenness (Dissimilarity)	1990 Exposure (Interaction)	1990 Concentration (Relative)	1990 Centralization (Absolute)	1990 Clustering (Spatial Proximity)
1980 % persons foreign born	.606 (2.25)	−1.24 (3.81)	−.0797 (.077)	.406 (.554)	.861 (2.92)
1980 % persons aged greater than four abroad in 1975	−1.34 (1.77)	2.45 (2.68)	−8.32 (2.88)	−3.89 (1.89)	−1.39 (1.67)
1980 % persons aged greater than four not in MSA of 1980 residence in 1975	−.468 (3.18)	.0721 (.405)	1.33 (2.37)	.0610 (.152)	−.174 (1.08)
1980 population	.0278 (3.33)	−.0478 (4.74)	.0337 (1.06)	.0482 (2.13)	.0823 (9.01)
1980 % black	−.0869 (1.03)	−1.31 (12.8)	−1.31 (4.05)	.148 (.643)	.745 (8.04)
1980 % year-round dwelling units vacant for rent	1.59 (2.30)	−2.46 (2.95)	8.47 (3.21)	3.79 (2.02)	.872 (1.15)
1980 % year-round dwelling units vacant not for rent	.762 (.941)	−.475 (.485)	−4.89 (1.58)	−1.28 (.580)	1.25 (1.41)
1980 % year-round dwelling units built 1975–80	−.188 (1.11)	.227 (1.11)	−2.13 (3.29)	.0522 (.113)	−.206 (1.11)
1980 % white persons older than twenty-four, > fifteen years school	.0677 (.359)	−.0117 (.051)	−1.75 (2.43)	−.0184 (.036)	.172 (.832)
1979 average white family income	−.00542 (.843)	.000589 (.076)	.0250 (1.02)	−.0190 (1.09)	−.0101 (1.44)
1979 % white families with incomes > $49,999	.112 (.218)	−.218 (.352)	2.37 (1.21)	.955 (.685)	.720 (1.28)

	(1)	(2)	(3)	(4)
1979 % white persons below poverty level	−.975 (3.28)	.377 (.332)	.171 (.212)	−.667 (2.05)
1980 % white-occupied rental units, rent > $300	.373 (3.15)	.302 (.667)	−.154 (.477)	.168 (1.30)
1980 % white households with no vehicle	−.354 (1.21)	−.105 (.054)	−.418 (.524)	−.238 (.744)
1980 % white-occupied units with no central heat	−.0194 (.182)	−.268 (.658)	−.305 (1.05)	.0479 (.411)
1980 % black persons older than twenty-four, > fifteen years school	−.345 (4.81)	.429 (1.56)	.171 (.875)	−.0894 (1.14)
1979 average black family income	−.00348 (1.36)	−.0438 (4.16)	−.0198 (2.83)	−.00213 (.758)
1979 % black families with incomes > $49,999	.580 (2.47)	2.79 (3.11)	1.18 (1.84)	−.125 (.487)
1979 % black persons below poverty level	.422 (4.07)	−.766 (1.93)	−.497 (1.76)	.157 (1.39)
1980 % black-occupied rental units, rent > $300	−.169 (2.53)	−.628 (2.46)	.0068 (.038)	−.0617 (.845)
1980 % black households with no vehicle	.191 (2.38)	1.16 (3.77)	.271 (1.24)	.191 (2.17)
1980 % black-occupied units with no central heat	−.0835 (1.12)	.243 (.852)	−.0094 (.046)	−.162 (1.98)
Intercept	.649 (4.41)	.480 (.853)	.932 (2.33)	1.17 (7.25)
Adjusted R^2	.699	.386	.338	.716
Mean of the dependent variable	.540	.573	.733	1.15

Notes: The sample contains 242 observations. Parentheses contain *t*-statistics. All equations include dummy variables for regions.

construction, the association suggests that segregation declines with increased housing market liquidity.

Vacancy rates depend on both the rate of residential turnover and the duration of vacancy spells. Higher turnover rates and vacancy durations imply, respectively, greater and lesser liquidity. The association between segregation and the proportion of dwelling units vacant for rent appears to capture the duration effect, increasing segregation as measured by the indices of dissimilarity, interaction, relative concentration, and absolute centralization.

In general, the 1980 characteristics of MSA white populations have few significant effects on 1990 segregation. However, holding constant the 1980 characteristics of black MSA populations, these effects imply that segregation increases with the welfare of the white MSA population. For example larger proportions of white-occupied rental units with the highest rental rates are significantly associated with higher values for the dissimilarity index and lower values for the interaction index. Lower proportions of white people below the poverty level are associated with similar changes in these indices as well as with increases in the index of spatial proximity.

The relationship between 1990 segregation and 1980 black characteristics is stronger. Holding constant white characteristics, many measures of increased black welfare imply reduced segregation. The dissimilarity index declines and the interaction index increases with increases in black educational attainment. Increases in average black family income are associated with reduced segregation as measured by the interaction, relative concentration, and absolute centralization indices. The dissimilarity and relative concentration indices decline, and the interaction index increases with increases in the proportion of black-rented housing units in the highest rent category. All indices with the exception of that for absolute concentration indicate reduced segregation with reductions in the proportions of black households with no vehicles.

However, some measures of increased black welfare imply increased segregation. Increases in the proportion of black families in the highest category of the black income distribution increase dissimilarity, relative concentration, and absolute centralization and reduce interaction. Reductions in the proportion of blacks in poverty are associated with reductions in the dissimilarity and increases in the interaction indices but also with increases in relative concentration and absolute centralization. These contrasts suggest that while increased black welfare may provide some of the means necessary to overcome segregation it may also encourage resegregation in higher-income black communities.[12]

Lastly, measures of immigration are significantly associated with all dimensions of segregation. Furthermore, the associations involving immigration are distinct from those of in-migration. This latter variable has associations that are significant, though contradictory, with only the dissimilarity and relative concentration indices. Both indices are also significantly associated with immigration.

MSAs with higher proportions of persons born abroad have significantly higher dissimilarity and spatial proximity indices and significantly lower interaction indices. Holding constant the population proportion abroad in 1975, this variable must predominantly reflect longer-term variations in immigration across MSAs. Increases in long-term immigration are therefore associated with greater segregation. This relationship may reflect the resistance of established white ethnic communities to neighbors from different minorities.

Similarly, holding constant the population proportion comprised by all foreign-born residents, variations in the proportion of 1980 MSA residents abroad five years previously must largely capture short-term variations in migration experiences. Short-term increases in immigration reduce segregation. Greater population proportions of those abroad in 1975 are significantly associated with higher values for the interaction index and lower values for all four of the other indices. This suggests that recent immigrants may compete in the some of the same housing markets as blacks, thereby reducing black residential isolation.

The regressions in table 7.5 demonstrate that, first, black residential segregation varies systematically across MSAs with different population characteristics. Second, they demonstrate that short-run immigration is associated with lower black segregation, but long-run immigration is associated with greater segregation. Third, the relatively sparse associations between in-migration and segregation suggest that migrants from abroad are more likely than those from within the United States to interact with blacks in metropolitan housing markets.[13]

SEGREGATION, IMMIGRATION, AND COMMUTING

The spatial mismatch hypothesis is based on the assumption that segregation imposes longer commutes on black workers. In general, black workers in metropolitan areas appear to experience longer commutes than do white workers (see Greytak 1974 and Leonard 1985 as examples). The STF3 files do not report commute times by race. However, the correlation between average commute times and the proportion black in the MSAs here is .410 in 1980 and .317 in 1990, both significant at better than 1 percent. MSAs with higher proportions of blacks tend to have higher average commute times.

Of course, this association may arise from many sources. In the absence of race-specific commuting time data, I will describe variations in

Table 7.6   Immigration, Segregation, and Commuting Times in MSAs with Low Levels of Segregation

	Level of Migration	Number of MSAs	Average % Black	Average Commute Time	Correlation; Commute Time, and % Black
MSAs with Low Relative Concentration Indices					
1980 % of persons foreign born	low	41	.194	18.5	.510*
	high	80	.0850	19.8	.130
1980 % aged greater than four abroad in 1975	low	33	.158	18.3	.402†
	high	88	.108	19.8	.117
1980 % aged greater than four not in MSA of 1980 residence in 1975	low	39	.159	19.3	.273‡
	high	82	.104	19.4	.0558
MSAs with Low Absolute Centralization Indices					
1980 % of persons foreign born	low	47	.160	18.5	.332†
	high	74	.0867	19.8	.0625
1980 % aged greater than four abroad in 1975	low	48	.125	18.5	.223
	high	73	.109	19.8	.0171
1980 % aged greater than four not in MSA of 1980 residence in 1975	low	55	.124	19.1	.189
	high	66	.108	19.4	−.0261

Notes: *, †, and ‡ indicate significance at 1 percent, 5 percent and 10 percent, respectively. MSAs with "low" levels of segregation have values below the median for the indicated segregation measure. MSAs with "low" and "high" levels of migration have values below and

these correlations associated with variations in segregation and immigration. Earlier in the study I associated immigration with four of the five segregation dimensions; however, relative concentration and absolute centralization appear to be the dimensions that have the most important associations with other measures of black welfare and the most important interactions with immigration. The rest of this study therefore focuses on them.[14]

The proportions black and average commute times are strongly and positively associated in highly segregated MSAs, regardless of levels of in-migration and immigration. Correlations among MSAs in the upper halves of the distributions of the various segregation indices exceed .46 and are statistically significant at better than the 99 percent level. More than half exceed .6.[15]

Table 7.6 examines the correlation between the proportion black and commuting time among the least segregated halves of the sample here through disaggregations by levels of immigration and in-migration. This correlation is generally lower in these MSAs than in those from the more segregated half of the sample, but it also varies substantially within this group. It remains large and significant among MSAs with low relative concentration indices and low levels of in-migration and immigration. It is also large, or at least sizable, among MSAs experiencing low mobility and with low absolute centralization indices. However, this correlation is both statistically insignificant and quantitatively negligible among MSAs with low levels of segregation that experience high levels of migration, regardless of segregation index.

In other words, the association between racial composition and average commute times is strong except among MSAs that have both low levels of segregation and high levels of in-migration and immigration. The contrast between MSAs with high and low proportions foreign born yields the sharpest contrast between correlation values. This evidence suggests the possibility that the presence of long-lived ethnic communities is associated with distinctive employment geographies. In MSAs with modest degrees of segregation, these geographies may have the consequence of improving the accessibility of workplace locations to black neighborhoods. In MSAs with high degrees of segregation, these communities are too small to have a noticeable effect.

SEGREGATION, IMMIGRATION, AND BLACK WELFARE

As is well known, blacks on average attain lower levels of economic welfare than do whites. Table 7.7 provides some simple comparisons for 1980 and 1990 in the MSAs examined here. In both years, black populations demonstrate lower levels of employment, average family or

Table 7.7   Labor Force Characteristics by Race in 1980 and 1990

Characteristics	1980 Means		1990 Means	
	for Blacks	for Whites	for Blacks	for Whites
% employed	.537	.693	.508	.606
% unemployed	.0740	.0435	.0780	.0339
% not in labor force	.325	.236	.383	.347
% with unemployment	.381	.258	—	—
Mean income per unit ($1000s)	15.8	23.5	24.7	37.4
Per capita income ($1000s)	—	—	8.32	14.5
% persons below poverty level	.280	.0967	.310	.106

Notes: "Unit" incomes are for families in 1980, households in 1990. Statistics for labor force status refer to the universe of persons older than sixteen years of age.

household incomes, and per capita incomes than do white populations. Average black rates of unemployment, nonparticipation in the labor force, and poverty are all greater than those of whites.

Some of these differences may depend directly on segregation. Individual labor market performance can depend on neighborhood characteristics such as the proportion of neighborhood residents on welfare (Corcoran et al. 1992), the incomes of schoolmates' parents, and the aspirations of friends (Rees and Zax 1997), and neighborhood racial composition (Datcher 1982). Segregation influences this last neighborhood characteristic, by definition, and may affect others by confining blacks to largely all-black neighborhoods.

Some of these differences may also be attributable to consequences of segregation for the geographical relationship between black residential areas and employment locations. Metropolitan spatial organization affects black labor-force experiences: as examples, central city residence appears to reduce black earnings (Price and Mills 1985; Reid 1985), and the variation of wages with distance from the city center may differ for white and black workers (Ihlanfeldt 1992).

Employer-based research suggests that black residences tend to be farther away from growing suburban employment centers than from workplaces in central cities (Fernandez 1994) and that this difference prevents some black workers from retaining jobs in the suburbs (Zax and Kain 1996). Moreover, blacks are less likely to appear in work forces located at greater distances from black residences (Leonard 1987; Holzer and Ihlanfeldt 1996). Recent individual-based research suggests that while white and black youth employment probabilities depend similarly on access to employment opportunities, the generally poorer access associated with black residences explains a substantial portion of the difference in black and white youth employment rates (Ihlanfeldt and Sjoquist 1990, 1991).[16]

The welfare implications of any spatial mismatch depend on the role of segregation in black labor-market performance. Without discriminatory barriers to black residential mobility, black residences with poor labor market access would be equilibrium choices, presumably as consequences of low incomes. The subsidies necessary to bring residences with better access within black budget sets would presumably be large, and the net social benefits of such policies would be small. In contrast, if mismatches are attributable to persistent housing disequilibria enforced through discrimination, remedies would require regulations and enforcement rather than subsidies and would surely improve welfare.

Surprisingly, the literature appears to contain only three studies in which segregation appears as an explanatory variable for black labor-market performance. O'Regan and Quigley (1991) find that MSA-level unemployment rates for black youth are greater in MSAs with higher levels of segregation among poor blacks. Cutler and Glaeser (1997) report that young black adults have lower incomes, are less likely to be in school or employed, and are more likely to be single parents in MSAs with higher contemporaneous segregation. Ihlanfeldt and Sjoquist (1989) report that the earnings of individual central city blacks are unrelated to the interaction index, as are the effects of job decentralization on these earnings.

In the sample here, descriptive regressions demonstrate strong negative associations between segregation, measured by relative concentration and absolute centralization, and black welfare, measured by per capita income, per household income, the proportion of black individuals below the poverty line, and the proportions of black families with incomes below 10,000 dollars or above 49,999 dollars.[17] Table 7.8 addresses the question of whether immigration intervenes in the relationships between segregation and black welfare. It presents, as examples, three regressions with black per capita income in 1989 as the dependent variable.[18] The three differ in the specification of variables measuring in-migration and immigration, and in the interactions between these variables and segregation measures. The explanatory variables also include an array of more conventional control variables.

This last set of explanatory variables reveals only a few important associations. As presented in the second part of table 7.8, there may be slight tendencies for black 1989 per capita incomes to be higher in MSAs that were larger and had longer average commute times in 1980. However, there is a very pronounced tendency for these incomes to be lower in MSAs whose 1980 populations were more heavily black. This association is both significant and substantial: an increase of approximately 15 percentage points in the 1980 black population share implies a reduction in 1989 per capita income of approximately 800 dollars, or approximately 10 percent.

Black per capita incomes in 1989 are largely unrelated to the four included measures of welfare among MSA white populations. There is a suggestion that they may be greater in MSAs where larger proportions of white families had earlier reported incomes above 49,999 dollars. Nevertheless, the absence of any stronger association may simply imply that MSA-level measures of welfare can evolve idiosyncratically over a span of ten years.

However, 1989 black per capita income is significantly and substantially lower in MSAs that had higher rates of black poverty in 1980. An increase of approximately 15 percentage points in this rate is again as-

Table 7.8   Regressions of 1989 Black Per Capita Income on
Segregation and Immigration Measures and Interactions

Explanatory Variables	Model 1	Model 2	Model 3
1980 relative concentration	−3087. (5.16)	−5414. (5.09)	−5276. (4.32)
1980 absolute centralization	3092. (2.73)	5213. (2.81)	5311. (2.60)
1980 % of persons foreign born	26637. (2.09)	28170. (2.82)	25979. (1.91)
1980 % of persons aged greater than four abroad in 1975	27261. (.947)	—	18800. (.483)
1980 % of persons aged greater than four not in MSA of 1980 residence in 1975	—	3587. (.783)	2063. (.334)
1980 relative concentration × 1980 % of persons foreign born	−20886. (1.55)	10593. (1.69)	−1984. (.122)
1980 absolute centralization × 1980 % of persons foreign born	−25448. (1.54)	−40590. (3.08)	−39015. (2.07)
1980 relative concentration × 1980 % of persons aged greater than four abroad in 1975	110560. (2.93)	—	44975. (.911)
1980 absolute centralization × 1980 % of persons aged greater than four abroad in 1975	−59991. (1.31)	—	−6248. (.100)
1980 relative concentration × 1980 % of persons aged greater than four not in MSA of 1980 residence in 1975	—	12827. (3.08)	11514. (2.05)
1980 absolute centalization × 1980 % of persons aged greater than four not in MSA of 1980 residence in 1975	—	−11937. (1.76)	−11647. (1.26)

P-Values for Tests of Joint Significance

1980 relative concentration and 1980 absolute centralization	.0001	.0001	.0001
1980 % of persons foreign born and 1980 % of persons abroad, 1975	—	—	.600
Interactions between 1980 segregation measures and 1980 % of persons foreign born	.0459	.0063	.0798

Table 7.8   *Continued*

Explanatory Variables	Model 1	Model 2	Model 3
Interactions between 1980 segregation measures and 1980 % of persons aged greater than four abroad in 1975	.0149	—	.621
Interations between 1980 segregation measures and 1980 % of persons aged greater than four not in MSA of 1980 residence in 1975	—	.0089	.119
All interactions with 1980 segregation measures	.0015	.0011	.0015
1980 population	297. (1.40)	451. (2.05)	349. (1.55)
1980 % black	−6008. (2.96)	−5810. (2.89)	−6285. (3.07)
1980 average commute time	153. (1.98)	119. (1.54)	139. (1.80)
1979 average white family income	−155. (1.06)	−185. (1.26)	−163. (1.09)
1979 % white families with incomes greater than $49,999	20534. (1.56)	24063. (1.82)	23274. (1.76)
1980 % white persons below poverty level	−6089. (.960)	−3921. (.614)	−3824. (.584)
1980 % white persons older than twenty-four, more than fifteen years school	1453. (.387)	3125. (.740)	1900. (.445)
1979 average black family income	−11.6 (.183)	−17.7 (.280)	−16.2 (.256)
1979 % black families with incomes greater than $49,999	6825. (1.22)	7829. (1.38)	7428. (1.30)
1980 % black persons below poverty level	−6163. (2.66)	−6576. (2.85)	−6032. (2.58)
1980 % black persons older than twenty-four, more than fifteen years school	159. (.101)	−370. (.232)	−133. (.083)
Intercept	9872. (3.06)	9888. (2.91)	9397. (2.67)
Adjusted R^2	.421	.421	.425

Notes: Average black per capita income in 1989 is 8,320 dollars. The sample contains 242 observations. Parentheses contain *t*-statistics. All regressions include dummy variables for region.

sociated with an approximately 10 percent per capita income reduction in 1989. This suggests that the welfare of the black populations in 1979 and 1989 are closely related. If so, the absence of intertemporal associations between white and black economic welfare may indicate that, though blacks and whites share the same metropolitan area, their economic activities are to some degree separate.

At the same time, 1980 measures of segregation, in-migration, and immigration and their interactions display many significant associations with 1989 black per capita incomes. These incomes are significantly and substantially lower in MSAs where blacks experienced higher levels of relative concentration in 1980. In model 1, an increase of one standard deviation in this measure, as given in table 7.2, is associated with a reduction in 1989 black per capita income of 1,222 dollars, or nearly 15 percent of its mean value. In models 2 and 3, the same increase implies a 1989 per capita income reduction of at least 2,089 dollars, or 25.1 percent.

In contrast, 1989 black per capita incomes are significantly and substantially greater in MSAs where blacks experienced higher levels of absolute centralization in 1980. Models 1 through 3, respectively, imply that an increase of one standard deviation in this measure, again as reported in table 7.2, is associated with increases of 807 dollars, 1,361 dollars, and 1,386 dollars in black 1989 per capita incomes. Respectively, these are equal to increases of 9.70, 16.4, and 16.7 percent.

As given in the second panel of table 7.8, the two segregation measures are jointly significant in all three specifications. Their effects, though of opposite sign and similar magnitudes, are not ordinarily canceling. As given in table 7.4, the 1980 correlation between the two is positive and significant, but only .391. In other words, a substantial proportion of the variance in either measure across MSAs is unrelated to the variance in the other.

The differences in the directions of these two effects therefore suggest some of the contemporary complexities of residential segregation. Comparing two MSAs in which the black populations experience equal degrees of absolute centralization, the MSA in which black neighborhoods are physically smaller will have poorer blacks. Analogously, between two MSAs in which the black populations experience equal degrees of relative concentration, blacks will be poorer in the MSA where the black population is more suburbanized.

In other words, black populations seem to benefit from access to both the center of the metropolis and ample geographic area. The impact of segregation on black economic welfare appears to be most severe when it forces blacks to live in small, suburban ghettos. The "gilded ghetto" (Kain and Persky 1975) is apparently one that is both central in location and large in expanse.

Black economic welfare is also significantly and positively associated with the presence of large long-term immigrant populations. Holding constant the rates of recent inflow into the MSA from both all origins and from those that are foreign, black per capita incomes are greater in MSAs where larger proportions of the population are foreign born. In models 1 through 3, an increase of one standard deviation in this proportion, as given in table 7.1, is associated with increases of between 1,190 dollars and 1,290 dollars.

These regressions do not reveal the structural basis for these increases. However, the estimated effects of long-term immigration hold constant extensive controls for 1979 incomes. Therefore, they are unlikely to be spurious in the obvious sense that MSAs with high incomes for all residents were especially attractive to immigrants prior to 1980. It seems more likely that large long-term immigrant populations change the nature of economic activity in a metropolitan area in such a way as to offer improved employment opportunities to black residents and perhaps to all others as well.

At the same time, measures of short-term in-migration and immigration have no significant direct associations with 1989 black per capita incomes. The 1980 proportions abroad and outside the MSA in 1975 are, in turn, individually insignificant in models 1 and 2. The second panel of table 7.8 reports that they are jointly insignificant in model 3 well as insignificant individually. Nevertheless, this panel demonstrates that both short-term and long-term immigration significantly alter the relationship between segregation and black incomes. Each model includes complete interactions between the two segregation indices and the included in-migration and immigration measures. The last line of this panel reports that these interactions are jointly significant in all three equations.

The interactions between the two segregation indices and the 1980 percentage of foreign born are themselves jointly significant in all three. Those between these indices and the two measures of short-term immigration are also themselves jointly significant except in model 3, which includes both. Even in that model, however, the test of the hypothesis that interactions with both short-term and long-term measures of in-migration and immigration are unimportant rejects at a much higher significance level than does the test of the analogous hypothesis for the interactions with the long-term measure of immigration, alone.

Individually, the coefficients for half of the interaction terms in these three models are statistically significant at 10 percent or better. Furthermore, in models 2 and 3 each segregation index is part of at least one significant interaction term. All of these significant coefficients indicate that the effects of increased in-migration or immigration are to mitigate the effects of segregation on black per capita income.

For example, models 2 and 3 indicate that the advantages of greater absolute centralization are significantly reduced in MSAs with larger 1980 proportions of foreign born. An increase of one standard deviation in this proportion reduces the net effect of 1980 absolute centralization by 1,859 dollars, or 34.3 percent, in model 2, and by 1,787 dollars, or 33.6 percent, in model 3. With the level of absolute centralization held constant, increases in long-term immigration must reduce the benefits blacks enjoy from access to MSA centers by intensifying competition for economic opportunities in these centers or by inducing a shift of those opportunities away from them.

This reduction is noteworthy both because it indicates that long-term immigration alters metropolitan spatial organization, and because it mitigates the positive direct effect of long-term immigration on black per capita incomes. The net effect of long-term immigration on these incomes becomes negative at values for 1980 absolute centralization as low as .694 in model 2 and .666 in model 3, both slightly below the 1980 average for this index. Black incomes benefit from the presence of long-term immigrants only in MSAs where black populations are relatively decentralized.

Models 1 through 3 indicate that between the two measures of short-term mobility only the 1980 population proportion that lived outside the MSA in 1975 has strong influence over the relationship between segregation and black economic welfare. While the interactions between the two segregation indices and the 1980 proportion that lived abroad in 1975 appear to be jointly significant in model 1, they are both jointly and individually insignificant in model 3. In this model the interactions between these indices and the 1980 proportion that lived outside the MSA in 1975 just fail to achieve significance at the 10 percent level. Furthermore, the individual interaction with 1980 relative concentration is significant at better than 5 percent.

This suggests that the overall level of short-term mobility in an MSA rather than the specific origins of in-migrants affects the relationship between segregation and black economic welfare. Again, the effects are substantial. An increase of one standard deviation in the 1980 population proportion that lived outside the MSA in 1975 reduces the net effect of 1980 relative concentration by 1,217 dollars, or 23.4 percent, in model 2, and by 1,093 dollars, or 20.6 percent, in model 3. In the absence of significant direct effects for this variable, its net effect on 1989 black per capita incomes is entirely positive.

MSAs with greater overall mobility probably have greater liquidity in housing markets. This would presumably imply that segregation is less of a binding constraint in these MSAs. If so, a given level of relative concentration would be associated with smaller subsequent losses in economic welfare in an MSA with greater overall mobility, compared to one with lesser mobility. Concentration in the latter would be more the consequence of segregation, while "unconstrained" black housing choices would have more influence on the spatial distribution of the black population in the former.

CONCLUSION

Though exploratory in nature, the results in this study are striking. Segregation is negatively associated with prior rates of short-term immigration and positively with prior rates of long-term immigration. Prior immigration and in-migration both reduce the strength of the association between contemporaneous segregation and average MSA commutes, but only in MSAs with low levels of segregation. Prior long-term immigration is significantly associated with higher subsequent black income. However, prior long-term immigration reduces the positive association between prior absolute centralization and black income.

In the absence of structural foundations, these results must be interpreted cautiously. Nominally, they suggest that well-established immigrant communities are especially resistent to black residents, but that new immigrants reduce the residential isolation of blacks. The effects of immigration on average commutes would appear to arise from shifts in workplace locations rather than in those of black residences: they are most consistent with respect to the MSA proportion foreign born, which is associated with greater rather than lesser black segregation.

The associations between prior segregation and black economic welfare suggest the presence of neighborhood but not spatial mismatch effects. The former would be represented by the effects of increased black relative concentration, which would appear to intensify the negative effects of black neighborhood contexts through increased residential densities. The absence of the latter would be represented by the positive effects of increased black absolute concentration, which would presumably reduce black access to workplaces other than those in central business districts.

With these segregation indices held constant, the effects of the interactions between prior segregation and prior long-term immigration on black incomes are difficult to attribute to orthogonal shifts in the distribution of black residences. Instead, they are probably attributable, as in the interactions with commute times, to shifts in workplace locations. In the absence of any confirmation that such shifts occur, this attribution must be taken as entirely speculative. However, its consistency with the observed affects of immigration on the associations between segregation and both commuting times and black welfare suggests that the spatial relationship between immigrant residences and workplace locations deserves immediate study.

Of course, speculations of this type cannot preclude alternative interpretations that attribute causality to underlying and here unmeasured MSA characteristics rather than to immigration and segregation themselves.[19] However, these interpretations would have to be consistent with the observed relationships: as examples, something about MSAs that were later to have low segregation and little association between racial composition and commuting times would have to be previously attractive to foreign-born individuals. Similarly, something about MSAs where black welfare would later be less positively influenced by prior black centralization would have had to have been especially attractive to recent immigrants.

Additional research might reveal plausible and even compelling alternative explanations for these associations. At the moment, though, there is little in them to contradict the hypothesis that the apparent links between immigration, segregation, commutes, and black economic welfare are causal. Tentatively, they demonstrate that short-term immigration has ambiguous affects on black welfare. It reduces segregation as measured by all indices, but the reductions in absolute centralization may be bad for black incomes. The effects of long-term immigration are more clearly negative. It increases many dimensions of segregation and except in cities where the foreign-born population is relatively small, reduces black incomes as well.

NOTES

1. Jencks and Mayer (1990a), Holzer (1991), and Kain (1992) provide comprehensive summaries of the literature discussing this hypothesis.

2. The official Census terms for metropolitan areas are SMSA (Standard Metropolitan Statistical Area) in 1980 and MSA in 1990. This discussion adopts the latter term. Intercensal comparisons of MSA data are notoriously complicated because of changes in MSA boundaries. The Harrison

and Weinberg (1992) indices for 1990 are largely but not completely based on Census retabulations that impose the 1980 boundaries where boundaries have changed. The requirement that their population totals roughly match those in the publicly available STF3C files presumably ensures that segregation indices and STF3C variables refer to roughly the same areas and populations. The sample also omits one MSA for which no measure of absolute centralization is available.

3. This discussion refers only to 1990 because the 1980 STF3 files do not tabulate year of entry.

4. The proportion living elsewhere five years prior to the Census includes the proportion abroad five years prior to the Census. The proportion abroad five years prior to the Census exceeds the proportion of foreign born arriving in the MSA in the previous five years because it includes individuals born in the United States but living abroad five years earlier.

5. The destinations of in-migrants and immigrants may differ more greatly in the long run. The correlation between the proportion foreign born and the proportion living elsewhere five years previously is small (.176 in 1980 and .195 in 1990).

6. Massey and Denton (1988b) define twenty different indices and discuss their properties in great detail. They choose the single representative for each dimension by subjecting all to a factor analysis. Massey and Denton (1989) also define and discuss their five preferred measures.

7. Massey and Denton (1988b, 1989) and Harrison and Weinberg (1992) state, evidently erroneously, that the relative concentration index has maximum and minimum values of positive and negative one. In fact, values larger than one in absolute value appear to be valid and the limits for this index appear to depend on MSA characteristics.

8. Black interaction rates with whites are well below those of Hispanics and Asians in 1970 and 1980 (Massey and Denton 1987) and below those of Hispanics, Asians and Pacific Islanders, and American Indians, Eskimos, and Aleuts in 1980 and 1990 (Harrison and Weinberg 1992). Harrison and Weinberg (1992) present values for nineteen of the twenty indices described in Massey and Denton (1988b). For all but one, average values indicate greater segregation for blacks than for any other minority group.

9. These statistics are unweighted and therefore accord equal influence to indices from MSAs that are small or have small minority populations. The averages in table 7.2 are therefore lower than those reported in Harrison and Weinberg (1992), which are weighted by MSA black populations.

Averages for this sample using these weights match the values in Harrison and Weinberg (1992).

10. Massey and Denton (1988a) also present multivariate regression analyses of intermetropolitan segregation differentials. However, their sample design is idiosyncratic and their specification omits income. Their results are therefore not comparable to those discussed here.

11. Economic theory provides little guidance as to the appropriate specification for these regressions or for those in later sections. The specifications throughout are examples drawn from a larger set of regressions that experiment with different measures of white and black welfare. The results of all these specifications are largely consistent, though naturally different in details. For these reasons, the regressions in this paper should be considered exploratory. At the same time, the specifications in table 7.5 provide a more comprehensive characterization of population characteristics than any previous multivariate analysis of segregation indices, with the possible exception of the stepwise regressions in McKinney (1989).

12. Galster (1987) and McKinney (1989) also find some evidence that segregation increases with higher black incomes. As noted above, Cloutier (1982) also reports that segregation declines with increases in incomes for blacks in the lower tail of the black income distribution but not with increases in the incomes of blacks in the upper tail.

13. The specifications of table 7.5, augmented with 1980 segregation indices as explanatory variables, are dominated if not overwhelmed by the intertemporal correlations in these indices, as reported in table 7.3. The reported specifications omit these indices because, while the indication that previously segregated cities tend to remain segregated is forcefully apparent in the data, it reveals little about the economic precursors of segregation or possible policy options. However, the results here must therefore be interpreted from the perspective that they may reflect this intertemporal relationship through associations between the included variables and contemporaneous segregation levels, rather than direct associations between these variables and subsequent segregation. Regressions specified as in table 7.5, but with changes in segregation indices between 1980 and 1990 as dependent variables, reveal few significant associations.

14. The author can provide parallel analyses using the other segregation indices.

15. Detailed tabulations of these correlations are available from the author.

16. The spatial mismatch hypothesis does not receive universal support. Jencks and Mayer (1990a), Holzer (1991), and Kain (1992) discuss some

of the negative evidence. Gordon, Kumar, and Richardson (1989) and Taylor and Ong (1995) are recent examples of dissenting work.

17. As discussed earlier in this study, "structural" estimations are beyond the scope of this analysis. The regressions summarized here are available from the author. Relative concentration and absolute centralization are the segregation indices that display the most consistent relationships with subsequent measures of economic activity.

18. Similar regressions with other measures of black economic welfare as dependent variables yield results that are roughly equivalent to but less definitive than those presented here.

19. The suspicion that these relationships are causal is strengthened by the fact that relative concentration and absolute centralization have the strongest associations with subsequent black welfare but the weakest associations to prior MSA characteristics.

REFERENCES

Benabou, Roland. 1993. "Workings of a City: Location, Education, and Production." *The Quarterly Journal of Economics* 108(3): 619–52.

Clark, W. A. V. 1986. "Residential Segregation in American Cities: A Review and Interpretation." *Population Research and Policy Review* 5(2): 95–127.

———. 1988. "Understanding Residential Segregation in American Cities: Interpreting the Evidence: A Reply to Galster." *Population Research and Policy Review* 7(2): 113–21.

Cloutier, Norman R. 1982. "Urban Residential Segregation and Black Income." *Review of Economics and Statistics* 64(2): 282–88.

Corcoran, Mary, Roger Gordon, Deborah Laren, and Gary Solon. 1992. "The Association Between Men's Economic Status and Their Family and Community Origins." *The Journal of Human Resources* 27(4): 575–601.

Cutler, David M., and Edward L. Glaeser. 1997. "Are Ghettos Good or Bad?" *Quarterly Journal of Economics* 112(3).

Datcher, Linda. 1982. "Effects of Community and Family Background on Achievement." *Review of Economics and Statistics* 64(1): 32–41.

Davis, DeWitt, Jr., and Emilio Casetti. 1978. "Do Black Students Wish to Live in Integrated, Socially Homogeneous Neighborhoods? A Questionnaire Analysis." *Economic Geography* 54(3): 197–209.

de Bartolome, Charles A. M. 1990. "Equilibrium and Inefficiency in a Community Model with Peer Group Effects." *Journal of Political Economy* 98(1): 110–33.

Denton, Nancy A., and Douglas S. Massey. 1988. "Residential Segregation of

Blacks, Hispanics, and Asians by Socioeconomic Status and Generation." *Social Science Quarterly* 69(4): 797–817.

Farley, Reynolds. 1977. "Residential Segregation in Urbanized Areas of the United States in 1970: An Analysis of Social Class and Racial Differences." *Demography* 14(4): 497–518.

Farley, Reynolds, and Diane Colasanto. 1980. "Racial Residential Segregation: Is It Caused by Misinformation about Housing Costs?" *Social Science Quarterly* 61(3,4): 623–37.

Fernandez, Roberto M. 1994. "Race, Space, and Job Accessibility: Evidence from a Plant Relocation." *Economic Geography* 70(4): 390–416.

Galster, George. 1982. "Black and White Preferences for Neighborhood Racial Composition." *Journal of the American Real Estate and Urban Economics Association* 10(1): 39–66.

———. 1987. "Residential Segregation and Interracial Economic Disparities: A Simultaneous-Equations Approach." *Journal of Urban Economics* 21(1): 22–44.

———. 1988. "Residential Segregation in American Cities: A Contrary Review." *Population Research and Policy Review* 7(2): 93–112.

———. 1989. "Residential Segregation in American Cities: A Further Response to Clark," *Population Research and Policy Review* 8(2): 181–92.

Gordon, Peter, Ajay Kumar, and Harry W. Richardson. 1989. "The Spatial Mismatch Hypothesis: Some New Evidence." *Urban Studies* 26(3): 315–26.

Greytak, David. 1974. "The Journey to Work: Racial Differentials and City Size." *Traffic Quarterly* 28(2): 241–56.

Harding, Robert R. 1983. "Housing Discrimination as a Basis for Interdistrict School Desegregation Remedies." *Yale Law Journal* 93 (December): 340–61.

Harrison, Roderick J., and Daniel H. Weinberg. 1992. "Changes in Racial and Ethnic Residential Segregation, 1980–1990." Working Paper, U.S. Department of Labor, U.S. Bureau of the Census, Washington, D.C.

Holzer, Harry. 1991. "The Spatial Mismatch Hypothesis: What Has the Evidence Shown?" *Urban Studies* 28(1): 105–22.

Holzer, Harry, and Keith R. Ihlanfeldt. 1996. "Spatial Factors and the Employment of Blacks at the Firm Level." *New England Economic Review* (May/June): 65–82.

Ihlanfeldt, Keith R. 1992. "Intraurban Wage Gradients: Evidence by Race, Gender, Occupational Class, and Sector," *Journal of Urban Economics* 32(1): 70–91.

Ihlanfeldt, Keith R., and David L. Sjoquist. 1989. "The Impact of Job Decentralization on the Economic Welfare of Central City Blacks." *Journal of Urban Economics* 26(1): 110–30.

———. 1990. "Job Accessibility and Racial Differences in Youth Employment Rates." *The American Economic Review* 80(1): 267–76.

————. 1991. "The Effect of Job Access on Black and White Youth Employment: A Cross-Sectional Analysis." *Urban Studies* 28(2): 255–65.

Jencks, Christopher, and Susan E. Mayer. 1990a. "Residential Segregation, Job Proximity, and Black Job Opportunities." In *Inner-City Poverty in the United States*, edited by Lawrence E. Lynn, Jr., and Michael G. H. McGeary. Washington, D.C.: National Academy Press.

————. 1990b. "The Social Consequences of Growing Up in a Poor Neighborhood." In *Inner City Poverty in the United States*, edited by Lawrence E. Lynn, Jr., and Michael G. H. McGeary. Washington, D.C.: National Academy Press.

Kain, John F. 1992. "The Spatial Mismatch Hypothesis: Three Decades Later." *Housing Policy Debate* 3(2): 371–460.

Kain, John F., and Joseph J. Persky. 1975. "Alternatives to the Gilded Ghetto." In John F. Kain, *Essays on Urban Spatial Structure*, pp. 199–210. Cambridge, Mass.: Ballinger Publishing Co.

Kain, John F., and John M. Quigley. 1975. *Housing Markets and Racial Discrimination: A Microeconomic Analysis.* New York: National Bureau of Economic Research and Columbia University Press.

Leonard, Jonathan S. 1985. "Space, Time and Unemployment: Los Angeles 1980." Working Paper, University of California at Berkeley.

————. 1987. "The Interaction of Residential Segregation and Employment Discrimination." *Journal of Urban Economics* 21(3): 323–46.

Marshall, Harvey, and Robert Jiobu. 1975. "Residential Segregation in United States Cities: A Causal Analysis." *Social Forces* 53(3): 449–60.

Massey, Douglas S., and Nancy A. Denton. 1987. "Trends in the Residential Segregation of Blacks, Hispanics, and Asians: 1970–1980." *American Sociological Review* 52(6): 802–25.

————. 1988a. "Suburbanization and Segregation in U.S. Metropolitan Areas." *American Journal of Sociology* 94(3): 592–626.

————. 1988b. "The Dimensions of Residential Segregation." *Social Forces* 67(2): 281–315.

————. 1989. "Hypersegregation in U.S. Metropolitan Areas: Black and Hispanic Segregation along Five Dimensions." *Demography* 26(3): 373–91.

Massey, Douglas S., and Brendan P. Mullan. 1984. "Processes of Hispanic and Black Spatial Assimilation." *American Journal of Sociology* 89(4): 836–73.

McKinney, Scott. 1989. "Change in Metropolitan Area Residential Integration, 1970–80." *Population Research and Policy Review* 8(2): 143–64.

McKinney, Scott, and Ann B. Schnare. 1989. "Trends in Residential Segregation by Race: 1960–1980." *Journal of Urban Economics* 26(2): 269–80.

Mieszkowski, Peter, and Richard F. Syron. 1979. "Economic Explanations for Housing Segregation." *New England Economic Review* (November/December): 33–39.

Montgomery, J. 1991. "Social Networks and Labor-Market Outcomes: Towards an Economic Analysis." *The American Economic Review* 81: 1408–1418.

Munnell, Alicia H., Geoffrey M. B. Tootell, Lynn E. Browne, and James Mc-Eneaney. 1986. "Mortgage Lending in Boston: Interpreting HMDA Data." *American Economic Review* 86(1): 25–53.

Newburger, Harriet B. 1989. "Discrimination by a Profit-Maximizing Real Estate Broker in Response to White Prejudice." *Journal of Urban Economics* 26(1): 1–19.

O'Regan, Katherine M., and John M. Quigley. 1991. "Labor Market Access and Labor Market Outcomes for Urban Youth." *Regional Science and Urban Economics* 21(2): 277–93.

Ottensmann, John R., David H. Good, and Michael Gleeson. 1990. "The Impact of Net Migration on Neighbourhood Racial Composition." *Urban Studies* 27(5): 705–17.

Price, Richard, and Edwin Mills. 1985. "Race and Residence in Earnings Determination." *Journal of Urban Economics* 17(1): 1–18.

Rees, Daniel I., and Jeffrey S. Zax. 1997. "Parents, Pals and Peers: Who's Responsible for Contextual Effects?" Working Paper (March).

Reid, Clifford E. 1985. "The Effect of Residential Location on the Wages of Black Women and White Women." *Journal of Urban Economics* 3 (November): 350–63.

Schnare, Ann B. 1980. "Trends in Residential Segregation by Race: 1960–1970." *Journal of Urban Economics* 7(3): 293–301.

Smith, Richard. 1989. "The Effects of Local Fair Housing Ordinances on Housing Segregation: Their Impact Is Small, But It's an Important Positive Change Toward Integration." *American Journal of Economics and Sociology* 48(2): 219–30.

Taeuber, Karl E., and Alma F. Taeuber. 1965. *Negroes in Cities.* Chicago: Aldine.

Taylor, Brian D., and Paul M. Ong. 1995. "Spatial Mismatch or Automobile Mismatch? An Examination of Race, Residence and Commuting in US Metropolitan Areas." *Urban Studies* 32(9): 1453–1473.

Van Valey, Thomas L., Wade Clark Roof, and Jerome E. Wilcox. 1977. "Trends in Residential Segregation: 1960–1970." *American Journal of Sociology* 82(4): 826–44.

Yinger, John. 1986. "Measuring Racial Discrimination with Fair Housing Audits: Caught in the Act." *American Economic Review* 76(5): 881–93.

———. 1995. *Closed Doors, Opportunities Lost: The Continuing Costs of Housing Discrimination.* New York: Russell Sage Foundation.

Zax, Jeffrey S. 1990. "Election Methods, Black and Hispanic City Council Membership." *Social Science Quarterly* 71 (June): 339–55.

Zax, Jeffrey S., and John F. Kain. 1996. "Moving to the Suburbs: Do Relocating Companies Leave Their Black Employees Behind?" *Journal of Labor Economics* 14(3): 472–504.

CHAPTER 8

Educational Crowding Out: Do Immigrants Affect the Educational Attainment of American Minorities?

Julian R. Betts

A large body of literature addresses the important question of how rapidly immigrants to the United States adapt to their new home in terms of labor-market performance. Perhaps an equally important question is how the presence of immigrants affects the economic well-being of American-born residents of the United States. This issue has received much less attention. To date, most research in this area has tested for an impact of immigrant flows on the wages of native-born Americans. Examples include Altonji and Card (1991), Bean, Lowell, and Taylor (1988), Borjas (1990), Grossman (1982), and LaLonde and Topel (1991). The typical conclusion from these studies has been that the presence of a large number of immigrants tends to lower the wages of natives, but by only a very small percentage. In a review of the literature, Borjas (1994) estimates that the average native wage elasticity with respect to the number of immigrants is -0.01 to -0.02.

To the best of my knowledge, no paper has yet studied whether the presence of immigrants in the local area affects the educational attainment of American-born workers. This link, if it exists, could provide an important mechanism through which immigrants affect the economic well-being of natives. Unfortunately, economic theory provides ambiguous predictions about the direction of the effect of immigrants on natives' educational attainment. The reason is simple: immigrants are likely to increase both the costs and benefits of education to natives. The marginal cost of education for natives may rise due to competition between immigrant and American-born students for school resources; the marginal benefit of education for natives may rise if the arrival of relatively unskilled immigrants increases the returns to education.

The goal of this study is to test whether immigration has affected the probability that American-born minority students complete high school. The analysis will proceed using 1980 and 1990 Census data.[1] I concentrate on estimating the impact of immigrants on educational attainment of two minority groups: native-born blacks and native-born Hispanics. There are three good reasons for doing so. First, families of higher income and socioeconomic status can "vote with their feet" if an influx of immigrants into the local area puts a strain on public services such as schooling. They can do this by moving to more affluent areas or by enrolling their children in private schools. It follows that the main impact of immigrants on natives may be felt by American-born minorities, simply because minorities are less likely to have the financial resources to move to affluent areas or to place their children in private schools. Second, *within* schools, minority students are more likely to be placed in classes with recent immigrants due to the grouping of students by initial achievement.[2] That is, since minority students are more likely to be placed in classrooms with lower average achievement, they are more likely to have immigrants in their classes than are students with higher levels of achievement. Third, disadvantaged immigrant students are eligible to participate in federally financed Chapter I programs. The goal of this spending is to provide remedial education to disadvantaged children. In a study of school districts in Oakland, Houston, Boston, and Washington, D.C., Fix and Zimmerman (1993) conclude that an influx of immigrants to each of these school districts in the 1980s did not crowd native-born students out of participation in Chapter I programs. They do find evidence that the influx of immigrant schoolchildren during this time expanded the number of children receiving Chapter I services, which had the effect of reducing spending per pupil on remediation. This reduction in remedial spending should have been felt most strongly by minority students.[3] For all three of these reasons, it is plausible that the effects of immigrants on educational attainment of natives should be greatest on minorities.

Because of the large and growing gap in earnings between high school graduates and high school dropouts, I will focus on high school completion.[4] The distinction between those with and without a high school diploma is becoming one of the great divides of American society. This is especially true for minorities. In 1992, among whites, blacks, and Hispanics aged eighteen to twenty-four, 12.2, 16.3, and 33.9 percent, respectively, had failed to graduate from high school. (U.S. Bureau of the Census 1994).

I will next discuss in more detail why economic theory suggests an ambiguous impact of immigration on the educational attainment of American-born minorities. I will then describe the data and present the results.

THE IMPACT OF IMMIGRANTS ON THE MARGINAL COSTS AND BENEFITS OF EDUCATION FOR NATIVES

As we have seen, the presence of a large number of immigrants in a city or state could induce native-born Americans to stay in school for either longer or shorter periods, depending on whether the marginal benefits of education or the marginal costs of education rise more in response. Consider first the costs. Young immigrants to the United States are typically not perfectly acculturated to American public schools. In particular, they often lack the ability to speak English fluently. The presence of a significant number of students in a school who cannot speak English fluently or who are otherwise not fully assimilated culturally can reduce the effectiveness of educational spending for *all* students. If separate classes are established for students with "Limited English Proficiency" (LEP), this drains resources away from native-born students. If on the other hand immigrant students are placed in classes with native-born students, the large gap in language proficiency between the two groups of students will make it difficult for the teacher to teach as effectively as if he or she had a more homogeneous class. Similarly, a large body of research indicates that parents have a large influence on the quality of the schools that their children attend. It thus becomes possible that immigrant parents, to the extent that their educational attainment and attitudes about schooling differ from those of native-born parents, could influence the effectiveness of schooling for both their own children and native-born children in the school.[5]

The idea that the presence of immigrants in the classroom can diminish the effectiveness of schools is by now widely accepted in the United States. Congress passed the Emergency Immigrant Education Act of 1984 in a bid to provide supplemental funding to school districts that had a large fraction of immigrant students.[6] Although the existence of this act illustrates public recognition that additional funding is needed to cope with inflows of immigrant schoolchildren, the funding disbursed under the law makes at best modest contributions to solving the problem. In the 1989 to 1990 school year, average disbursements under the act were only sixty-two dollars per eligible immigrant student (General Accounting Office 1991). This sum is slightly more than 1 percent of the current expenditures per pupil ($4,939) in average daily attendance in public schools in that year (National Center for Education Statistics 1991, 155).[7]

If it is more expensive to teach a given set of skills and knowledge to immigrant students than to native-born students, and if, as appears to be the case, government funding has not risen to reflect fully these additional costs, it is likely that native-born students' rate of learning at school will fall. The cost to American students of acquiring a given set of skills thus rises. Once immigrant students arrive in a school, native-born students would either have to exert more independent effort or stay in school longer in order to acquire a given amount of human capital. The induced rise in the marginal costs of schooling suggests that

American-born students will on average reduce the amount of education they acquire. In other words, "educational crowding out" might reduce the educational attainment of natives.

It is also possible that the presence of immigrants in the area might increase the marginal benefits of education to natives, thus rendering the overall direction of the impact on the educational attainment of natives ambiguous. To see why the marginal benefits of education to natives might rise after an inflow of immigrants, consider a simple model with two types of workers, skilled and unskilled. Borjas (1994) outlines such a model. The wages of skilled and unskilled workers are both likely to change after immigrants arrive in the country. If the proportion of immigrants who are unskilled is greater than the proportion of natives who are unskilled, then it is likely that the wage of skilled workers will rise and the wage of unskilled workers will fall. Since, as documented in Borjas (1995), about 37 percent of immigrants in both the 1980 and 1990 Census were high school dropouts, compared to just 23 percent of natives in 1980 and 15 percent of natives in 1990, it seems fair to argue that immigrants are "unskilled" relative to natives. Consequently, the presence of immigrants in the American labor market should increase the gap between the earnings of high school graduates and high school dropouts. In this way, immigrants can increase the marginal benefits of education for natives. Indeed, Borjas, Freeman, and Katz (1992) estimate that the arrival of less-skilled immigrants could have decreased the wages of high school dropouts relative to high school graduates by about 3 percent between 1980 and 1988.

If both of these forces are at work—educational crowding out that increases the marginal cost of education to natives, and rising returns to education due to an influx of less skilled immigrants—the average educational attainment of natives could either rise or fall in response to immigration. Given the aforementioned studies, which tend to show no or small effects of immigrants on the wages of local natives, the crowding-out effect may dominate in the real world, thus leading natives to obtain less education.

DATA

The regressions use a pooled sample of young people taken from the 5 percent samples of the 1980 and 1990 versions of the Census of Population and Housing. The regression samples include all American-born blacks and Hispanics aged nineteen to twenty-five at the time of the Census.[8] In the regressions, the dependent variable is a dummy indicating whether the person has obtained a high school diploma or higher on one hand, or less than a high school diploma on the other. In the case of people from the 1980 Census, if a person reported twelve years of education but indicated that he or she had not completed the given year of education I set the graduation variable to zero.

I choose young people aged nineteen to twenty-five in order to ensure that the person is likely to have attended school in the state of current residence. In other words, given that I seek to estimate the immigrant-to-population ratio in the area where each person spent his or her childhood and adolescence, using the person's current state of residence will produce more accurate estimates for younger workers than for older workers. Studying the group of people who attended grade school in the 1980s is especially interesting because of large increases in immigration during that decade.

Based on each person's place of residence, measures of the immigrant-to-population ratio were calculated. In the main regressions, these and other demographic variables were calculated for the state of residence. But additional regressions were run in which immigration rates were calculated for the metropolitan area of residence. In these latter regressions, people were assigned to one of 132 metropolitan areas, based on code generously provided by Susanna Loeb, Sarah Turner, and David Jaeger (see Loeb, Turner, and Jaeger 1996 for a summary of their method of creating consistent definitions of metropolitan areas across the 1980 and 1990 editions of the Census). In 1980, metropolitan area was derived from the person's county group; in 1990 the metropolitan area was derived from the PUMA code for each person.

Regressors include a dummy for whether the person at the time of the Census was living in a city, which was determined using the four-digit SMSA codes in the 1980 Census and the four-digit MSA/PMSA codes in the 1990 Census. Other regressors are described later in this study.

Unlike the 1980 Census, the 1990 Census is not self-weighting. That is, each person in the sample did not have an equal probability of being included in the Census. Therefore, all model estimates are weighted, using the person weights contained in the 1990 Census data (which have a mean of roughly 20, given that the sample is a 5 percent sample), and using a constant weight of 20 in the 1980 sample.

RESULTS
Basic Results

This section begins by presenting simple OLS results and then proceeds to more complex difference-in-difference models that use variations over time in each state to identify the impact of immigrants on the educational attainment of minorities.

The basic estimates are linear probability models for the probability that a given individual has obtained twelve years of schooling by the time of the Census. The simple OLS and the fixed-effect models are given by the following equations, where i, s and t are subscripts for the individual, his or her state of residence, and the year of the Census observation (1980 or 1990):

$$(8.1) \quad GRAD_{ist} = c + \alpha CENSUS90_{ist} + \beta IMM_{ist} + X_{ist}\Gamma + \varepsilon_{ist}$$

and

$$(8.2) \quad GRAD_{ist} = \sum_{j=1}^{51} STATE_{ist}\gamma_j + \alpha CENSUS90_{ist} + \beta IMM_{ist} + X_{ist}\Gamma + \varepsilon_{ist},$$

respectively.

The dependent variable is a dummy variable set to one if the person has finished at least twelve years of schooling. In the OLS regressions without state dummies, regressors include a constant, $CENSUS90_{ist}$, which is a dummy variable for whether the observation derives from the 1990 Census, IMM_{ist}, which is a measure of the proportion of the state population that consists of immigrants, and X_{ist} which is a vector of other variables. This vector initially includes a dummy for whether the person was living in a city at the time of the Census, calculated as described earlier, a dummy for whether the person was female, and age at the time of the interview. Equation (8.2) is a fixed-effect estimator that replaces the constant with a set of dummy variables for each state (and the District of Columbia).

A variety of measures of the proportion of immigrants in the local population were calculated. The first was the proportion of people aged nineteen to twenty-five in the area who reported being born abroad of foreign parents. Note that this age range corresponds exactly to the members of minority groups whose educational attainment is being modeled. This measure should capture any "crowding-out" effects experienced by these young blacks and Hispanics while they were in school and at the same time will control for any changes in the returns to education for young workers due to immigration. It makes sense to calculate a second immigration ratio over a broader age group for three reasons. First, the quality of grade-school education that was enjoyed by natives aged nineteen to twenty-five could have been adversely affected if a large number of younger immigrant children had attended the school district at the same time, as it might have diverted resources from upper grade levels to the lower levels.

(Conversely, when these minority students were in primary school, a large influx of immigrants of high school age could have diverted the resources of the school district away from primary schools.) Second, to the extent that younger and older workers of a given level of education are substitutes in the labor market, the returns to education for young workers should depend on the overall ratio of immigrants in the population, not just in the population aged nineteen to twenty-five. Third, to the extent that adult immigrants affect the quality of local schooling through indirect neighborhood effects, it may be relevant to include older people in the calculation of immigrant ratios. Therefore a second measure of the extent of immigration was calculated: the proportion of the entire population aged six to sixty-four who were born abroad of foreign parents.

The OLS results without state fixed effects are presented for young blacks and Hispanics in tables 8.1 and 8.2, respectively. Although, as will be discussed later in this study, these models appear to be misspecified due to the neglect of significantly different intercepts by state, these regressions provide a logical starting place. Table 8.1 shows that black women were significantly more likely to have completed high school than black men, by about 6 to 7 percent. Similarly, blacks living in cities and older blacks were more likely to have graduated. In column (1), which includes the proportion of the state's population aged nineteen to twenty-five who are immigrants, this variable enters positively and significantly. Column (2) instead uses the overall immigrant ratio among the population aged six through sixty-four. The coefficient is still positive and significant, but both the coefficient and its *t*-statistic fall by over half.

A common finding throughout the tables to be presented is that when the immigrant ratio for ages nineteen to twenty-five is replaced by the ratio for the population aged six to sixty-four, the coefficient falls. There are two ways to interpret this pattern. The first is that immigrants affect the educational attainment of natives of their own age only, so that using broader age groupings introduces measurement error. This explanation does not seem wholly accurate, since measurement error should bias the coefficient toward zero. As will be shown below, in the typical case the use of the broader age grouping leads to a larger *negative* coefficient on the immigration variable, which is not consistent with the explanation of measurement error. A second and more reasonable explanation is that the educational attainment of young natives aged nineteen to twenty-five is affected by immigrants of a much broader age group than just ages nineteen to twenty-five. Since the effect of immigrants becomes smaller or more negative when using

Table 8.1   Linear Probability Models of the Probability of Attaining at Least Twelve Years of Schooling for Native-Born Blacks Aged Nineteen to Twenty-Five

Variable	(1)	(2)	(3)	(4)
Constant	0.4643 (50.20)	0.4646 (50.22)	0.3825 (37.70)	0.3697 (36.40)
Female	0.0663 (39.82)	0.0661 (39.69)	0.0672 (40.39)	0.0672 (40.38)
Age	0.0093 (22.73)	0.0093 (22.80)	0.0094 (22.91)	0.0094 (22.95)
Live in city	0.0423 (17.25)	0.0446 (18.07)	0.0319 (12.49)	0.0327 (12.78)
1990 Census	−0.0199 (−11.64)	−0.0177 (−10.43)	−0.0669 (−26.05)	−0.0701 (−27.22)
Proportion age 35–64 with high school diploma			0.3953 (23.86)	0.4114 (25.10)
Mean income/1000 (35–64)			−0.0102 (−13.18)	−0.0090 (−11.50)
Immigrant/population (19–25)	0.1139 (8.07)		−0.0473 (−2.77)	
Immigrant/population (6–64)		0.0480 (3.08)		−0.1604 (−8.30)
R-square	0.0096	0.0094	0.0118	0.0120
Adjusted R-square	0.0096	0.0094	0.0118	0.0120
Number of observations	278282	278282	278282	278282
P-value: F-test for exclusion of state dummies	<0.00001	<0.00001	<0.00001	<0.00001

Note: t-statistics appear in parentheses.

this measure, it suggests that the presence of adult (or very young) immigrants may decrease educational attainment of native-born minorities, perhaps by inducing reallocation of the school district's resources between grade levels.

The two specifications presented so far are rather sparse. It seems quite likely that omitted-variable bias could be biasing the coefficients. It seems particularly likely that if immigrants tend to settle in economically vibrant states, and if minorities tend to obtain relatively more education in such states, then the coefficients on immigrant ratio will be biased upward.

As a first attempt to solve this problem, consider other demographic variables that might influence the educational attainment of young

Table 8.2   Linear Probability Models of the Probability of Attaining at Least Twelve Years of Schooling for Native-Born Hispanics Aged Nineteen to Twenty-Five

Variable	(1)	(2)	(3)	(4)
Constant	0.4661 (31.64)	0.4692 (31.82)	0.2049 (12.66)	0.2099 (13.03)
Female	0.0282 (10.85)	0.0282 (10.86)	0.0307 (11.91)	0.0308 (11.94)
Age	0.0083 (12.89)	0.0083 (12.89)	0.0084 (13.16)	0.0084 (13.19)
Live in city	0.0252 (5.69)	0.0280 (6.29)	0.0443 (9.92)	0.0469 (10.46)
1990 Census	0.0140 (4.96)	0.0174 (6.29)	−0.0780 (−20.24)	−0.0772 (−20.03)
Proportion age 35–64 with high school diploma			0.5258 (23.78)	0.5090 (22.89)
Mean income/1000 (35–64)			0.0046 (4.05)	0.0052 (4.62)
Immigrant/population (19–25)	0.0292 (1.69)		−0.2359 (−11.90)	
Immigrant/population (6–64)		−0.0351 (−1.66)		−0.3146 (−13.14)
R-square	0.0029	0.0029	0.0153	0.0155
Adjusted R-square	0.0029	0.0029	0.0152	0.0155
Number of observations	125664	125664	125664	125664
P-value: F-test for exclusion of state dummies	<0.00001	<0.00001	<0.00001	<0.00001

Note: *t*-statistics appear in parentheses.

blacks. Research has consistently shown that the socioeconomic status of a person's parents is a significant determinant of that person's educational attainment (see for instance Taubman 1989). It is not possible to obtain such information from the Census unless the person is still living in the same residence as his or her parents; but proxies can be obtained by measuring the average socioeconomic status of people in the local area who are in the age group likely to have offspring who would be in the regression sample (aged nineteen to twenty-five and of the given race). Therefore, in some regressions, two measures were included to capture the characteristics of the older population of the given race in the person's area of residence. The first was the average total income of people in the local area of the given race who were American-born and who were aged thirty-five to sixty-four at the time of the Census. The second measure was the proportion of members of the given race who were American-born and aged thirty-five to sixty-four and who had at least twelve years of schooling. Separate measures were obtained for blacks and Hispanics.

Columns (3) and (4) replicate the first two models with these two proxies for the income and education of parents of young blacks added. Strikingly, the coefficients on the immigrant ratios reverse and are significantly different from zero. This reversal suggests that omitted variable problems of the sort discussed earlier may have biased the coefficients of the immigration variable upward. As expected, if a larger proportion of the older black population in the state has at least twelve years of schooling, young blacks are more likely to have completed high school. However, a somewhat troubling result is that income per capita of this older generation is significantly *negatively* correlated with the probability of high school completion by young blacks.

One indicator of a potential reason for this puzzling result is shown in the bottom row of the table, which lists the probability value for the hypothesis that model (1) is correctly specified, with model (2), which adds state fixed effects, as the alternative. In all cases the null is overwhelmingly rejected. I will return to this issue later in this study.

Table 8.2 presents the same four specifications using the sample of young Hispanics. As for young blacks, those who are female, older, or who live in a city are significantly more likely to have completed at least twelve years of schooling. Column (1) indicates a positive correlation between high school completion and the proportion of immigrants in the state's young population, but the link is not significant. In column (2) the coefficient reverses sign but remains insignificant. In columns (3) and (4), which add measures of the socioeconomic status of older Hispanics in the state, the immigrant ratios become negative and highly significant, just as was found for blacks. Unlike for blacks, both proxies for parents' socioeconomic status are positively and significantly related to educational attainment of the younger generation. A notable difference between the results for Hispanic and black youth is that the estimated (signed) impact of immigrants on the probability of graduating is uniformly lower for Hispanics. In other words, there is greater evidence of an adverse impact on outcomes for Hispanics than for blacks.[9]

An immediate concern in the search for an impact of immigrants in the local area on the educational attainment of minorities is that a correlation between these two variables might not be causal but instead might reflect correlation with an underlying trait of the local area. One plausible example is a situation in which immigrants tend to settle in

Table 8.3   Linear Probability Models of the Probability of Attaining at
Least Twelve Years of Schooling for Native-Born Blacks
Aged Nineteen to Twenty-Five, with State Fixed Effects

Variable	(1)	(2)	(3)	(4)
Female	0.0691	0.0691	0.0691	0.0691
	(41.62)	(41.61)	(41.61)	(41.61)
Age	0.0093	0.0093	0.0093	0.0093
	(22.87)	(22.88)	(22.85)	(22.86)
Live in city	0.0535	0.0536	0.0530	0.0530
	(19.95)	(19.97)	(19.76)	(19.77)
1990 Census	−0.0083	−0.0072	−0.0696	−0.0658
	(−3.95)	(−3.27)	(−6.32)	(−6.09)
Proportion age 35–64 with high school diploma			0.2473	0.2196
			(4.45)	(4.00)
Mean income/1000 (35–64)			0.0064	0.0085
			(3.36)	(4.17)
Immigrant/population (19–25)	−0.3026		−0.2449	
	(−6.34)		(−3.75)	
Immigrant/population (6–64)		−0.4561		−0.4718
		(−6.57)		(−4.78)
R-square	0.0102	0.0102	0.0103	0.0103
Adjusted R-square	0.0101	0.0102	0.0103	0.0103
Number of observations	278282	278282	278282	278282

Note: *t*-statistics appear in parentheses.

thriving areas of the country. If the returns to education are higher in such areas, young American-born citizens are more likely to obtain their high school diplomas. In such a situation, a spurious positive correlation will emerge between the ratio of immigrants to total population and the probability that an American-born citizen will have completed high school. To the extent that any such unobserved traits of the local area are fixed over time, this spurious correlation can be purged from the model by including a fixed effect for each area.

Indeed, for both blacks and Hispanics, the hypothesis of a common intercept across states was uniformly rejected with a p-value < 0.00001. Accordingly, tables 8.3 and 8.4 show the results when dummies for state of residence are added, as in model (2) earlier. In this specification, which as before includes a time dummy, variations across states in educational attainment no longer contribute to the identification of the parameters; rather, this model uses changes between 1980 and 1990 within each state to identify the coefficients. The inclusion of a time dummy means that the identification is further limited to the parts of

Table 8.4   Linear Probability Models of the Probability of Attaining at Least Twelve Years of Schooling for Native-Born Hispanics Aged Nineteen to Twenty-Five, with State Fixed Effects

Variable	(1)	(2)	(3)	(4)
Female	0.0317	0.0317	0.0318	0.0317
	(12.30)	(12.29)	(12.33)	(12.32)
Age	0.0084	0.0084	0.0084	0.0084
	(13.21)	(13.21)	(13.21)	(13.21)
Live in city	0.0571	0.0572	0.0569	0.0569
	(12.21)	(12.22)	(12.17)	(12.16)
1990 Census	0.0426	0.0424	0.0330	0.0384
	(9.73)	(9.12)	(2.40)	(2.75)
Proportion age 35–64 with high school diploma			−0.0509	−0.0742
			(−0.84)	(−1.22)
Mean income/1000 (35–64)			0.0129	0.0135
			(4.67)	(4.79)
Immigrant/population (19–25)	−0.4263		−0.5758	
	(−7.51)		(−8.93)	
Immigrant/population (6–64)		−0.6045		−0.8831
		(−6.82)		(−8.46)
R-square	0.0046	0.0045	0.0048	0.0047
Adjusted R-square	0.0045	0.0045	0.0047	0.0046
Number of observations	125664	125664	125664	125664

Note: *t*-statistics appear in parentheses.

these within-state changes that vary from the average changes over time at the national level.

In these tables the ratio of immigrants to total population is in all cases negatively and significantly related to the probability that the young person finishes at least twelve years of schooling. The models also seem better specified in that the troubling negative and significant coefficient on mean income per capita of the older black generation in table 8.1 is reversed in table 8.3, once one controls for unobserved differences across states.[10]

Recall that the coefficient on the immigration variables changes radically in the OLS specifications in tables 8.1 and 8.2 once proxies for parental socioeconomic status are added. This appears to indicate that in the simpler models in tables 8.1 and 8.2, the immigration ratio was biased upward by correlation with these and other measures of the socioeconomic level of state residents. Once the state fixed effect is added in tables 8.3 and 8.4, the coefficients on the immigration ratios are much more robust to addition of the two socioeconomic variables. This suggests that the addition of the state fixed effects does a good job of controlling for socioeconomic determinants of the educational attainment of young blacks and Hispanics.

Note that in the fixed-effect estimates, as was the case in the simpler models, the adverse impact of immigrants appears to be larger for native-born Hispanics than for native-born blacks. For instance, based on columns (3) and (4), an increase of 0.1 in the share of immigrants in the state population aged nineteen to twenty-five is predicted to lower the probability of high school completion for blacks by 0.024, or 2.4 percent. For Hispanics, the predicted drop is much larger, 5.8 percent. Using the overall immigration ratio, the predicted drops in graduation probabilities after a 10 percent increase in the immigrant ratio are 4.7 percent for blacks and 8.8 percent for Hispanics.

Interpreting the Size of the Coefficients

What is the economic import of the coefficients on the immigration variables? Table 8.5 presents estimates of how the probability of graduation would change when the immigrant-to-population ratio changes. Given that the hypothesis of no fixed effects was strongly rejected, and that the two proxies for parental socioeconomic status are in general significant, the table uses the estimated impact of immigration from columns (3) and (4) of tables 8.3 and 8.4. The first row shows the proportion of the regression sample that had graduated from high school. The next three rows in the table show the immigrant-to-population ratio for blacks and Hispanics in 1980 and 1990. These are based on the immigrant-to-population ratios that were calculated for each state using the population of each state between ages nineteen and twenty-five, or between six and sixty-four, which are the ratios used in the previous regressions. Separate estimates of the "average" exposure of blacks and Hispanics to immigrants were then obtained by taking a weighted average of these state immigrant ratios, using the numbers of native-born blacks and Hispanics in each state. The immigrant share in total population rose substantially during the 1980s, with both the initial level and the subsequent increase proving especially large for Hispanics. (As will become apparent from the later analysis, this in large part reflects a major increase in the immigrant-to-population ratio in California, a state in which slightly over one-quarter of the Hispanic natives in the regression sample resided.)

The first "experiment" simply estimates the predicted drop in the probability of graduating from high school for blacks and Hispanics based on the coefficient estimates and the observed changes in immi-

Table 8.5   Estimates of the Predicted Drop in the Probability of
Graduation Given a Rise in the Ratio of Immigrants to the
Overall Population

Row	Immigration Measure	Black Age 19–25	Black Age 6–64	Hispanic Age 19–25	Hispanic Age 6–64
1	Proportion of regression sample of given race which graduated	0.737	0.737	0.695	0.695
2	Mean immigration ratio, 1980	0.045774	0.04931	0.085048	0.085705
3	Mean immigration ratio, 1990	0.075413	0.072448	0.148837	0.130947
4	change, 1980–1990	0.029639	0.023138	0.063789	0.045242
	Experiment (1): Effect of 1980–1990 Increase in Immigration Ratio				
5	Coefficient on immigration × change, 1980–1990 (row 4)	−0.2449	−0.4718	−0.5758	−0.8831
6	= Predicted change in probability of graduation	−0.00726	−0.01092	−0.03673	−0.03995
	Experiment (2): Effect of Increasing Immigration Ratio from 0 to 1990 Level: Row 3 × Row 5				
7	= Predicted change in probability of graduation	−0.01847	−0.03418	−0.0857	0.11564

Notes: Estimates are based on the coefficients in columns (3) and (4) in tables 8.3 and 8.4. Mean immigration ratios are calculated using weighted means for blacks and Hispanics aged nineteen to twenty-five in 1980 and 1990.

gration. For blacks, the probability of high school graduation is predicted to have dropped by approximately 1 percent during the 1980s due to immigrant inflows. For American-born Hispanics, the estimates are much higher, on the order of a 3 to 4 percent drop. These estimates are higher for Hispanics than for blacks as a result of both higher estimated marginal effects and a greater increase in exposure to immigrants. These predicted drops in graduation rates are meaningful when compared to the actual sample averages of the graduation rate, which as shown in row (1) of table 8.5, are roughly 70 percent for both blacks and Hispanics.

The second experiment is outlined in the bottom portion of the table. It shows that if the immigrant-to-population ratio rose from zero to its actual level for each race in 1990, the predicted drop in the probability of high school graduation would be 1.8 to 3.4 percent for blacks, and an astonishing 8.5 to 11.5 percent for Hispanics. These estimates should of course be treated with some caution. Since the coefficients underlying this analysis are identified using actual changes between 1980 and 1990, the estimates from this second, bolder experiment are probably less accurate than are the estimates based on the actual, more limited changes in immigration in the 1980s.

Robustness

The remaining tables probe the robustness of the results. Four sorts of respecifications are carried out. First, I rerun the fixed-effect models while conditioning on a measure of public school resources in each state. Second, I attempt to reduce the measurement error caused by young people migrating from the area in which they attended school. Third, I rerun the difference-in-difference model, this time using the metropolitan area as the unit of observation for gathering geographic data such as the immigrant ratios. Finally, given that the immigrant-to-population ratio rose particularly strongly in California during the 1980s, I rerun the key models without observations from California.

Controlling for School Resources   Models (3) and (4) in tables 8.3 and 8.4 control for unobserved but constant factors in each state through use of a state fixed effect. They also control for the socioeconomic status of the parents' generation in the state by including measures of the older generation's level of education and income, both specific to race. It is possible that not only family background but also school spending influences the probability that a student will graduate from high school. Betts (1996) reviews the literature on the link between school resources and educational attainment of students. Evidence is mixed, with the strongest positive result being the finding in five of seven studies that a negative and statistically significant link exists between the pupil-teacher ratio and students' years of schooling. Class size is also one of the school inputs that has changed the most over the last thirty years. At the national level the average pupil-teacher ratio declined from 26.4 in 1960 to just 16.8 in 1990 (National Center for Education Statistics 1991).

To test whether the models suffer from omitted variable bias of this sort, the average pupil-teacher ratio in each state was calculated based on data published by the National Center for Education Statistics (various years) in the *Digest of Education Statistics* and the *Biennial Survey of Education in the United States* (Federal Security Agency, various years). For several years in the 1960s, data were linearly interpolated using surrounding observations. In the sample of natives aged nineteen to twenty-five in 1980, the oldest would have attended grades 1 through 12 between fall 1961 and spring 1973, while the youngest would have graduated from grade 12 in spring 1979. So for this cohort the simple average of the pupil-teacher ratio in each state was taken over the school years 1961 to 1962 through 1978 to 1979. Similarly, for the sample of people aged nineteen to twenty-five in 1990, the pupil-teacher ratio was calculated as the mean for all school years between 1971 to 1972 and 1988 to 1989.[11]

I then repeated models (3) and (4) from tables 8.3 and 8.4 for blacks and Hispanics, adding the mean pupil-teacher ratio to the models that already contain controls for education and income among the older generation of the given race as well as a fixed effect for each state. The results appear in the top part of table 8.6. Several conclusions emerge from the table. First, the pupil-teacher ratio does not appear to be significantly related to the probability of graduation. Second, the coefficients and level of significance on the immigration variables and measures of socioeconomic status are highly similar to those reported in the earlier tables. The *t*-statistics and the coefficients on the immigration variables are slightly smaller in absolute size.

In the fixed-effect specification the coefficients on the immigration variables and the pupil-teacher ratio are identified by changes in these variables between the two cohorts represented in the 1980 and 1990 Census. It is useful to examine the difference in the immigration ratios and the pupil-teacher ratio between the 1990 and 1980 Census periods. Figure 8.1 shows the change in the immigration-to-population ratio for each state among the population aged nineteen to twenty-five between 1980 and 1990 plotted against the change in the calculated pupil-teacher ratio for this age group. The figure reveals three facts. First, the states varied considerably in how they changed the pupil-teacher ratio over time, with some states decreasing class size by only one or two and many others decreasing class size by four or five pupils. This finding suggests that a lack of variation in the pupil-teacher ratio cannot explain why this measure of school resources is not significantly related to the probability that black or Hispanic students graduate from high school. Second, the figure reveals a positive correlation between

Table 8.6   Robustness Tests of the State Fixed-Effect Models

Variable*	Blacks (1)	Blacks (2)	Hispanics (3)	Hispanics (4)
Pupil-teacher ratio	−0.0023 (−0.85)	−0.0009 (−0.33)	−0.0001 (−0.03)	−0.0030 (−0.72)
Immigrant/population (19–25)	−0.2039 (−2.71)		−0.5706 (−6.47)	
Immigrant/population (6–64)		−0.4440 (−3.94)		−0.8111 (−5.84)
R-square	0.0103	0.0104	0.0048	0.0047
Adjusted R-square	0.0103	0.0103	0.0047	0.0046
Number of observations	277464	277464	125043	125043

Variable†	Blacks (5)	Blacks (6)	Hispanics (7)	Hispanics (8)
Immigrant/population (19–25)	−0.3353 (−3.82)		−0.5949 (−6.96)	
Immigrant/population (6–64)		−0.6339 (−4.78)		−0.9343 (−6.65)
R-square	0.0122	0.0123	0.0043	0.0042
Adjusted R-square	0.0122	0.0123	0.0042	0.0041
Number of observations	175286	175286	83093	83093

*The regressions are identical to models (3) and (4) in tables 8.3 and 8.4 except that the pupil-teacher ratio is an added regressor and observations from Hawaii and Alaska have been dropped.
†There are no added regressors. The subsample reported living in the same state five years before the Census year.

changes in the immigration ratio and the pupil-teacher ratio. This may explain why the *t*-statistics and the coefficients on the immigration-to-population ratio decline somewhat when the pupil-teacher ratio is added, even though the latter does not enter significantly itself. (The correlation between the changes in the immigration ratio and the pupil-teacher ratio is 0.32.) Third, the figure reveals that California was very much an outlier over the 1980s, with its immigrant-to-population ratio rising by 0.132, far above the simple mean (0.015) for the remaining states. This is an important issue that will be addressed later.[12] The conclusion from this analysis is that the observed negative relation between the immigration-to-population ratio and educational attain-

Figure 8.1.   Changes by State in the Immigration-to-Population Ratio and the Pupil-Teacher Ratio, 1980 to 1990

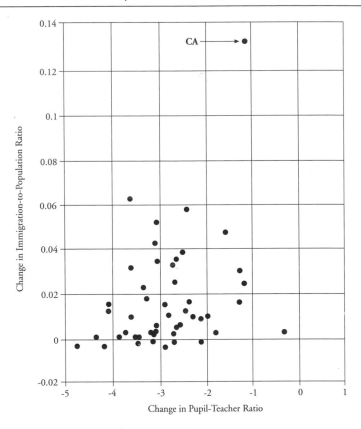

Notes: The immigration ratio is calculated among people aged nineteen to twenty-five in each state. The pupil-teacher ratio is calculated as an average for those aged nineteen to twenty-five in the given Census year during the time they were attending grades one to twelve.

ment is robust to controls for the pupil-teacher ratio among both blacks and Hispanics.

Replication of Results Using Subsamples of Nonmovers   In the state-level regressions, measurement error in the state-level variables, including the immigration-to-population ratios, could be biasing upward (toward zero) the estimated effects of immigrants on natives' probability of finishing high school. One way to control for this is to use data available in the Census indicating the location in which the person was living five years before the Census year in order to eliminate those who have moved. In theory, this should increase the absolute size of the co-efficients on the variables measured at the state level (such as the immi-gration ratio) since these variables are calculated based on current loca-tion and not the actual location in which the person grew up. But removing those who have moved is not without costs. First, the sample drops, in part because movers are removed from the sample but also be-cause in the 1980 Census questions about the person's location in 1975 were made available for only one-half of the 5 percent sample. Thus the precision of the estimates will drop. Second, it is possible that movers are a nonrandomly selected sample, so that regressions on this subsam-ple could be biased in an unknown direction.

I repeated models (3) and (4) from tables 8.3 and 8.4 after drop-ping those who reported living in a different state five years before the Census year well as the 50 percent of 1980 observations for which lo-cation five years earlier was not available. Accordingly, in the regres-sions the weights on those remaining in the 1980 Census sample were doubled to forty, while weights on observations from the 1990 Census were left unchanged, with an average value of approximately twenty. This has the effect of representing both years equally in the regression sample.

The results appear in the bottom portion of table 8.6 (regressions 5 through 8). About one-third of the observations are lost due to the sample restriction. The table indicates that for Hispanics the results are very little changed when people who lived in a different state five years prior to the Census year are excluded, with the coefficients on the im-migration variables becoming slightly more negative. In the regressions for blacks, the coefficients on the immigration variables remain nega-tive and significant but become about one-third larger in absolute value. The direction of these changes is consistent with the presence of some measurement error in the full sample due to internal migration of natives.

Replicating the Results Using Metropolitan Areas   A problem with using state-level estimates of the immigrant-to-population ratio is that immigrants are not evenly distributed within the typical state. It would be reassuring if the flavor of the above estimates were retained in analy-ses based on less geographically aggregated areas. For this reason, the re-gressions in tables 8.3 and 8.4 were repeated for the subsample of blacks and Hispanics who reported living in one of the 132 metropolitan areas for which I could obtain consistent coding between 1980 and 1990.

Table 8.7   Estimates of the Probability of Attaining at Least Twelve Years of Schooling for Native-Born Blacks and Hispanics Aged Nineteen to Twenty-Five, with Metropolitan Area Fixed Effects

	Blacks			
Variable	(1)	(2)	(3)	(4)
Immigrant/population (19–25)	−0.2443 (−5.53)		−0.2555 (−4.47)	
Immigrant/population (6–64)		−0.1767 (−5.93)		−0.2068 (−5.58)
R-square	0.0102	0.0102	0.0103	0.0103
Adjusted R-square	0.0102	0.0102	0.0103	0.0103
Number of observations	211039	211039	211038	211038

	Hispanics			
Variable	(1)	(2)	(3)	(4)
Immigrant/population (19–25)	−0.2647 (−5.12)		−0.4147 (−6.98)	
Immigrant/population (6–64)		−0.2075 (−5.64)		−0.3470 (−7.95)
R-square	0.0038	0.0039	0.0041	0.0042
Adjusted R-square	0.0038	0.0038	0.0040	0.0042
Number of observations	102749	102749	102749	102749

Notes: The four specifications for each group are identical to the four specifications given in tables 8.3 and 8.4, except that the regressors describing the level of education and income of those aged thirty-five to sixty-four in the given group, which appear in the third and fourth regressions, are now calculated at the metropolitan level rather than the state level. Also, the dummy variable for people who live in a city is dropped.

Using less geographically aggregated measures has both advantages and disadvantages. The advantage is that more precise estimates can result. The disadvantages are twofold. First, it is likely that the metropolitan area in which members of the nineteen to twenty-five cohort live at the time of the Census differs from the metropolitan area in which they attended school. This is of course an issue in the state-level analysis as well but is necessarily of less importance since interstate migration is less frequent than is interurban migration. Second, the matching of metropolitan areas across Census years is an inexact science, as borders of cities and groups of cities within metropolitan areas evolve over time. For both of these reasons, the metropolitan-level regressions could prove to be *less* precise than the state-level regressions and possibly biased in an unknown direction.

Table 8.7 shows the metropolitan-level regressions for blacks and Hispanics. The regressions are identical in form to those in tables 8.3 and 8.4 with three exceptions. First, the state dummies are replaced by dummies for metropolitan areas. Second, the dummy for whether the person lives in a city is dropped in this metropolitan-level sample. Third, the immigrant ratios, and in the replications of models (3) and (4) the proxies for the education and income of older blacks and Hispanics, were calculated at the level of the metropolitan area rather than at the level of the state. Of course, the sample size is lower, since only those living in one of the 132 metropolitan areas are included.

For blacks, in all four specifications the link between the immigrant-to-population ratio and the probability of high school graduation remains negative and highly significant. The coefficients using the immigration ratio among young people are quite close to those reported in table 8.3. The coefficients on the immigration ratio for all people aged six to sixty-four drop by about 60 percent but remain highly significant.

For Hispanics, the coefficients on the immigration variables remain negative and highly significant. The coefficients fall considerably in all cases, however. One potential explanation for the lower coefficients is that in these metropolitan-area regressions there is greater measurement error in assigning people to geographic locations than occurred in the state-level analysis, both due to changes in the metropolitan boundaries and changes in the places where people live.

Overall, this metropolitan-area analysis bolsters the conclusions in the state-level analysis, suggesting that a higher proportion of immigrants in the local area over time is associated with declining probabilities of high school graduation among blacks and Hispanics. Recall that in the state-level analysis the estimated effects on graduation probabilities were much higher among Hispanics than blacks. The metropolitan-level models yield the same pattern, but the crowding-out effects are now only slightly higher for native-born Hispanics than for native-born blacks.

Table 8.8 addresses the valid concern that migration between cities has introduced measurement error in the immigrant ratios and other demographic variables, biasing the coefficients toward zero. The table presents the results when models (3) and (4) from table 8.7, which used metropolitan-level fixed effects, are repeated on a subsample of natives who reported that they lived in the same metropolitan area five years before the Census. Again, half the 1980 sample drops out because the information about the respondent's location in 1975 is provided by the

Table 8.8   Replication of Metropolitan Fixed-Effect Models in Table
8.7, Models (3) and (4), with Subsample Reporting They
Lived in Same Metropolitan Area Five Years Before Census
Year

	Blacks	Blacks	Hispanics	Hispanics
Variable	(3)	(4)	(3)	(4)
Immigrant/population (19–25)	−0.2590 (−2.86)		−0.4274 (−4.73)	
Immigrant/population (6–64)		−0.2410 (−4.16)		−0.3758 (−5.55)
R-square	0.0113	0.0113	0.0038	0.0040
Adjusted R-square	0.0112	0.0113	0.0037	0.0039
Number of observations	101918	101918	47123	47123

Notes: This table replicates models (3) and (4) from table 8.7. Column numbers refer to the model from table 8.7 being replicated.

Bureau of the Census for only one-half of the 5 percent sample in 1980. In the 1980 sample, the weight of those for whom this information is available is doubled accordingly. For blacks, both the level of significance and the size of the immigration coefficients are quite similar to the full sample regression in table 8.7. Similarly, in the regressions for Hispanics, the results are little changed. In all cases, the coefficients on the immigration variables become somewhat larger (more negative), as would be expected if moving results in measurement error.

The conclusion from these robustness tests is that the observed impact of immigrants on the probability that minorities graduate from high school is robust to the level of geographical detail and to removal of people who have moved between metropolitan areas in the five years before the Census.

Are the Observed Effects Purely a California Phenomenon?   As figure 8.1 revealed, the rise in the immigrant-to-population ratio among the age group nineteen to twenty-five in California between 1980 and 1990 was 0.132, more than double that of any other state. It therefore becomes important to test whether the results presented earlier depend crucially upon the extraordinary rise in the proportion of immigrants in California's population. Table 8.9 replicates the state-level and metropolitan-level fixed-effect models in tables 8.3, 8.4, and 8.7, models (3) and (4) once those living in California at the time of the Census are excluded. In the state-level sample this restriction drops

Table 8.9 Replication of State and Metropolitan Fixed-Effect Models in Tables 8.3, 8.4 and 8.7 with Subsample Living Outside California

Variable*	Blacks (3)	Blacks (4)	Hispanics (3)	Hispanics (4)
Immigrant/population (19–25)	−0.2052 (−1.83)		0.0811 (0.45)	
Immigrant/population (6–64)		−0.4915 (−3.44)		0.1176 (0.51)
R-square	0.0105	0.0105	0.0056	0.0056
Adjusted R-square	0.0105	0.0105	0.0056	0.0056
Number of Observations	258212	258212	90857	90859

Variable†	Blacks (3)	Blacks (4)	Hispanics (3)	Hispanics (4)
Immigrant/population (19–25)	−0.1374 (−1.62)		0.5445 (3.85)	
Immigrant/population (6–64)		−0.1830 (−3.68)		−0.0338 (−0.44)
R-square	0.0106	0.0106	0.0053	0.0051
Adjusted R-square	0.0105	0.0106	0.0052	0.0050
Number of Observations	191343	191343	69284	69284

Notes: This table replicates models (3) and (4) from tables 8.3, 8.4, and 8.7. Column numbers refer to the model from tables 8.3, 8.4, or 8.7 being replicated.
* State fixed effects added.
†Metropolitan fixed effects added.

the sample of blacks by 7.2 percent, but the sample of Hispanics drops by fully 27.7 percent.

Consider first the results for blacks. In the models with state-level fixed effects, shown in the top part of the table, both the coefficients and *t*-statistics are very similar in the regressions to those reported in table 8.3, although in model (3) in table 8.9 the immigration ratio becomes only marginally significant. The bottom part of table 8.9 shows the results in the models with fixed effects for metropolitan areas. The coefficient on the immigration to population ratio in the age group nineteen to twenty-five drops considerably both in size and in significance once Californians are excluded; but in specification (4), the coefficient on the overall immigrant ratio is very similar to that in table 8.7, and it remains highly significant. The evidence among the non-California population is clearly stronger when the overall immigration ratio is used rather than the immigration ratio in the age group nineteen to twenty-five. Overall, the conclusion that immigrants crowd out blacks from secondary school seems to be a national phenomenon and not restricted solely to California.

Although the results for blacks seem quite robust, the same cannot be said for the results for Hispanics. In none of the regressions in table 8.9 is immigration negatively and significantly related to the probability that Hispanics graduated from high school. The change in the results in the models with metropolitan fixed effects once California residents are dropped is particularly dramatic. The overall immigrant ratio becomes insignificantly related to the probability of graduation for Hispanics, and the immigrant ratio in the age group nineteen to twenty-five becomes positively and significantly related to the probability of graduation. This last result should probably be viewed with some caution, as it is the only specification in the paper that yields such a result.

What do these regressions suggest? For blacks, they indicate that the observed negative impact of immigration on the educational attainment of native blacks is a national phenomenon. Among Hispanics, the observed negative impact appears to be almost purely a California phenomenon. This finding does not necessarily mean that the observed negative impact of immigration on the probability that native Hispanics graduate is spurious. Indeed, it is not particularly surprising that the effect weakens so much once Hispanics from California are removed from the regression sample: over one-quarter of all young native Hispanics in the sample live in California.

CONCLUSION

This study uses a difference-in-differences strategy to identify the effect of immigration on the educational attainment of American-born minorities by using pooled Census data from 1980 and 1990 combined with state-level estimates of the share of immigrants in the local population. Evidence emerges that there is a negative link between immigration and the probability of high school graduation for both blacks and Hispanics. The effects are meaningful. Based on the leading specifications, the rise in immigrants' share in the population observed in the 1980s is predicted to have decreased the probability that blacks graduate from high school by roughly 1 percent; for American-born Hispanics the predicted drop is closer to 3.5 to 4 percent. This compares with graduation rates of 73.7 percent and 69.5 percent among blacks and Hispanics in the regression sample. These results are similar to findings by Hoxby in this volume of strong evidence that immigrants crowd native-born minorities out of American universities.

Economic theory is ambiguous as to whether immigration should decrease the educational attainment of natives, since both the marginal benefits and the marginal costs of education are likely to rise when less-skilled immigrants enter the country. The state-level evidence presented here supports the "educational crowding-out" hypothesis, whereby an influx of immigrants reduces the effectiveness of public education for minorities who attend the same schools, discouraging them from completing school. This effect appears to outweigh any increase in high school graduation that theory suggests could result among natives if immigration serves to boost the returns to education. This is not particularly surprising given that earlier research suggests that immigration has only small effects on the wages of natives.

The conclusions of the state-level analysis are largely supported when subjected to a number of tests for robustness. The results are virtually unchanged when controls for the pupil-teacher ratio in each state are added. I repeated the analysis using the metropolitan area as the unit of observation for the immigrant-to-population ratio and again obtained highly similar results. I also reanalyzed the models on a subsample that excluded people who reported moving between states (or metropolitan areas) in the five years before the Census year. This was done in an attempt to reduce measurement error in the variables designed to characterize the immigrant ratio in the area in which each individual grew up. The immigration variables remained negative and highly significant. Finally, I reestimated the models with a sample that excluded people residing in California, on the grounds that the immigrant-to-population ratio had grown over twice as fast in the 1980s in California as in any other state. The results for blacks weakened somewhat but continued to indicate the existence of a crowding-out effect. In contrast, the negative link between immigration and the probability of finishing high school among Hispanics appears to derive solely from trends in California. Given that over one-quarter of young native-born Hispanics in the sample lived in California, the finding of a negative impact of immigration on the educational achievement of Hispanics within California is still important from a policy perspective.

The results have important implications for public policy. If schools have become less effective as a result of immigrant inflows during the 1980s, it raises the question of whether federal aid for school districts with large numbers of immigrants, mandated under the Emergency Immigrant Education Act of 1984 and under Title VII spending on bilingual education, is sufficient to meet the rising need. Recent trends in immigration also raise the question of whether native-born children who are disadvantaged have seen a dilution in Chapter I spending, as suggested by the work of Fix and Zimmerman (1993). This could provide a direct mechanism for the crowding-out phenomenon documented earlier.

Overall, the results of this study are strongly suggestive of the hypothesis that immigrants crowd out investments in public education by American-born minorities. But the results are not definitive. The state-level analysis identifies the effect of immigrants using, in effect, fifty-one observations by state (and the District of Columbia) on changes in the ratio of immigrants to population between 1980 and 1990. The metropolitan-level analysis involves far less geographical aggregation, but again identification of the effect of immigrants derives from changes in the immigrant-to-population ratio in 132 metropolitan areas. In spite of my attempt to control for changes in the demographic traits of each area and for changes in the resources devoted to schools, it is certainly a possibility that the strong crowding-out effect detected in this analysis is a proxy for other unmeasured changes within states and cities during the 1980s.

Clearly, further research, possibly conducted at the school level, would be advisable to confirm the finding of a crowding-out effect. Of greatest importance to this task, but arguably also of greatest difficulty, is research to understand how resources are reallocated within schools and school districts when schools experience large inflows of immigrant students.

NOTES

1. See Hoxby in this volume for a careful study that tests whether immigrants crowd minority students out of colleges.

2. The use of tracking to group together students who are at similar levels of achievement is a widespread practice in American public schools. Betts and Shkolnik (Forthcoming), using a representative national panel of six thousand students from 1987 to 1992, find that approximately three-fourths of school principals reported that a formal tracking policy was used in math classes. Yet the range of mean academic achievement across classes was virtually identical in schools that reported using tracking and those that claimed that they did not. This finding suggests that virtually all American schools track students, even if no formal tracking policy is in place.

3. For instance, Fix and Zimmerman (1993) report that in 1989 to 1990, 29 percent of Chapter I enrollees were black and 23 percent were Hispanic.

These proportions are far larger than the proportions of blacks and Hispanics in the overall population.

4. Blackburn, Bloom, and Freeman (1990) document that between 1979 and 1987 the ratio of annual earnings of high school dropouts to high school graduates among white male full-year workers aged twenty-five to thirty-four fell from 0.797 to just 0.743.

5. For a review of the impact of family background and the characteristics of the student body on the achievement of individual students, see Hanushek (1986, 1163).

6. See U.S. Government Printing Office (1984) for text of the original bill.

7. For recent Congressional testimony that confirms that funding from the federal government has not adequately accounted for increases in the numbers of immigrant schoolchildren, see Morra (1994).

    A larger program directed toward immigrant schoolchildren is Title VII funding for bilingual education. In 1990–1991 spending in this program amounted to 158.5 million dollars, or about 70 dollars per Limited English Proficiency student in the country. Even though the number of LEP students rose by 51.8 percent between 1985 and 1990, between 1980 and 1990 total Title VII spending on bilingual education fell by 5.1 percent in nominal terms and 47.8 percent after accounting for inflation. Most of the drop occurred in the first half of the 1980s. (Author's calculations based on tables 3.2 and 3.3 of Fix and Zimmerman 1993.)

8. By "American-born" I mean those born in the United States or born abroad of American parents. Hispanics are defined as those who state that their ancestry is Spanish (in 1980) or Hispanic (in 1990) and that their race is white or "other" (and not Asian, native American, or black).

9. The models in tables 8.1 and 8.2 were reestimated using a probit instead of a linear probability model. The signs and level of significance of the coefficients were extremely close to the OLS results presented in tables 8.1 and 8.2.

10. In table 8.4 the proxy for parental education becomes negative, but it is insignificant.

11. Pupil-teacher ratios were calculated for all states except Hawaii and Alaska, so that the regressions to be discussed below which use this variable have slightly fewer observations than those in the earlier part of the study.

12. When California was omitted, the correlation between the changes in the immigration ratio and the pupil-teacher ratio remains positive but is much smaller at 0.190. A similar analysis using the immigration ratio

among the entire population aged six to sixty-four yields a correlation of 0.218 for all states and 0.066 without California.

REFERENCES

Altonji, Joseph G., and David Card. 1991. "The Effects of Immigration on the Labor Market Outcomes of Less-Skilled Natives." In *Immigration, Trade, and the Labor Market*, edited by John M. Abowd and Richard B. Freeman. Chicago: University of Chicago Press.

Bean, Frank D., B. Lindsay Lowell, and Lowell J. Taylor. 1988. "Undocumented Mexican Immigrants and the Earnings of Other Workers in the United States." *Demography* 25(1): 35–52.

Betts, Julian R. 1996. "Is There a Link between School Inputs and Earnings? Fresh Scrutiny of an Old Literature." In *Does Money Matter? The Effect of School Resources on Student Achievement and Adult Success*, edited by Gary Burtless. Washington. D.C.: Brookings Institution.

Betts, Julian R., and Jamie L. Shkolnik. Forthcoming. "The Effects of Ability Grouping on Student Math Achievement and Resource Allocation in Secondary Schools." *Economics of Education Review.*

Blackburn, McKinley L., David E. Bloom, and Richard B. Freeman. 1990. "The Declining Economic Position of Less Skilled American Men." In *A Future of Lousy Jobs? The Changing Structure of U.S. Wages*, edited by Gary Burtless. Washington, D.C.: Brookings Institution.

Borjas, George J. 1990. *Friends or Strangers: The Impact of Immigrants on the U.S. Economy*. New York: Basic Books.

———. 1994. "The Economics of Migration." *Journal of Economic Literature* 32(4): 1667–1717.

———. 1995. "Assimilation and Changes in Cohort Quality Revisited: What Happened to Immigrant Earnings in the 1980's?" *Journal of Labor Economics* 13(2): 201–45.

Borjas, George J., Richard B. Freeman, and Lawrence F. Katz. 1992. "On the Labor Market Effects of Immigration and Trade." In *Immigration and the Work Force: Economic Consequences for the United States and Source Areas*, edited by George J. Borjas and Richard B. Freeman. Chicago: University of Chicago Press.

Federal Security Agency. Various years. *Biennial Survey of Education in the United States*. Washington D.C.: Office of Education.

Fix, Michael, and Wendy Zimmerman. 1993. "Educating Immigrant Children." In *The Changing City*, chapter 1. Washington D.C.: Urban Institute Press.

General Accounting Office. 1991. *Immigrant Education: Information on the Emergency Immigrant Education Act Program: Report to Congressional Committees*. Washington D.C.: U.S. General Accounting Office.

Grossman, Jean Baldwin. 1982. "The Substitutability of Natives and Immigrants in Production." *Review of Economics and Statistics* 64(4): 596–603.

Hanushek, Eric A. 1986. "The Economics of Schooling: Production and Efficiency in Public Schools." *Journal of Economic Literature* 24(3): 1141–1177.

LaLonde, Robert J., and Robert H. Topel. 1991. "Labor Market Adjustments to Increased Immigration." In *Immigration, Trade, and the Labor Market*, edited by John M. Abowd and Richard B. Freeman. Chicago: University of Chicago Press.

Loeb, Susanna, Sarah Turner, and David Jaeger. 1996. "Coding Geographic Areas Across Census Years: Creating Consistent Definitions of Metropolitan Areas." Department of Economics, University of Michigan. Unpublished manuscript.

Morra, Linda G. 1994. *Immigrant Education: Federal Funding Has Not Kept Pace with Student Increases*. Statement of Linda G. Morra, Director, Education and Employment Issues, Health, Education, and Human Services Division, Before the Subcommittee on Education, Arts and the Humanities, Committee on Labor and Human Resources, U.S. Senate. Washington, D.C.: U.S. General Accounting Office.

National Center for Education Statistics. Various years. *Digest of Education Statistics*. Washington D.C.: U.S. Department of Education.

Taubman. Paul. 1989. "Role of Parental Income in Educational Attainment." *American Economic Review* 79(2): 57–61.

U.S. Bureau of the Census. 1994. *Statistical Abstract of the United States*. Washington, D.C.: U.S. Government Printing Office.

U.S. Government Printing Office. 1984. *Hearing on Emergency Education Act*. Subcommittee on Elementary, Secondary, and Vocational Education of the Committee on Education and Labor, House of Representatives, 98th Congress, Second Session. Washington D.C.: U.S. Government Printing Office.

CHAPTER 9

Do Immigrants Crowd Disadvantaged American Natives Out of Higher Education?

Caroline M. Hoxby

Many Americans think of higher education as a bridge that those who are born disadvantaged must cross to gain access to the full range of income, professional, and social opportunities in the United States. This notion may be somewhat simplistic, but it is widely held and has undoubtedly motivated a variety of policies intended to increase access to higher education for the disadvantaged. The best-known of these policies are the Pell grants, federal tuition subsidies for low-income students, and affirmative action, admissions preferences for racial and ethnic minorities. These policies are merely the most conspicuous of a host of access programs aimed at the disadvantaged in American colleges and universities. Others include financial aid and counseling from the institution, remedial education, academic counseling, funding for racial and ethnic support groups, work-study subsidies, and state and federal student loans.

Today these programs are a common ground shared by disadvantaged American natives and immigrants to the United States, who, if they attend college, are likely to make use of one or more of them. Regardless of whether the policies were originally intended to provide equally for natives and nonnatives, many of them do provide for both groups, and policymakers need to know the degree to which immigrants "crowd" disadvantaged American natives out of obtaining higher education. This information would be useful, for instance, in the current debate over whether immigrants should pay in-state tuition at California state colleges.

There are two possible routes by which immigrants may crowd out disadvantaged natives. The first is simply that the two groups compete for scarce access resources, such as grants that institutions make to needy students. The second is through affirmative action, since affirmative action targets do not necessarily distinguish between American natives and nonnatives who fall into the same racial or ethnic group.

Competition between immigrants and disadvantaged natives for low-wage jobs and social benefit programs is now much studied, but we equally need to understand competition in access to college education.[1] The number of people affected in any given year is much smaller, of course, but this is largely the difference between stocks and flows. It is by sending a small absolute number of people to college each year that the education and incomes of disadvantaged and minority populations are gradually transformed. However, *very* little is known about whether immigrants actually crowd disadvantaged natives out of higher education; and the very little known up to now has taken the form of anecdote rather than empirical evidence. One might object that the lack of evidence merely reveals that immigrants are too negligible a force in higher education to much affect anyone's college access. But, this is a mistake based on the viewpoint of middle-class, white natives—from whose perspective *both* groups (disadvantaged natives in higher education and immigrants in higher education) are small. What matters is the scale of the two groups relative to one another. For example, in the large group of colleges that are less selective, 29 percent of students who take remedial reading classes are foreign born.[2] At the opposite end of the spectrum, in the small group of colleges that are very selective, 29 percent of all Hispanics are foreign born.

A better reason why so little evidence exists is that college and university reporting is simply not equipped to deal with this question. Despite the fact that institutions of higher education report a substantial amount of enrollment information each year, the lack of distinction between natives and nonnatives in the breakdown of enrollment by race, financial aid, and curriculum would have made it almost impossible to answer this question—until the advent of the survey used in this paper (the National Postsecondary Student Aid Study, hereafter referred to as NPSAS).

What little evidence we do have comes from case studies of fourteen institutions carried out by the Rand Corporation and reported in Gray, Rolph, and Melamid (1996) (hereafter referred to as GRM). An advantage of the GRM case study method is that their conversations with college staff suggest a number of mechanisms through which immigrant-native crowding out might occur. Prominent among the mechanisms discussed are displacement of natives from Equal Opportunity Support (EOP) programs that offer academic and financial support to "educationally and economically disadvantaged populations" and whose criteria many immigrants almost automatically meet because their poor language skills make them do sufficiently poorly on access tests in reading and writing. Additionally, some faculty worry that remedial reading and writing classes are reoriented implicitly away from the needs of natives and toward the needs of foreign-born students, whose reading and writing problems are not general but are based on their limited English proficiency. Another mechanism discussed is the displacement of black and Hispanic natives in affirmative action targets by black and Hispanic students from elite Caribbean and Latin American families. Some college officials worry that immigrants who already have university educations conceal this fact in order to use access programs that will refine their cultural and language skills. Others worry that immigrants monopolize academic and financial counseling services not only by competing directly for time and resources but also by redirecting interest toward a set of problems distinct from those of the typical disadvantaged native student. Conversely, some staff report that immigrants are more assertive and vocal than disadvantaged natives about pursuing aid, and thus they provide spillovers for the natives by drawing more of the college's attention and monies toward the needs of the disadvantaged. Evidence is required to show whether the size of the pie for the disadvantaged increases sufficiently that natives' smaller share is not a smaller slice.

The major empirical challenge for this study is that the percentage of students in a college who are foreign born may be correlated with unobservable characteristics of the college that independently affect the enrollment of native-born students. The resulting omitted variables bias is a particular problem for colleges that draw from a localized area (typically, these are colleges with low selectivity) because they enroll foreign-born and native-born students who are unobservably "alike." To address the omitted variables problem, I exploit a court case that produced plausibly exogenous variation in the percentages of foreign-born students attending California's colleges. As a result of this case, the University of California system and the California community college system began charging many foreign-born students the out-of-state tuition rate in 1990. California's state college and university system, however, continued to charge them the much lower in-state tuition rate. California's private colleges have tuition policies that have never distinguished between in-state and out-of-state residents or native- and foreign-born students.

The NPSAS makes this study possible because it links an impressive array of student surveys, institutional reports, and individual student records and forms on file with colleges and the federal government. Yet, the NPSAS was not designed to answer this question—that would have required longitudinal data and oversampling of nonnatives. So, I regard the empirical evidence presented here as not definitive but exploratory. I find sufficient evidence of crowding out through access resources and affirmative action to warrant more investigation, although this will require institutions to report more detailed enrollment and application figures.

It is important to understand that evidence on crowding out does not tell us whether it is *better* to extend college access to disadvantaged natives or immigrants. The evidence is useful because it informs us about how the college-going behavior of natives depends on whether immigrants can make use of college access programs. However, unless we can say decisively what college access programs *are supposed to do* to maximize social welfare, we cannot say whether the interaction of immigrants with them is good or bad. For instance, if one thinks the social welfare–maximizing function of affirmative action is to give minority natives disproportionately easy access to college as a counterbalance to past discrimination, then the foreign born (who allow colleges to circumvent this policy) might decrease social welfare. On the other hand, if one thinks that affirmative action programs reduce social welfare because they interfere with the efficient distribution of college education among individuals, then the foreign born might increase social welfare.

The plan of the remainder of this study is as follows: I first discuss two simple models of crowding out, one that depends on affirmative action and another on competition for access resources. These provide structure for the empirical tests that follow. I then discuss the two major empirical challenges for this study (omitted college characteristics associated with the foreign born and measurement error) and how I meet them. I next consider the data and give a snapshot of native and immigrant college-going in the United States through descriptive statistics. Finally, I present results and conclusions.

A MODEL OF THE RELATIONSHIP BETWEEN IMMIGRANT AND NATIVE COLLEGE-GOING

The fundamental question that this study attempts to answer is, "How is the college-going of natives affected by exogenous increases in the number of foreign-born people who are in the pool of potential students for American colleges?" The model I will present here formalizes the mechanisms by which these effects may operate. It does not attempt to suggest a new theory of college-going behavior. Its goal is modest: to describe the mechanisms with just enough precision to clarify their implications for empirical evidence. Before I set up the model, however, a few overarching points need to be made.

We are interested in who is "college-going"—that is, who is enrolled in college for a first degree. This is a reduced-form analysis, since college-going behavior is actually the result of at least three decisions: an individual's decision to apply to a college, the college's acceptance and its decisions regarding financial aid for that individual, and the individual's decision to enroll once accepted. Reduced-form analysis is appropriate because these three decisions are simultaneous: for any given crowding-out mechanism (such as competition for scarce need-based financial aid), the decision to not go to college can occur at any of the three stages. This is because the college application behavior of individuals depends on their expectations about admissions and financial aid decisions. Colleges' financial aid decisions depend on their expectations about the enrollment behavior of individuals. Since individuals' decisions depend on what they expect of the other decisions, we cannot meaningfully identify the stage at which crowding out occurs. For the same reason, econometric identification of the separate decisions is also nearly impossible, even in the most propitious data circumstances.

In the model of crowding out, there is no need to distinguish between the three types of immigrants, who are (1) foreign-born people who have become naturalized U.S. citizens, (2) foreign-born people who are U.S. residents, and (3) "nonresident aliens"—foreign-born people who are undocumented or on student visas. The basic mechanisms of crowding out usually do not depend on which of these types the immigrants are. Policies for which citizenship or residency status does make a difference (such as the Pell grants) do not make for much crowding out—precisely because they are administered at a federal rather than an institutional level. However, since policymakers might wish to weigh the welfare of the three groups differently (the latter two groups are significantly less attached to the United States), I do distinguish among the three types of immigrants in the equations that are estimated.

The Basics

Start with a basic model of higher education in which there is no crowding out. Students are assumed to be able to calculate their potential (private) net benefits from college attendance, given their own abilities and characteristics and the college's policies regarding tuition, financial aid, curriculum, and so on. This calculation comes from a standard Becker-Rosen model of human capital investment, assuming that colleges' policies are perfectly known. If student i's potential net benefits from attending college j are positive, he is in its pool of potential applications, the set P_j:

(9.1) $i \varepsilon P_j$ if $nb_i^j > 0,$

where nb_{ij} indicates the net potential benefits from college j for person i (note lowercase "nb").

For each student in its pool, the college calculates the potential net benefits *for the college*, NB_{ij} (note uppercase), in the Rothschild and White (1995) sense. The calculation of the potential gross benefits from student i for college j, B_{ij}, includes the tuition he would pay, the federal or state monies he would bring with him, the net present value of any direct contributions he would make to the endowment, and the positive spillovers he would provide for others that the college could internalize (through getting other students to pay higher tuition, getting other donors to make greater contributions to the endowment, getting faculty to work for less), and so on. The gross costs of having him as a student, C_{ij}, are a function of his academic and social needs *and* any costs associated with the effect his presence would have on the college's size. That is, the supply of places at an individual college is not perfectly elastic because additional students crowd the campus and decrease other students' benefits. Also, colleges commonly have disproportionately high costs of expanding relative to maintaining current size, since their land and locations are historically determined and protected from the real estate market by their nonprofit (nontaxable) status.

For now, the calculation does *not* include any benefits the student may give the college purely because he is a member of a disadvantaged group whose access to higher education has historically been limited. Finally, the college calculates the probability that the student will attend if admitted, p_{ij} (a function of nb_{ij} and NB_{ij} for all colleges j). It then maximizes total expected net benefits for the college by admitting N_j students in expectation:

(9.2) $max_{Nj}\ \Sigma_i p_{ij}(N_j) NB_{ij}(N_j)$ where $\Sigma_i p_{ij} = N_j$.

Notice the adding up constraint at the end of equation (9.2). Notice also that p_{ij} and NB_{ij} are functions of the number of students admitted in expectation. This is because every N_j determines an expected distribution of students in the college, thus determining the expected level of spillovers for every student, the tuition he can be charged, and so on.

Let X be a vector of student characteristics, such as family income, that influences NB_{ij} and nb_{ij} for all j (and therefore p_{ij}). Let Z be a vector of inherent college characteristics, such as location, that influence NB_{ij} and nb_{ij} for all i (and therefore p_{ij}). Then, for the college's choice of N_j, the student body of college j has a predictable joint distribution of characteristics, $F_j(X)$.

"Benchmark Crowding Out"

All this might occur in the absence of immigrant students. If the pool of potential applicants facing college j increases because of an influx of immigrant applications with $nb_{ij} > 0$, some displacement of native students who would otherwise have been admitted will occur. Marginal native students (those with low net benefits, NB_{ij}, previously) will be the first to go, and the displacement will appear as an increase in the college's admissions standards (a rise in natives' average characteristics from X_j^* to X_j^{**}). The better the immigrant students' characteristics are, the greater will be the rise in the college's admissions standards.

I describe this crowding out as "benchmark crowding out," noting that there is nothing about it peculiar to immigrants. Similar crowding out would occur, for instance, if social change prompted women with previously low college-attendance rates to go to college. In the long term, benchmark crowding out is observable at individual colleges but not in general, because the supply of college places can eventually expand through the addition of marginal, less-selective colleges (as it currently does in the United States, where much of the elasticity of supply is in the participation of colleges that are not selective).

If we examine the population of students at each college, benchmark crowding out would empirically appear as follows. Let enrollment N_j be divided between native enrollment, N_j^n, and foreign-born enrollment, N_j^f. Let a subset of these groups be classified as disadvantaged according to a standard that is a function of student characteristics. That is,

$$(9.3) \quad N_j^{nd} = \sum_{i=1}^{N_j^n} I_{ij}, \, I_{ij} = 1 \text{ if } f(X_{ij}) < D.$$

For instance, among the total number of native students, N_j^n, how many (N_j^{nd}) come from families in which neither parent has more than a high school education $(X_{ij} < D)$? The share of natives who are disadvantaged is decreasing in the share of immigrants in the expected-attendance-weighted pool—or in the actual student body—*but only because the immigrants raise the admissions standards for everyone and natives who are disadvantaged are probably more marginal students.* For a given level of admissions standards, the percentage of immigrants in the student body has no effect on the percentage of natives who are disadvantaged. That is, $\beta = 0$ in:

$$(9.4) \quad \frac{N_j^{nd}}{N_j^n} = \beta \frac{N_j^f}{N_j} + \delta S_j(X) + Z_j \gamma + \varepsilon_j$$

where $S_j(X)$ is exactly the admissions standard, as a function of student characteristics, that achieves the optional N_j students in expectation.

Of course, if S_j were omitted from equation (9.4) and equation (9.4) were otherwise correctly specified, the coefficient on N_j^I/N_j would pick up benchmark crowding out—the crowding out of natives that occurs purely because immigrants can raise admissions standards. This study is not, however, only focused or even mainly focused on benchmark crowding out. Therefore, equations that test for other crowding-out mechanisms (such as affirmative action) do contain measures of S_j, so that a negative, significant estimate of β will indicate the presence of a crowding-out mechanism other than benchmark crowding out. This is an important distinction, because benchmark crowding out is unlikely to have the interesting efficiency implications that the other crowding-out mechanisms may have.

Crowding Out Through Competition for Access Programs

Consider what happens if the college is subjected to a system of rewards and penalties for facilitating access for the disadvantaged. The rewards and penalties may exist because society benefits more than a college does from a disadvantaged student's going to college. This would occur if some of the societal benefits are spillovers that fall outside the college and are thus not internalized by it. In practice, some rewards and penalties come explicitly from governments (for example, EOPs), some implicitly from governments (for example, federal grants for science), and some from private donors such as foundations.

There are numerous possible formalizations of the rewards and penalties for providing access programs, but a simple one will make the necessary point. Let the college's objective function be revised to be:

$$(9.5) \quad \Sigma_i p_{ij}(N_j)NB_{ij}(N_j) - p \; max(Z^{k*} - Z_j^k, 0),$$

where Z^k is the element of the college's characteristics, Z, that indicates what share of the college's resources are going to disadvantaged students. Z^{k*} is the target share, and in this simple specification, colleges are only penalized for being below the target, not rewarded for being above the target. This is a stark way of noting that society does not particularly want colleges entirely composed of disadvantaged students, since part of the benefit of college-going is supposed to be integration with more advantaged students.

Since the college has incentives to do so, it sets Z^k higher under the regime given by equation (9.5) than when there is no reward for providing access programs. Thus, the expected net benefits of college are now more positive for students from disadvantaged backgrounds:

(9.6) $\dfrac{\partial nb_{ij}}{\partial Z_j^{\,k}} > 0$ for i such that $f(X_i) < D$.

The share of the college's students who are disadvantaged, N_j^{nd}/N_j^n, is higher, and the access programs achieve some of their intended effects.

Again, consider an influx of immigrants. They are particularly likely to qualify as disadvantaged and thus disproportionately affect the net benefits from college enjoyed by disadvantaged natives. This is because they swell the ranks of disadvantaged students, inducing crowding in the access programs and reducing the benefits available to potential native students.[3] The empirical prediction when there is competition for access resources is that β in equation (9.4) is negative. That is, if colleges provide access programs up to some level Z^{k^*}, even when we control for the college's admissions standards, the share of native students who are disadvantaged decreases in the share of the college's total enrollment that is foreign born. *Moreover, the more disadvantaged the immigrants are, the more a given number of immigrants crowds out disadvantaged native students.* This implication is the *reverse* of what the benchmark model implies.

Crowding Out Through Affirmative Action Targets

Only a small twist to the above model is required to show how crowding out can occur through affirmative action targets. Instead of a system of rewards and penalties for providing access resources, suppose that a college is penalized for not meeting its affirmative action targets with respect to racial/ethnic groups $\bar{g} = 1, \ldots, G$. The college's objective function might now be,

(9.7) $\displaystyle\sum_i p_{ij}(N_j)NB_{ij}(N_j) - \theta \sum_{\bar{g}=1}^{G} \max(N_j^{g^*} - N_j^g, 0),$

where N^{g^*} is the target population for group $\bar{g}$, AND N^g is the college's actual enrollment of students from group $\bar{g}$. Everything goes through as earlier, with the outcome that students from each group will face a group-specific admissions standard, $S_j(X, \bar{g})$. Underrepresented groups will face lower admissions standards:

(9.8) $\dfrac{\partial S_j}{\partial (N_j^{g^*} - N_j^g)} < 0.$

The college may admit students who produce net benefits—other than the benefits to the college of not being penalized for missing an affirmative action target—that are negative for the college ($NB_{ij} < 0$). But these students will not enroll unless they have positive net benefits from attendance ($nb_{ij} > 0$). So the affirmative action target achieves some of its goal of inducing greater numbers of underrepresented groups to gain (positive) benefits from higher education.

Again, consider what happens when immigrants enter the scene. Suppose there is a group of potential students who are foreign born, would produce positive net benefits for the college, and fit into underrepresented racial/ethnic groups. So long as the affirmative action targets are not county-of-birth specific, the college will not admit some native members of the underrepresented groups who would otherwise have been admitted. Instead, it will admit their foreign-born counterparts. (Note that affirmative action targets are typically implicit, rather than a set of explicit rules. Even in reporting their progress in affirmative action to the federal government, colleges are allowed a good deal of discretion in how they set up their targets. For instance, selective colleges may choose to compare their students' racial composition not to that of the general public but to that of likely college students.)

The empirical prediction when affirmative action targets work this way is that β in equation (9.4) is negative. That is, even when we control for the college's admissions standards, the share of native students who are members of underrepresented groups (blacks and Hispanics) decreases in the share of the college's total enrollment that is foreign born. *Moreover, each group of natives, black and Hispanic, will be disproportionately affected by a change in the supply of potential immigrants from its own group.* This implication is not a prediction of the benchmark model of crowding out.

EMPIRICAL CHALLENGES

There are two major challenges to successful estimation in this study. The first, omitted-variables bias, has already been mentioned. The second is measurement error.

Remedying Omitted-Variables Bias and Other Sources of Endogeneity

So far, the discussion has assumed that Z (the vector of inherent college characteristics) is properly specified. If it is not, and omitted college characteristics are correlated with N_j^f/N_j, the estimate of β will be biased away from the truth. A few examples will show that the probable sign of the omitted-variables bias is positive (that is, estimates of β will be biased against the finding of crowding out). The reason for this prediction is that "like" students attend the same colleges, so that disadvantaged natives and immigrants cluster in the same colleges. For example, among both Hispanics who are native born and Hispanics who are foreign born, colleges in California, Florida, and the Southwest are more popular than colleges elsewhere. Or, the same college characteristics that appeal to black native-born students—black faculty or a social atmosphere receptive to blacks—may appeal to black foreign-born students. Or, the same college characteristics that attract disadvantaged natives may attract disadvantaged foreign-born students—for instance, low tuition, proximity to an area where low-income people live, or class schedules designed for part-time and evening enrollment.

Negative omitted-variables bias is less likely because it would only occur when native-born and foreign students who are apparently alike are actually dissimilar in their preferences. For example, suppose I could observe whether people were poor but not whether they lived in rural or urban areas. If I naively assumed that native-born poor people were equally likely to be urban and attend urban colleges as foreign-born poor people, I would be wrong. Fortunately, the example does not arise because the data allow us to describe people quite accurately. Most of the variables that remain are inherently unobservable: motivation, tastes unrelated to income, and so on.

Many of the variables that would cause bias if they were omitted are locational. For this reason, I include several covariates in Z that describe a college's location: state indicator variables, center-city campus, urban campus, metropolitan-area campus, and rural campus. Another group of variables that would cause bias if they were omitted are institutional characteristics. Therefore, I include covariates in Z that describe a college's selectivity, type of control (private or public), enrollment size, and degree-granting programs.

Even with these covariates, the possibility of omitted-variables bias still exists. It is especially possible for colleges that draw from a localized area (like a community college), since students who are likely to be neighbors are also likely to share unobserved characteristics. In the United States, it is generally the least selective colleges that have the most local draw.[4] Thus, omitted-variables bias is most likely to cause a finding of "no crowding out" among colleges with low selectivity.

The best method of eliminating omitted-variables bias and other sources of endogeneity in the independent variable is to find an explicit cause of plausibly exogenous variation in the percentage of students in a college who are foreign born. I take advantage of an unusual policy change in California between 1986 and 1992 that caused plausible exogenous variation in the pool of foreign-born people applying to California's colleges. California has extensive public higher education that is divided into three systems. Its University of California system, California state college and university system, and California community college systems are administered separately. For all three systems, a perennial controversy is whether immigrants (especially recent immigrants and nonresident aliens) should qualify to pay the low in-state tuition rather than much higher out-of-state tuition. A particularly sore issue is whether undocumented aliens should automatically qualify for in-state tuition while legal immigrants must satisfy more stringent residency requirements. This issue not only affects "typical" undocumented aliens; people on other immigrant visas can become undocumented aliens simply by letting their visas lapse. By the 1986–1987 school year, all three California systems were allowing all undocumented aliens to pay the in-state tuition. This uniform treatment was the result of a 1985 Superior Court ruling in *Leticia A. et al.* v. *Regents of the University of California*. In 1990, however, this decision was reversed in *Regents of the University of California* v. *Bradford*. Interestingly enough, the outcome of the new decision was that in 1990 the University of California and California community college systems switched to making undocumented aliens pay the out-of-state tuition, but the California state system *did not switch*. In brief, between 1986 and 1993, the California state colleges and universities became relatively attractive to nonresident aliens compared to the University of California and California community college systems. Over the period, the cost of attending a University of California school or a California community college was dramatically raised for nonresident aliens while California state colleges and universities offered them in-state tuition. Private colleges' tuitions were not directly affected by any of the policy changes since they do not charge in-state and out-of-state tuitions.

The policy change creates the opportunity for differences-in-differences estimation. The identifying assumption is that basic immigration and demographic patterns between 1986 and 1992 similarly affected California state colleges and universities, private California colleges and universities, universities that are part of the University of California, and California community colleges. (The "similarity" is only assumed *conditional* on selectivity and other observable college characteristics.) Though experiencing the same immigration and demographic patterns, California state institutions should have had an increased number of foreign-born people in their pool of potential applicants. Evidence of crowding out would take the form of native-born, disadvantaged students *differentially* reducing their enrollment at California state institutions between 1986 and 1992 *relative* to how much they reduced their enrollment at private colleges, University of California institutions, and California community colleges. Notice that the tripartite "control" group of colleges (private, University of California, and California community colleges) spans the entire selectivity range and offers a number of colleges comparable in selectivity to the California State colleges and universities.

In practice, this strategy requires instrumental-variables estimation of a first-differenced version of equation (9.4) where the identifying instrument is a college's membership in the California state system. The two implied stages of the instrumental-variables estimation are a first-differenced equation that spans the policy change (the 1992–1993 school year versus the 1986–1987 school year):

$$(9.9) \quad \left(\frac{N^{nd}_{j92}}{N^{n}_{j92}} - \frac{N^{nd}_{j86}}{N^{n}_{j86}} \right) = \beta \left(\frac{N^{fd}_{j92}}{N_{j92}} - \frac{N^{fd}_{j86}}{N_{j86}} \right) + \delta (S_{j92} - S_{j86}) + (Z_{j92} - Z_{j86}) \gamma + (\varepsilon_{j92} - \varepsilon_{j86}),$$

and the equation showing how being in the California state college system affected a college's percentage of students who were foreign born:

$$(9.10) \quad \left(\frac{N^{fd}_{j92}}{N_{j92}} - \frac{N^{fd}_{j86}}{N_{j86}} \right) = \mu \; CalStat_j + \nu (S_{j92} - S_{j86}) + (Z_{j92} - Z_{j86}) \kappa + (\iota_{j92} - \iota_{j86}).$$

Remedying Division Bias Due to Measurement Error

A study of this kind can suffer from two distinct biases related to measurement error. The first is the familiar problem of attenuation bias (bias against finding a statistically significant effect of either sign) due to the fact that the percentage of students in a college who are foreign born is measured with error. Attenuation bias might prevent finding evidence for crowding out even if it were truly quantitatively important. Attenuation is a real possibility, because the foreign-born percentage must be calculated from a *sample* of students in each college.

A more worrisome form of measurement error bias, often called "division bias," is also possible. Division bias occurs when a variable that is measured with error is used to calculate both the dependent variable and an independent variable. In equation (9.4), the bias occurs because the native, nondisadvantaged student population is the denominator of the dependent variable and is part of the denominator of the independent variable that measures immigrant college-going. Though the denominators are not identical, error in the measure of native, nondisadvantaged students is likely to make the two variables positively correlated with one another. Such bias would make the estimates *understate* the true amount of crowding out.

A remedy for both of these measurement error problems is instrumenting each college's 1992 percentage of students who are foreign born by its 1989 percentage of students who are foreign born. Intuitively, when the 1992 estimate of immigrant college-going is instrumented by the 1989 measure, error in the measure of native, nondisadvantaged students cannot be propagated from the instrumented independent variable to the dependent variable. Note that not only the percentage of students who are foreign born but all sample-based covariates must be instrumented using the 1989 data. This remedy will produce unbiased estimates so long as the sampling error in one year is uncorrelated with the sampling error in the other year. This condition will hold if random sampling is the source of sampling error (and the NPSAS does use random sampling to the best of its ability).[5]

DATA AND DESCRIPTIVE STATISTICS

Before introducing the data used in this study, I discuss the general data requirements for answering questions about immigrant crowding out. This discussion clarifies why many of the more familiar longitudinal and institutional data sets are not useful. It also clarifies the importance of the NPSAS data, which are imperfect for answering this question but much more informative than any other data.

The ideal data would be longitudinal, following students from before their college-going decisions. Since the behavior of immigrants as well as natives determines whether crowding out occurs, nonnative students would need to be included in the sample. In fact, the longitudinal data would almost certainly have to oversample immigrants, just as minority students are routinely oversampled, because sampling error can otherwise overwhelm the true variation recorded for a small group. To differentiate among the models discussed in the previous section, at least some curricular and financial-aid information about the students would be necessary. Finally, the survey would have to be linked to colleges' institutional records, in particular the breakdown of college enrollment into immigrant-race-ability-income cells.

The major longitudinal surveys cannot meet these criteria at all because their samples are limited to students who attended junior high or high school in the United States.[6] The numbers of foreign-born students in the samples are far too small and not sufficiently representative for answering crowding-out questions. The major panels of data from college and university records, do not break out enrollment by immigration status.[7] They do break out nonresident aliens, but do not break out race, income, or financial aid within this category. Finally, surveys like the Census of Population or the Current Population Survey cannot be linked to specific colleges' information and tend to produce college enrollment rates that are seen to be inaccurate when compared with colleges' administrative records.

The NPSAS does meet many of the criteria. It has been conducted every three years since 1986, so that the three school years currently available are 1986 to 1987, 1989 to 1990, and 1992 to 1993. Its student survey is large (approximately fifty-two thousand in each year's undergraduate sample) and it includes about one thousand undergraduate institutions each year. These represent about one-fourth of the total number of undergraduate institutions in the United States but about one-half of the total number of undergraduate students in the United States. Of these institutions, which represent over three-eighths of undergraduate students in the United States, 762 are included in all three surveys so that we have panel data at the college level.

The size of the survey is important because immigrants, racial and ethnic minorities, and disadvantaged students are all small shares of the college population, and some estimates of the characteristics of a college's population must be calculated from the sample. Sample-based population estimates are particularly important for immigration, since the NPSAS is the only microdata sample of higher education that contains detailed immigration status, thus allowing us to divide the foreign born into naturalized citizens, residents, and nonresident aliens. Note that the differing accuracy of the sample-based estimates (owing to different-sized samples at different colleges) requires use of weighted estimation to account for heteroskedasticity.

The NPSAS student data are unusually accurate because students' administrative records, both those of colleges and those of the federal government, were used to validate student responses. For instance, the student's actual federal financial aid form was used, whenever possible, to determine what aid the student was receiving.

I matched the NPSAS data to colleges' institutional data for the same school year from the Integrated Post-Secondary Education Data System (IPEDS). The institutional data contain a number of population statistics, which were used whenever possible for estimation and for validating sample estimates of the population statistics. Over the entire sample of colleges, the correlations between sample estimates and the available population statistics were consistently above 0.95.

The main limitation of the NPSAS is that it is not longitudinal for individual students. This precludes us from identifying the sequence of choices summarized by college attendance.[8] Descriptive statistics for the variables used are shown in appendix table 9a.1.

Immigrants in College

Table 9.1 shows that, compared to the entire population of native college students, immigrants are disadvantaged and make heavy use of colleges' access resources. The table is partitioned based on colleges' selectivity, judged by the average SAT score (or converted ACT score) in the college sample. The table also divides immigrants into the three detailed subgroups: naturalized citizens, residents, and nonresident aliens. As one moves across the table to the right (toward immigrants less attached to the United States), use of access resources increases. For instance, in the second-most selective group, institutional aid covers only 7.7 percent of natives' tuition and fees, but 10.5 percent of foreign-born residents' tuition and fees, and 17.3 percent of nonresident aliens' tuition and fees. The pattern of increase is clear in all the categories of selectivity, but it is most dramatic in the two middle categories. This is apparently the result of two opposing forces. As colleges become more selective, they are more differentially generous toward relatively needy students; but they have relatively few needy students, because most needy students do not make it through the selection process. Thus, nonresident aliens at highly selective colleges are much less needy than the typical nonresident alien. At the other end of the spectrum, nonselective colleges have many needy students and small endowments. They cannot afford to be differentially generous.

Tables 9.2 and 9.3 show, however, that if one looks *within* black students or Hispanic students, the picture that emerges is very different. Compared to these disadvantaged groups of natives, immigrants do not look particularly needy. Consider table 9.2, which covers black students. Among selective schools with average SAT scores greater than 1100, students who are natives and naturalized U.S. citizens come from families with lower combined parental incomes ($32,488 and $25,397) than are typical for the families of foreign-born residents ($42,185) and nonresident aliens ($40,404). Also, within the selective colleges, students' SAT scores are higher among the foreign-born residents and the nonresident aliens than among natives and naturalized citizens. In the category of nonselective colleges, there is no indication of such a pattern.

A somewhat similar picture emerges for Hispanics in table 9.3. In all the categories of college selectivity, nonresident aliens have the highest SAT scores and have parents with the highest educational attainment.

Table 9.1   Natives and Foreign Born in College

All Students	U.S. Native	Foreign Born but U.S. Citizen	Foreign Born, Noncitizen but U.S. Resident	Foreign Born Noncitizen, Nonresident Alien
College's Average SAT ≥ 1200				
% of tuition/fees from institutional need-based aid	7.25	10.85	11.28	10.43
% of tuition/fees from all institutional financial aid	11.37	14.19	16.92	19.78
Limited English home background 6.51	53.8	82.19	81.25	
Took remedial writing	1.05	3.03	4.22	12.76
College's Average SAT ≥ 1100 and ≤ 1200				
% of tuition/fees from institutional need-based aid	4.24	4.87	6.82	9.43
% of tuition/fees from all institutional financial aid	7.72	7.66	10.52	17.26
Limited English home background	2.51	45.45	74.07	83.84
Took remedial writing	1.33	2.59	7.97	8.07
College's Average SAT ≥ 900 and ≤ 1100				
% of tuition/fees from institutional need-based aid	2.09	2.87	3.91	3.07
% of tuition/fees from all institutional financial aid	5.04	5.12	6.80	11.54
Limited English home background	3.30	47.97	78.10	79.68
Took remedial writing	1.85	4.33	11.11	10.93
College's Average SAT ≤ 900 or College Does Not Use an Admissions Test for Selection				
% of tuition/fees from institutional grants and loans	1.37	1.65	1.61	1.91
% w/ financial aid for the disadvantaged (Pell grants, etc.)	2.66	2.78	2.38	4.44
Limited English home background	4.92	59.03	80.58	82.96
Took remedial writing	3.21	7.36	16.0	16.0

Notes: Unweighted means. See appendix table 9.1 for number of observations in each category and standard deviations.

Table 9.2 Black Natives and Black Foreign Born in College

Black	U.S. Native	Foreign Born but U.S. Citizen	Foreign Born, Noncitizen, but U.S. Resident	Foreign Born, Noncitizen, Nonresident Alien
	College's Average SAT ≥ 1100			
Parents' income	32,488 [10,087]	25,397 [9,865]	42,816 [10,234]	40,404 [11,986]
Parents' highest grade completed	14.7 [1.5]	15.2 [1.9]	14.4 [1.9]	14.3 [2.0]
SAT score[1]	952 [40]	923 [44]	960 [42]	1022 [43]
	College's Average SAT ≥ 900 and ≤ 1000			
Parents' income	25,096 [9,246]	24,684 [9,452]	17,360 [11,765]	24,720 [10,452]
Parents' highest grade completed	13.9 [1.4]	13.2 [1.8]	12.2 [2.0]	13.6 [2.2]
SAT score[1]	847 [42]	841 [42]	881 [43]	896 [44]
	College's Average SAT ≤ 900 or College Does Not Use an Admissions Test for Selection			
Parents' income	25,269 [9,987]	29,389 [9,786]	20,098 [11,452]	26,384 [12,235]
Parents' highest grade completed	13.3 [1.7]	13.3 [1.8]	12.2 [2.0]	13.3 [2.0]
SAT score[1,2]	782 [95]	789 [98]	818 [105]	783 [109]

Notes: Unweighted means. See appendix table 9.1 for number of observations in each category.

[1] For those students who took only the ACT test and not the SAT test, the SAT score is predicted from the ACT score.

[2] In the "Less Selective to Not Selective" category, approximately 75 percent of students do have a recorded SAT or ACT score.

Table 9.3 Hispanic Natives and Hispanic Foreign Born in College

Hispanic	U.S. Native	Foreign Born but U.S. Citizen	Foreign Born, Noncitizen, but U.S. Resident	Foreign Born, Noncitizen, Nonresident Alien
	College's Average SAT ≥ 1100			
Parents' income	33,884	25,606	28,999	33,651
	[9,765]	[9,976]	[9,762]	[10,236]
Parents' highest grade completed	14.4	14.2	13.8	15.4
	[1.7]	[2.0]	[1.9]	[2.01]
SAT score[1]	1076	1053	894	1083
	[41]	[44]	[42]	[45]
	College's Average SAT ≥ 900 and ≤ 1000			
Parents' income	27,264	20,169	21,774	26,369
	[8,765]	[10,256]	[9,711]	[9,452]
Parents' highest grade completed	13.8	13.6	12.1	16.1
	[1.5]	[1.6]	[2.0]	[2.2]
SAT score[1]	924	852	811	943
	[47]	[48]	[47]	[50]
	College's Average SAT ≤ 900 or College Does Not Use an Admissions Test for Selection			
Parents' income	24,015	19,055	19,737	22,558
	[9,913]	[9,901]	[9,876]	[10,632]
Parents' highest grade completed	12.6	12.9	11.7	14.5
	[1.8]	[1.9]	[2.0]	[2.2]
SAT score[1,2]	818	759	729	882
	[97]	[98]	[100]	[104]

Notes: Unweighted means. See appendix table 9.1 for number of observations in each category.

[1]For those students who took only the ACT test and not the SAT test, the SAT score is predicted from the ACT score.

[2]In the "Less Selective to Not Selective," category, approximately 75 percent of students do have a recorded SAT or ACT score.

Natives generally come next, followed by foreign-born residents. Naturalized citizens appear to be the most economically and educationally disadvantaged group.

One might worry that parents' income and education are not exactly comparable across the United States and foreign countries. This worry should make us focus on the differences in parents' educational attainment that are shown in tables 9.2 and 9.3. Focusing on education is sensible because we know the direction of the bias from other studies of education and skills. America has an educational system that gives opportunities to failing students much longer than most other countries would. As a result, a foreigner with ten years of education, say, is likely to be more truly educated than an American with the same measured education. In short, the education differences in table 9.2 are likely to *understate* the extent to which the education of parents of foreign-born residents and nonresident aliens exceeds the education of parents of natives.

Tables 9.1, 9.2, and 9.3 demonstrate that the two proposed channels for crowding out, affirmative action and competition for access resources, are at least plausible. Immigrants certainly do make relatively heavy use of access resources, and colleges—especially selective colleges—may reach their affirmative action targets by substituting less-disadvantaged immigrants for more-disadvantaged natives. If it exists at all, we expect crowding out through affirmative action to be more pronounced in more selective colleges. If crowding out through competition for access resources occurs, it is likely to be most pronounced in the middle of the selectivity spectrum (state colleges, for instance), where there exist institutional resources to be differentially distributed among students and there are numbers of needy students.

RESULTS

I will now examine results that test the affirmative action channel for crowding out and then discuss results related to competition for access resources. This order does not imply anything about the relative importance of the two possible channels. Instead, it is convenient because all of the tables have the same basic form, but the "access resources" tables present a greater variety of options; thus, it is helpful to become familiar with the simpler tables first.

All of the tests have a form based on equation (9.4). All are estimated by weighted least squares to account for the different degrees of precision in estimates of colleges' student compositions (due to the different number of student observations). The coefficient on the immigrants' share of enrollment—the coefficient relevant for crowding out—is allowed to be different for colleges in different selectivity categories (the left-out category is always the nonselective college category). This is because affirmative action and access program targets are unlikely to be equally binding across the spectrum of college selectivity. In the tables presented, the coefficients on the interaction terms are always added to the coefficient on the left-out category—so that the estimate for each category of school can be read directly off the table.

Recall that the estimates obtained are probably biased in a positive direction simply because students who are alike go to school with one another. That is, the results probably underestimate the true amount of crowding out. One simple, partial test of this hypothesis is comparison of the estimated coefficients in tables 9.4 through 9.7 with estimated coefficients from a regression that is identical *except* for the omission of college characteristics, like the state fixed effects, the indicator for a private college, and the locational descriptors. Under the assumption that the unobserved omitted variables are like the variables that we observe (location, for instance), the direction in which the coefficient changes as we add control variables to the regression indicates the sign of the omitted-variables bias. Of course, this can only be a partial test, but it is shown in footnotes to each table, and it consistently indicates that the omitted-variables bias is positive.

The Baseline: Results Using OLS Estimation on Cross-Section Data

Tables 9.4 through 9.7 show the baseline results. College characteristics are included, but omitted variables bias may still exist (especially for the results based on less selective colleges), and no remedy for measurement error is attempted. Table 9.4 shows tests for crowding out of black natives by black immigrants and nonblack immigrants. I use both the comprehensive measure of immigrants (all foreign born) and the finer measure, nonresident aliens. Both the descriptive evidence of table 9.2 and the anecdotes related in GRM suggest that nonresident aliens—for instance, students from well-off Caribbean and Latin American families—could be particularly important for satisfying affirmative action targets at selective colleges. Columns (2) and (4) test for cross-ethnicity crowding out by seeing whether the percentage of natives who are black responds to the share of nonblack immigrants in the college. Column (2) does show some crowding out between nonblack immigrants and black natives. The coefficient is statistically significant at the 0.05 level, but the effect is quantitatively small.[9] A 1-percentage-point increase in the share of the college's students who are nonblack immigrants decreases the share of native students who are black by 0.15 percentage points.

Table 9.4   Tests: Crowding Out of Black Natives by Immigrants (Dependent Variable: Percent of College's U.S.-Born Students Who Are Black)

	Measure of Foreign Born Is Percent of College's Total Students Who Are			
	Nonblack and Foreign Born	Black and Foreign Born	Nonblack, Nonresident Aliens	Black Nonresident Aliens
(Above) × college's average SAT ≥ 1200	−0.021 (0.044)	−0.407 (0.163)	0.048 (0.212)	−1.421 (0.362)
(Above) × college's average SAT ≥ 1100 and ≤ 1200	0.035 (0.052)	−0.328 (0.121)	0.353 (0.303)	−0.381 (0.228)
(Above) × college's average SAT ≥ 900 and ≤ 1100	−0.119 (0.700)	1.089 (0.323)	0.056 (0.229)	−0.449 (0.312)
(Above) × college's average SAT < 900 or no SAT required	−0.152 (0.031)	1.504 (0.086)	−0.199 (0.148)	0.655 (0.166)
College's average SAT ≥ 1200	−9.308 (3.443)	−4.460 (2.242)	−6.803 (2.850)	−5.640 (2.261)
College's average SAT ≥ 1100 and ≤ 1200	−8.841 (2.139)	−5.414 (1.594)	−8.602 (2.047)	−7.183 (1.630)
College's average SAT ≥ 900 and ≤ 1100	−7.627 (1.590)	−5.692 (1.321)	−6.734 (1.563)	−6.486 (1.354)
College is a private college	−3.662 (0.991)	−4.336 (1.593)	−4.412 (1.048)	−4.625 (1.034)
State indicator variables	yes	yes	yes	yes
R-squared	0.319	0.401	0.326	0.329
Number of observations (colleges)[1]	1337	1337	1337	1337

Notes: Covariates not shown are: college is located in a center city, in an urban area, in a metropolitan area; college's enrollment per class is < 1000, > 1000 and < 2000, > 2000; university has professional degree programs, doctoral programs, education program, undergraduate business or vocational degrees. Standard errors in parentheses. Estimates are weighted by sample size in the colleges to correct for heteroskedasticity. If all the covariates below the fourth row of this table were dropped, the estimated coefficients for the most selective category of college (SAT > 1200) would be (respectively for the four columns): 2.005 (0.456), 2.997 (0.405), 1.338 (0.457), 3.078 (0.412). The estimates for the next most selective category of college (1100 < SAT < 1200) would be (respectively for the four columns): 2.674 (0.437), 3.401 (0.439), 2.311 (0.450), 3.876 (0.442).
[1]Historically black colleges are omitted.

More interestingly, columns (3) and (5) show quantitatively important crowding out of black natives by black immigrants—particularly in very selective schools and in response to nonresident aliens. In the most selective category of college, a 1-percentage-point increase in the share of students who are black immigrants reduces the share of native students who are black by 0.41 percentage points. Moreover, a 1-percentage-point increase in the share of students who are black, nonresident aliens reduces the share of native students who are black by 1.42 percentage points. We cannot statistically reject that one-for-one crowding out occurs between black, nativeborn students and foreign-born students.[10] In the next two categories of college selectivity, there is evidence of less substantial crowding out: a 0.4-percentage-point fall in black, native college-going for a 1-percentage-point rise in black, nonresident alien college-going. For the least selective colleges, there is no evidence of crowding out. The positive estimate is likely explained by omitted-variables bias.

Table 9.5 presents the same exercise for Hispanics. Again, there is evidence in column (2) of a very small amount of crowding out across ethnic groups, but the important evidence is in columns (3) and (5). A 1-percentage-point increase in the share of students who are Hispanic and foreign born reduces the share of natives who are Hispanic by about 0.5 of a percentage point in the most selective colleges. Most of the crowding out apparently occurs through nonresident aliens. For the two most selective categories of college, we cannot reject at 0.05 significance the hypothesis that one-for-one crowding out of Hispanic natives for Hispanic nonresident aliens occurs. There is no evidence of crowding out in the two less selective categories of colleges, either because it does not occur or because of omitted-variables bias.

In summary, the results suggest that crowding out through affirmative action targets occurs at colleges that are selective or very selective—with average SAT scores in excess of 1100. Particularly important in this crowding out are nonresident aliens, who—in selective schools—are largely individuals on student visas. The affirmative action crowding out appears almost entirely within racial/ethnic groups, suggesting that there is little substitution among affirmative action targets (for instance, exceeding the Hispanic affirmative action target while falling short of the black affirmative action target).

Basic Tests of Crowding Out Through Competition for Access Resources

The advantage of testing the affirmative action channel is that the measure of the student's "disadvantaged" background is chosen for us: race

Table 9.5   Tests: Crowding Out of Hispanic Natives by Immigrants (Dependent Variable: Percent of College's U.S.-Born Students Who Are Hispanic)

	Measure of Foreign-Born Is Percent of College's Total Students Who Are			
	Non-Hispanic and Foreign Born	Hispanic and Foriegn Born	Non-Hispanic, Nonresident Aliens	Hispanic, Nonresident Aliens
(Above) × college's average SAT ≥ 1200	−0.297 (0.076)	−0.474 (0.198)	0.080 (0.199)	−1.588 (0.672)
(Above) × college's average SAT ≥ 1100 and ≤ 1200	−0.280 (0.087)	−0.303 (0.145)	−0.297 (0.103)	−1.317 (0.602)
(Above) × college's average SAT ≥ 900 and ≤ 1100	−0.248 (0.078)	0.949 (0.104)	0.071 (0.153)	−0.370 (0.436)
(Above) × college's average SAT < 900 or no SAT Required	−0.094 (0.031)	0.992 (0.123)	0.015 (0.080)	1.723 (0.264)
College's average SAT ≥ 1200	0.030 (2.470)	−0.001 (1.127)	−2.877 (1.788)	−1.785 (1.393)
College's average SAT ≥ 1100 and ≤ 1200	−1.514 (1.634)	−0.173 (0.859)	−2.569 (1.183)	−2.936 (0.939)
College's average SAT ≥ 900 and ≤ 1100	−0.719 (1.151)	−0.818 (0.668)	−2.362 (0.943)	−1.848 (0.805)
College is a private college	−1.739 (0.697)	−1.074 (0.531)	−1.018 (0.685)	−1.037 (0.675)
State indicator variables	yes	yes	yes	yes
R-squared	0.618	0.828	0.672	0.676
Number of observations (colleges)[1]	1337	1337	1337	1337

Notes: Covariates not shown are: college is located in a center city, in an urban area, in a metropolitan area; college's enrollment per class is < 1000, > 1000 and < 2000, > 2000; university has professional degree programs, doctoral programs, education program, undergraduate business or vocational degrees. Standard errors in parentheses. Estimates are weighted by sample size in the college to correct for heteroskedasticity. If all the covariates below the fourth row of this table were dropped, the estimated coefficients for the most selective category of college (SAT > 1200) would be (respectively for the four columns): 1.433 (0.522), 1.687 (0.529), 1.189 (0.519), 1.825 (0.530). The estimates for the next most selective category of college (1100 < SAT < 1200) would be (respectively for the four columns): 1.876 (0.510), 3.897 (0.598), 1.452 (0.566), 4.987 (0.504).
[1]Historically black colleges are omitted.

and ethnicity. It is harder to choose the best indicator(s) for a generally disadvantageous background. Table 9.6 shows the results of regressing a number of indicators on the percentage of total students who are foreign born and allowing the coefficient to vary with the college's selectivity. Basically, the equations estimated are the same as in column (2) of tables 9.4 and 9.5, except that the dependent variable is a general measure of disadvantage and the immigrant percentage includes all races. In order to show a greater number of dependent variables, the table has been turned on its side (so that each row is an equation). As in the previous tables, the coefficients on the interaction terms have been added to the coefficient on the left-out category, so that the estimate for each category of school can be read directly off the table.

Across its variety of measures of disadvantage, table 9.6 shows a consistent pattern of some crowding out of disadvantaged native students in the two middle categories of colleges. The "Very Selective" category of colleges (average SAT scores greater than or equal to 1100 and less than 1200) shows the most crowding out. The "Somewhat Selective" category (average SAT scores greater than or equal to 900 and less than 1100) shows less but still consistent crowding out. The two extreme categories ("Not Selective" and "Extremely Selective") show no evidence that the foreign born generally crowd out disadvantaged students.

For instance, a 1-percentage-point increase in the share of students who are foreign born reduces the share of native students whose parents' combined income is less than twenty thousand dollars by 0.75 percentage points in "Very Selective" schools and 0.33 percentage points in "Somewhat Selective" schools. A 1-percentage-point increase in the share of students who are foreign born lowers the share of native students who have no parent with a college degree (including an Associate's degree) by 0.51 percentage points in "Very Selective" schools and 0.14 percentage points in "Somewhat Selective" schools.

One question raised by table 9.6 is whether we ought to expect one-for-one crowding out. The answer is that the more alike the immigrants "doing" the crowding out and the natives whose crowding out we are measuring, the more one-to-one crowding out is the relevant benchmark. Table 9.7 examines this issue by varying the measure of immigrants, only including immigrants as disadvantaged (and competing with disadvantaged natives) if they are, say, from low-income families. Table 9.7 has the same structure as tables 9.4 and 9.5.

Looking across the row that shows the effect for the crucial "Very Selective" schools, it looks as though there are certain choices of disadvantage that will generate estimates such that we cannot reject the hypothesis that crowding out is one-for-one. In particular, crowding out

Table 9.6   Tests: Crowding Out of Disadvantaged Natives by
Immigrants, with Various Indicators for Being
Disadvantaged (Dependent Variable: Percent of Native
Students Who Are Disadvantaged)

	Estimated Coefficient on Percent of Total Students Who Are Foreign Born for Colleges That Are			
Dependent Variable	Not Selective[1]	Somewhat Selective	Very Selective	Extremely Selective
% of native students' whose parents' combined income is < $10,000	−0.016 (0.061)	−0.217 (0.086)	−0.558 (0.131)	0.208 (0.158)
% of native students whose parents' combined income is < $20,000	−0.057 (0.086)	−0.329 (0.109)	−0.748 (0.134)	0.034 (0.298)
% of native students whose parental household receives food stamps	−0.006 (0.015)	−0.023 (0.061)	−0.172 (0.099)	0.088 (0.102)
% of native students who meet Pell grant eligibility requirements	−0.089 (0.043)	−0.330 (0.097)	−0.212 (0.087)	0.013 (0.091)
% of native students *neither* of whose parents has a high school diploma	−0.024 (0.021)	−0.351 (0.063)	−0.370 (0.071)	0.023 (0.096)
% of native students *neither* of whose parents has any education beyond high school	−0.019 (0.031)	−0.334 (0.099)	−0.365 (0.102)	0.024 (0.167)
% of native students *neither* of whose parents has an associate degree or any higher college degree	−0.013 (0.029)	−0.141 (0.101)	−0.511 (0.172)	0.073 (0.120)

Notes: All other covariates in the equations estimated for this table are the same as those in tables 9.4, 9.5, and 9.7. This table varies the measure by which a native is classified as disadvantaged. Compare to table 9.7. The covariates not shown are thus: indicator variables for average SAT category of college; indicator variable for private college; state indicator variables; college is located in a center city, in an urban area, in a metropolitan area; college's enrollment per class is < 1000, > 1000 and < 2000, > 2000; university has professional degree programs, doctoral programs, education program, undergraduate business or vocational degrees. Standard errors in parentheses. Estimates are weighted by sample size in the college to correct for heteroskedasticity. Historically black colleges are omitted.
[1]Extremely Selective, average SAT score > 1200; Very Selective, average SAT score > 1100 and < 1200; Somewhat Selective, average SAT score > 900 and < 1100, Not Selective, average SAT score < 900 or admissions tests not used.

Table 9.7   Tests: Crowding Out of Disadvantaged Natives by Immigrants (Dependent Variable: Percent of College's U.S.-Born Students Who Come from Low-Income Families)[1]

	Measure of Disadvantaged Foreign Born Is Percent of College's Total Students Who Are			
	Foreign Born and from Very Low Income Families	Foreign Born and Have No Parent with More Than High School	Foreign Born and Come from a Limited English Home	Foreign Born and Take Remedial Writing
(Above) × college's average SAT ≥ 1200	0.211 (0.154)	0.122 (0.802)	0.375 (0.338)	−0.417 (1.576)
(Above) × college's average SAT ≥ 1100 and ≤ 1200	−0.153 (0.122)	−0.812 (0.264)	−0.828 (0.204)	−1.120 (0.636)
(Above) × college's average SAT ≥ 900 and ≤ 1100	−1.571 (0.168)	−0.185 (0.203)	−0.146 (0.141)	−1.214 (0.631)
(Above) × college's average SAT < 900 or no SAT required	−0.058 (0.079)	−0.074 (0.125)	0.080 (0.100)	−0.119 (0.244)
College's average SAT ≥ 1200	−22.430 (4.176)	−15.073 (6.033)	−16.575 (6.722)	−13.800 (5.038)
College's average SAT ≥ 1100	−16.381 (2.915)	−10.266 (4.372)	−9.862 (4.287)	−13.260 (3.623)
College's average SAT ≥ 900 and ≤ 1100	−8.786 (2.448)	−11.411 (3.401)	−9.744 (3.278)	−8.627 (2.927)
College is a private college	−12.875 (2.042)	−16.371 (2.233)	−17.071 (2.236)	−16.514 (2.229)
State indicator variables	yes	yes	yes	yes
R-squared	0.348	0.320	0.342	0.330
Number of observations (colleges)[1]	1337	1337	1337	1337

Notes: Covariates not shown are: college is located in a center city, in an urban area, in a metropolitan area; college's enrollment per class is < 1000, > 1000 and < 2000, > 2000; university has professional degree programs, doctoral programs, education program. undergraduate business or vocational degrees. Standard errors in parentheses. Estimates are weighted by sample size in the college to correct for heteroskedasticity. If all the covariates below the fourth row of this table were dropped, the estimated coefficients for the most selective category of college (SAT > 1200) would be (respectively for the four columns): 8.086 (3.143), 8.870 (3.211), 9.675 (4.019), 8.432 (3.786). The estimates for the next most selective category of college (1100 < SAT < 1200) would be (respectively for the four columns): 11.652 (4.069), 10.777 (3.605), 9.562 (4.199), 10.891 (4.004).

[1]Historically black colleges are omitted.

appears to be about 0.8-for-one between low-income (parents' income less than twenty thousand dollars) natives and foreign-born students who have no parent with more than a high school education. It is also about 0.8-for-one between low-income natives and foreign-born students who come from a family with limited English skills.

The last column of table 9.7 is not like the others, because the measure of the immigrant student disadvantage is not predetermined. The measure is the percentage of students who are both foreign born and take a remedial writing class in college. This measure is partly endogenous to crowding out. If foreign-born students "convert" remedial writing classes to their particular needs and crowd out disadvantaged native students, the writing classes are likely to become more attractive to foreign-born students. The remedial writing measure will reflect this greater attractiveness and overstate the *initial* impact of immigrants on the composition of writing classes. However, the endogenous increase in the share of remedial students who are immigrants will cause further crowding out of natives. Thus, if remedial-class conversion is a real method by which natives and immigrants compete, then an initial increase in the percentage of foreign-born students who take remedial classes has a multiplier effect on the percentage of native students who are disadvantaged. This "muliplier" is reflected both in the remedial-writing measure and the dependent variable, so the last column of table 9.7 effectively presents a reduced-form estimate. These reduced-form estimates suggest that a 1-percentage-point increase in the share of students who are foreign born and taking a remedial writing class reduces the share of native students who have low-income parents by 1.1 percentage points in "Very Selective" colleges and by 1.2 percentage points in "Somewhat Selective" colleges.

Overall, tables 9.6 and 9.7 demonstrate that crowding out does appear to go on through competition for access resources. The more the immigrants look like people who would need access resources, the more disadvantaged natives are crowded out. This type of crowding out appears to be irrelevant at extremely selective colleges. This is probably because such colleges can afford to be relatively generous with each of their relatively few needy students—in terms of giving them remedial help, counseling, and financial aid. This type of crowding out also appears to be irrelevant at colleges that are not selective. Two explanations are possible. The first is omitted-variables bias. The second is that these colleges have meager access resources that come *from the institution* (as opposed to the federal government). In this case, little crowding out occurs because the meager resources from the institution do not make much difference, so that spreading them over a larger, competing group of students has little effect. Federal access resources such as Pell grants may be the key resources in these schools, and the ability of one student in a college to get a Pell grant does not depend on the number of similarly needy students in his college. Most crowding out through competition for access resources occurs at colleges between the two extremes, selective but not extremely selective. This includes many state universities, state colleges, and good private colleges; it does not include community colleges.

Correcting for Attenuation and Division Bias with Instrumental Variables

Table 9.8 summarizes the results of instrumenting for a college's 1992 immigrant share by its 1989 immigrant share. Compared to the point estimates in tables 9.4 through 9.7, the instrumental-variables estimates indicate slightly more crowding out. This is what we expected, given the fact that both measurement-error bias and division bias would make the estimates in tables 9.4 through 9.7 understate the true amount of crowding out. However, the estimates in table 9.8 display the same general pattern as those in tables 9.4 through 9.7. It still appears that crowding out through access resources occurs at colleges of middling selectivity and that crowding out through affirmative action occurs at very selective colleges.

Correcting for Omitted-Variables Bias and Endogeneity with California's Policy Changes

Table 9.9 summarizes the results of the instrumental-variables strategy estimated on California colleges. The number of observations is smaller than in previous tables because only California colleges are included. The smaller number of observations generates large standard errors, which preclude definitive results. Nevertheless, the estimates are an important addition to the results of tables 9.4 through 9.8. Of all the results in the study, the California results are the most cleanly and explicitly identified (least likely to suffer from omitted-variables bias or endogeneity of colleges' percentages of students who are foreign born). The standard errors are too large for statistically significant results, but the point estimates suggest more crowding out due to competition for access resources than is suggested by table 9.8. For instance, one-for-one crowding out appears to occur between low-income natives and foreign-born students who have no parent with more than a high school education. We do not see and do not expect to see much crowding out due to affirmative action in the California state system, since its

Table 9.8 Estimates with IV Treatment of Measurement Error (Tests: Crowding Out of Minority and Disadvantaged Natives by Immigrants)

| Dependent Variable
Independent Variable | Estimated Coefficient on Independent Variable for Colleges That Are | | | |
	Extremely Selective[1]	Very Selective	Somewhat Selective	Not Selective
% of U.S.-born students who are black				
% of total students who are nonblack and foreign born	−0.042 (0.060)	−0.009 (0.066)	−0.014 (0.744)	−0.226 (0.068)
% of total students who are black and foreign born	−0.545 (0.270)	−0.398 (0.173)	−0.122 (0.531)	−0.103 (0.308)
% of total students who are nonblack, nonresident aliens	−0.010 (0.401)	−0.009 (0.423)	−0.079 (0.432)	−0.287 (0.248)
% of total students who are black, nonresident aliens	−1.309 (0.452)	−0.724 (0.339)	−0.394 (0.405)	0.029 (0.134)
% of U.S.-born students who are Hispanic				
% of total students who are non-Hispanic and foreign born	−0.299 (0.132)	−0.301 (0.143)	−0.320 (0.117)	−0.121 (0.060)
% of total students who are Hispanic and foreign born	−0.785 (0.294)	−0.613 (0.215)	0.023 (0.145)	0.088 (0.076)
% of total students who are non-Hispanic, nonresident aliens	−0.135 (0.288)	−0.397 (0.179)	0.019 (0.200)	−0.108 (0.122)
% of total students who are Hispanic, nonresident aliens	−1.386 (0.661)	−1.311 (0.653)	−0.538 (0.576)	−0.141 (0.459)
% of U.S.-born students who come from low-income families				
% of foreign-born students who come from very low income families	0.090 (0.203)	−0.482 (0.193)	−1.332 (0.387)	−0.045 (0.127)

Table 9.8   *Continued*

Dependent Variable *Independent Variable*	Estimated Coefficient on Independent Variable for Colleges That Are			
	Extremely Selective[1]	Very Selective	Somewhat Selective	Not Selective
% of foreign-born students who do not have a parent with more than high school	−0.169 (0.984)	−0.628 (0.300)	−0.610 (0.310)	−0.100 (0.142)
% of foreign-born students who come from limited-English homes	−0.056 (0.467)	−0.804 (0.316)	−0.619 (0.203)	−0.027 (0.156)
% of foreign-born students who take remedial writing	−0.578 (2.114)	−1.319 (0.719)	−1.255 (0.686)	−0.551 (0.337)

Notes: Except for constant, all covariates are shown. (College characteristics drop out in first-differenced specification.) Standard errors in parentheses. Estimates weighted by sample size in the college to correct for heteroskedasticity and exacerbation of attenuation bias in first differences (see text). Historically black colleges omitted. See equation (9.9) in text. Observations totaled 762.

[1]Extremely Selective, average SAT score > 1200; Very Selective, average SAT score > 1100 and < 1200; Somewhat Selective, average SAT score > 900 and < 1100; Not Selective, average SAT score < 900 or admissions tests not used.

colleges and universities do not fall into the "Very Selective" or "Extremely Selective" categories.

Of course, it is possible that the identifying assumption for this instrumental-variables strategy does not strictly hold. The California state system could have coincidentally changed some feature (unrelated to immigrants) that made its colleges less appealing to native-born students relative to other California colleges. However, there is no apparent policy change of this type during the 1986–1992 period.

CONCLUSIONS

This study provides some of the first empirical evidence on the question of whether immigrants crowd disadvantaged American natives out of higher education. Although neither group—immigrants or disadvantaged natives—forms a large share of the college-going population in any given year, college education is an important route by which both groups gradually transform themselves into higher-skilled, better-

Table 9.9   Instrumental Variables. First-Differenced Estimates (Tests: Crowding Out of Disadvantaged Natives by California Colleges That Are More Accessible to Immigrants)

Dependent Variable *Independent Variable*	IV Estimated Coefficient on Independent Variable for Colleges That Are	
	More Selective	Less Selective
% of US.-born students who are black		
% of total students who are black, nonresident aliens	−0.969 (0.675)	0.009 (0.186)
% of U.S.-born students who are Hispanic		
% of total students who are Hispanic, nonresident aliens	−1.212 (0.899)	−0.130 (0.404)
% of U.S.-born students who come from low-income families		
% of foreign-born students who come from very low income families	−0.639 (0.308)	−0.243 (0.128)
% of foreign-born students who do not have a parent with more than high school	−0.543 (1.033)	−0.191 (0.155)
% of foreign-born students who come from limited-English homes	−0.699 (0.587)	−0.172 (0.190)
% of foreign-born students who take remedial writing	−0.588 (1.909)	−0.239 (0.402)

Implied First-Stage of Instrumental Variables Estimation

Dependent Variable	Estimated Coefficient on Indicator for California State University for Colleges That Are	
	More Selective[1]	Less Selective
% of total students who are black, nonresident aliens	0.200 (0.049)	0.153 (0.054)
% of total students who are Hispanic, nonresident aliens	3.104 (0.706)	2.868 (0.654)
% of foreign-born students who come from very low income families	1.539 (0.608)	2.043 (0.644)
% of foreign-born students who do not have a parent with more than high school	1.817 (0.667)	2.314 (0.749)

(Table continues on p. 314.)

Table 9.9   *Continued*

Dependent Variable *Independent Variable*	IV Estimated Coefficient on Independent Variable for Colleges That Are	
	More Selective	Less Selective
% of foreign-born students who come from limited-English homes	2.899 (0.787)	2.720 (0.811)
% of foreign-born students who take remedial writing	1.838 (0.709)	1.977 (0.746)

Notes: Except for constants, all covariates are shown. (College characteristics drop out in first-differenced specification.) Standard errors in parentheses. Estimates weighted by sample size in the college to correct for heteroskedasticity and exacerbation of attenuation bias in first differences (see text).

[1] See equations (9.9) and (9.10) in text. Observations totaled 87, all in California. More Selective, average SAT score > 950; Less Selective, average SAT score < 950.

integrated individuals. Disadvantaged natives and immigrants are sufficiently large groups relative to one another and relative to the resources devoted to improving their access to college that immigrants actually do crowd disadvantaged natives out of higher education.

Crowding out takes a few forms. In very selective colleges, black and Hispanic natives appear to be crowded out by foreign-born students who fill the same racial/ethnic affirmative action targets but who come from more advantaged circumstances than their native counterparts. In particular, foreign-born blacks and Hispanics who are nonresident aliens are significantly better off than the native blacks and Hispanics, and we cannot reject the hypothesis that they crowd out native blacks and Hispanics one-for-one. Crowding out through the channel of affirmative action targets does not appear to happen much outside of very selective colleges.

Crowding out also occurs through immigrants and disadvantaged natives competing for scarce access resources such as financial aid and remedial classes. This phenomenon is relevant mainly for colleges that are selective, but not extremely selective. In this "central" group, the colleges do have some discretionary resources to distribute over their needy students, and these resources are stretched by competing groups of disadvantaged natives and immigrants, who often have particular needs related to their English-language skills. Crowding out through competition for access resources probably does not occur as much at nonselective colleges because their key access resources are not discretionary but come from federal government programs such as the Pell grants.

Generally, it is hardest to draw conclusions about crowding out (or the lack of it) at nonselective colleges. We cannot obtain results for this particular group of colleges that are not likely to suffer from omitted-variables that bias estimates toward a finding of "no crowding out."

Empirical evidence on crowding out cannot tell policymakers whether access resources or affirmative action should or should not distinguish between natives and immigrants. Difficult social welfare analysis (because immigrants are a marginal part of society, so that society itself is endogenous) is really required. Nevertheless, this evidence can give policymakers a sense of whether their decisions involve trade-offs between immigrants and disadvantaged natives. For instance, crowding-out evidence is relevant to the continuing debate in California about whether undocumented immigrants should qualify for in-state tuition (University of California 1993). It is also relevant to the debate about whether need-based grants should be equally used for courses in English as a Second Language (Zook 1994). Certainly, the empirical evidence should help the federal government decide how colleges should report their efforts to meet affirmative action targets.

APPENDIX

Appendix Table 9a.1

	U.S.-Born Citizen	Foreign-Born U.S. Citizen	Foreign-Born, Noncitizen Resident	Foreign-Born, Noncitizen, Nonresident Alien
Very Selective 1				
White	83.68	35.20	27.39	33.68
Black	5.19	5.10	6.84	5.26
Asian	4.87	46.42	57.53	51.57
American Indian	0.44	0.51	0.00	0.00
Hispanic	5.80	12.75	8.21	9.47
Parents' income	52432.58	38280.56	31025.12	32185.60
	[12673.11]	[10472.81]	[9872.74]	[10525.71]
Parents' highest	16.48	16.21	15.46	15.55
grade completed	[1.43]	[1.80]	[2.15]	[2.30]
Limited-English				
home background	6.51	53.80	82.19	81.25
SAT Score[1]	1186.65	1198.51	1105.91	1194.29
	[39.54]	[40.45]	[41.42]	[50.30]
Took remedial				
writing	1.05	3.03	4.22	12.76

(Table continues on p. 316.)

Appendix Table 9a.1   *Continued*

	U.S.-Born Citizen	Foreign-Born U.S. Citizen	Foreign-Born, Noncitizen Resident	Foreign-Born, Noncitizen, Nonresident Alien
Took remedial math	0.85	2.02	1.42	3.22
Took remedial study skills	0.93	2.03	1.42	2.15
Took remedial reading	1.05	1.51	5.63	9.47
Public college/ university	39.73	44.22	50.68	30.20
Private college/ university	60.26	55.77	49.31	69.79
New England region[2]	9.01	8.04	2.73	6.25
Mid-East region[2]	27.76	22.11	24.65	46.87
Great Lakes region[2]	17.25	20.60	13.69	11.45
Plains region[2]	0.00	0.00	0.00	0.00
South-East region[2]	26.47	15.57	12.32	13.54
South-West region[2]	0.60	2.51	0.00	3.12
Rocky Mountain region[2]	0.92	0.50	0.00	3.12
Far West region[2]	15.52	24.12	46.57	15.62
Number of observations this category	5010	399	352	395
Very Selective 2				
White	89.01	37.69	31.01	24.22
Black	4.08	3.66	5.69	3.96
Asian	2.41	46.59	51.26	66.51
American Indian	0.74	0.52	0.00	0.00
Hispanic	3.73	11.51	12.02	4.40
Parents' income	45392.38	33730.34	29554.78	21347.00
	[11626.41]	[9872.47]	[9272.98]	[10613.87]
Parents' highest grade completed	15.46	15.36	14.76	14.75
	[1.40]	[1.63]	[1.65]	[2.05]
Limited-English home background	2.51	45.45	74.07	83.84
SAT score[1]	1047.77	1052.30	924.57	989.41
	[43.26]	[39.45]	[43.21]	[42.46]
Took remedial writing	1.33	2.59	7.97	8.07
Took remedial math	1.91	2.08	1.86	2.25
Took remedial study skills	1.26	1.30	1.87	1.80
Took remedial reading	1.30	3.11	6.13	8.00

Appendix Table 9a.1 *Continued*

	U.S.-Born Citizen	Foreign-Born U.S. Citizen	Foreign-Born, Noncitizen Resident	Foreign-Born, Noncitizen, Nonresident Alien
Public college/ university	64.78	63.21	77.30	67.82
Private college/ university	35.21	36.78	22.69	32.17
New England region[2]	8.16	11.65	5.52	5.65
Mid-East region[2]	15.89	14.24	19.63	12.60
Great Lakes region[2]	19.21	10.62	13.49	15.21
Plains region[2]	10.98	6.21	10.42	6.95
South-East region[2]	17.20	14.76	7.97	13.91
South-West region[2]	13.35	18.65	17,79	20.43
Rocky Mountain region[2]	3.05	1.03	0.61	3.04
Far West region[2]	12.11	22.79	24.53	22.17
Number of observations this category	13261	772	728	852
Somewhat Selective				
White	89.13	45.93	28.78	31.55
Black	5.03	4.06	6.56	2.45
Asian	0.62	26.79	45.95	56.14
American Indian	0.67	1.19	2.02	0.40
Hispanic	4.52	22.00	16.66	9.42
Parents' income	36333.79	32385.08	26016.20	15674.17
	[9872.06]	[10762.20]	[9814.10]	[9736.15]
Parents' highest grade completed	14.63	14.55	14.11	15.27
	[1.21]	[1.30]	[1.59]	[1.60]
Limited-English home background	3.30	47.97	78.10	79.68
SAT score[1]	957.86	939.82	880.16	855.36
	[49.02]	[50.45]	[52.12]	[50.01]
Took remedial writing	1.85	4.33	11.11	10.93
Took remedial math	3.95	2.89	9.18	2.03
Took remedial study skills	1.72	1.69	5.67	2.86
Took remedial reading	2.19	3.85	10.60	10.16
Public college/ university	77.38	71.83	70.64	82.86
Private college/ university	22.28	27.20	29.35	17.13
Private, for-profit college	0.32	0.95	0.00	0.00

(Table continues on p. 318.)

Appendix Table 9a.1   *Continued*

	U.S.-Born Citizen	Foreign-Born U.S. Citizen	Foreign-Born, Noncitizen Resident	Foreign-Born, Noncitizen, Nonresident Alien
New England region[2]	1.94	2.62	1.49	1.19
Mid-East region[2]	8.03	9.78	18.40	9.96
Great Lakes region[2]	22.28	16.94	20.39	20.31
Plains region[2]	17.23	10.26	4.97	9.56
South-East region[2]	30.60	29.35	25.87	33.86
South-West region[2]	11.93	14.08	13.93	17.13
Rocky Mountain region[2]	3.92	2.62	3.98	3.98
Far West region[2]	2.81	8.11	10.44	3.98
Number of observations this category	22412	843	1007	962
Less Selective to Not Selective				
White	76.67	33.56	21.16	27.42
Black	13.84	10.22	13.58	8.65
Asian	1.09	29.54	29.96	49.69
American Indian	1.21	0.81	0.52	0.61
Hispanic	7.16	25.84	34.75	13.60
Parents' income	33277.51	27510.36	22509.96	18603.33
	[9234.77]	[9943.82]	[9768.08]	[10812.44]
Parents' highest grade completed	13.92	13.95	13.08	14.43
	[2.06]	[2.19]	[2.32]	[2.14]
Limited-English home background	4.92	59.03	80.58	82.96
SAT score[1]	875.78	861.50	820.53	889.15
	[105.67]	[109.78]	[105.67]	[130.62]
% with no ACT/ SAT score	71.76	85.61	91.59	90.68
Took remedial writing	3.21	7.36	16.00	15.90
Took remedial math	6.38	5.85	9.83	4.56
Took remedial study skills	1.98	3.25	4.83	4.80
Took remedial reading	3.99	7.53	17.71	15.98
Public college/ university	60.83	58.34	52.14	55.87
Private college/ university	23.55	26.08	22.46	33.80
Private, for-profit college	15.60	15.56	25.38	10.32
New England region[2]	5.49	5.03	3.66	2.63
Mid-East region[2]	18.55	24.72	32.94	26.92

Appendix Table 9a.1 *Continued*

	U.S.-Born Citizen	Foreign-Born U.S. Citizen	Foreign-Born, Noncitizen Resident	Foreign-Born, Noncitizen, Nonresident Alien
Great Lakes region[2]	12.74	6.75	6.42	5.87
Plains region[2]	4.73	2.03	0.62	1.61
South-East region[2]	25.12	17.08	10.80	19.23
South-West region[2]	12.32	11.47	7.32	4.85
Rocky Mountain region[2]	4.21	3.18	0.89	1.82
Far West region[2]	16.08	27.53	37.14	37.04
Number of observations this category	49934	3362	2436	1028

Notes: For variables that are not indicator variables, the numbers in square brackets are standard deviations. "Very Selective 1" includes colleges/universities whose average composite SAT score is greater than 1200; "Very Selective 2" includes those whose average composite SAT score is between 1100 and 1200; "Somewhat Selective" includes those whose average composite SAT score is between 900 and 1100; "Less Selective to Not Selective" includes (1) those whose average composite SAT score is lower than 900 and (2) those with fewer than 30 percent of students taking SAT or ACT tests.

[1]For those students who took only the ACT test and not the SAT test, the SAT score is predicted from the ACT score.

[2]The location of the college or university, not necessarily of the student's residence.

NOTES

1. See, for instance, Borjas, Freeman, and Katz (1992), LaLonde and Topel (1992), and Altonji and Card (1991), and the studies in Part I of this volume.

2. This statistic is for colleges that are less selective or not selective—those that do not typically use admissions test scores for admissions or have an average SAT score less than 900. These are the colleges most relevant to students whose secondary schooling is deficient.

3. It is possible that the presence of the immigrants increases the target because they are vocal members of the pool of potential applicants. But, it is unlikely that targets will keep up with immigrant additions to the population of disadvantaged, especially since nonnaturalized immigrants have little political influence.

4. Hoxby (1997).

320 Help or Hindrance?

5. Sampling error due to unintended, non-random sampling is unlikely to be remedied by instrumental variables. If a college unintentionally has non-random sampling one year, the problem that caused the non-randomness may crop up again in the next year of the survey.

6. The National Educational Longitudinal Study, the National Longitudinal Study of Youth, High School and Beyond.

7. The Higher Education General Information System, the Integrated Postsecondary Education Data Set (IPEDS), and CASPAR.

8. However, starting with the 1992–1993 survey, a portion of the students do enter a longitudinal survey. This will be useful in the future, though it does not help us identify decisions that take place before a student enters his or her first college. The longitudinal survey would have to "back up" to help us there.

9. Hereafter, the asymptomatic 0.05 level, unless specified otherwise.

10. Note that this calculation requires adjustment for the fact that the dependent variable (N_j^{ng}/N_j^n) has a different base (denominator) than the independent variable (N_j^f/N_j). However, this adjustment is quite small.

REFERENCES

Altonji, Joseph, and David Card. 1991. "Effects of Immigration on the Labor Market Outcomes of Less-Skilled Natives." In *Immigration, Trade, and the Labor Market*, edited by John Abowd and Richard Freeman. Chicago: University of Chicago Press.

Borjas, George, Richard Freeman, and Lawrence Katz. 1992. "On the Labor Market Effects of Immigration and Trade." In *Immigrants and the Work Force*. Chicago: University of Chicago Press.

Gray, Maryann Jacobi, Elizabeth Rolph, and Elan Melamid. 1996. *Immigration and Higher Education: Institutional Responses to Changing Demographics*. Santa Monica, Cal.: Rand.

Hoxby, Caroline. 1997. "The Changing Market Structure of U.S. Higher Education." Working Paper. Cambridge, MA: National Bureau of Economic Research.

Kerschner, Lee. 1992. "Immigration: Recognizing the Benefit, Meeting the Challenges." In *A Challenge of Change: Public Four-Year Higher Education Enrollment Lessons from the 1980s for the 1990s*, edited by American Association of State Colleges and Universities. Washington, D.C.: American Association of State Colleges and Universities.

LaLonde, Robert, and Robert Topel. 1992. "The Assimilation of Immigrants in the U.S. Labor Market." In *Immigrants and the Work Force*. Chicago: University of Chicago Press.

Manski, Charles, and David Wise. 1983. *College Choice in America.* Cambridge, Mass.: Harvard University Press.

National Center for Education Statistics. 1995. *The National Postsecondary Student Aid Study 1992–93* (Users Manual, codebooks, and restricted-access machine-readable data files). Washington, D.C.: U.S. Department of Education.

Rothschild, Michael, and Lawrence White. 1995. "The Analytics of the Pricing of Higher Education and Other Services in Which the Customers are Inputs." *Journal of Political Economy* 103(3): 573–86.

University of California, *Latino Student Eligibility and Participation in the University of California.* Santa Cruz: University of California.

Zook, Jim, "Pell Grant Protest: Proposal to Bar Use for English-as-a-Second-Language Training Raises Concern." *The Chronicle of Higher Education,* September 21, 1994, p. A35.

CHAPTER 10

Immigration and Crime Among Young Black Men: Evidence from the National Longitudinal Survey of Youth

Jeffrey T. Grogger

Immigration and crime are two of the most pressing public policy problems of the 1990s. New immigrants have arrived in the United States recently in numbers not seen since early in the century, and the evidence suggests that their labor-market skills are lower than those of immigrants from the 1950s and 1960s (U.S. Immigration and Naturalization Service 1991; Borjas 1985). Reported crime rates have fallen a bit in the last few years but remain roughly three times higher than they were just thirty years ago (U.S. Federal Bureau of Investigation, various years). Discussions in the press and comments by public officials often suggest that these problems are linked, and that recent immigration has caused crime to rise (Ostrow 1992; Gallegly 1992; Lauter and Ostrow 1993).

As contemporary as the problem may seem, however, attributing crime to immigrants reiterates an argument often debated in the history of American politics. Steinberg (1981) cites pre-Revolutionary concerns about the connection between immigration and crime, and the issue was vigorously debated during the antebellum period (Sanderson 1856). Earlier in this century, the argument that immigrants were causing a crime wave was cast in remarkably inflammatory terms (Orebaug 1922). In the 1920s, it was one of the principal arguments offered by supporters of the National Origins Act (Steinberg 1981).

Despite the perennial popularity of the notion that immigration causes crime, the issue has received little recent attention from researchers. A few studies have asked whether immigrants are more likely to commit crime than natives, and one study has analyzed the correlation between crime rates and immigration rates across cities (Butcher and Piehl 1995a, b; Los Angeles County 1992). As far as I can tell, however, no one has asked whether immigrants cause U.S. natives to commit more crime.

In the context of economic models of crime (Becker 1968; Grogger Forthcoming), it is easy to see how this could happen. In a utility-maximization model, individuals' decisions to commit crime depend on their rewards from crime and on their opportunity costs. Since crime is time-consuming, their opportunity cost is their wage: what they could earn if they spent their time working rather than committing crime. If immigration lowers the wages of natives, then immigration could cause natives to commit more crime.

In light of the numerous findings that immigration has only small effects on native wages, however, one might wonder how important this link could be (LaLonde and Topel 1991; Altonji and Card 1991; Borjas, Freeman, and Katz 1996). Moreover, in the context of an economic model, immigration could equally well cause natives to commit *less* crime. Just as an increase in labor supply due to immigration may cause wages to fall, an increase in the supply of criminals may reduce the returns to crime. Presumably, if immigration causes the number of criminals to rise, more stolen goods will circulate, and the prices that criminals can fetch for them will fall. The economic model predicts that as the returns to crime fall fewer natives will commit crime. Thus the effect of immigration on crime committed by natives is theoretically ambiguous.

In this study I examine the question empirically. For a number of reasons, I focus on the link between immigration and crime committed by young black men. First, young black men are among the most crime-prone members of the population. Studies of police data generally estimate that young black males are 50 to 100 percent more likely to be arrested than young white men, and they are vastly overrepresented in the nation's jails and prisons (Wolfgang, Figlio, and Sellin 1972; U.S. Bureau of Justice Statistics 1990). Moreover, because many young black men have relatively low levels of education and low wages, they are likely to be among those most affected by competition from recent immigrants. Thus the specific goal of this paper is to test whether immigration affects crime committed by young black males.

THEORETICAL FRAMEWORK

In this section I briefly discuss a theoretical model of the consumer's choice between work and crime, or more specifically, between work and crimes that may result in financial gain for the criminal. The model serves two important purposes. First, it yields insights into the means by which immigration may affect participation in crime on the part of natives. Second, as will be elaborated later in the study, the model provides guidance in developing a reduced-form approach to estimating the effect of immigration on native crime participation.

The model is similar to that in Grogger (Forthcoming), which is itself a variant on Gronau's (1977) model of the consumer's time-alloca-tion problem. The consumer is assumed to maximize utility U, a func-tion of consumption c and leisure L. The utility function has positive first partial derivatives and negative second own-partial derivatives. To maximize utility, the consumer allocates his time T between leisure, market work h_m, and crime h_c. If he works in the market, he receives the competitively determined wage w. If he commits crime, he receives a price p for every unit of stolen goods s that he produces. The price of stolen merchandise is assumed to be competitively determined in the (black) market by the intersection of the demand for and supply of stolen goods. Time spent committing crime, however, is subject to di-minishing returns: more time devoted to crime produces more goods, but at a decreasing rate. The production function relating time to stolen goods is given by $s = f(h_c)$, where $f' > 0$ and $f'' < 0$. Formally, the consumer's problem can be written as:

$$\max U(c, L)$$

$$\text{s.t. } c = w\, h_m + p\, s + A$$

$$s = f(h_c)$$

$$T = L + h_m + h_c,$$

where A is nonlabor income.

As shown in Grogger (Forthcoming), this model yields a particularly simple crime participation rule, at least for the majority of criminals who spend at least some time working in the labor market. Specifically, a worker commits crime if and only if the returns to the first hour of crime exceed the wage, that is, if $pf'(0) > w$.

This observation motivates the linkage between immigration and native crime. Write the worker's crime-participation rule as:

$$(10.1) \quad P(h_c > 0) = P(pf'(0) > w),$$

where $P(z)$ denotes the probability of the event z. In words, this says that the probability that the worker commits crime is equal to the prob-ability that returns to the first hour of crime exceed the wage.

The first way that immigration could affect the crime participation of natives is through the labor market. More immigrants mean more workers. This shifts out the labor-supply curve, lowering the wage. If wages fall, then native workers are more likely to participate in crime. The second is through the market for stolen merchandise. If more im-migrants mean more thieves—absolutely, not relatively—then immigrants shift out the supply curve of stolen goods, driving their price down.[1] If stolen goods fetch lower prices, then native workers are less likely to participate in crime.

Thus the time-allocation model of crime yields an important insight: immigration could either raise or lower crime among natives.[2] The net result will depend on which effect dominates, the labor-market effect or the black-market effect. The model also motivates a reduced-form approach to estimating the net effect of immigration, a point to which I return later in this study. For now, I turn to a description of the data to be used in the empirical analysis.

DATA

Crime Data

Studying the link between immigration and crime imposes stringent data demands. The analyst requires data on the criminal activity of young men that can be linked to immigration data on the cities where they live. Ideally, one would use measures collected at more than one point in time in order to control for unobservable characteristics of cities that might be correlated with both immigration and crime. Valid measures of youth crime, however, are hard to come by. Most self-reports are tainted by obvious incentive problems, whereas police records and the like capture only a fraction of all crime. There is no ideal solution to this problem. Ultimately, the researcher must choose between objectivity and completeness.

The National Longitudinal Survey of Youth (NLSY) provides several potential sources of data. The NLSY began in 1979 as a survey of 12,686 youths age fourteen to twenty-one. It is stratified, providing an oversampling of minorities. Survey respondents have been reinterviewed annually. One source of crime data in the NLSY is its 1980 crime module, which queried respondents as to whether they had committed a number of specific crimes over the previous year. A problem with most of these data, however, as with most self-reported offending (SRO) data, concerns their validity. Criminologists have noted that SRO data differ in several ways from police records. Most notably, in SRO surveys, blacks and whites appear to participate in crime in roughly the same proportion, a feature that stands in sharp contrast to estimates based on police records (Blumstein et al. 1986). While in principle a number of explanations could reconcile this discrepancy, an extensive cross-checking study of self-reports and police records concluded that it was due largely to underreporting by young black men (Hindelang, Hirschi, and Weis 1981).

Because of these validity issues, I use three other measures of crime available from the NLSY. The first is a binary measure constructed from a question in the 1980 crime module that asked respondents about how much money they had earned from crime in the previous year. Specifically, it equals one if the consumer reported any income from crime in the previous year, and equals zero if he reported none. As I discuss in detail elsewhere (Grogger Forthcoming), this measure yields a black-white participation ratio well above one, and reasonably close to estimates taken from police records. It thus has greater prima facie validity than all of the other measures one could construct from the 1980 crime module. It also has the advantage of tying in fairly closely to the theoretical model discussed earlier. Recalling that the model pertains only to crimes committed for income, we see from the left-hand side of equation (10.1) that the theoretically ideal measure of crime participation would be a dummy variable equal to one if and only if the consumer spent any time committing crime. Under the assumption that one can only earn money from crime by devoting some time to it, this is essentially what the income-from-crime dummy represents.

The other crime measures come from a completely different part of the NLSY questionnaire. Each year, the NLSY interviewer codes the type of residence in which the respondent was living at the time of the interview. A surprisingly large number of respondents were interviewed in jail at least once.

These jail interview data have the benefit of objectivity, although this benefit comes with a cost. First, the data limit much of the scope of the analysis to incarceration rather than more general aspects of crime. Furthermore, they provide no information about the offense that led to the observed jail spell. Finally, I observe only those jail spells that are ongoing at the time of the annual interview. As a result, I may miss many short stays in jail.

From these data I construct two incarceration dummies. One is equal to one if the respondent was interviewed in jail at any time between 1979 and 1982. The other is equal to one if the respondent was interviewed in jail at any time between 1988 and 1992. These variables coincide temporally with my immigration measures, which are constructed from the 1980 and 1990 Censuses. I merge the 1979 to 1982 incarceration measure (and the measure of income from crime in 1979) to immigration rates constructed from the 1980 Census, and I merge the 1988 to 1992 incarceration dummy to immigration rates constructed from the 1990 Census.

Analyzing these three measures together helps to overcome some of the shortcomings involved with crime data. In the first place, by comparing estimates based on the income-from-crime dummy and the early incarceration dummy, I can check to see whether my estimates depend on the particular way in which crime is measured. If the estimates are similar, then one can have a reasonable amount of confidence that they reflect the effect of immigration on crime and not merely the idiosyncratic features of the different crime variables. By comparing the estimates from the earlier and later incarceration dummies, I can check whether the relationship between immigration and incarceration has changed over time. Finally, because the incarceration measure is longitudinal, I can pool the data over time and control for city effects using the variation in immigration rates over time to estimate the effect of immigration on crime. I can thus control for any city-specific factors that affect both immigration and crime.

Immigration Data

In wage studies the immigration intensity of a particular area is typically measured as the number of foreign-born residents relative to the total number of residents. Here I measure immigration rates similarly, although I refine the typical measure a bit by limiting attention to people who are likely to provide the greatest competition for young black men. I use the ratio of male immigrants to males, of recent male immigrants to males, of Hispanic male immigrants to males, and of recent Hispanic male immigrants to males, each in different specifications. I restrict the measures to males because males are most likely to compete with young black men. I construct the measures of recent and Hispanic immigrants because research has shown that these groups tend to have low education levels and hence are most likely to compete with young blacks with low education levels—the segment of the black population most likely to commit crime.[3]

These measures are constructed for 132 metropolitan areas (MAs) from 1-percent samples of 1980 and 1990 Census PUMS data.[4] The exact definitions of these MAs, and the computer code to aggregate Census microdata into these units of geography, were generously provided by David Jaeger. These MAs are a hybrid of Consolidated Metropolitan Statistical Areas (CMSAs), New England County Metropolitan Areas (NECMAs), and the smaller Metropolitan Statistical Areas (MSAs). Roughly, they correspond to CMSAs in those few areas of the country where CMSAs are defined, and otherwise correspond to MSAs, except in New England, where some of them correspond to NECMAs. The virtue of using Jaeger's MAs is that they are defined consistently across the two Censuses. Jaeger (1995) provides details.

The Geocode version of the NLSY provides codes for the residence of each respondent in each year that map almost exactly into Jaeger's MAs. I assign to each sample member the modal MA of residence during the 1979 to 1982 period and link the sample member's income-from-crime dummy and early incarceration dummy to immigration data for that MA. I link each sample member's 1988 to 1992 incarceration dummy to his modal MA of residence between 1988 and 1992. In both cases, I exclude from the sample all persons who had no distinct mode, who lived in rural areas over the entire period, or who were survey nonrespondents or lived abroad for a majority of the period.

One might worry that this approach would be less likely to assign to an MA those respondents who spent longer times in jail. In practice, this approach assigns the great majority of respondents who spend time in jail at about the same rate as it assigns respondents who were never interviewed in jail. There were 1,265 black men in the NLSY who were eligible to be assigned to an MA for the period 1988 to 1992: respondents who both took part in the survey and were living in the United States during at least three of the five years. Of these, 171 were interviewed in jail at least once. Among those who never were interviewed in jail, 71.3 percent were assigned to an MA. Among those who were interviewed in jail one, two, or three times and who account for 84 percent of the sample ever interviewed in jail, 70.8 percent were assigned to an MA. Only among respondents interviewed in jail four or five times was under-assignment a problem: of these twenty-seven people, fifteen were assigned to an MA rather than the nineteen who would have been assigned if the assignment rate were 71 percent. It seems doubtful that this level of under-assignment could impart much bias to the results.

Summary Statistics

The sample I analyze here consists of black men (1) who were not in the military subsample of the NLSY and (2) for whom a modal MA could be determined over either the 1979 to 1982 or 1988 to 1992 subperiod. Table 10.1 presents means and standard deviations of the crime and immigration measures. In the top panel, we see that nearly 30 percent of the sample admitted to earning income from crime in 1979. Only 4.4 percent were interviewed in jail between 1979 and 1982, however. By the end of the sample period, many more were spending time behind bars: 13 percent of the sample were interviewed in jail at some time between 1988 and 1992. These data are consistent

Table 10.1   Crime and Immigration Means

	Ciminal Justice Outcomes	
Variable	1979 to 1982 Sample	1988 to 1992 Sample
Any income from crime in 1979[a]	0.293 (0.455)	
Interviewed in jail	0.044 (0.206)	0.130 (0.337)
Sample sizes	854	897
	Immigration Rates (×100)	
Immigration Measure	1979 to 1982 Sample	1988 to 1992 Sample
Male immigrants/males	7.84 (6.70)	12.39 (10.57)
Recent male immigrants/ males	3.43 (3.04)	8.76 (8.07)
Hispanic male immigrants/ males	2.31 (3.25)	5.26 (6.56)
Recent Hispanic male immigrants/males	1.14 (1.43)	3.94 (5.10)
Sample sizes	854	897

Note: Figures in parentheses are standard deviations.
[a]Sample size is 744 due to item nonresponse.

with widely reported results about the age distribution of crime and incarceration. Crime participation generally peaks in the late teens, although the peak age for incarceration does not occur until much later, when the offender has accumulated a criminal record. In 1980, the sample members ranged in age from fifteen to twenty-two; in 1990, they ranged from twenty-five to thirty-two.

The immigration rates in the bottom panel of the table show large increases in immigration between 1980 and 1990, which is consistent with other research findings (Borjas 1995). In the urban areas sampled here, the fraction of males who were immigrants rose from 7.8 percent in 1980 to 12.4 percent in 1990. The stock of immigrants became more Hispanic over the time period and consisted of more recent immigrants as well. In 1980, 44 percent of male immigrants were recent, and 29 percent were Hispanic; in 1990, the figures were 71 percent and 42 percent, respectively.

THE ECONOMETRIC MODEL
The Statistical Model

I begin by motivating a reduced-form estimating equation based on the crime-participation rule presented earlier. Denote the income-from-crime dummy by C. Then $C = 1$ if $h_c > 0$ and $C = 0$ if $h_c = 0$. For the ith person in the jth MA, equation (10.1) can be rewritten as:

(10.2) $P(C_{ij} = 1) = P(pf'_{ij}(0) > w)$.

The problem with equation (10.2) as an estimating equation is that the returns to the first hour of crime $f'_{ij}(0)$, and in the case of nonworkers, the market wage w_{ij}, are unobserved. To solve this problem I assume that both the returns to the first hour of crime and the wage can be written as functions of observable explanatory variables and an unobservable disturbance term with a components-of-error structure. Thus I have:

(10.3) $w_{ij} = X_{1ij} \beta_1 + \beta_2 I_j + \mu_{1j} + \varepsilon_{1ij}$

(10.4) $pf'_{ij}(0) = X_{2ij} \gamma_1 + \gamma_2 I_j + \mu_{2j} + \varepsilon_{2ij}$.

The vector X_{1ij} contains market human capital variables and other determinants of the consumer's market productivity. The vector X_{2ij} contains criminal human capital variables which similarly determine the consumer's productivity as a criminal. The variable I_j is an immigration measure for the jth MA. The terms μ_{1j} and μ_{2j} are MA-specific effects that reflect components of variation in the labor market and the criminal environment, respectively, that vary between MAs but are common to all consumers within an MA. Substituting equations (10.3) and (10.4) into (10.2) leads to:

$$P(C_{ij} = 1) = P[X_{2ij} \gamma_1 + \gamma_2 I_j + \mu_{2j} + \varepsilon_{2ij} > X_{1ij} \beta_1 + \beta_2 I_j + \mu_{1j} + \varepsilon_{1ij}]$$
$$= P[\varepsilon_{2ij} - \varepsilon_{1ij} > -(X_{2ij} \gamma_1 - X_{1ij} \beta_1 + (\gamma_2 - \beta_2) I_j + \mu_{2j} - \mu_{1j})]$$
$$= P[\varepsilon_{ij} > -(X_{ij} \delta_1 + \delta_2 I_j + \mu_j)],$$

where X_{ij} contains all the elements of X_{1ij} and X_{2ij}. For elements of X common to X_1 and X_2, $\delta_1 = \gamma_1 - \beta_1$; for elements unique to X_1, $\delta_1 = -\beta_1$; and for elements unique to X_2, $\delta_1 = \gamma_1$. We also have $\delta_2 = \gamma_2 - \beta_2$, $\mu_j = \mu_{2j} - \mu_{1j}$, and $\varepsilon_{ij} = \varepsilon_{2ij} - \varepsilon_{1ij}$. Assuming that ε_{ij} is normally distributed with zero mean and unit variance, we arrive at our probit estimating equation:

$$(10.5) \quad P(C_{ij}=1)=\Phi(X_{ij}\delta_1+\delta_2 I_j+\mu_j) \quad i=1,\dots,n_j; j=1,\dots,m,$$

where Φ is the unit normal c.d.f., there are m MAs in the sample, and the number of individuals in each MA is given by n_j. The δ_1 and δ_2 terms are parameters to be estimated. The term δ_2 is proportional to the effect of immigration on the individual's participation in crime. Positive values for δ_2 indicate that immigration increases crime among young black men; negative values indicate that immigration decreases youth crime.

The MA-specific effect μ_j warrants some discussion. If μ_j is independent of both the immigration rate I_j and the person-specific regressors X_{ij}, then μ_j serves merely to reflect the dependence that may arise among observations within an MA because the immigration rate varies only at the level of the MA, whereas the outcome and the other regressors vary at the level of the individual. In the presence of such group dependence, the ordinary probit estimator yields consistent estimates of δ_1, and δ_2 but inconsistent estimates of their standard errors (Moulton 1986; Borjas and Sueyoshi 1994). For this reason, I report robust standard errors below that are consistent in the presence of such group dependence.

A more serious problem arises if μ_j is correlated with I_j, that is, if there are MA-specific factors that are correlated both with the level of immigration to the MA and with the level of crime committed by its residents. An example might be the level of law enforcement. In this case, ordinary probit methods yield inconsistent estimates of the effect of immigration on crime.

This problem can be solved with repeated observations on the same individuals. Pooling the incarceration data across time periods gives rise to within-MA variation in immigration, since immigration varies over time. With the pooled sample, therefore, I can treat the MA-specific effects as fixed, including a separate dummy variable for each MA. This removes the influence of any time-invariant MA-specific factors that may be correlated with both immigration and crime. This approach uses the temporal variation in immigration rates within each MA to obtain consistent estimates of the effects of immigration. I fit the reduced-form probit model given by equation (10.5) to the incarceration dummies as well as the income-from-crime dummy.

The Empirical Specification

As mentioned earlier, the variables in X_1 and X_2, and hence X, include determinants of the consumer's wage and returns to crime. Determinants of wages include such standard human capital measures as education and age (as a proxy for experience). I also include a marriage dummy and a union dummy to capture effects widely documented in previous analyses and the local unemployment rate as a measure of demand-side conditions in the local labor market. I measure these variables at the beginning of the period over which the outcome variable is constructed. In other words, I include 1979 values of education, age, marriage, union status, and unemployment in the models for the income-from-crime dummy and the 1979 to 1982 incarceration dummy, and 1988 values of these variables in the model for the 1988 to 1992 incarceration dummy.

Determinants of the returns to crime, in contrast to wage determinants, have received very little study. In other work using the NLSY, I have included measures of past involvement in crime, which act much as past labor-market experience in a wage regression to pick up the effects of learning-by-doing (Grogger Forthcoming). Unfortunately, those variables were constructed from 1980 crime module responses and hence are available only for the earlier crime outcomes.

One available measure that is time-invariant and hence useful for all the outcomes I analyze here is a dummy variable indicating that the respondent's brother is a criminal. This measure is available because the NLSY employed a household sampling frame and drew into the sample all youths in sampled households who fell in the target age range. Specifically, the variable labeled "Brother is a criminal" equals one if the respondent had a brother in the sample who was ever interviewed in jail, or who, in the 1980 crime module, indicated that he had earned money from crime in the past year or had ever been arrested, convicted, or jailed for a crime. The notion here is that having a brother who is a criminal may be a good way to learn the trade: he may provide information on techniques, targets, or means of avoiding police that raise one's returns to crime. Because only about one-third of the sample had brothers who had also been surveyed, I also include a "No brother" dummy in the regression to serve as a statistical control.

Table 10.2   Probit Coefficients from Baseline Specifications

	Dependent Variable		
Variable	Any Income from Crime in 1979 (1)	Ever Interviewed in Jail, 1979 to 1982 (2)	Ever Interviewed in Jail, 1988 to 1992 (3)
Education	−0.073 (0.028)	−0.133 (0.048)	−0.188 (0.028)
Married	−0.043 (0.381)	0.006 (0.449)	−0.502 (0.185)
Union	0.397 (0.144)	0.096 (0.239)	−0.456 (0.168)
Brother is a criminal	0.110 (0.195)	0.845 (0.276)	0.411 (0.176)
Unemployment rate	−0.015 (0.019)	−0.076 (0.040)	−0.043 (0.042)
Age	−0.022 (0.031)	0.133 (0.044)	0.026 (0.035)
lnL	−440.3	−141.2	−304.0
Sample size	742	854	897

Notes: Standard errors are in parentheses. In addition to the variables shown, all regressions include region dummies, a dummy equal to one if the respondent had no brother in the sample, and are missing value flags for the education and unemployment variables.

RESULTS

Baseline Estimates of the Determinants of Crime Participation

Although the primary focus of this study concerns the effect of immigration on crime, it is instructive to examine briefly estimates from crime-participation models that exclude the immigration variables. Results are presented in table 10.2. The effect of education is strongly and significantly negative across all three crime measures. Marriage has no significant effect on participation until the end of the sample period. Union effects are positive in the income-from-crime equation, insignificant in the early incarceration model, and then significantly negative in the later incarceration equation. The positive effect on the income-from-crime measure has been noted previously and may arise because young workers find that unionized shops provide better grounds for drug dealing or gambling rackets than nonunionized shops (Grogger Forthcoming). By the end of the sample period, the wage-enhancing effects of unionization dominate, reducing participation in crime. The criminal human-capital coefficient is positive in all three models and significant in both incarceration equations. Apparently, crime runs in families. The unemployment rate has a surprising negative coefficient in all three equations, though only one of them is statistically significant.

The age coefficient is negative, though insignificant, in the income-from-crime equation, positive and significant in the early incarceration equation, and insignificant in the later incarceration equation. All of these results are consistent with what is known about age-crime and age-incarceration profiles. Participation in crime generally peaks in the late teens, falling thereafter (Blumstein, Roth, and Visher 1986). The negative coefficient in the income-from-crime model is consistent with this widely observed pattern. Incarceration, however, peaks well after the modal age for crime participation, reflecting the fact that offenders with short criminal records generally get lighter sentences, whereas jail and prison terms are generally reserved for those with more extensive past involvement. This would explain the positive age coefficient in the early incarceration model. By the end of the sample period, however, all sample members range from their mid-20s to their mid-30s. The insignificant estimate in the later incarceration model indicates that, over that age range, the age-incarceration distribution is fairly flat.

In summary, most of the variables included in the crime-participation models perform roughly as expected for at least some of the outcomes. Of course, the focus of this study is not on these variables, but rather on the effects of immigration. I turn now to cross-sectional estimates of the effects of immigration on crime among young black males.ß

Cross-Sectional Estimates of the Effects of Immigration

Table 10.3 presents estimates of the effects of immigration on the three crime outcomes, using various measures of immigration. Each coefficient is from a separate regression; all are obtained by applying ordinary probit methods to equation (10.5). In addition to the immigration measure, each regression includes all of the regressors from table 10.2. The standard errors, enclosed in parentheses, are robust to arbitrary forms of groupwise dependence that may arise from the presence of multiple sample members in each MA.

Table 10.3   Cross-Sectional Probit Estimates of the Effect of
Immigration on Crime

	Dependent Variable		
Immigration Measure (×100)	Any Income from Crime in 1979 (1)	Ever Interviewed in Jail, 1979 to 1982 (2)	Ever Interviewed in Jail, 1988 to 1992 (3)
Male immigrants/males	−0.012	−0.038	−0.007
	(0.009)	(0.011)	(0.006)
	[−0.004]	[−0.003]	[−0.001]
Recent male immigrants/ males	−0.026	−0.058	−0.008
	(0.019)	(0.024)	(0.008)
	[−0.009]	[−0.005]	[−0.002]
Hispanic male immigrants/ males	−0.018	−0.057	−0.008
	(0.013)	(0.030)	(0.008)
	[−0.006]	[−0.005]	[−0.002]
Recent Hispanic male immigrants/males	−0.034	−0.091	−0.009
	(0.038)	(0.055)	(0.011)
	[−0.012]	[−0.008]	[−0.002]
Sample sizes	742	854	897

Notes: Each coefficient is from a separate regression. In addition to the immigration measure, each regression includes all the variables listed or mentioned in table 10.2. Standard errors are in parentheses; mean marginal effects are in square brackets.

Consider first the estimates in column (1), which are based on the income-from-crime measure. All of the coefficients are negative, suggesting that immigration serves to reduce crime among young black men. This is consistent with the notion that immigrants have a greater effect on the supply of criminals than on the supply of workers, and thus reduce the returns to crime by more than they reduce wages.

To measure the magnitude of this effect, I have calculated the mean marginal effects of the immigration variables, presented in square brackets. These numbers are based on the probit coefficients and express how a one-unit change in the immigration rate affects the probability of participating in crime. For example, the marginal effect of the broadest immigration measure, reported in the first row of column (1), indicates that on average, a 1-percentage-point increase in the ratio of male immigrants to males would lower the likelihood that a young black native commits crime by four-tenths of 1 percentage point. Equivalently, a 10-percentage-point increase in the male immigration rate would reduce crime among young black males by 4 percentage points.

Moving down column (1), we see that the immigration rates that capture the immigrant groups most likely to compete with young, particularly low-skilled blacks, such as recent or Hispanic immigrants, have slightly greater effects than the broadest immigration measure. The marginal effect of an increase in the ratio of Hispanic immigration is −0.006, 50 percent larger than the effect of the male immigration ratio. The effect of recent immigration is even stronger, three times the effect of male immigration generally.

An important caveat to the above discussion is that none of the results based on the income-from-crime measure is significant at conventional levels. In fact, the significance levels of the more specific immigration measures are lower than that of the most general measure, even though the effects of the specific measures are stronger. This is probably because the variance of the more specific measures is lower than the variance of the broadest measure, as seen in table 10.1. Based on the significance of these coefficients, the appropriate conclusion to draw would be that immigration has no effect on crime participation among young blacks.

The estimates based on the early incarceration measure, however, presented in column (2), are largely significant. Moreover, although the magnitudes of the coefficients differ between the two outcome measures, the marginal effects of the immigration variables are similar. The estimate in the first row indicates that, on average, a 1-percentage-point increase in the male immigration rate lowers the likelihood of incarceration among young black men by three-tenths of a percentage point. The pattern in the effects of immigration across the different immigration measures is similar to that in column (1) as well. Recent immigration has a greater negative effect on incarceration among black men than immigration measured more generally. The same is true for immigration by Hispanics.

The general conclusion to be drawn from the estimates in columns (1) and (2) is that the quantitative effect of immigration on crime participation is similar, regardless of how crime is measured. In both cases, a 10-percentage-point increase in male immigration is predicted to reduce crime participation by young black males by 3 to 4 percentage points. Using measures of immigration that focus on groups most likely to compete with young blacks raises the estimated effect of immigration.

Both of these crime measures are based on events that occurred during the early 1980s. The third measure, equal to one if the respondent was interviewed in jail between 1988 and 1992, is based on events that occurred roughly a decade later. Over that time, the sample aged by ten years, and a substantial number of new immigrants entered the country. Column (3) of table 10.3 presents estimates of the effects of immigration based on this later incarceration dummy. As with the earlier measures, all of the immigration coefficients are negative. The coefficients are all insignificant, however, and the estimated marginal effects are much smaller than those from columns (1) or (2).

In the context of the economic model of crime, this decrease in the negative effect of immigration is consistent with one of two explanations. First, immigration may have had a lesser negative impact on native wages in the early 1990s than it had in the early 1980s. Alternatively, immigration may have had a smaller negative effect on natives' returns to crime in the 1990s than in the 1980s.

This latter notion is supported by some recent findings by Butcher and Piehl (1995a). They report that earlier cohorts of immigrants are generally more likely to go to jail than more recent cohorts. They also find that immigrants who arrived in the 1970s were more likely to be incarcerated in 1980 than in 1990. If, for either reason, the pool of immigrants in the United States was sufficiently less crime prone in 1990 than in 1980, then their effect on the supply of criminals may have been lower in 1990 than in 1980, even though they were present in greater numbers.

Estimates with MA-Specific Fixed Effects

Of course, the negative immigration coefficients may not reflect the effects of immigration per se but rather of MA-specific effects that are correlated with both immigration and crime on the part of young black men. For example, if areas with higher levels of immigration employ more police on average, and police deter crime among young blacks, then the negative coefficients in the crime probits above may be spurious. In this section, I pool the data across the two incarceration measures. This allows me to include separate dummy variables for each MA in the regression, which control for all time-invariant MA-specific factors that are correlated with both crime and immigration.[5]

Table 10.4 displays the results.[6] In the first column are ordinary probit estimates from the pooled sample. These models do not include the MA dummies. For each of the immigration measures, the estimated coefficient is negative and lies between the estimates obtained from each of the separate samples. The *t*-statistic for the broadest immigration measure is −1.66; the other coefficients are less significant.

To include a particular MA in the fixed-effects regression, there must

Table 10.4   Probit Estimates of the Effect of Immigration on Incarceration from Pooled Sample

| | Dependent Variable: Ever Interviewed in Jail | | |
| | Specification and Sample | | |
Immigration Measure (×100)	Ordinary Probit; Full Sample (1)	Ordinary Probit; Sample for Which MA Fixed Effects Can Be Estimated (2)	Probit with MA Fixed Effects (3)
Male immigrants/males	−0.0108	−0.0184	−0.0057
	(0.0065)	(0.0070)	(0.0153)
	[−0.0015]	[−0.0027]	[−0.0008]
Recent male immigrants/ males	−0.0104	−0.0206	−0.0046
	(0.0084)	(0.0089)	(0.0147)
	[−0.0015]	[−0.0031]	[−0.0006]
Hispanic male immigrants/ males	−0.0116	−0.0229	−0.0081
	(0.0099)	(0.0111)	(0.0216)
	[−0.0016]	[−0.0034]	[−0.0011]
Recent Hispanic male immigrants/males	−0.0101	−0.0250	−0.0086
	(0.0127)	(0.0136)	(0.0209)
	[−0.0014]	[−0.0037]	[−0.0012]
Sample sizes	1751	1571	1571

Notes: Each coefficient is from a separate regression. In addition to the immigration measure, each regression includes all the variables listed or mentioned in table 10.2, plus a period dummy for observations drawn from the 1988 to 1992 period. Standard errors, robust to the dependence that arises from drawing multiple observations per household, are in parentheses. Mean marginal effects are in square brackets.

be variation in the dependent variable within the MA. Otherwise the probit method cannot estimate the coefficient associated with the MA's dummy variable, because the maximization algorithm attempts to drive the coefficient either to infinity or minus infinity, and the algorithm fails to converge. In the pooled sample, there were 43 MAs, accounting for 180 observations, within which the incarceration dummy did not vary. Column (2) reports the estimated immigration coefficients from ordinary probit models fit to the sample from which those observations have been deleted. The immigration coefficients are more negative than those obtained from the full sample, and nearly all are significant at the 5 percent level.

Column (3) reports estimates from the fixed-effects probit model which includes the MA-specific dummies. The immigration coefficients are an order of magnitude smaller than their ordinary probit counterparts. None of the estimates is even one-half the magnitude of its standard error.

The F-statistics that test for the significance of the MA-specific dummies ranged from 199 to 221, with 43 numerator degrees of freedom. Thus all were significant at arbitrary confidence levels. This indicates that there are indeed MA-specific factors correlated with both immigration and crime. It appears that those factors, rather than a causal link between immigration and crime committed by young black males, are responsible for the negative coefficients obtained in the ordinary probit models. Based on the fixed-effects estimates, I conclude that immigration has no effect, positive or negative, on crime committed by young black men.

CONCLUSIONS

Throughout most of American history policymakers and the public have feared that immigrants cause crime. In the early part of our history, jails and prisons indeed were occupied disproportionately by arrivals from overseas (Steinberg 1981). Evidence from the recent period, however, suggests that immigrants today are less likely to be found behind bars than natives (Butcher and Piehl 1995a).

Furthermore, my analysis has provided no evidence that immigrants cause crime among young black natives. Cross-sectional estimates show a negative correlation between immigration rates and crime; fixed-effects estimates that control for unobservable differences between cities show no association whatsoever. This finding is consistent with the repeated findings in the literature that immigrants have little effect on wages (see, for example, the Butcher and Reimers papers in this volume). The results from this analysis provide no reason to think that crime among immigrants is spilling over into the native population of young black men.

NOTES

1. Of course, immigrants also may demand stolen goods. Strictly speaking, in order for immigration to decrease the price of stolen goods, the supply effect must exceed the demand effect.

2. Although the discussion has focused on workers, the model also predicts that decreases in the wage or increases in the returns to crime tend to increase participation in crime among nonworkers.

3. I also analyzed a set of youth immigration ratios in which both the numerator and denominator were restricted to males between sixteen and thirty-four years old. Results based on the youth immigration ratios were nearly identical to those based on the broader measures reported below.

4. Only eighty-six of these MAs actually were home to any of the black men in my analysis sample.

5. One might be concerned that pooling across outcomes measured over exposure periods of different lengths would affect the results. To check, I constructed a dummy equal to one if the respondent was interviewed in jail between 1989 and 1992 and pooled it with the 1979–1982 incarceration dummy. Estimation results obtained using this alternative measure were nearly identical to those reported below.

6. The standard errors reported in this table are robust to the dependence that arises from including multiple observations from the same individual.

REFERENCES

Altonji, Joseph G., and David Card. 1991. "The Effects of Immigration on the Labor Market Outcomes of Less-Skilled Natives." In *Immigration, Trade, and the Labor Market*, edited by John M. Abowd and Richard B. Freeman. Chicago: University of Chicago Press.

Becker, Gary S. 1968. "Crime and Punishment: An Economic Approach." *Journal of Political Economy* 76 (March/April): 169–217.

Blumstein, Alfred, Jacqueline Cohen, Jeffrey A. Roth, and Christy A. Vischer. 1986. *Criminal Careers and "Career Criminals."* Washington, D.C.: National Academy Press.

Borjas, George J. 1985. "Assimilation, Changes in Cohort Quality, and Earnings of Immigrants." *Journal of Labor Economics* 3 (October): 463–89.

———. 1995. "Assimilation and Changes in Cohort Quality Revisited: What Happened to Immigrant Earnings in the 1980's?" *Journal of Labor Economics* 13 (April): 201–45.

Borjas, George J., and Glenn T. Sueyoshi. 1994. "A Two Stage Estimator for Probit Models with Structural Group Effects." *Journal of Econometrics* 64 (September/October): 165–82.

———. 1996. "Searching for the Effect of Immigration on the Labor Market." *American Economic Review* 86 (May): 246–51.

Butcher, Kristin F., and Anne Morrison Piehl. 1995a. "Immigration and Incarceration." Manuscript, Boston College (October).

———. 1995b. "Cross-City Evidence on the Relationship Between Immigration and Crime." Manuscript, Boston College (October).

Gallegly, Elton. 1992. "'Illegals' in Jail: A Double Slap to the Taxpayer." *Los Angeles Times*, August 16, 1992, p. M5.

Grogger, Jeff. Forthcoming. "Market Wages and Youth Crime." *Journal of Labor Economics*.

Hindelang, Michael J., Travis Hirschi, and Joseph G. Weis. 1981. *Measuring Delinquency*. Beverly Hills, Cal.: Sage Publications.

Jaeger, David A. 1996. "Skill Differences and the Effect of Immigrants on the Wages of Natives." Working Paper 273, BLS Working Paper Series, U.S. Department of Labor, U.S. Bureau of Labor Statistics, Office of Employment Research and Program Development (March).

LaLonde, Robert, and Robert Topel. 1991. "Labor Market Adjustments to Increased Immigration." In *Immigration, Trade, and the Labor Market*, edited by John Abowd and Richard Freeman. Chicago: University of Chicago Press.

Lauter, David, and Ronald J. Ostrow. 1993. "Mexico Prison Deal Is Linked to NAFTA Votes." *Los Angeles Times*, November 12, 1993, p. A1.

Los Angeles County. 1992. *Impact of Repeat Arrests on Deportable Criminal Aliens in Los Angeles County*. Los Angeles: Countywide Criminal Justice Coordination Committee, July 15, 1992.

Moulton, Brent R., 1986. "Random Group Effects and the Precision of Regression Estimates," *Journal of Econometrics* 32: 385–97.

Orebaugh, David A. 1922. *Crime, Degeneracy, and Immigration: Their Interrelations and Interactions*. Boston: The Gorham Press.

Ostrow, Ronald J. 1992. "Faster Deportation of Criminals Sought." *Los Angeles Times*, June 24, 1992, p. A3.

Sanderson, John P. 1856. *Republican Landmarks: The Views and Opinions of American Statesmen on Foreign Immigration*. Philadelphia: J. B. Lippincott and Co.

Steinberg, Allen. 1981. "The History of Immigration and Crime." In Select Commission on Immigration and Refugee Policy, *U.S. Immigration Policy and the National Interest*, Appendix A.

U.S. Bureau of Justice Statistics. 1992. *Correctional Populations in the United States, 1990*. Washington, D.C.: U.S. Government Printing Office.

U.S. Federal Bureau of Investigation., Various years. *Crime in the United States*. Washington, D.C.: U.S. Government Printing Office.

U.S. Immigration and Naturalization Service. 1992. *Statistical Yearbook of the Immigration and Naturalization Service, 1991*. Washington, D.C.: U.S Government Printing Office.

Wolfgang, Marvin E., Robert M. Figlio, and Thorsten Sellin. 1972. *Delinquency in a Birth-Cohort*. Chicago: University of Chicago Press.

PART III

IMPLICATIONS BEYOND THE LABOR MARKET

CHAPTER 11

Immigration and Native Minority Workers: Is There Bad News After All?

Marta Tienda

Well before econometric studies of the labor-market consequences of immigration became fashionable, Vernon Briggs (1973) warned that Mexican immigration makes poor Chicanos poorer by undercutting wages and displacing workers. Such warnings were dismissed by pro-immigration advocates who argued that foreign workers take jobs that native-born workers refuse. Briggs's position implied that immigrants and domestic minority workers were substitutes in production, while opponents argued that immigrants are complements in production, even in areas that receive large volumes of immigrants such as southern California and Texas. Until recently it appeared that Briggs was wrong, not only with respect to Chicanos, but also African Americans. This is because the vast majority of studies that investigated the labor-market consequences of immigration using 1970 and 1980 decennial Census data found little evidence of adverse impacts of immigration on domestic workers; that the most deleterious labor-market impacts were experienced by prior immigrants; and that women were stronger substitutes for male workers than immigrants (for comprehensive reviews of this literature, see Greenwood and McDowell 1986; Greenwood, McDowell and Hunt 1997). Yet, the puzzle of the declining economic fortunes of African Americans, despite their visible educational progress, implicated immigration as a contributing, if not the major, cause.

Three major trends justified revisiting the labor-market consequences of immigration. First, immigration accelerated during the 1980s, reaching a new post–World War II high. Of course, the U.S. economy is much larger and more complex now compared to the turn of the century. However, contemporary immigrants are more residentially concentrated than their predecessors at the turn of the century, and today's source countries imply greater racial diversification than was true historically. Consequently, contemporary immigration has dramatically transformed the ethnic landscape of several cities, including Miami (Portes and Stepick 1993) and Los Angeles (Waldinger and Bozorgmehr 1996) as well as the historic immigrant destinations of

Chicago and New York. Although none of the papers undertakes a case study of a heavy immigrant-receiving city, a plausible hypothesis is that the impacts of immigration differ depending on the volume and settlement patterns of new arrivals.

Second, wage dispersion between skill groups, which rose after 1973, increased during the 1980s as the returns to education rose appreciably. This is important because immigrants' educational composition also became more polarized during the 1970s and 1980s (Chiswick and Sullivan 1995). Because immigrants from Asia and Africa are positively selected on the basis of skill, and those from Latin America are negatively selected on educational attainment, recent trends in wage inequality imply very different fortunes for the two major "skill" groups. At a minimum, this well-documented trend warrants caution in drawing inferences about immigrants as an undifferentiated skill group. Although it is common to make blanket generalizations about immigrants as an unskilled labor flow, the skill distribution of immigrants reported by Borjas (this volume) reveals that immigrants are more dissimilar from blacks than blacks are from whites.

Third, the rise of persistent poverty and chronic joblessness in inner-city black ghettos rekindled the hypothesis that immigrants were competing with some groups of domestic workers, particularly minorities with low levels of education. Although the racial gap in education narrowed appreciably since 1960 (Mare 1995), educational disparities between Latinos and whites have persisted because unskilled immigration from Mexico, Central America, and the Caribbean continually replenished the low-educational segments of these populations (Mare 1995; Waldinger and Bozorgmehr 1996).

Despite the massive attention devoted to the problems of the urban underclass, there were no real policy breakthroughs and no answers about why new immigrants appeared to be more successful in the labor market than U.S.-born blacks. Massey and Denton (1993) identified residential segregation as the single most important reason for the worsened economic status of African Americans. Wilson (1987) emphasized the massive loss of jobs in central cities where African Americans were disproportionately concentrated. Wilson has not changed his position about the structural forces undergirding the rise of concentrated urban poverty, but his recent treatise finally acknowledged that immigration may contribute to the declining fortunes of African Americans (Wilson 1996). Still, his emphasis on mobility of capital, and thereby jobs, as the primary mechanism responsible for the declining fortunes of inner-city blacks leaves unanswered a fundamental question about why African Americans have not followed jobs to the suburbs. Massey and

Denton (1993) claim that the legacy of segregation and persisting discrimination prevents this option. Wilson claims it is lack of access to transportation. Yet, in Chicago, the site of Wilson's ideas and fieldwork, recent Mexican immigrants have infiltrated the manufacturing and service jobs inside and around the central city, and they have begun to spill over into the surrounding suburbs that experienced vigorous job growth during the 1970s and 1980s. For example, from 1970 to 1990, the outlying counties of the Chicago SMSA experienced a staggering 267 percent increase in nonmanufacturing jobs, compared to increases of 128 percent in the non-central-city part of Cook County. Comparable job growth within the city limits was a mere 20 percent.

Recent demographic trends have made Chicago a distinctly minority city: in 1990, over 40 percent of the city's population was black and an additional 20 percent was Hispanic. The population of Mexican origin remains the most educationally disadvantaged. In Cook County, the proportion of adults without a high school diploma declined from 40 percent in 1970 to just over 20 percent in 1990. Moreover, the educational level of Cook County's labor force rose faster than that of the adult Mexican population, such that by 1990 the share of adults without a high school education was nearly three times greater for the Mexican population than it was among all job holders. Based on these trends and in light of the rising returns to skill after 1973, one might predict that Mexicans would fare worse in the local labor market than blacks. Just the opposite occurred. Mexicans enjoyed the greatest increases in labor-force participation rates, which rose from 86 to 91 percent between 1970 and 1990 among men in their prime working ages, while labor-force activity rates of black and white men fell slightly or remained stable. In 1990, black men were unemployed at over twice the rate of men of Mexican origin. The distinctly favorable labor-market standing of men of Mexican origin, despite their lower levels of education, suggests that race presents barriers to labor-market opportunity that supersede group disparities in education. I belabor this point to underscore the continuing tension surrounding the exchange value of achieved characteristics, notably education, and ascribed characteristics, such as race, national origin, and nativity.

These anomalies speak to several issues addressed by the papers and others that are ignored. The major theme undergirding the studies is that the economic plight of African Americans dramatized by the emergence and growth of an urban underclass warrants further explanation. Although both Wilson (1987, 1996) and Massey and Denton (1993) downplayed the role of immigration in explaining the declining economic fortunes of African Americans, it is worth asking whether blacks would be better off in the absence of unskilled immigration. Prior studies implied that African Americans would not be much better off, if at all, had unskilled immigration been halted during the 1970s and 1980s. However, the papers included in this volume qualify this interpretation in substantial ways; at a minimum, they suggest that trends in wage inequality, inner-city poverty, and immigration warrant further scrutiny despite the rising consensus during the 1980s that immigration was not responsible for the plight of inner-city blacks. A focus on the distributional consequences of immigration, as Borjas has pursued, represents a significant advance over prior interest in wage and employment impacts.

Although Reimers, Butcher, and Borjas provide many useful new insights, clever methodological extensions, and innovative twists on previous findings, it is fair to ask whether the area approach has been sufficiently fruitful to warrant further extensions. Are its assumptions tenable, and is the restriction to four labor inputs plus capital adequate to tease out the relationships that the researchers want to untangle? If analysts were not constrained by estimation strategy, how many labor inputs would be needed to represent the spectrum of competing and complementary groups, and what are the relevant groups? How are gender, national origin, age, and skill balanced off one another in defining the labor inputs for such models?

At first blush it appears that the value added from area approaches is still positive, albeit small, just like the estimated net impact of immigration on the aggregate economy (Smith and Edmonston 1997). Still, these papers break new ground in different ways, even though they may not go far enough. One important contribution is their explicit focus on unskilled workers and African American workers. The extensive study of wage trends has generally concluded that skill-biased technological change may be responsible for the declining fortunes of unskilled workers, but the worsened labor-market position of black workers has not been well explained. Although several papers now indicate that unskilled immigration has had deleterious consequences on African Americans, it is also conceivable that the economic fortunes of black workers would have declined even in the absence of immigration. This counterfactual warrants further scrutiny. Another contribution of these papers is the consideration of women as an important force in the labor market since 1970. These considerations represent clear improvements over past studies, but in light of the conclusion by Borjas, Freeman, and Katz (1996) that inferences about the impact of immigration on domestic workers depend crucially on the level of aggregation of the analysis (for example, region, state, or SMSA), would it not be more productive to focus on specific labor markets to learn how and why unskilled immigrants often face better labor-market prospects than their better-educated domestic workers? Case studies of labor markets that have been heavily impacted by recent immigrant flows (for example, Los Angeles, Chicago, and Miami) would complement insights generated from econometric analyses that employ a production function methodology.

Reimers capitalizes on cross-MSA variation in changes in unskilled immigration to estimate wage impacts on native whites, Mexican Americans, and African Americans. She concludes that unskilled immigrants are substitutes for white and black dropouts, but that Mexican American dropouts are complements with unskilled immigrants in the labor market. Reimers speculates that this may reflect an "enclave" effect, whereby Mexican Americans may shelter Mexican immigrants in the labor market. While this post hoc explanation is plausible, it is not entirely convincing without more evidence that Mexican Americans in supervisory positions or those who are self-employed actually hire Mexican immigrants at higher rates than their Anglo counterparts. Also, Mexicans tend not to work in their neighborhood of residence, which is one important condition for an enclave to emerge. An alternative hypothesis is that immigrants are preferred workers for certain types of jobs—formerly agricultural jobs, but increasingly a wide variety of unskilled service jobs in urban labor markets (Smith and Edmonston 1997). Yet, suppose employers are indifferent between unskilled Mexican immigrant and Chicano workers but quite discriminating between them and white or black high school dropouts. Why would this be so? Unfortunately, this is not a question that can be pursued with Census data of any sort, but interviews with Chicago employers certainly support the hypothesis that immigrants (Mexicans in Chicago) are preferred workers to native blacks (Wilson 1996).

Perhaps the big lesson is that future researchers should attempt to unpack the demand side of the equation. In other words, are some jobs "typecast" as immigrant jobs, and if so, and how does this process evolve as the industrial composition of employment changes? Do employers make distinctions between Chicanos and Mexican immigrants or between Central American and Mexican immigrants when making hiring decisions, or is immigrant status a sufficient attribute to distinguish more- from less-preferred workers? And, might these distinctions become more fine-grained depending on the demographic composition of the work force of specific labor markets? More generally, will the lessons about the terms of competition among minority and immigrant groups differ in Los Angeles, San Antonio, and Chicago because of the distinct demographic profiles of these cities? Again, in-depth study of all labor markets that have been transformed by immigration seems warranted to answer these and related questions.

Butcher's chapter goes beyond most studies about the impact of immigration by including women, but her results are highly disappointing in that she finds *no* effects of immigration on changes in employment, weeks worked, hourly wages, or annual earnings of black men. The notable exception is the significant effect of immigration on the black-white earnings gap, which suggests a testable hypothesis—namely, that this effect may be driven by distinct patterns of employment instability among blacks and immigrants. Hsueh and Tienda (1995, 1996) have documented both appreciable race and ethnic differences in labor-force instability among both men and women and quite substantial annual earnings losses associated with intrayear episodes of joblessness. Blacks sustain the largest earnings losses from chronic joblessness, while Hispanics incur the greatest earnings losses from frequent jobless spells over the course of a year (Hsueh and Tienda 1995). If blacks and immigrants are unequally sorted into undesirable jobs, then it is also important to ask whether it is the marginal workers (unskilled) or marginal jobs (seasonal, unstable, and low-amenity jobs) that undergird Butcher's finding that immigrants increase the white-black annual earnings gap.

Both Hamermesh and Johnson consider aspects of this question, albeit in different ways. And their papers have great value added for what they accomplish, especially for opening up promising lines of inquiry about the nature of labor-market competition. Hamermesh's focus on amenity differences is original in a field that has become cluttered with repetition and marginal increments around the general topic of employment and wage competition. Although the two measures of amenities examined—shifts and injury rates—may not be the most important or best discriminators between good and bad jobs, the idea of documenting differences in the quality of jobs in terms other than wages promises new answers to the age-old question about whether immigrants take jobs that U.S. natives refuse. If this were so, Hamermesh claims, then we should expect immigrants to work less desirable shifts and in more dangerous jobs than U.S.-born whites and blacks. Hamermesh finds the opposite, namely that native-born blacks have the worst jobs as measured by these two amenities. And although he focuses only on employed blacks—those selected into the labor force—they work in more dangerous jobs and at less-convenient hours than comparably skilled immigrants. Hamermesh's lead on trying to pinpoint the working conditions that undergird wage and employment conditions is an important new direction for understanding the labor-market impacts of immigration.

Johnson's paper picks up on this theme in a different way by examining the occupational distributions of immigrants and blacks to determine whether and how much they may be insulated from competition by virtue of their segregation in the labor market. Although market-segmentation theory fell into disfavor during the 1980s largely over methodological quibbles, a focus on changes in labor demand invites reconceptualizing whether and how labor demand is coupled with ascriptive traits. Stated as a question, has labor demand become group-specific as well as skill-specific? If both jobs and demographic groups become "typecast" because of selective sorting and network recruitment into particular lines of work, then labor demand may become group-specific as well as skill-specific. This line of inquiry requires longitudinal data about network recruitment patterns and would be a welcomed addition to the study of labor-market competition and occupational segregation.

The study of occupational and industrial segregation has deep roots in sociology. During the 1970s and 1980s sociologists developed elaborate statements about occupational sex-typing and identified both positive and negative consequences. One positive benefit is that typing of jobs by ascriptive traits (gender, nativity, race) reserves slots for members of the preferred group. The downside, usually, is that group-typed jobs usually commanded lower wages. The causal mechanisms producing this result were never fully unraveled, although numerous researchers documented inverse correlations between wages and the gender (or immigrant) composition of occupations. A better understanding of the mechanisms that produce lower wages in jobs where women and immigrants are concentrated may help clarify why the econometric literature shows strong negative effects of recent immigration on earlier arrivals.

A revival of market-segmentation research that heeds the lessons and false starts of the earlier debates could shed some insight into these questions. Although they do not dwell on this point, both Hamermesh and Johnson's results are consistent with the idea that discrimination is a major reason for the poor labor-market standing of blacks. I would go further by insisting that *immigrants are preferred to blacks in many jobs*. It is not simply a matter of education or skill, because African Americans are English-speaking, whereas the majority of unskilled immigrants are from Spanish-speaking countries. Both scenarios imply considerable race and ethnic tension unless these trends are reversed by improvements in economic opportunities. Fortunately, the vigorous economic growth during the early 1990s appears to have provided some relief for potentially explosive intergroup relations.

REFERENCES

Briggs, Vernon M. 1973. *Chicanos and Rural Poverty*. Baltimore: Johns Hopkins University Press.

Borjas, George J., Richard B. Freeman, and Lawrence Katz. 1996. "Searching for the Effect of Immigration on the Labor Market." *American Economic Review* 86 (May): 246–51.

Chiswick, Barry R., and Teresa Sullivan. 1995. "The New Immigrants." In *State of the Union*, vol. 2, edited by Reynolds Farley. New York. Russell Sage Foundation.

Greenwood, Michael, and John McDowell. 1986. "The Factor Market Consequences of U.S. Immigration." *Journal of Economic Literature* 24(4): 1738–1772.

Greenwood, Michael, John M. McDowell, and Gary L. Hunt. 1997. *The Economic Consequences of U.S. Immigration*. Report prepared for the Organization for Economic Co-Operation and Development, Economics Department (February).

Hsueh, Sheri, and Marta Tienda. 1995. "Earnings Consequences of Employment Instability Among Minority Men." *Research in Social Stratification and Mobility* 14: 39–69.

———. 1996. "Gender, Ethnicity and Labor Force Instability." *Social Science Research* 25(1): 73–94.

Mare, Robert D. 1995. "Changes in Educational Attainment and School Enrollment." In *State of the Union*, vol. 1, edited by Reynolds Farley. New York: Russell Sage Foundation.

Massey, Douglas S., and Nancy Denton. 1993. *American Apartheid*. Cambridge, Mass.: Harvard University Press.

Portes, Alejandro, and Alex Stepick. 1993. *City on the Edge: The Transformation of Miami*. Los Angeles: University of California Press.

Smith, James P., and Barry Edmonston. 1997. *The New Americans: Economic, Demographic, and Fiscal Effects of Immigration*. Washington, D.C.: National Academy Press.

Waldinger, Roger, and Mehdi Bozorgmehr, eds. 1996. *Ethnic Los Angeles*. New York: Russell Sage Foundation.

Wilson, William J. 1987. *The Truly Disadvantaged: The Inner City, the Underclass, and Public Policy*. Chicago: University of Chicago Press.

———. 1996. *When Work Disappears: The World of the New Urban Poor*. New York: Knopf.

CHAPTER 12

What Does Labor Economics Contribute to Debates Over Immigration?

Richard B. Freeman

E conomic analysis offers three major insights into the perennial debate over the appropriate level of immigration into a society.

The first insight is that the benefits and costs of immigration are closely interrelated—two sides of the same coin, as it were. If the benefits to receiving countries from immigration are large, so too are the costs of immigration. If the costs are small, so too are the benefits. You cannot readily argue that immigration raises economic output without harming *some* native workers, nor, on the other side, that it harms some natives without improving the lot of others.

The second insight is that the economic effects of immigration depend critically on how immigration relates to trade and capital flows. In an open economy, trade or capital flows can substitute for immigration, so that changes in immigration may have little or no economic effects on the immigrant-receiving country. If the United States were to reduce immigrant flows, say to improve the incomes of low-paid native workers for whom immigrants are good substitutes, it might simply increase imports or investments overseas, offsetting the benefits to low-paid Americans of reduced immigrant competition at home.

The third insight is that the national social welfare function for assessing how immigration affects the well-being of natives depends significantly on factors beyond the effect of immigration on native incomes. Native assessments of the benefits of immigration to immigrants and of the effects of immigration on nonimmigrants in immigrant source countries, and native tastes toward cultural diversity, may readily dominate the social assessment.

INSIGHT ONE: BENEFITS AND COSTS ARE INTERCONNECTED

Much economic analysis, including Reimers and Butcher in this volume, examine the effects of immigration on native substitutes. Since immigration reduces the incomes of native substitutes and is thus a cost of immigration, it might seem to the outsider that economists are implicitly biased against immigration. If I devote my professional expertise to "searching desperately" for the impacts of unskilled immigration on low-skill Americans, you might wonder if I've got some bias against immigration. Where are the benefits? Why not devote similar professional effort to estimating the benefits of immigration?

In fact, there is no bias in the economic studies of the costs of immigration for the simple reason that the benefits and costs of immigration are intrinsically related. You don't get the benefits without the costs, and vice versa. Economists focus on the costs of immigration because the costs are potentially easier to identify in data. If the United States lets in one thousand Ph.D. mathematicians from Russia, the wages of native mathematicians are likely to fall. The costs to natives are simply the reduction in pay (or employment opportunities) to that well-identified group and are potentially observable in data. The benefits to the rest of society from having more plentiful and cheaper mathematicians are harder to find: how much did your income rise last year because of the influx of immigrant mathematicians? Economists look where the effects of immigration are most likely to be found.

Why are the benefits and costs of immigration intrinsically related? Essentially because of the interconnection between native workers and immigrants through the production process. Assume that national production is governed by a constant returns to scale production function $GDP = GDP\ (S,C)$, with $S =$ substitutes for immigrants and $C =$ complements. Letting MP_S and MP_C be the marginal product of substitutes and complements, respectively, constant returns implies:

$$(12.1) \quad GDP = MP_S\ S + MP_C\ C.$$

This implies that an increase in the number of immigrant substitutes has the following effect on GDP:

$$(12.2) \quad \Delta GDP/\Delta S = MP_S = S\ MP_{SS} + C\ MP_{SC} + MP_S.$$

where $MP_{SS} < 0$ is the fall in the marginal product of substitutes due to the supply of immigrants, $MP_{SC} > 0$ is the gain in the marginal product of complements due to the supply of immigrants, and Δ is the difference operator.

But this reduces to:

$$(12.3) \quad MP_{SS}\ (Sn + I) + MP_{SC}\ C = 0,$$

where $Sn =$ the native substitutes, and I are the new immigrants ($S = Sn + I$ after immigration). Then the change in the incomes of natives is:

(12.4) $MP_{SS} \, S + MP_{SC} \, C = - \, MP_{SS} \, I > 0.$

Equation (12.4) shows that the reduction in the pay of native substitutes that economists generally study (MP_{SS}) is directly related to the gain in pay of native complements with a proportionality factor depending on the size of the two groups (S/C). It also shows that native GDP rises from immigration. Standard economic analysis thus predicts that immigration is an economic plus to the country and immigration redistributes income in ways that are intrinsically related to the gain in native GDP. Native substitutes lose while complements gain (more) from immigration.

The model in equations (12.1) through (12.4) is the standard model of immigration. It has strong implications because it makes strong assumptions about the production process. Constant returns to scale is critical in making explicit predictions. Changing this assumption leads to more complicated analyses. If you believe that national production is governed by increasing returns, immigration would be even more beneficial to native GDP than indicated in equation (12.4) and might even raise the incomes of native substitutes. If you believe that congestion and environmental costs imply that national production is governed by decreasing returns, immigration would be less beneficial than indicated in equation (12.4) and potentially harmful even to native complements. The other key assumption is that immigrants substitute for at least some natives: if immigrants did work that no native would or could do (at any plausible wage), either because the immigrants are super-talented or willing to do jobs that no native would take, immigration would benefit all natives.

As there is little evidence for major deviations from constant returns to scale or for immigrants ending up in jobs that no native would undertake (see Hamermesh in this volume), the standard model is the standard by which most economists assess the economic effects of immigration.

INSIGHT TWO: THE EFFECTS OF IMMIGRATION DEPEND ON TRADE AND CAPITAL FLOWS

But there is more to the economic story. Assume that the United States reduced immigration to zero. Would this have the effects on native incomes indicated by the model in equations (12.1) through (12.4)? The model assessed immigration in isolation, as if the flow of people was the sole linkage between the United States and other countries. But there are linkages through trade and capital flows, and these linkages might very well compensate for the effects attributed to immigration in the model. Specifically, if immigrants could not come to the United States, where they compete with native substitutes in our job market, they might produce goods that compete with the output of native substitutes in their native countries, increasing the flow of imports to the United States. From the perspective of immigration, imports are simply immigrants "embodied" in goods. If business cannot hire immigrants in the United States, firms might set up plants overseas, reducing the capital-labor ratio in domestic production and raising it overseas, with similar effects on the demand for substitute native labor as immigration has on the supply of substitute labor.

In the standard factor–endowment model of international trade, capital flows, trade, and immigration are alternative ways to equalize factor proportions across countries. They produce the same income outcomes: factor-price equalization around the world in the strongest situation. If this model accurately predicted how the global economy affected us, analyses of the effects of immigration on the economy would be moot. Immigration would have no effects on our economy. Only the sum of immigration, trade, and capital flows would affect our economy, and the only way to control these effects (if we so wanted) is to control them all.

But the world is more complicated than the standard trade model. Trade, immigration, and capital flows are not perfect substitutes. Most trade is with advanced countries who have similar factor proportions as the United States. Traded goods are only a segment of what Americans consume. Most of our work force is in service jobs, the bulk of which cannot be traded. You buy goods, including imports, in stores located in your neighborhood, not in Calcutta, travel to the store on a U.S. transportation system, and so on. And there are even complications to capital flows. Many investors exhibit a home-country bias in their investment decisions: a U.S. firm will likely as not try to produce in the United States if it can, since it knows the society, has access to social capital, and prefers to conduct business in the dollars that its shareholders will spend on consumption goods.

While we lack a well-grounded analysis of the differences in the economic effects of trade, immigration, and capital flows, what we do know suggests that immigration will have larger effects on native workers than trade and capital flows. The reason is that native workers can "escape" the adverse effects of imports by finding work in nontraded sectors. Some foreign goods—such as bananas or cheap children's toys—are not produced in the United States. No American competes with low-paid foreign labor in these sectors. Low-skilled Americans who might have produced these goods are employed in nontraded services, such as flipping hamburgers in fast food restaurants. When we increase the imports of those goods, all Americans benefit and no one loses. Similarly, while some forms of capital can flow overseas (in fact the United States in recent years has benefited from net foreign investment in our country), you cannot build a supermarket for residents of Des Moines, Iowa, in Korea. Much capital is localized in the United States.

But there are no such natural limits on competition from immigrants. Immigrants can work in nontraded services that provide an alternative to low-paid Americans who face import competition. They can compete for the job in the local supermarket, even in Des Moines. Since immigrants can compete with natives in traded-goods sectors and in nontraded-goods sectors, they are likely to have a larger effect on natives than trade. The only jobs for which an immigrant cannot compete are president and vice president, which are limited to native-born citizens.

Thus it is likely that immigration has some independent effects on GDP and native incomes. But, given the possibilities for trade and capital flows, studies that focus on immigration effects by themselves probably overestimate both the costs of immigration to native substitutes and the benefits of immigration to native complements.

INSIGHT THREE: WHAT MATTERS MOST IN THE SOCIAL WELFARE FUNCTION

The most general framework for examining the pros and cons of immigration to the United States or any other country is a social welfare function that measures the well-being of current natives. This analysis necessarily differentiates between natives whose income rises from immigration (complementary inputs) and those whose income falls from immigration (substitute inputs). If natives care only about their own economic well-being, and if the social welfare function values the income of all natives equally (as does GDP, which is widely used as an indicator of broad economic well-being), the welfare analysis is simple. The welfare calculus judges immigration as good because the increased income of complementary inputs exceeds the decreased income of substitute inputs.

But if the social welfare function weighs the incomes of different groups of Americans differently, the welfare calculation is more complicated. It must consider the distribution of the change in incomes as well as the overall gain in native GDP. Immigrants to the United States from the 1970s through the 1990s have been disproportionately less skilled, so that the issue becomes one of weighing the increase in the income of the wealthy who benefit from immigration against the decrease in the income of the lower paid who lose from immigration. Democratic societies generally value the income of the lower paid more than that of the rich—one person/one vote puts a greater weight on well-being of the larger group (though the role of money in politics in the United States may be reversing this normal rule of democratic governments)—so that the dollar gains to the wealthy would be less important than the dollar losses to the poor. Immigration that increased Bill Gates's income by 10 million dollars while reducing the incomes of everyone else by 9 million dollars might be judged a social loss rather than a social gain.

Still, if natives cared solely about the incomes of natives (their own and those of others), the social welfare analysis of immigration becomes a "simple" exercise in income distribution and redistribution. Since immigration raises GDP, it is possible to redistribute income from winners to losers, implying that immigration plus some redistribution is likely to be in the interests of the entire society. But redistribution can be costly. Increased taxes on the rich will affect their labor supply or induce them to avoid if not evade taxation, causing a deadweight loss. Increased social benefits to the poor will affect their labor supply, also with potential deadweight losses. It may be more expensive to redistribute incomes post-immigration than to limit immigration. Alternatively, from a political economy perspective, the gains in income to the rich from immigration may increase their political power and ability to prevent any redistribution of incomes.

If economic studies found that immigration had massive effects on native substitutes and thus on national output, these distributional factors would dominate the social welfare function for assessing immigration. But nearly all economic studies find that immigration has only modest effects on income distribution and GDP. Borjas, Katz, and Freeman estimate a gain to GDP of about 3.5 to 9 billion dollars in a 7 trillion dollar GDP—or around .01 percent of GDP. The Panel on Immigration of the NAS-NRC gives a higher estimate of about 10 billion dollars. In this volume, George Johnson comes up with an estimate of just over 1 billion dollars. These studies differ in how much they postulate that immigration changes, and in the specific way they simulate the effect of immigration on GDP. But they all come up with numbers of similar magnitude—the sort of numbers that could easily be dwarfed by measurement error in GDP.

What, then, might dominate the social welfare function for immigration? The primary beneficiaries from immigration are immigrants and their descendents. A low-skilled immigrant to the United States might increase his or her family income by a factor of five to tenfold.

You earn two thousand dollars in Mexico or Nicaragua or the Dominican Republic and fifteen thousand dollars in the United States. In terms of the model of equations (12.1) through (12.4), the gain to immigrants is their marginal product or wage in the United States (MPS) minus their wage in their native country, which, given the U.S. lead in world production, is likely to be much lower. The immigrant's living standard is vastly improved, and his or her children become Americans and obtain the benefits of American schooling and culture. There are, to be sure, risks and dangers: crime is high in many poor U.S. communities where immigrants might live, and American culture has its problems, particularly in inner-city poverty neighborhoods. But that immigrants benefit greatly from immigration is a sine qua non for their coming to the United States. Immigrants who do not benefit can usually return to their native land, as perhaps a third of immigrants in fact do.

Assume for simplicity that each immigrant to the United States enjoys an income gain of ten thousand dollars. Then the six million or so immigrant workers who came since 1979 earn sixty billion dollars more in the United States than they would earn in their native countries. Even ignoring the benefits to their children, these figures dwarf the estimates of gains to native complements and native GDP. The big beneficiaries of immigration are immigrants.

But, you say, immigrant incomes do not enter the national social welfare function. Correct. We do not operate the United States for the benefit of noncitizens. But while immigrant incomes do not enter the welfare direction directly, they do enter indirectly *if* natives care about the well-being of immigrants. Think about the hard-working immigrant from Mexico who came to the United States to better his life and that of his family. How much do you value the improvement in his life that our country offers him? Even if you value it at just 10 percent as much as you value the income of a native American, this valuation will weigh heavily in the social welfare function, simply because that improvement is so big.

There is one other potentially important term in the welfare function. Some natives value immigration for its own sake, independent of its effects on their economic well-being or on the economic well-being of immigrants. Perhaps you find it unpleasant that immigrants look or talk differently from the way you do: "Just ride the N.Y. subways and you know our immigration policy is wrong." But perhaps you find diversity a pleasure: "N.Y. or L.A. or London would be dull without ethnic restaurants and celebrations and cultural events." Given that the effects of immigration on GDP are relatively modest, it doesn't take all that much independent demand for immigration for that term to play an important part in any welfare assessment. Finally, if natives care about the well-being of persons in countries that send immigrants, the effect of immigration on those people should also enter the social welfare function.

In short, there are several elements in any social welfare assessment of immigration, and some of these elements are likely to carry as much or greater weight in that assessment than the effect of immigration on GDP and on the distribution of income of natives.

CONCLUSION: THE MISSING PIECE OF EVIDENCE

Assume that we came up with an estimate of the social welfare effects of changing the number of immigrants coming into the United States and decided to act on this social assessment.

If our welfare assessment was that the country would benefit from more immigration, it would be relatively easy to effectuate such a policy. There are huge queues for entering the United States, and an announcement that we welcomed more immigrants would surely draw a big supply response from the rest of the world. We could easily implement a policy of increasing immigrant flows.

If our welfare assessment was that the country would benefit from reduced immigration of highly skilled persons, it would also be relatively easy to effectuate such a policy. Most highly skilled immigrants are socially visible and enter the country legally. Changes in immigration law could easily reduce the flow of skilled immigrants into the country.

But if, as is more likely, our welfare assessment was that the country would benefit from a reduction in less-skilled immigration, it would not be so easy to effectuate such a policy. Many less-skilled workers have come into the country illegally, and reductions in the legal flow of immigrants might simply induce greater illegal flows. Unfortunately, little is known (at least by economists) about alternative ways to control immigration, much less about the costs of these alternatives. More border police. Greater penalties on employers who hire illegal immigrants. Identification cards for citizens and legal immigrants. Electronic surveillance of borders. Until we have detailed information on the costs of different ways to limit unskilled immigration, even the best social welfare assessment of how various changes in the number of immigrants affect national well-being will not suffice to guide policy. So, at best, our job is just half done.

CHAPTER 13

Reflections on the Effects of Immigrants on African Americans—and Vice Versa

Peter H. Schuck

Most of the chapters in this book deal with the economic effects of immigration on African Americans, but as a lawyer I have little to contribute to that particular debate. Instead, I shall reflect on other possible effects that immigration may have on the native-born African American population. The book's subtitle uses the term "African Americans" to refer to American blacks. In common parlance, of course, this is perfectly conventional; we use these two referents pretty much interchangeably. But scholars do not always engage in common parlance, and when we discuss how immigration to the United States affects a group of people who have been citizens for at least six or seven generations and at the heart of American life (however marginalized by traditional law and practice) for much longer, it seems noteworthy, and not a little odd, that we classify them as "hyphenated Americans," as if they had just gotten off the boat or were only recently naturalized. (For purposes of this discussion, I shall use the term "hyphenated American," even though contemporary dictionaries and style manuals have dropped the hyphen in favor of the unpunctuated "African American.")

The vast majority of American blacks, after all, are neither immigrants nor the descendants of immigrants, at least as defined in the conventional sense of those who migrate voluntarily. (Recent black immigrants from the Caribbean are discussed below.) What do we mean by "voluntary migration"? Many distinctions seem appropriate. Immigrants have come here under a variety of compulsions, ranging from the slavemaster's bond and lash, to the refugee's fear of torture or persecution, to the landless peasant's fear of starvation, to the spouse's fear of family separation, to the computer programmer's fear of underemployment, to the investor's fear of confiscatory taxation. We show no disrespect in calling attention to the common feature of compulsion so long as we recognize, as we must, that each of these compulsions was different in its effect on the immigrants who were subjected to it and that some were far more cruel and dehumanizing than others. (It is chastening to realize both how controversial even this last observation can be and how much psychic and intellectual energy groups continue to in-

vest in such maudlin comparisons. To cite an extreme but perhaps revealing example, Daniel Jonah Goldhagen, in his recent book, *Hitler's
Willing Executioners*, argues that even slaves were treated as less "socially
dead" than Jews were in Germany during the Nazi period.)

Even if the distant ancestors of American blacks, brought here under the most brutal conditions, are nevertheless considered immigrants for some purposes, the fact is that no other immigrant group re-
tains its "hyphenated" status beyond the second or, at most, third
generation in America. By that time, the descendants are native English speakers, typically ignorant of their ancestral tongue. (Blacks, who
can only recover their ancestors' polyglot African languages through
the most strenuous exertions, are especially vulnerable to this shedding
of the original culture.) By the third generation, the hyphen is likely to
be more a functional construction of demographers, sociologists, and
Census officials than a reflection of some vestigial, deeply felt immigrant identity or consciousness to which the individual tenaciously
clings. Indeed, cultural historians have shown that many of the ethnic
"traditions" that the postimmigrant generations celebrate are actually
latter-day inventions.

Still, labels are symbolically important; they can also be psychologi-
cally revealing, especially about the labeler. They are even more revealing when people select the labels that they wish to have applied to
themselves. Black leaders often refer to the group as African Americans,
and the rest of us, who are anxious to latch on to any label that seems
authoritative and promises to avoid controversy or indignity, happily
go along with it. We do so even though only a small percentage of
blacks actually describe themselves as hyphenated Americans. For those
who do, the hyphen's reference to an ancient lineage may be a source of
some pride and satisfaction. But the referent may be considerably more.
This is a time when American social leaders and institutions transmit
increasingly clear signals that multicultural identities and primordial
ties are not only entitled to society's respect but may actually be channels to cultural leadership, perceived group legitimacy, and even political power. In such a milieu, the hyphen is even more attractive.

There is a certain poignancy in the fact that these identities and ties
are, for most of their invokers, likely to be somewhat contrived. The ar-
tificiality of blacks' conjuration of offshore roots is shared by that of
many other Americans who find ourselves, often to our dismay, thor-
oughly assimilated into American culture but yearning for something
more emotionally satisfying and authentic. But the mythic nature of
blacks' quest seems more poignant than that of most other groups. In
his forthcoming book, Jim Sleeper cites Harvard's (and Ghana's)

Kwame Anthony Appiah: "[w]e do not have a common traditional culture, common languages, a common religious or conceptual vocabulary. . . . [W]e do not even belong to a common race." Sleeper adds the important insight that "[p]recisely because [blacks] had not chosen to join this society, could not dominate it, and could not leave it, they had the highest possible stakes in redeeming its oft-stated, oft-violated ideal."

This brings us back to the persistent issue of the hyphen. Is it useful, at least for certain purposes, to think of American blacks as an immigrant group, like other immigrant groups in some respects but different in others? I have already alluded to the common experience of compelled migration, while noting that different compulsions exert different effects on the immigrants subjected to them. In another kind of convergence, American blacks, several generations after Emancipation and formal citizenship, shared the traumas of modernization and urbanization with most of the immigrants who migrated from traditional, rural societies to cities in the United States. In this sense, then, today's urban blacks are not as distant from this central aspect of the immigrant experience as their six generations of formal citizenship would suggest. Still another convergence is the slow but steady rate of social and economic progress that blacks, along with most immigrant groups, have experienced in the United States. Again, however, the disparities in the rates and patterns of mobility among different immigrant groups, and between those groups and American blacks, are at least as striking as the commonalities. Some immigrant groups have done better than blacks while others—Puerto Ricans, many illegal aliens, and certain refugee groups, for example—seem to be doing worse. Does the use of the term "African American" take some of the sting out of these comparisons, make the sting worse, or just make the comparisons that much more complicated?

A book concerned with the interaction of immigrants and American blacks has numerous salient and intersecting contexts which cannot be easily disentangled. The *policy* context is the most straightforward, in the sense that it presents discrete questions of obvious importance to policymakers and citizens concerning immigration's effects on Americans, including blacks. These questions can be investigated through more or less agreed-upon methodologies and yield answers that can be reported. The studies in this volume report answers to some of these questions: how blacks are affected by immigrant competition for secondary and postsecondary education resources, for housing, and for criminal opportunities; how immigration affects black self-employment; and the distributional impacts of immigration.

But the effects of immigration on blacks extend well beyond even these important issues to implicate virtually every area of public policy. The significance of these effects is magnified, of course, by the historically high levels of current immigration to the United States; legal flows are near the record levels reached early in the century, while the number of illegals residing here, now over five million, approaches or exceeds the best estimates of the number that resided here at the time when the 1986 law, with its employer sanctions and amnesty provisions, was enacted. The share of the foreign-born population in the United States is approaching 10 percent, twice the share in 1970.

The *political* context, which of course is an integral part of the policy context, has also been dramatically transformed within the last year. Immigration policy is very much on the collective minds of Congress and the public. Ample evidence of this is contained in the strong public support for new laws reforming the welfare system and the immigration enforcement system. Because each of these laws was debated in part in terms of how current immigration was affecting low-income blacks (the dominant assumption being that it was significantly harming them), each is part of the policy context in which the issues discussed by the conference papers are being debated.

The welfare reform legislation enacted in August 1996 expressed profound dissatisfaction with the conception of citizenship implicit in the contemporary welfare state, a dissatisfaction that is evidently far deeper and more widespread than most of us, including many astute politicians like Bill Clinton, had imagined. Immigrants were a major target of this dissatisfaction. Indeed, welfare-dependent immigrants, along with non-working mothers, came to symbolize for many Americans a flagrant breach of the social contract. Congress singled immigrants out for particularly harsh treatment for a number of reasons. The most obvious one is that as nonvoters they are politically vulnerable to shifts in political winds. This factor, however, is easily exaggerated; the pro-immigration lobby, after all, was powerful enough to defeat bipartisan legislation that would have reduced legal immigration below the levels established by the 1990 act. (The enactment of the expansionist 1990 act was itself testimony to the growing power of the diverse pro-immigration coalition in the face of public opinion that consistently favors reduced immigration.) There were other important reasons why these laws passed. Once the politicians had decided that welfare outlays must be severely reduced, immigrants were seen as competing in a zero-sum game with low-income Americans, including blacks, whom the public thinks should have higher claims on limited public resources than newcomers should. Moreover, reducing public benefits for immigrants was where much of the money for the desired budgetary savings could be found (à la Willie Sutton). Finally, immigrants on public assistance were seen to violate an explicit but previously unenforceable promise that they would rely on secure, identified sources of support in the United States rather than depend on public need-based programs. In short, the legislative outcome was overdetermined.

The political context also reflects the recent enactment of two far-reaching reforms of the Immigration and Nationality Act. The second, the Illegal Immigration Reform and Immigrant Responsibility Act of 1996, is only now going into effect. Compared to the legal regime that it replaced, this may be the most fundamental, indeed radical, restructuring of immigration enforcement and immigrants' rights in our history. Among other things, it eliminates the ancient distinction between exclusion and deportation; severely restricts judicial review of enforcement actions and challenges to INS practices; greatly limits the relief from deportation available to aliens; requires the detention, often for long periods or even indefinitely, of illegal aliens and of legal aliens who have been convicted of crimes in the United States; and provides for summary exclusion of most documented asylum seekers.

The political convulsions that fueled these radical statutory changes have profoundly altered the *legal* context as well. Congress has struck a radically new balance among the competing values of national sovereignty, state initiative, substantive equality, and procedural due process. Litigation is already testing the constitutional validity of these arrangements in an entirely novel legal setting, one in which Congress has adopted an explicit policy preference requiring discrimination against aliens in federal programs and further authorizing and in some cases mandating the states to adopt this discrimination in their own programs. These new policies have set the stage for major constitutional debates that only the Supreme Court can ultimately resolve.

There is, moreover, a new *ideological* context for these debates. I am struck by the growing convergence of liberals and conservatives on the proposition that the fuller integration of blacks into the mainstream of American life is essential to both the future of American democracy and the flourishing of liberal values. The persistent pathological social conditions that many conservatives and others ascribe to a culture of poverty and associate with some low-income blacks—violence, crime, drugs, family dissolution, urban decay, welfare dependency, inadequate job skills, teenage pregnancy, and the like—are increasingly seen to pose profound threats to the quality and security of the suburban middle-class life that most Americans now lead, and to worsen the genuinely dangerous conditions of life in urban ghettos.

There is little agreement, of course, either on the ultimate causes of these dire conditions or on the particular policy approaches that might ameliorate them. But the bitter political divisions over affirmative action, welfare policy, and the ingredients of a balanced budget should not obscure the fact that a larger ideological convergence is occurring. More politicians seem to agree that these conditions are endangering our society's future and that current social policies are not solving the problem and may well be aggravating it. Liberals, exemplified by the coalition of forces supporting Bill Clinton's election and reelection, increasingly accept the traditional conservative position that generating sustained economic growth is as important (or more important) to durable progress among blacks than redistribution through entitlements. Mainstream conservatives, exemplified by the coalition that supported George Bush and Bob Dole in the last three presidential elections, increasingly accept the legitimacy of traditional antidiscrimination laws, acknowledge many of the social gains wrought by the civil rights revolution that some of them had earlier opposed, and support legal immigration in part in the belief that it tends to advance, rather than retard, black progress by spurring economic growth.

Finally, the issue of immigration's impacts on blacks arises in a distinctive *economic* context. There is widespread agreement (buttressed by George Borjas's study here) that legal immigration increases aggregate social welfare, especially in terms of economic growth and urban revitalization, and that illegal aliens pay and generate more in taxes than they take out in services, although a severe fiscal mismatch exists between the net gains of the federal government on the one hand and net losses of certain states and localities on the other. What is far more debatable are the distribution of the net economic benefits that immigration produces and the distribution among particular groups, especially low-income blacks, of the job displacement and other costs. Borjas provides some good theoretical reasons for predicting that these costs are especially high for blacks. As I indicate in the final section of my comments, blacks themselves have traditionally been convinced that this is so.

In order to gain a more refined understanding of how immigration affects American blacks, it is imperative that the two categories—immigrants and blacks—be disaggregated as much as the data permit, which unfortunately may not be very much. Caroline Hoxby's analysis usefully distinguishes among three types of immigrants—those who have become naturalized U.S. citizens; legal permanent resident aliens; and other aliens—but much more unpacking is needed if we are to understand how immigration affects natives, including blacks.

Immigrants are an exceedingly diverse category. Consider some of the variables that can plausibly be expected to affect their social behavior and economic performance. Their *legal status* is critical, as is their *skill level* and *English language fluency* at the time of entry. Although a surprisingly small percentage of legal immigrants are selected for their skills, even those admitted in family unification categories are likely nonetheless to enjoy a number of advantages over illegal aliens. But the often significant differences that exist among skills-based, family-based, refugee, "diversity," and investor admissions suggest that the legal immigrant category itself needs further disaggregation. An immigrant's *time in the United States* and *age* are also correlated with important performance-related variables: English fluency; social ties; job skills and continuity; income; ability to convert illegal into legal status; and so on. *Locality in the United States* also affects immigrants' progress because of geographical differences in economic conditions, concentrations of labor-market competitors, public benefit levels, and so on. The *racial-ethnic group* to which an immigrant belongs is also correlated with the economic performance and rate of assimilation of its members, as is the immigrant's *nationality group*. Again, these groupings are broad enough to conceal important intragroup differences. Immigrants differ significantly in their *utilization of public benefits* and indeed in the particular public programs in which they participate. The *political resources* available to immigrants also vary and may affect their progress, albeit in complex ways.

Like immigrants, American blacks are a highly diverse group. The differences among them, moreover, can be quite relevant to the ways in which they are affected by immigration. An important variable is *nativity*. Many American blacks, now naturalized, were immigrants or the children or grandchildren of immigrants. At least 6 percent of blacks in the United States—more than two million people—are of black, non-Hispanic, Caribbean origin. About 86 percent of them are foreign born, half live in New York City, and two-thirds are West Indian. For many decades, sociologists have been studying Caribbean-born blacks and comparing their culture and economic behavior with that of American-born blacks. The recent work of Orlando Patterson, Mary Waters, and Philip Kasinitz, like earlier studies, finds significant differences in educational achievement, family structure, political behavior, and occupational mobility between the two groups. Indeed, Waters's current research finds striking differences between these groups *in the same workplace*. Another study, by health researcher Selma Taffel, reveals that the incidence of low birth weight is much higher for native blacks than for foreign-born ones, even after controlling for the mother's socioeconomic status.

The greater success of foreign-born blacks as a group thus raises difficult but important questions about the role of racial discrimination in explaining group differences in achievement, about the nature of competition and conflict within racial groups, and about the ways in which immigration selects for, and in turn shapes, certain aspects of character and behavior. But even this distinction between foreign-born and native blacks is still too crude. For even within the category of Caribbean-born blacks, the researchers find important differences in achievement between the first wave (late nineteenth and early twentieth centuries) and the second wave beginning in the 1960s. Indeed, as Patterson has recently emphasized, this second wave is notably more complex in social origin than the first wave, in that it draws from both extremes of the islands' talent pool rather than simply from the elite. Ideally, it too would be disaggregated for analytical purposes.

Age is another revealing variable. Most older black Americans who entered the work force during the era of Jim Crow reflect the low educational and occupational attainment so tragically characteristic of that period and carry the psychic scars inflicted by pervasive discrimination. The legacy of racism was impounded in their limited education and job mobility until they reached an age when it was too late to rise much above it. The mobility of young blacks who have attained maturity during the last twenty-five years, when their high school completion rates have begun to equal or exceed those of whites and when many have received postsecondary education, is not constrained to nearly the same extent. This is particularly true of black women, whose occupational and income levels now exceed those of their white (and black male) counterparts on average.

Class, of course, is always a powerful variable in predicting almost anything of policy interest, including how people will be affected by immigration. This is perhaps especially true of American blacks. The rapid growth of the black middle class during the post–World War II period has been a striking feature of American social change. Among young intact families, blacks have essentially achieved parity with whites in income (although not in wealth), a remarkable achievement given their vastly inferior position only a short time ago. And though still vulnerable to discrimination, most notably in housing, many blacks have acquired new class interests that separate them from those whom they left behind in the inner city. These upwardly mobile blacks, like their white class counterparts but unlike many lower-income blacks, have important economic stakes in increased immigration, which tends to increase their wealth without threatening their jobs. Indeed, immigration probably increases their job opportunities on balance, especially since they disproportionately are public employees who provide a variety of education, health, welfare, and other social services to immigrants. One result of this class differentiation among blacks is that their positions on immigration issues have become more diverse, making it even more difficult to speak with a unified political voice and preserve group cohesion.

With respect to both immigrants and blacks, it is likely that the main social forces driving differentiation within these two groups are gaining additional strength. The legal immigration stream is increasingly diverse in terms of national origins; indeed, the 1990 act established an explicit "diversity" program of fifty-five thousand annual admissions for immigrants from low-admissions countries. Legal immigrants in recent decades have traditionally resided initially in a relatively few metropolitan areas. Although this concentration certainly persists, we may see more residential changes in the future as immigrants mimic the pronounced mobility patterns of Americans. The 1996 legal reforms are likely to increase the number of immigrants in illegal status in the short term; it is more doubtful whether these changes will succeed any more than their predecessor reforms did in reducing illegal migration in the long term. Moreover, the gender and age composition of the illegal immigration stream appears to be becoming more diverse, as more women and children enter illegally to join their families in taking up residence here.

For American blacks, the engine of future differentiation is also powerful. It is fueled by growing residential mobility to the suburbs (although it is still much lower than that of other ethnic groups at comparable levels of income), the persistent deterioration of conditions in the inner cities from which higher-income blacks are desperately seeking to flee, steadily rising intermarriage rates, and the continuing educational and economic progress being achieved by most young blacks, especially females. This latter progress is occurring notwithstanding the disturbing evidence in the chapters by Julian Betts and, to a lesser extent, by Caroline Hoxby that immigration may be reducing educational attainments among native minorities below the levels they would otherwise reach.

My final reflections identify some issues that have not been addressed here but which may help to constitute a future research agenda for social scientists concerned about immigration's impacts. Broadly speaking, I wish to note three categories of questions. First, immigration affects blacks in some important ways not discussed in the chapters of this volume, which of course properly focus on certain policy domains and not others. Some of these effects are impossible to measure yet are exceedingly far-reaching. Several deserve special mention. Second, we must ensure that these authors' preoccupation with the obviously critical question of how immigration affects American blacks does not obscure an equally or perhaps even more important question for the future: how immigration is affecting Americans of Latino (particularly Mexican and Central and South American) descent. Finally, we should turn the theme of the studies around and inquire into how American blacks are affecting immigrants, not just the reverse.

Immigration has profoundly affected the public's attitudes toward the pathological social conditions that afflict many low-income black communities. The common but dramatic chronicles of immigrant progress in the United States have inspired Americans' admiration for immigrants in general (and their own immigrant ancestors in particular). A central element of the immigrant mythos is the belief that millions of immigrants confronted racial discrimination, religious intolerance, an unknown language, family separation, and grinding poverty, yet through hard work, sacrifice, and suffering managed to enter the American mainstream within a few generations without relying on special favors from either government or markets. It is also a basic motif in our popular culture and public philosophy.

This view of the immigrant experience tends to undermine the group claims and status of American blacks by engendering group comparisons. This discourse of group comparison occurs in many different venues: among political elites or ordinary citizens, through the writings of scholars or those of journalists, in polite company or on freewheeling radio call-in shows. Such comparisons often focus on the most sensitive topics, including economic status; attitudes toward school, work and welfare dependency; family values and stability; crime and violence; entrepreneurial spirit; and labor-force attachment. Those making the comparisons share a strong normative consensus, a conventional ideology of group behavior that holds that all social groups should be held to the same standards of public and private rectitude and accomplishment that other groups are thought to have met in the past.

How does a pluralistic, individualistic society think and talk about groups and their differences? Broadly speaking, we might distinguish between two approaches to analyzing group differences: social science and folk wisdom. Social scientists, of course, methodically gather, analyze, and report large bodies of data bearing on group and subgroup achievement, attempting to control for those socioeconomic factors that correlate with, but do not necessarily cause, observed differences in achievement. The results of such analyses often show quite dramatic disparities among different groups in their levels of achievement.

Specifically, they tend to show that American blacks as a group have not done as well as most immigrant groups (although, as noted earlier, they have done better than some), "doing well" being defined here in terms of conventional indices of social status and behavior.

Even the best social scientific analyses, however, are likely to be uncertain in their ability to support firm comparative conclusions. Suppose we control for intergroup disparities in education, the variable most highly correlated with income, and find that income differences largely disappear. This finding hardly resolves the dispute over the causes of group differences in socioeconomic achievement. Education level, even more than most control variables, reflects human choice; it is a costly investment in human capital that invites value judgments rather than muting them. Indeed, Americans value this choice so highly that we view groups that have made it as being more socially and morally praiseworthy than those that have not.

But education level is shaped by more than autonomous choice; it is also *socially* determined to some degree, reflecting discrimination's effects on the student's family stability, self-image, and aspirations. Thus the fact that some recent immigrant groups, notably Asians, attain higher education levels than blacks only raises another set of questions. One such question—the extent to which a better-educated group possessed this advantage before its members came to the United States—can be answered empirically. Other questions, however, are harder to resolve. If the members of an immigrant group did not bring their educational advantage with them but acquired it here, did they face obstacles to educational attainment comparable to those that discrimination created for blacks? How much does discrimination actually affect educational choices? Why does a history of having suffered discrimination seem to spur achievement for some groups more than others? (Such differences are indicated by Thomas Sowell's studies covering an enormous range of societies across time and space.) Why are the performance differentials *within* groups often even greater than those between and among groups?

Where social science is inconclusive on such questions, folk wisdom often speaks with smug clarity. Impressionistic, anecdotal, and subjective, folk wisdom seems authenticated by vivid personal experience and emotional engagement. For precisely these reasons, of course, it also carries higher risks of bias, overgeneralization, and other sources of error. Folk wisdom tends to stress cultural-attitudinal explanations for group differences rather than demographic or historical ones. This emphasis tends to make the comparisons more morally charged and invidious, since folk wisdom often assumes that values are simply matters of choice.

It is significant, then, that social scientists, who appreciate how deeply embedded values can be, are increasingly converging on cultural-attitudinal explanations. This turn toward cultural explanation is observable not only among liberal sociologists like Christopher Jencks and William Julius Wilson and more radical commentators like Cornel West, who might be expected to find a focus on group values congenial. Economists, who usually prefer "harder" variables, also seem to be finding a larger role for irreducibly cultural explanations of behavior. Thomas Sowell, Robert Frank, Richard Posner, and Robert Shiller are among those who come first to mind.

Regardless of how and by whom group comparisons are made, they will certainly become more common in public and private discourse. Pressed into political service by the newer, more mobile immigrant groups who wish to fortify their own competitive positions against blacks, these comparisons will probably also be more pointed. As their political influence grows, for example, Asians and other groups whose immigrant ancestors also faced virulent racial discrimination here and who bear no group responsibility for black slavery or subordination may be somewhat less sympathetic to traditional affirmative action claims, especially when these claims conflict with their own claims based on their own deeply felt sense of group victimization.

The immigrant mythos, then, presents a particularly cruel paradox to black demands for race-based preferences: such demands invite the very group comparisons that increasingly discredit those demands in the public mind. When a group demands an entitlement qua group—whether that entitlement be for affirmative action, for legislative districting that protects group members from political competition, or for public benefits—it calls attention to its underlying claims about the group's uniqueness, moral desert, lack of opportunity, and achievement. Other groups that feel themselves disadvantaged by the preferential policies that such claims purport to justify are bound to reflect on their own group experiences and find them at least as deserving of preferment. In a meritocratic society that glorifies upward mobility and economic success, group claims necessarily lead to group comparisons, which in turn underscore group differences in achievement. In this way, black calls for group preferences have given such comparisons, long a staple of private conversation, greater salience, visibility, and legitimacy in the public domain as well.

The importance of studying Latinos is so obvious that I can be very brief. According to a recently released Census Bureau report, Hispanic Americans will outnumber blacks and become the largest minority group by the year 2005. Beginning in 2020, more Hispanic American children will be added to the population each year than blacks, Asian Americans, and American Indians combined. Hispanics will also have the lowest death rate by virtue of their relative youth.

The Hispanic grouping, of course, is the most polyglot, hence the most analytically meaningless, of all. (Latinos is only slightly better, but it is not an official Census grouping.) But precisely because of its diversity, its component elements—especially Mexicans, who now number more than 7 million, constitute almost two-thirds of the total, and are also the fastest growing subgroup—deserve discrete study. For example, some of Frank Bean's findings concerning the educational trends among Mexican immigrants and Mexican-origin Americans are extremely disturbing. School completion rates for Hispanic youngsters continue to be low, even when compared to blacks of comparable income level. The RAND study on the economic mobility of different nationalities also documents dismaying trends for some of the Hispanic subgroups in the United States.

Although these studies are properly concerned with how immigrants affect blacks, it is equally important to investigate the effects of blacks on immigrants. Many of the studies in this volume confirm that frequent and momentous interactions between these groups are inevitable. For example, Jeffrey Zax's paper shows that new immigrants tend to reside in areas of high black concentration, a circumstance that he views optimistically as "bad for ghettos" and thus good for blacks, while George Borjas maintains that immigrants and blacks possess similar occupational skills and thus tend to compete for the same jobs. Such interactions, of course, are bound to exert influences in both directions. Of the many effects of blacks on immigrants, I shall mention only two here. They concern how black Americans' attitudes toward immigration affect U.S. immigration politics and policy, and how certain deviant aspects of black lower-class culture affect immigrants' children (the second generation).

In tracing the reactions of black leaders, media, and public to immigration throughout American history, Lawrence Fuchs has documented a consistent pattern (until the 1980s) of determined opposition, primarily because of immigrants' competition for jobs at the bottom of the economy but also, at least well into this century, often on grounds that we would now condemn as racist. Black spokesmen from Frederick Douglass to Booker T. Washington vigorously opposed immigration, whether by whites, Asians, or Mexicans. Blacks were among the strongest supporters of the infamous Chinese Exclusion Act of 1882 and of the restrictions that in the 1920s took the form of the national origins quotas that prevailed until 1965.

For a variety of reasons, black leaders' hostility to immigration softened by the 1980s as they desperately attempted to nurture coalitions with Latino groups that were firmly opposed to employer sanctions and other immigration restrictions and that strongly supported amnesty for illegal aliens. Fuchs, who was director of the Select Commission on Immigration and Refugee Policy that reported to Congress in 1981, notes that the black congressional caucus supported the Mexican American leadership on every major vote despite substantial sentiment among American blacks against legalization and for employer sanctions. Equally interesting, however, black leaders showed little interest in influencing policy on legal immigration and did not even advocate expanding black immigration from the Caribbean, partly reflecting the long-standing pattern of tension between native and immigrant blacks.

Although Fuchs's account, which ends in the late 1980s, points out that black attitudes toward immigration had become more favorable (and were more favorable than those of whites), he doubted that this represented a permanent change. The large increases in immigration that have occurred during the last decade may have increased black opposition, tending to restore the more traditional pattern. Peter Skerry, for example, notes that almost half of the black voters in California supported Proposition 187 in 1994 despite the black leadership's categorical opposition to the measure, and that Governor Pete Wilson, who made Proposition 187 a centerpiece of his campaign, won 20 percent of the statewide black vote, twice the historic level of black support for Republican candidates. With the Asian and Latino populations growing more rapidly than the black cohort, we are likely to see more political conflict with blacks over legislative redistricting and the remnants of affirmative action, as well as more intense competition in the more traditional areas of jobs, housing, and public resources.

The last issue concerns the second generation. Some sociologists of immigration point to a dynamic of cultural transfer. In this pattern, first- and second-generation immigrants, particularly second-generation children, are inducted into American subcultures that transmit some of the subcultures' social pathologies to the newcomers. In this way, dysfunctional behavior that is relatively rare in the country of origin may, with exposure to these subcultures, become more common among immigrant children as they seek to mimic what they perceive as the American norm. Alejandro Portes and his colleagues describe this as a downward or "segmented" assimilation process in which new immigrants locate in areas that bring their children into close contact with native minorities. Influenced by the native children's seductive street culture, many immigrant children acquire a cluster of self-defeating attitudes and behaviors, including negative views of education that contrast sharply with the optimism and socially adaptive strategies that immigrants usually bring to the United States and seek to transmit to their children. According to Portes, "[t]he confrontation with the culture of the inner-city places second generation youth in a forced-choice dilemma: to remain loyal to their parents' outlook and mobility aspirations means to face social ostracism and attacks in schools; to become 'American' means often to adopt the cultural outlook of the underclass and thus abandon any upward mobility expectations based on individual achievement."

Portes and his colleagues claim to find support for this theory in comparing Cuban, Haitian, Sikh, and other immigrant communities in south Florida and California. They find that different immigrant communities evolve various strategies for insulating their children from this threat, which the immigrants associate with menacing black and other native underclass cultures, and that some of these protective strategies are more successful than others. If these sociologists are correct (their research is ongoing), then this may indeed be the most important immigrant-black interaction of all.

CHAPTER 14

Reflections on Family Issues in Immigration

Linda Datcher Loury

Increasing interest in the effects of immigration on native blacks and Hispanics largely results from recent growth in the numbers of immigrants, concerns about competition between these groups, and speculation about the influence of the immigrants on the socioeconomic environment in which many blacks and Hispanics live. Five studies in this volume provide considerable insight into these questions in the areas of criminal behavior, residential segregation, self-employment, and education. One general conclusion that can be drawn from examining the results is that a complete understanding of the consequences of immigration requires both disaggregated, detailed analysis as well as an aggregated broad overview of its effects.

Disaggregation is important in three respects: which native-born groups are the focus of analysis, which types of immigrants have an impact on natives, and which geographic areas are examined. A more disaggregated, detailed analysis along these lines is required for both conceptual and statistical reasons. On the statistical side, focusing on more detailed trends or changes reduces the degree to which results are contaminated by spurious correlation between immigration and the outcomes of interest. Several examples illustrate the importance of this issue. First, Grogger focuses on the effects of immigration on crime comparing native blacks and Hispanics. Theoretically immigration could either increase crime by reducing the wage of low-skilled native workers thereby making crime more attractive. On the other hand, it could reduce crime by increasing the supply of criminals and correspondingly lowering the return to criminal activity. Grogger's initial analysis uses variations in recent and Hispanic immigration across metropolitan areas to determine whether crime is smaller among blacks in MAs with limited immigration compared to similar blacks in MAs where immigration is much more substantial. He finds that these cross-section estimates imply that immigration serves to reduce the likelihood of incarceration among young black men. This suggests that immigration increases the relative supply of criminals and thus lowers the payoffs that blacks receive from criminal activity.

376

Grogger's second analysis makes use of repeated observations on the same individuals over time and examines how individuals within a given MA change in response to variations in immigration in that MA over time. This procedure disaggregates geographically to control for unobserved differences across MAs that might affect both crime and immigration. For example, MAs with more immigration may also hire more police. In this case, a negative correlation between native crime and immigration is not due to immigration itself but instead results from a greater police presence. The results of doing this more detailed analysis show that the effects of immigration on crime are insignificant and much less than the original estimates. Grogger concludes that the more aggregated approach that fails to take into account unobserved differences between metropolitan areas provides a misleading view of the effects of immigration on crime, and that there is no evidence that immigration has an effect, positive or negative, on crime committed by native blacks or Hispanics.

Betts studies whether immigration affects the high school completion rates of native blacks and Hispanics. As in the case of Grogger, the theoretical effects are ambiguous. Immigrants may increase the benefits of education by lowering the wages of low-skilled workers and thereby raise the returns to schooling. They may, on the other hand, reduce school resources available to native students. Also, as in the case of Grogger, Betts begins with the results of a cross-section analysis that relies on differences in immigration between states to determine its effects. These cross-section estimates imply that immigration *increases* the proportion of native-born blacks and Hispanics who graduate from high school. Betts then reports the results of adding state and time dummies to his analysis. With these additions, the new estimated effect of immigration is disaggregated to capture the consequences of within-state changes between 1980 and 1990 rather than overall differences across states in the levels of immigration. Betts now finds that the effects of immigration are large, *negative*, and significant. Thus, while the aggregated estimates imply increased schooling for blacks and Hispanics, the disaggregated estimates point to substantial reductions in native schooling due to immigration.

Fairlie and Meyer examine the effects of immigration on self-employment. Following a slightly more complicated estimation procedure than Grogger or Betts to eliminate spurious cross-section effects, they find that initial positive cross-section estimates of immigration on black self-employment become insignificant.

These applications using more detailed analysis were prompted by statistical problems. However, there are also conceptual reasons for using more detailed analyses. Hoxby studies competition among immigrants and blacks and Hispanics for enrollment into elite colleges. One implication of the theoretical part of her study is that crowding out should be largest for those who are close substitutes for affirmative action target groups. She finds evidence for this hypothesis. While the coefficient of the immigrant's share of enrollment in elite institutions of higher learning is negative and significant using a comprehensive measure of immigrants (all foreign-born), it is quantitatively small. In contrast, foreign-born or nonresident aliens who are black have a much greater crowding-out effect on blacks at very selective schools, and Hispanic foreign-born or nonresident aliens have a similarly larger crowding-out effect on native Hispanics. This crowding out is not just limited to blacks and Hispanics but applies more widely to native students who are disadvantaged. At less selective colleges and universities, more immigrants reduce the number of disadvantaged students. Furthermore, immigrants who themselves are disadvantaged appear to have the largest effects. Thus, looking at the aggregate effects of immigration on college enrollments would underestimate the extent of the competition experienced by particular native groups.

Zax studies the effects of a variety of measures of immigration on residential segregation. The most aggregated measures, the percentage of all persons in 1980 in a given Metropolitan Statistical Area (MSA) born abroad, is an indicator of long-term immigration into the MSA. A more disaggregated measure, the percentage of all persons in 1980 who were abroad in 1975, is an indicator of more recent immigration. Zax finds that the effects of long-term immigration increase segregation. This may result from resistance from established white communities. On the other hand, the effects of short-term immigration help reduce segregation. This may result from competition between blacks and immigrants for the same housing stock or increased liquidity in the housing market.

All of the above-mentioned examples point to the dangers inherent in using an aggregated level of analysis to examine the effects of immigration. The results from aggregated analyses are often contrary to the actual effect that immigration has on native blacks and Hispanics. While these studies examine a limited set of outcomes—crime, self-employment, education, and residential segregation—it is likely that similar issues arise in areas where immigrants may affect native populations.

Having argued for looking at the disaggregated effects of immigration, it is useful to note that there are also dangers inherent in this approach. If analysis of the effects of immigration is narrowly confined to particular spheres of activity, there is a greater likelihood that individuals harmed in one arena may have alternatives that are nearly as attractive, or that they may benefit indirectly from immigration. For example, if natives are crowded out of particular economic activities (for example, retail self-employment or housing in particular communities) there may be other alternatives that are close substitutes in the form of different types of self-employment, employment in businesses owned by others, or housing in nonimmigrant communities. Thus, it would be unclear what policy implications, if any, should be drawn from observing a given effect of immigrants on native blacks or Hispanics.

There may also be indirect effects through changing the socioeconomic composition of neighborhoods and the extent of business activity. Suppose, for example, immigrant businesses reduce the proportion of all business owned by natives. This change would not necessarily lower the fraction of natives who were self-employed if immigrant businesses revitalize and encourage greater business development in low income communities. The growth in immigration may, as a result, raise the overall level of economic activity. Not only would there be spillovers on native self-employment but on other measures of community cohesion and social development. Suppose also that immigration reduces short-term segregation, as found by Zax. The effects on the socioeconomic status of natives in these more integrated communities would clearly depend on the characteristics of the immigrants with whom they share their communities. Given differences in the attitudes, behaviors, and socioeconomic status of immigrants from white natives, general findings about the effects of less housing segregation may not apply in this case.

The effects of competition between immigrants and natives in the areas of schooling at elite colleges and in high school graduation are less likely to be mitigated by the moving of individuals harmed in one arena to alternatives that are nearly as attractive. There are no obvious substitutes available for the high school completion studied by Betts. In the case of Hoxby's analysis, immigrants appear to crowd out native blacks and Hispanics from all but the least-selective schools. This implies that problems of disaggregation may be less important for schooling. However, using a narrow focus also ignores longer-run implications of immigration in the form of the children of immigrants. There is anecdotal evidence that a large percentage of attendees at some elite colleges are the children of West Indian immigrants. While this is not crowding out in the usual sense, since these individuals are natives, there is a potentially large effect on the children of native-born blacks from the children of immigrants.

The basic conclusion to be drawn is that while disaggregation can generate more precise answers about the effects of immigration it is unclear what implications for policy can be drawn. The disaggregated results may overlook the positive or negative indirect effects of immigration, may overstate the actual harm done to natives with suitable alternative choices, or may understate the negative consequences of immigration for the next generation.

INDEX

Boldface numbers refer to tables and figures.